A FINE BROTHER

A FINE BROTHER

The Life of Captain Flora Sandes

LOUISE MILLER

ALMA BOOKS

ALMA BOOKS LTD
London House
243–253 Lower Mortlake Road
Richmond
Surrey TW9 2LL
United Kingdom
www.almabooks.com

First published by Alma Books Limited in 2012
Copyright © Louise Miller, 2012
This mass-market edition first published by Alma Books Limited in 2014

Louise Miller asserts her moral right to be identified as the author of this
work in accordance with the Copyright, Designs and Patents Act 1988

Extract from 'Many Sisters to Many Brothers' from *Poems of Today* by
Rose Macaulay reprinted by permission of Peters Fraser & Dunlop
(www.petersfraserdunlop.com) on behalf of the Estate of Rose Macaulay

Front-cover photograph: Photographer Charles Wellington Furlong, with
thanks to Charles R. Furlong. From James Bruce Papers, Special Collections, University of Maryland Libraries

Author picture: Clear Photography

Printed in England by CPI Group (UK) Ltd, Croydon CR0 4YY

Typesetting and eBook by Tetragon

ISBN: 978-1-84688-245-6
eBook ISBN : 978-1-84688-230-2

Contents

For my father, Tony Miller,
who also liked a good adventure

A FINE BROTHER

Oh it's you that have the luck, out there in blood and muck:
You were born beneath a kindly star;
All we dreamt, I and you, you can really go and do,
And I can't, the way things are.
In a trench you are sitting, while I am knitting
A hopeless sock that never gets done.
Well, here's luck, my dear – and you've got it, no fear;
But for me… a war is poor fun.

Rose Macaulay,
'Many Sisters to Many Brothers', 1914

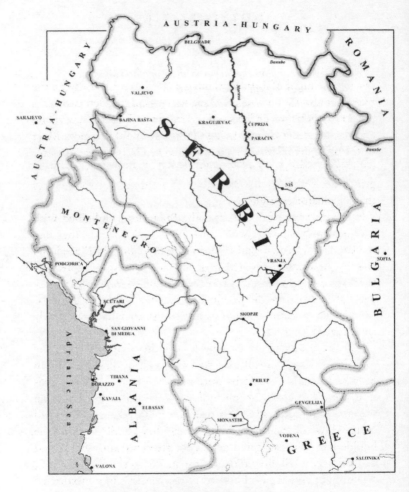

MAP OF SERBIA, 1915

PROLOGUE

During the night of 15th November 1916, snow fell softly on the bare hills and mountains of Macedonia. Had it fallen two years previously, none would have noticed except perhaps the few villagers who scraped a meagre living in this inhospitable region. Most of the unhappy inhabitants by now had fled in the wake of bitter fighting between the Serbian and Bulgarian armies, who were both grimly determined to lay claim to territory that they believed was theirs by historical right.

In the autumn of 1915, after the Bulgarians had sided with the Germans to declare war on the British-allied Serbs, they had marched their brown-clad soldiers into Serbian-held Macedonia to seize the strategic town of Monastir. The following September the Serbs had counter-attacked in an attempt to recapture this key location. By the middle of November, after fighting a series of vicious battles in the mountains to the east, they had very nearly succeeded.

Hill 1212, which rose to a peak over the plain on which the town lay, was now one of only two mountain strongholds still in Bulgarian hands. The Serbs were halfway up this remove elevation, named solely for its altitude, after days of dogged fighting over the rough ground. Their orders were to take the Hill at all costs. Ahead of their impending attack they huddled behind the boulders that lay scattered across the steep terrain. Others had dug themselves shallow trenches for shelter in the hard earth.

During the night, five hundred reinforcements in a mixture of horizon-blue and khaki uniforms joined their compatriots in the front lines. As they moved into position, indistinguishable in her uniform among them was a forty-year-old woman from Suffolk, Flora Sandes, the granddaughter of an Irish bishop. She took her place behind a pile of rocks alongside the men and lay shivering on the snow in her heavy overcoat. Eventually, despite the bitter cold, she fell asleep.

At the break of dawn she woke abruptly to the sharp crack of rifle fire. In a surprise pre-emptive assault, the Bulgarians had attacked under the cover of the early-morning mist that now accompanied the snow. Flora jumped up and grabbed her rifle. To the shouts of her commandant ordering *"Drugi Vod napred!"* ("Second Platoon forward!") she joined the men as they scrambled up the hillside. They advanced, taking cover behind the rocks that dotted the barren, snow-covered terrain. As she paused, panting from the excitement and exertion, she could see the men of her regiment sheltering behind similar outcrops from the withering enemy rifle and machine-gun fire. Although she could hear how close the Bulgarians were by their shouts, she was unable to see them through the thick fog that lay atop the mountain.

The Serbian defence began to disintegrate into chaos in the face of the ferocity of the attack. The men refused to leave their cover, despite the efforts of their officers to dislodge them. In a desperate effort to save their positions from being overwhelmed, a captain was valiantly attempting to organize a counter-attack. He ordered the regimental bugler to signal his men into battle, but the man was so terrified that he was unable to make a noise. The exasperated captain seized the instrument from his shaking hands, stood up against the skyline and began to blow with all his might. His example was enough to rally the soldiers, including Flora. She left her shelter with the men of her platoon and raced ahead for a few paces before throwing herself flat on the snow alongside them. Just then, a group of Bulgarians emerged from the mist a few steps away and hurled a well-aimed grenade into their midst.

PART ONE

CHAPTER 1

DEPARTURE

1914

On 12th August 1914, a mere eight days after war had been declared between Britain and Germany, a group of nurses gathered on the platform at Charing Cross station. Around them swirled bustling crowds of uniformed Territorial soldiers returning from training, Naval Reserve men who had just been called up and civilians wearing little flags on their lapels, clutching the latest edition of the newspapers.[1] The eight women were a mixed group. Some, properly speaking, were not even nurses. In the excitement and enthusiasm of the early days of the war all that was needed to lay claim to the title was a uniform, the correct bearing and a patriotic desire to serve one's country.

Among them was Flora Sandes, a tall, thirty-eight-year-old Englishwoman who spoke with a soft Irish accent. She too was not a qualified nurse — she had enjoyed far too privileged an upbringing to have trained for a commonplace career – but her leisured background had given her the time to take up nursing as a hobby. It was one at which she was supremely competent, although at times her unbridled enthusiasm tempered her ability. She had sailed through numerous St John Ambulance Brigade courses. She was also one of the few women who had been trained specifically to give first aid in wartime conditions through her membership of two quasi-military women's organizations, the First Aid Nursing Yeomanry (FANY) and the Women's Sick and Wounded Convoy Corps.

When, a week before, she heard the news that Britain was at war, she was camping with her family and a couple of friends near Rye in Sussex. Leaving everyone behind, she leapt into her French racing car and sped back to her home in Thornton Heath, then a prosperous suburb of London.[2] That week, she had joined the throngs of women all frantically looking for war work at the offices of the British Red Cross in London's Vincent Square.[3] There she had been put in touch with Mabel Grouitch,[4] the elegant forty-one-year-old American wife of Slavko Grouitch, the Under-secretary of Foreign Affairs for Serbia. Mabel was scrambling to enrol a corps of volunteer surgeons and nurses willing to travel to Serbia with her "Anglo-American Unit" but, in the two weeks she gave herself, her efforts at recruitment had been a disappointment. She was only able to hire those who could leave at a moment's notice and had failed to attract a single surgeon. Short of trained volunteers, she had agreed to interview Flora, who was determined to join the Unit and had argued her case hard. Despite her experience, she had already received her first rejection by the time she sat nervously before Mabel. A day or two earlier she had eagerly applied to become a Voluntary Aid Detachment (VAD), an assistant attached to a British hospital, fully expecting to be hired immediately. Instead, to her disbelief, the interviewing matron had "snubbed" her. "There are others who are better trained than you. And anyway, the war will only last six months," she told her brusquely.[5]

Although the matron had rejected her on the grounds of insufficient experience, Flora also had the *wrong* sort of experience. Few hospitals at the time were willing to hire women doctors, let alone a former member of the FANY and Women's Sick and Wounded Convoy Corps, organizations with strong links to the suffrage movement. Her prospective employers would have written her off as a potential troublemaker, unlikely to submit meekly to the discipline of an Edwardian hospital ward. And Flora was anything but meek. But Mabel, desperate for all the competent help she could get, agreed to take her on. She may not have been a nurse, she reasoned, but her training in first aid had been comprehensive. She also needed women who were practical and adaptable, able to serve under potentially gruelling conditions, and Flora was both to a fault.

On the day the Anglo-American Unit left England, Austria-Hungary attacked Serbia. The assassination of Franz Ferdinand, the heir to the Austro-Hungarian throne, at the hands of a Bosnian

Serb provided the pretext that it had been waiting for to teach the fledgling but troublesome kingdom a lesson in humility it believed it sorely needed. The dynamic Serb state to its south had been an irritant for years. Flush with its territorial gains from the Balkan Wars of 1912 and 1913, it had served as an increasingly attractive magnet for the large Slav population in the south of Austria-Hungary who desired, if not union with Serbia, then certainly a closer alliance. The Serbs knew exactly what they wanted – the formation of a Greater Serbia within the territories that had formed their medieval empire, including parts of Austria-Hungary. On 28th June 1914, the night of the assassination, the Austro-Hungarian army turned its spotlights threateningly across the Sava River on Belgrade.

The flurry of diplomatic activity in the wake of the murder was unable to prevent Austria-Hungary from issuing an ultimatum designed to be impossible for Serbia to accept. Mabel Grouitch's husband Slavko was one of two representatives of the Serbian government to be handed the ultimatum.[6] Anxious to avoid further warfare after two years of fighting in the Balkan Wars, the government accepted its humiliating terms with only three reservations, which they offered to submit to international arbitration. But these reservations were enough to give Austria Hungary the excuse they required to declare war, on 28th July. That day, when they lobbed their first shell on Belgrade, they set in motion a chain of events that led to full-scale global conflict.

The train carrying the Anglo-American Unit pulled out of Charing Cross just before three o'clock on a hot summer's afternoon. Flora was waved off by several members of her large and tight-knit family. The youngest child of eight, she was the epitome of the independent, forthright and determined "new woman", with an interest in fast cars, gruelling physical challenges and, above all, travel. A seasoned camper, she had used her experience to prepare herself well for this trip. In addition to her violin, she had packed a tea basket, a portable rubber bath, a hot-water bottle, a campbed, a first-aid kit and all the cigarettes she could carry.[7]

Among the women travelling with her was Emily Simmonds, a spirited, competent and conscientious "private duty" nurse in her early thirties, of British origin but American training. She was newly versed in the latest techniques, having transcended an impoverished upbringing to specialize as a surgical assistant.[8] When war was declared she had been on holiday in Paris. Cancelling her return trip, she had joined the throngs of excited passengers leaving the French capital for London. On arrival, she approached the British Red Cross for work, only to be refused forthwith on the grounds that she was American-trained.[9] Her options curtailed, she volunteered for Mabel Grouitch's Unit to work under the auspices of the Serbian Red Cross, who had no such qualms about nationality.

Mabel had warned the women before they left that they would face a difficult and comfortless trip. They had also been told by all who ventured an opinion that it was "impossible to get a party of women across Europe at that time". Trains throughout France were being diverted for military use, towns were crowded, hotels were full and that August was one of the hottest months in years. They were also travelling on a shoestring budget. Mabel had not been able to find time to raise funds for the expedition and was forced to finance the party herself. Still, the women shrugged off the warnings of discomfort. "We were all very proud of the fact that our boat was the first to cross the Channel after the British Expeditionary Force," remembered Flora.[10]

Early that evening they arrived in Folkestone, lugging their bags from the train to a boat and, once across the Channel, from the boat to a Paris-bound train. They pulled into the dark station, exhausted, at five o'clock in the morning. By the time they caught the 6.16 p.m. train south in the "awful" heat, they had thirty Serbian students with them who wanted to join their country's army but were unable to travel to Serbia through neutral countries without an alibi. When Mabel had visited the Serbian legation earlier that day, the Minister had asked her if she would take the students with her and tell any authorities who asked that they were part of her Unit. After she readily agreed, the students were kitted out with Red Cross armbands.[11]

To save what little funds they had, the women travelled mainly third-class in the relentless August heat, in the spirited company of the students. At every stop, Mabel and her eight nurses – Flora, Emily, Mrs Ada Barlow, Miss Violet O'Brien, Miss Ada Mann, Mrs Rebecca Hartney, Mrs Barber and Miss Grace Saunders[12] – had to push their way through platforms seething with soldiers and civilians, with their baggage and medical supplies in tow. Finding accommodation in the crowded towns along the route was no less of a struggle; the disruption to train schedules played havoc with any attempts they made to plan ahead.

From Paris their sleeping arrangements became increasingly makeshift. They spent some nights sleeping on the floor of their train, wrapped in their overcoats. At other times, they shared rooms in inexpensive and none-too-clean hotels. "Mrs Barlow and I shared a room with four beds. I broke two of them. Bugs galore," wrote Flora in her diary after one particularly sleepless night. But not all nights were so miserable, thanks to the considerable charms of Mabel Grouitch. "Importantly she had very fascinating manners and was extremely pretty," Flora recalled. "We used to get stuck at some little wayward station, with nobody to meet us and nowhere to go, and Mme Grouitch used just to go up to the Military Commander and *smile* at him, and in five minutes there would be motor cars to fetch us and we'd be taken up to the best hotel in town and everything done for us, and the next morning there would be the Military Commander to see us off all smiles and bows – and bouquets of flowers for Mme Grouitch."[13]

Nonetheless, despite Mabel's best efforts the ad-hoc travel arrangements took their toll on the women. "All looked rather the worst for wear [sic]," Flora reported, before commenting soon after that they were all "hot and cross".[14] They had set out from Paris for Marseilles, from where they intended to catch a ship to Salonika. However, on arrival they were turned away from its busy port, which had been closed to allow Indian troops to land. Mabel Grouitch improvised. She took her nurses by train through neutral Italy while trying to keep the Serbian students quiet and as inconspicuous as possible.[15]

The Italian authorities soon grew highly suspicious at the sight of a small group of Englishwomen in the company of a large group of Serbian men of military age. They first threatened to lock all the women up as "spies", before deciding that the best thing to do would be to get the group out of their country as rapidly as possible. On the second of their two-day trip through Italy, the authorities posted a soldier outside the door of each of their railway carriages, with orders not to allow the women out. "Well, I don't like sitting still too long without moving about," commented Flora, "so I had the presence of mind to give the sentry nearest to me a drink – after that *I* was allowed to move about wherever I liked."[16]

By the time the group had reached Italy any initial reticence they felt in each other's company had vanished. "Sandy" and "Americano", as Flora and Emily had nicknamed each other, formed an immediate friendship. Flora, at thirty-eight, was the older of the two, round-faced, brown-eyed and a fairly sturdy 5'7". To the other nurses, at first glance, she appeared the picture of propriety. However, her prematurely greying hair was too short to be properly ladylike, she had a penchant for what she called "galumphing" (which almost always involved alcohol) and she smoked far too much.

Emily, at 5'5", stood slightly shorter than Flora. Born in London to an English mother,[17] her home was New York, where she had remained after graduating from the Roosevelt Hospital Training School in 1911. She was slender and attractive, "a blue-eyed, delicate, small-featured, curly-haired, pink-cheeked, soft-voiced slip of a girl".[18] Like Flora, she had seized the chance to join Mabel's Unit. It promised an opportunity to put her training to full use and offered far more variety and excitement than her work as a private-duty nurse, which involved looking after a single patient at a time, could ever give her. Mabel could not provide her with a salary – and Emily was far from financially self-sufficient – but she had placed any pecuniary concerns to the back of her mind as she set out with the others.[19]

Despite their differences in age and financial standing, Flora and Emily found they had much in common. Thoughts of courageous work for the Allied cause were, for the moment, far from their minds and both were determined to enjoy their trip, come what may. And enjoy it they did. "Miss Saunders lost her purse and Americano her reputation – neither ever found again," wrote Flora in her diary as they travelled through Italy.[20]

Flora and Emily's disregard of proper decorum (and numerous shopping trips) soon incurred the disapproval of their stolid and duty-bound colleagues. When they missed their ship due to a "mistake" at their next stop, Corfu, the other nurses simply left them behind. After they rejoined them in Athens, they did their threadbare reputations even more damage when a bouquet arrived

for them from a war correspondent they had befriended. It "nearly
caused a battle", recorded Flora. Undeterred, they spent the evening
in his company and that of "sundry others", being driven about in
the balmy heat of a late summer's evening. The other nurses were
so scandalized by Flora and Emily's escapades that the following
day they would barely speak to them. There was an "awful frost
after last night", Flora noted tersely in her diary.[21]

From Athens the women made the short journey to Piraeus,
its busy, industrial port. There they boarded a filthy Greek cattle
steamer and piled into one large cabin. The ship travelled north
through the Aegean Sea, past the scenic Greek islands, straight into
the heart of a raging thunderstorm. "Of the eight who were in one
cabin, all were ill; half of them were lying on the floor, and the
rest in the bunks," recalled nurse Ada Mann, from Dartford, Kent.
"Some of the bunks were full of rainwater. The luggage, which
was on one deck, was piled in confusion, large trunks on top of
small bags, etc., smashed and broken, and everything was soaked
and spoilt in water."[22] Thirty-six hours later, they arrived. "I never
want to do another journey like it," commented Flora abruptly.[23]

Flora and Emily's first experience of Salonika was brief. They
were overwhelmed more by a sense of relief at having reached the
horseshoe-shaped harbour than by the awe that so many felt upon
arrival. From the sea, the town was imposing. Graceful white minarets vied with the cupolas of Greek Orthodox churches against a
backdrop of rugged hills. Along the modern quayside, dominated
by the fortress-like White Tower, hundreds of brightly painted
fishing boats were moored, overlooked by hotels, restaurants and
cinemas. Once the women stepped shakily ashore they were ushered
past the crowded quay and through its narrow, dirty streets to a
hotel. This time even Flora collapsed into bed. The shops would
have to wait, she thought to herself.

It was now nearing the end of August. After one night's rest in
Salonika the women caught a slow train north that took them
alongside the marshland that bordered the muddy waters of the
Vardar River, over the arid plains and low hills of Macedonian
Greece and through the mountains of southern Serbia. They
stopped overnight in Niš, Serbia's second largest city, to receive
their orders from Colonel Subotić, the Vice-President of the Serbian Red Cross, then climbed back aboard a train for the final leg

of their journey. Early in the morning of 29th August, the women clambered off the train at Kragujevac, a town that was rapidly becoming a main hospital centre by virtue of its position astride transportation routes.[24] Sixty miles south of Belgrade, it was also the closest town of any size to the fighting in the north-west. Although the journey had taken them fourteen long days, they had defied the predictions of those who had told them they could never do it. Their success, praised Flora, was due to the "pluck and perseverance" of Mabel Grouitch.[25]

CHAPTER 2

ANTEBELLUM

1876–1914

"I was the youngest, and the only one to disgrace the family, at least according to my brothers, by being born in England," said Flora, when asked about her childhood.[1] The granddaughter of the Bishop of Cashel, she came from a Protestant Anglo-Irish family from Cork who, while not wealthy, were comfortably off. Her father, Samuel Dickson Sandes, was educated prestigiously at Eagle House School in Hammersmith, Rugby and Trinity College Dublin and eventually followed in his own father's footsteps by graduating from theological college, although he did not succeed in mirroring the latter's success. In 1856, he married Sophia Julia Besnard, the daughter of a prominent Cork family of Huguenot origins with eccentric connections. Sophia's first cousin was Sir Samuel Baker, explorer of the Nile, who, when his first wife died, simply purchased another at a Bulgarian slave market. His brother, Valentine Baker, was convicted of assaulting a woman on the train to Waterloo. After serving a short prison term, he transferred his career to the Turkish and Egyptian armies, where previous convictions for sexual assault were no impediment to promotion.[2]

Sophia and Samuel's first child, Stephen, was born the year after their marriage, in 1857. Sophia, Mary (known as Meg), John, Sam, William and Fanny followed at two-year intervals. In 1874, seventeen-year-old Stephen died at sea on a voyage to Melbourne, Australia.[3] His death affected the family deeply and the first child to be born to one of his siblings, Sophia's son, was named after him. Flora's birth, two years after Stephen's death and seven years after the arrival of Fanny, the next youngest, had all the signs of being

unplanned. She was born on 22nd January 1876, in the Parish of
Nether Poppleton, County of York, where her fifty-four-year-old
father was rector for a couple of years. Her mother was forty-three.
The family had left Ireland for good four years earlier after being
caught up in the rising tide of violence against the Anglo-Irish
community. "On the night of 23rd December 1867 the fenians
burned us out," recorded Flora's father in his sketchy diary.[4] Her
parents had clung on to their home for a further five years, before
joining the throngs of Protestants to cross the Irish Sea to Britain.

Flora's early life was unusually unsettled, which may at least
partly account for the wanderlust that would characterize her
adulthood. Her father's attempts to establish himself in several
parishes clearly failed, although the reasons remain unclear. In
1878, having failed to find a permanent job, he advertised in the
English press. "A clergyman, for upwards of twenty years a vicar,
is willing to serve as curate without any remuneration," he wrote,
evidently worried about finding a permanent home for his large
family.[5] His appeal does not appear to have met with great success,
as he moved his unwieldy household at least five times in the following years, including a spell in Boulogne in France.

The family made the best of it in each of the towns and villages
that provided them with a temporary home. They organized fêtes
to raise funds for improvements to their parish church, allowed
the parishioners free use of the glebe meadows for games of lawn
tennis, cricket and quoits, ran the Sunday school and church choirs
and held Christmas parties for the local children.[6] All members
of the family were drafted in to help. At a concert organized in
Monewden, Suffolk, in 1881, several members of the Sandes family
took a turn on the stage, along with a succession of local talents.
Even Flora, "a young lady not yet six years", was pushed forward
to sing her own composition, the 'Floating Scow'. Her efforts were
"vociferously applauded and encored", recorded a local paper.[7]
When they left each parish, their departure was marked by genuine
sorrow. "They have, by their courtesy to all and extreme kindness
to the poor, won the esteem and affection of its inhabitants," wrote
one paper in tribute.[8]

In 1885, when Flora was nine years old, the family finally settled
in Marlesford, Suffolk, when her father found a position as rector
of its small church dedicated to St Andrew. The rural village, set

on a stream amid rolling land, was small but not isolated. At the
time they arrived it had a population of nearly four hundred, most
of whom made a comfortable living from farming. The village was
important and prosperous enough to boast its own small railway
station, which allowed its residents to travel easily to other towns
in the district as well as to London. It was even big enough to
support its own grocer, blacksmith, bootmaker and "thatcher and
vermin killer". The Reverend Sandes took charge of its low, twelfth
century grey-stone church and moved his family into the adjacent
rectory, an elegant, cream-coloured house of high ceilings, large
windows and many fireplaces.[9] Its inhabitants, who lived along its
quiet lanes in two-storey stone, brick and painted cottages, soon
came to know the Irish rector, his wife and their many children.

Flora's childhood in the village was a happy one, spent amid a
close-knit tumble of family members, parishioners and various
pets, including the improbably named Womary Tizey the cat, and
Dicky the dog. Like all families of their standing they also had servants, although they managed on the bare minimum for a household
of their size, employing only a young female cook and parlour
maid when Flora was very young, and later a sole "ladyhelp".[10]
The activities of the family were centred on the village and the
Reverend Sandes's position as rector. Flora's sister Meg described
a comfortable, carefree and happy existence of "frequent trips to
[nearby] Framlingham and Ipswich, much walking, visiting the sick
and elderly, and village activities in the tithe barn adjacent to the
rectory".[11] The girls were home-schooled by governesses and Flora
was later sent to finishing school in Switzerland, while her brothers
attended public school and university. It was an education designed
by the standards of the day to turn her into a well-rounded but
leisured young lady, able to manage a household, play an instrument – in her case, the violin – paint and attract a suitable husband.
Crucially, it catered to her aptitude for languages. By the time she
left the school she could speak both French and German, skills that
would in the coming years prove vitally important.

Flora read avidly and developed an early preference for heady
tales of imperial glory and far-flung adventure, which fired her
desire for excitement and to see the world for herself. While other
girls of her age and standing spent their hours practising sewing,
painting and dreaming of their wedding day, Flora immersed herself

in Tennyson's 'Charge of the Light Brigade', wondering what it would be like to be "Storm'd at with shot and shell". As she grew older, she spent long hours in the rolling Suffolk countryside galloping through the lanes on horseback, imagining that she was rushing into battle against the Russians at Balaklava, all the while practising her field skills by shooting rabbits. Her choice of reading material also reflected the obsession with travel that took hold of her from a young age. From the time she was a child she kept a scrapbook into which she avidly pasted her favourite cuttings and poems. Many of the latter were by "R.K." – Rudyard Kipling – and almost all were devoted to one overarching theme: 'Vagrant's Epitaph', 'The Spell of the Road', 'Wander Thirst', 'Wanderlust', 'The Vagabond', 'A Camp', 'The Traveller'. One of the poems that Flora carefully transcribed into her book was Dora Sigerson Shorter's 'A Vagrant Heart':

> Ochone! to be a woman, only sighing on the shore –
> With a soul that finds a passion for each long breaker's roar,
> With a heart that beats as restless as all the winds that blow –
> Thrust a cloth between her fingers, and tell her she must sew;
> Must join in empty chatter, and calculate with straws –
> For the weighing of our neighbour – for the sake of social laws.

Somewhat incongruously, Flora also collected recipes – some pasted from newspapers or magazines, some handwritten – all her life, which by all accounts never apparently translated into any real cooking ability. Inside the front cover of her first recipe book is written "Flora Sandes Her Book" in a child's painstaking but awkward script. Even the domestic staff helped her. Kate Jones, the young "ladyhelp" from Wales who lived with the family, contributed a recipe for scones to Flora's second book, in her own neat and careful handwriting.[12]

Flora, or "the brat" as she was called by her brothers and sisters, displayed the stubbornness early on that would characterize her for the rest of her life. Many of the pictures of her in her childhood and teenage years show her looking impatient at having to stand still for long enough for the photograph to be taken. In another, taken when she was around fifteen, she looks defiantly at the camera, head slightly cocked and lifted, half-smiling with eyebrows raised in amusement, as if challenging the photographer to do his or her worst. She envied her brothers their freedom from social disapproval and, in her early childhood, "used to pray every night that I might wake up in the morning and find myself a boy". "Fate," she commented further while reflecting on her youth, "plays funny tricks sometimes, so that it behoves one to be careful of one's wishes. Many years afterwards, [I] realized that if you have the misfortune to be born a woman it is better to make the best of a bad job, and try not to be a bad imitation of a man."[13]

She was lucky at least that the countryside surrounding Marlesford gave her the perfect base to practise her beloved pursuits of riding and shooting, in which she soon became proficient. She was also fortunate to have been born into a liberal family that valued athleticism and a love of the outdoors, while giving an unusual amount of independence to all the children, irrespective of gender. Her father was remembered as a "kindly old chap" by his grandchildren, who illustrated his later letters to his children with various stories that he thought might amuse them.[14] He was also a keen reader of the *Times*, contributing one letter to the editor arguing the need for tolerance to others in matters of religion and another advocating the "habitual and temperate" taking of alcoholic drinks.[15] Little is known of Flora's mother Sophia Julia, except that she suffered periods of ill health when Flora was still young and when able occupied herself with her children, managing the household and organizing community and charitable events. Flora's sisters appear to have stepped into the gap left by their mother's indisposition, indulging her as the baby of the family. Sophia Julia died in 1911, when Flora was thirty-five.

Flora's sister Fanny shared her enthusiasm for physical challenges and became one of the first women to climb Mount Fuji. Meg, another sister, travelled as a pioneer to Canada in 1887 with her new husband before moving to the Australian bush. Her brother Sam, a master mechanic, left for Canada in the same year and soon found a job with a mining company in Van Anda, British Columbia, before he moved to Papua New Guinea. Another brother, William, worked as a teacher in Norway. Only Flora's sister Sophia remained permanently in England.

William was the only other member of the immediate family to enlist in the armed forces during the First World War, although his modest contribution to the war effort was soon eclipsed by that of his younger sister. Listing his occupation as "independent gentleman", he joined the Bedford Regiment in May 1916, aged forty-nine. To improve his chances of being accepted, he fibbed about his age, telling them he was forty-one. He served for the duration of the war on English soil. In 1919, fifty-one-year-old Private Sandes was discharged as no longer fit for war service. His minor ailments were listed as "shortness of breath on exertion" and gout, indicating that he likely shared the familial appreciation of alcohol.[16]

The most professionally successful of Flora's siblings was her brother "Johnnie". John, a graduate of Magdalen College, Oxford, attained widespread public recognition in Australia as a writer of verse and popular novels and as a contributor to the *Sydney Daily Telegraph*. In 1919 he became the paper's London correspondent and reported from the Versailles Peace Conference. He was a man of firm opinions, many of them "determinedly patriotic, Christian, [and] anti-socialist", and was considered something of a theatre-loving, affable "literary genius" by those of his colleagues who enjoyed his company, and "sleepy and bad-tempered" by those who did not.[17]

Flora's remaining family stayed in Marlesford until 1894. That year, they moved to Thornton Heath, near Croydon, where Flora's sister Sophia was now living with her new husband.[18] The main purpose of the move was almost certainly to ensure that eighteen-year-old Flora and her sister Fanny, both of whom then aspired to become writers, were in commuting distance of London. There they would have access to training and employment opportunities that would be unavailable to them in Marlesford.[19]

Others had the same idea. By the time the Sandes family moved to their two-storey semi-detached house, Thornton Heath was quickly changing from a quiet rural hamlet to an affluent London suburb, while the open countryside that surrounded it was rapidly being swallowed up by roads, houses and new amenities. By the early years of the twentieth century the residents could visit the local library, play tennis on one of the grass courts in the recreation grounds and join the customers who thronged the many brick-fronted shops along the busy high street. There were also the swimming baths, whose charges varied according to how long it had been since the water was last changed. Then, in 1911, Thornton Heath's first cinema, the white-fronted, ornately decorated "Electric Palace", opened its doors to feature "The World and Its Wonders Week by Week".[20] Flora made the most of her new-found opportunities. After completing a course in secretarial training, she began work in the capital.[21]

By the time she reached adulthood Flora showed scant desire to lead the respectable and leisured life that was expected of a woman of her background. Easily bored, she had little interest in domesticity and, in search of adventure, worked as a typist in Cairo for a year.[22] In September 1903 she set off again, this time for New York.[23] Along with her friend Bessie Stear, a fellow typist and stenographer who was every bit the thrill-seeker she was, Flora planned to "type" her way "around the world". It was a first, "a record in the way of travel", reported a professional journal of their exploits. The "two young lady typists" were "working their way along from city to city and from country to country".[24]

A year later Flora was still traipsing happily around the States. She had stopped temporarily in the Midwestern town of St Louis, Missouri, to work at the Irish Industrial Exhibit at the 1904 World's Fair, but left on 8th August. "Miss Florence Sandes [sic]," the local paper reported, "started from the World's Fair Grounds... to walk to San Francisco, whence she will sail for Hong Kong, thence to Australia and back to Ireland. Miss Sandes carries baggage weighing ten pounds and will be armed to protect herself while on the long journey."[25] By later that autumn she had made her way to Cripple Creek in Colorado, likely drawn there by curiosity about the famed "Miners' War" that saw gold miners rise up against their oppressive overlords.[26]

In December 1904 Flora's Canadian sister-in-law, Rose Sandes (née Allison), died of heart failure, aged only twenty-nine.[27] She left a five-year-old son, Dick, and a husband (Flora's brother Sam) with little time or inclination for childcare. Flora, Sam knew, was somewhere in the American hinterland. He needed her urgently to take the young boy from Van Anda to their parents in England. The problem was that no one knew quite where to find her. "It

appears that when my mother died my father was aware of the
fact that Flora was somewhere in the States but [had] no positive
address and he therefore employed the famous agency of Pinkerton
to find her," recollected Dick years later.

> She was eventually located working in a box factory in a very distant
> town, she received the message that she was urgently required but had
> no money with which to travel and promptly started to travel by goods
> van on the railways until she had an unpleasant experience with a guard
> or brakesman who she is alleged to have shot – and this delayed her
> journey to join my father, I asked her years later about this experience
> but only received a reply that it was something that happened long ago
> and she could not remember.[28]

Flora stepped off a small steamer in Van Anda in January 1905
apparently no worse for wear. For the next month, she stayed with
Sam and Dick. Van Anda was just the sort of rough-and-tumble
place that she liked. Halfway between a mining camp and a town,
many of its five hundred inhabitants were hard-living miners who
drank and played cards late into the night.[29] One of the many
amusing pastimes, recorded a local paper, was to sit and "watch
a young hopeful try to blast the head off his dog by getting it to
retrieve lighted firecrackers".[30] Almost certainly against her will,
Sam assigned Flora a bodyguard, "Buskie", to protect her from the
more lively individuals. "Not that she needed much protection,"
commented Dick later. Despite any initial irritation she may have
felt at Buskie's assignment, she soon became fast friends with the
"old-timer", who began to teach her everything he knew about
living in the outdoors. She listened avidly to every word. "He was
about 70 years of age," recorded Dick,

> [and] wore a very dirty Stetson hat out of which he constantly offered
> my aunt a drink whenever she was thirsty and which out of politeness
> she had to accept – Buskie lived in a decked-over boat which had been
> beached and used to take Flora on long trips on which he taught her to
> use an old Winchester .45 rifle and to hunt deer, I distinctly remember
> her first kill and the elation when it was brought home. It was there
> that she also learnt to become a good hand in a boat and to handle a
> fishing rod in the approved backwoodsman style.[31]

In February the small boy was kitted out to travel to England but, still fired by the thought of adventure, Flora had no wish to return directly home. "It's up to you," Sam told her, when she proposed taking Dick with her on her travels. In early February she boarded a small steamer with her young nephew, who brought with him his two most treasured possessions, a Brownie box camera and a pet white rat that he carried in the camera case. With money given to them by Sam they set off first for San Francisco, visiting it only the year before the great earthquake. They then began working their way south along the western coast of the United States, before crossing first into Mexico and then, reputedly, into Central America.[32] From there, they followed the coast north through the southern states of Texas, Louisiana, Alabama and Florida before travelling up the eastern seaboard to New York.

Having a five-year-old in tow restricted Flora's freedom considerably, particularly after she "became friendly with a Captain McCarthy of the US Navy".[33] Likely under the impression that five was a perfectly good age to learn some self-sufficiency, her solution was to go out on her own, leaving him locked in a hotel room with only his white rat for company.[34] Finally, in April, they reached Thornton Heath. Dick's rat arrived with them, to the utter horror of Flora's mother and her sister Fanny. "On arrival it was quietly got rid of," remembered Dick. "It's escaped," they told him.[35]

Around the time of Flora's return a wealthy, unmarried uncle died, leaving her and her brothers and sisters a considerable legacy. "She proceeded to enjoy life," wrote Dick. "I remember she joined several clubs and was continually at the opera."[36] One of the clubs was an underground rifle range for both men and women in Central London's Cork Street. Her Australian sister-in-law, Clare Sandes (née Berry) joined too. "Flora was a fairly good shot with the ordinary service rifle, but she was not by any means the best in the club," Clare recalled. "[She] was a capital shot with the big service revolver – a terribly difficult weapon to hit the target with, as I discovered for myself."[37]

In 1908, with part of the inheritance, she also bought her first motor car. Flora's interest in cars took precedence over all else. "There seemed to be many admirers in the offing," recollected Dick, "and amongst them being Capt. Mellelieu (from South

Africa), a Mr Brook, but they all seemed to fade away. She seemed more and more interested in motor cars and [later] purchased a Caesare Naudine [Sizaire-Naudin] racing car which she took to Brooklands and I believe entered some races."[38] To his delight, she allowed Dick, aged fourteen, to race it round the track until reprimanded by the officials. Even when she showed some enthusiasm for her suitors, Flora's car (and her fast driving) did not mix at all well with her romantic involvements. One relationship, Dick recalled, came to an abrupt end when she took her suitor out in her car, crashed, and put him in hospital. When he later came down with tuberculosis, rumours flew that he had caught it in the wards.[39] Fortunately for Flora's conscience and reputation, he was a taxidermist and almost certainly caught the disease in his line of work.

She also entered the two-seater in reliability trials. "Once she entered it for a reliability non-stop race from Edinburgh to London, and drove it herself," commented Clare. "She would have won the race if she had not taken the wrong road in the middle of the night."[40] And she was furious when regulations barring women from entering prevented her from driving a borrowed Deemster at the Royal Automobile Club Light Car Reliability Trial in Harrogate in the spring of 1914. "I have driven my own cars for eight or nine years, and have done all running repairs entirely myself," she scribbled in an angry letter to the *Autocar*, a magazine whose readership was otherwise almost exclusively male. "On the light car which I am still driving every day I have covered a distance of over 70,000 miles. Experience, after all, is the thing that counts, and, given the necessary experience, it would be absurd to suggest that a woman driver is not as good as a man, except in handling a large car, which requires physical strength."[41]

Flora's Sizaire-Naudin was her pride and joy. Whenever she could she packed her camping gear and spent weeks at a time motoring to far-flung places across England, including Land's End. On many such trips, she was accompanied by a friend, Annie ("Nan") MacGlade, the free-spirited daughter of a Belfast-based businessman who, unusually for the time, was the manageress of an engineering works.[42] In May 1911, they took the Sizaire on their first driving holiday abroad. They packed their things in the car's box, strapped their two suitcases on top and set off across the

Channel to Boulogne. Over the subsequent days, on a hot, dusty drive through central France that took them south all the way to the French Riviera and back, they lost a suitcase off the back, drove the car up three thousand feet to the top of Mont Agel, raced others on the roads, got lost several times and squandered money at the Casino in Monte Carlo. They slept at hotels and inns and, when none could be found, in sleeping sacks and rugs under the skies. Photographs from the trip show Flora with windswept brown hair, dressed in pantaloons, with baskets, blankets, cutlery, boxes, cooking tins, clothing and shoes strewn across the ground. Another shows one of them, dressed in long skirts, sunglasses and a scarf, outside the presciently named "Café de l'Orient".[43]

The Sizaire, to their dismay, "went very badly". Within two hours of arriving in France they had their first of what would be "daily" punctures, which they patched themselves by the side of the road. Over the days that followed they also changed the sparking plug and dealt as best they could with a clutch that threatened to "give up the ghost", an unreliable brake and lamps that stopped working after the car got drenched one time too many. So much time did they lose fixing the series of problems that, on the return journey, Flora was forced to drive almost continuously from nine o'clock one morning to three o'clock the following afternoon to catch the boat back to England. "We arrived at our destination covered with dust and dead tired," wrote Nan. In around two weeks, they had driven the twelve-horsepower Sizaire two thousand miles.[44]

Flora spent more of her inheritance buying the lease on the old guardroom at Beau Port Battery to use as family holiday cottage near St Brélade's Bay, Jersey. It was an "extraordinary little place", recalled her sister-in-law. "It had been a small square fort, built of solid masonry, and it dated back to the Middle Ages, or thereabouts. It stood at the extreme edge of the cliff at the farthest point of St Brélade's Bay... It had long slits in the masonry – loopholes for arquebuses and demi-culverins, and other clumsy weapons with which people used to kill each other."[45] They spent wonderful summer weeks there, recollected Dick. The days were filled with cycle rides, swimming, poaching rabbits on a nearby estate and living "in luxury on rabbit stews, lobster... and Jersey cider". Flora was "very fond" of the latter, he remembered. She could drink "more

than the average man could take & never turn a hair – in all the
years I knew her I never saw her the worse for liquor."[46]

Her holidays in Jersey gave her the opportunity to prove to
herself how hardy she was. She bought a dinghy in St Heliers and
rowed it single-handedly six miles back along the coast through
dangerous currents to St Brélade's Bay, recalled Dick. "We would
go out with the St Brélade's fishermen all night in all weathers
and she never seemed to tire of physical exercise," he added. "She
made me accompany her on a cycle to every bay and inlet on the
island. She always took a bath in the open... at the back of the
[cottage] often having to break the ice before she could bath in a
tin tub." She did her best to get her young nephew to follow her
example. "Flora encouraged me to harden up," Dick remembered.
"On several occasions I had to take my sleeping bag outside and
sleep in the snow just to get to know what it was like." But there
was another side to her character, he commented. "Whenever she
was in funds (which seemed to be quite often) she would indulge
in the best hotel accommodation she could find whilst travelling
and liked comfort."[47]

By the time Flora reached her thirties, the rector's daughter was still
living at home, single, and had a penchant for decidedly unfeminine
pursuits which made her exciting company to those with similarly
liberal inclinations. "She was hot-tempered, full of fun, and possessed an amazing amount of vitality," described her sister-in-law.
"When she became excited – which was frequently – she spoke
with a marked Irish accent, although she was born and educated
in England."[48] But there were many who took a dim view of what
they regarded as her wayward antics. Some of the disapproval
clearly got to her. "For anyone to say they are proud of anything
I do is such a novel experience – it's generally so much the other
way," Flora scribbled plaintively in a letter in 1916.[49]

Still, she had no intention whatsoever of letting convention prevent her from doing what she wanted. In 1907 or 1908 she brought
yet more disapproval upon herself by joining the First Aid Nursing Yeomanry (FANY), an organization formed by the self-styled
"Captain" Edward Charles Baker in the autumn of 1907. That year,
he advertised in the national press for members, with the vision of
putting together a body of women to gallop onto the battlefields

of a future war to rescue the injured.[50] The women attracted to
Baker's pioneering group were a diverse collection of middle- and
upper-class suffragists, eccentrics and those, like Flora, who were
seeking excitement wherever they could find it. By 1909 she was a
"corporal" and one of the most active members of the organization, which was London-based.[51]

The FANY was one of many associations then established with
the aim of increasing Britain's readiness for war. With the rise of
Germany as a military power it was widely believed that the country was both vulnerable to attack and grossly unprepared for such
an eventuality. "War fever" reached such a pitch that an invasion
was "expected every morning at breakfast time with the arrival
of the *Daily Mail*".[52] All across the country, public and grammar
schools began to form their own Officers' Training Corps while
the War Office launched a scheme of Voluntary Aid Detachments
to assist in hospitals in the event of war.[53] Even the Boy Scouts
were founded to instil in the soldiers of tomorrow the right sort
of military zeal.

Although the motives behind the formation of the FANY reflected the same mood of concern, it was one step too far for many
to see women in marching formation, subject to army discipline
and attending military-style camps. There were instances of naked
hostility to the uniformed women, who were mistaken for "———
suffragettes" (which many of them actually were) and had things
thrown at them.[54] More frequently, the women were ridiculed
gently by the press. "Being women, however, as well as soldiers,
they have smuggled in some comforts," reported a journalist about
one such military camp. "There are carpets on the wooden floors
and easy chairs. Some of the tents have cottage-size pianos. The
mess tent serves salads and pie, and other dainties."[55]

Despite such press reports implying otherwise, membership
of the FANY involved much hard work. The women were given
training in first aid, horsemanship, camp cookery and signalling.
They attended organized camps where they slept in tents, took
part in night marches to hunt for "casualties" and practised their
battlefield skills. There was little that Flora enjoyed more. Her
enthusiasm was such, according to a family anecdote, that it lost
her a "wounded rescue race" despite finishing well ahead of her
competition. She had lined up on horseback with the other women,

a wheeled stretcher harnessed behind each. At the signal, she galloped off, selected her "patient", bandaged him up, bundled him
into her stretcher and raced back. But when the winner's name was
announced she was crestfallen to find that she had been disqualified
on the grounds that, had he been a genuine patient, her reckless
speed would more than likely have killed him.[56]

By 1909 a number of the members, including Flora and the
suffragist Mabel St Clair Stobart, were becoming increasingly
dissatisfied with Baker's impractical leadership. Along with two
others they formed a "tougher and more practical" faction to
spearhead a rebellion against it.[57] Matters came to a head after
a charity matinee in London to raise funds for the organization.
The event, which the famous Harry Lauder headlined, was a great
success financially. It raised £170, much of which was earmarked
for the purchase of an ambulance wagon. But the money ended
up in the hands of Flora and the rebels, not Baker. While details
of what happened next are sketchy, the end result was that the
FANY split that summer.[58] Flora and Mabel became part of the
"Executive Committee of the Women's Sick and Wounded Convoy
Corps" which kept half of the £170. They also took with them the
majority of the members. Baker did not get his ambulance wagon
and the FANY was left in a state of near collapse.[59] In a letter to a
friend in 1910, the harried Baker rued the day that he let "elderly
women" join.[60] This unflattering description would certainly have
been directed at Mabel Stobart, who was in her late forties. It may
also have encompassed Flora who, at thirty-three, would have been
considerably older than the majority of the members.

Due to the influence of Flora, Mabel and the other members
of the Executive Committee, the Women's Sick and Wounded
Convoy Corps had a decidedly pragmatic bent. Their grey-green
uniforms were designed for practicality rather than elegance and,
in addition to training in horsemanship and first aid, the women
were taught military skills like trench-digging, tent-pitching and
formation marching. To prove to the members that they could
do without things normally considered essential, in their annual
fortnight's "camp" they slept on the ground without mattresses
or beds and were taught to improvise with basic supplies. During
the First Balkan War of 1912, the Corps formed the first all-female
medical mission when they sent a unit in aid of the Bulgarian army

under Mabel Stobart's leadership. For reasons unknown, Flora was not with them.

By the time Britain declared war on Germany on 4th August 1914, thirty-eight-year-old Flora was living at home with her fifteen-year-old nephew Dick, her bedridden elderly father, his Irish "butler, secretary and nurse" Moffat, two housemaids and Cullen, a former sea chef on the Castle Line, who had been employed after Flora had fallen out with a succession of female cooks. The house was "in turmoil", remembered Dick. The housemaids were virtually unsupervised and Flora "knew nothing about housekeeping at that time and could not care less".[61] Above all, by 1914, Flora needed a change. She received the news of war with a thrill of excitement. She had been training for years to serve her country, via the FANY and the Women's Convoy Corps, and knew at once that this was her opportunity, at long last, to put her knowledge into practice.

The First World War held out the prospect of great adventure abroad for thousands more British women who were keen to "do their bit" for a suitably patriotic cause, just like their brothers. It provided a chance for them to live and travel independently and work in fields that had hitherto been restricted to men, while its fluid circumstances gave unheard-of opportunities to women with courage and initiative. For the more adventurous of them, often their potential was more easily realized in the campaigns in the Balkans and Russia than in the west because, where the British, French and Belgians controlled access, women were barred from working near the front.[62] Paradoxically, their desire to "protect" women who did not want to be protected meant that many ended up working in some of the most dangerous sectors of the war. Many would pay with their lives, among them twenty-one British women in Serbia alone.[63]

The majority of the women who left Britain for Serbia during the First World War were volunteers with the Scottish Women's Hospitals, an organization formed in Edinburgh in 1914 after its head, the suffragist Dr Elsie Inglis, was told by an official upon offering her services to the War Office, "My good lady, go home and sit still." Flora would come to know many of them, including Dr Katherine MacPhail, who became a lifelong friend. Katherine had also experienced the prevailing hostility to professional women. The daughter of a Scottish doctor, she had graduated in medicine from Glasgow University, winning several prizes during the course of her studies, but found most general hospitals unwilling to appoint a woman to their staffs and few opportunities in general surgery. She too had been rebuffed by the War Office upon the outbreak of war. After the British Red Cross also refused her assistance, she became one of the early recruits of the Scottish Women's Hospitals.[64] "Well, I hardly knew where Serbia was, but from what I had read I knew that they were having a very hard time in the war, and so I said to Dr Elsie Inglis that I'd be very willing to go," recalled Katherine, who had never been abroad before. "Most of us had the vaguest idea of what Serbia was like, we had read it was a wild country with wilder people. Therein lay half the attraction for the more adventurous of us."[65]

The aim of the Scottish Women's Hospitals was both political and patriotic. Like Mabel Stobart, its organizers set out to prove that women were fit to work in the theatre of war and thus deserved the full rights of citizenship, including the ability to vote.[66] They were run and staffed by women, from doctors, nurses and X-ray technicians to stretcher-bearers, orderlies and drivers. Men, however, were not necessarily excluded from membership: although some units were doctrinaire, taking pride in not accepting male help, a couple of men became fully-fledged members, most units had a "handyman" and male prisoners-of-war were accepted to work as orderlies.[67] Nevertheless, men were kept "in a thoroughly subordinate position; they were the labourers, the odd men of the hospital, and did as they were told!"[68]

During the war, a myriad of British relief organizations in addition to the Scottish Women's Hospitals offered their services in Serbia and the Balkans, in which many British men and women distinguished themselves both as doctors and relief workers. Others travelled independently to Serbia and worked courageously as "freelancers". Irrespective of their background or motivation in leaving Britain, the suffering, stoicism and quiet courage of the Serbs would make a deep impression on them all. Politically, socially and economically disenfranchised in Britain, the women volunteers were treated with great courtesy within Serbia and, more importantly, as equals. The Serbs in turn were almost pathetically grateful for their assistance and bestowed awards and honours upon them.

Although the most important medical help given to Serbia during the war was British, other countries – some Allied, some neutral – also sent units. Significant missions arrived from America, France, the Netherlands, Greece and Switzerland. Even Russia, which was struggling to find enough medical staff and supplies for its own armies, sent generously equipped and well-staffed units. The Serbians themselves, ravaged by disease and war, did what they could under the auspices of organizations like the Serbian Red Cross.

Like Flora, almost all of the British women who volunteered for overseas service were financially self-sustaining.[69] Many were professionally trained and a number in turn were heavily involved in the fight for the right to vote. Although there is no record of Flora having been actively involved in the suffrage movement, she mixed widely before the war with its supporters in the FANY and the Women's Sick and Wounded Convoy Corps. At the very least she was influenced by the spirit of the movement, recalled Dick. "At dinner she would insist on smoking (which was not done in those days)," he wrote of a fund-raising show that he had attended with her for one of these organizations. "I remonstrated and was promptly told to go home alone. I rather fancy at the time she was in some way mixed up with Sylvia Pankhurst and had an idea that women must stick up for their own rights." Flora soon forgave him. "A few nights later I was allowed to see the show," he remembered.[70] At best, Flora was a passive supporter of the suffragists. Although it is improbable that she would have been a founding member of the Women's Convoy Corps, whose watchword was "loyalty to country and to womanhood", if she felt any antipathy to the movement, more than likely she was simply indifferent. Throughout her life, she remained motivated more by the thought of adventure than politics.

For the first time in their lives, many such women and men were free from the constraints of Edwardian morality and the prying eyes of their friends and neighbours. Although most distinguished themselves in their work, the rigid discipline and hierarchy found in hospitals along the Western Front was just as notable for its absence in Serbia. The directors of the units were often the sole authority. Theirs was an unenviable task. Not only was it difficult to send their charges all the way back to Britain for misconduct, they knew that any transgressors with enough initiative had the option of leaving their unit to work directly for the Serbs.

And there were transgressions aplenty, most of which were successfully hushed up in the press at the time. But the gossip about the behaviour of the volunteers flew wildly. "Most of them are grand but two doctors and a parson had to be sent home on account of drunkenness and two others were deported for spying," wrote two members of one of the organizations. "Mrs X—— seems to have made an almost international reputation, somebody said, 'She breaks all the commandments every night.' A nurse is living openly with one of the interpreters. One of the London hospital committees is reported to have said, 'Don't be too particular about whom we send or we won't get anybody to go at all.'"[71] What is described in this account was merely the tip of the iceberg. Life in Serbia for medical and relief workers was a bit of a free-for-all. It was just the kind of environment where a headstrong and determined English nurse could join the Serbian army.

CHAPTER 3

KRAGUJEVAC

1914

Bags in hand, the women of the unit walked across the cracked, baked earth bordering the First Reserve Military Hospital, past the litter that fluttered in dusty heaps against its walls. They were welcomed through the front doors by the portly and middle-aged hospital director, Dr Vučetić, with a grandiose sweep of his hand.[1] They stepped out of the searing heat of the afternoon sun into the gloom of the poorly lit building, squinting while their eyes adjusted, and breathing in for the first time the fetid smell that permeated every room, of crowded human bodies, badly infected wounds, antiseptic, tobacco and stale food.[2]

The hospital, on the outskirts of Kragujevac, was overflowing with patients, both Serbs and POWs. They had been placed side by side in the small, unventilated rooms, which were connected by dark and seemingly interminable corridors. These too were packed full of gaunt, tired men. "Over a thousand rough iron cots had been placed with sacks stuffed with straw for mattresses, one small pillow also of straw, one sheet and one thick army blanket to each," wrote Emily later, describing the dismay she felt on getting her first good look at the surroundings. "We had none of the equipment or conveniences of an ordinary hospital, not even running water. All had to be carted from the village, half an hour's journey away."[3]

What was now one of the largest military hospitals in Serbia had been hurriedly converted from an army barracks. Its twelve hundred patients were housed in a pair of two-storey buildings that were identical in design and relatively modern. One was set aside for six hundred sick, the other for the same number of wounded.[4]

Like many official constructions of the time, the buildings were finished in cream-coloured stucco. They were otherwise simply adorned and stood plainly, marked by row upon row of evenly spaced windows and capped by low, red-tiled roofs. They stretched out lengthwise, dominating spacious and tree-bordered grounds that had been well kept before the war.[5]

The women of the Anglo-American Unit were given as enthusiastic a welcome as the energies of the exhausted staff permitted. Surgeon Dr Roman Sondermeyer, the immaculately dressed head of the Military Medical Service of the Serbian army, stepped forward smartly to meet them, while Dr Vučetić introduced them to his wife, who was also a doctor, and their young daughter, who assisted in the wards. Other than a few untrained Serbian women, the staff included a mere five orderlies and, briefly, Catharina Sturzenegger, a Swiss-German nurse of indelicate build. "Twelve hundred patients and we were only two surgeons, eight nurses and some five hospital orderlies!" wrote Emily of her shock upon realizing how many patients there were and how few staff.[6]

On 30th August, the day after her arrival, Flora rose early with the others and attempted to turn herself out as smartly as possible in her uniform. She eased uncomfortably into a starched, high-collared, ankle-length grey dress, over which she wore a plain white coat. Then she pinned a white nurse's cap onto her unruly brown-grey hair.[7] After running her hands down her uniform one final time, she hurried with Emily to the five wards that they had jointly been assigned to by Dr Vučetić. He had also given them all the men in the corridors to care for, one hundred and forty patients in all.[8]

With the aid of gestures and the few words of Serbian she had been taught by Mabel, Flora set to work. "Gave several baths etc., and rubbed backs," she scribbled in her diary one week after arrival.[9] On a typical day she began work in the morning, stopped for lunch, and then returned to the wards mid-afternoon, finishing in the early evening. Every sixth day she took her turn at night duty in one of the two dimly lit hospital buildings. In practice, this meant an exhausting "36 hours on duty without sleep".[10] The shift was daunting even for the trained nurses. "It has been an agitating night," wrote one of them near the end of one such shift. "A man suddenly had an arterial haemorrhage, and I had to hold on to him for nearly half an hour before the doctor was awake and dressed, pressing with all my might on the artery. I am drenched in blood and cannot go and change till my night duty is done. We see some pretty awful things."[11]

At the end of each long, hard day, Flora returned to the sparsely furnished room that she shared with the other women. It had one table, two backless benches and a makeshift bed for each of them, which was nothing more than wooden planks raised on bricks, covered with the same lumpy straw mattress given to patients and a single, coarse soldier's blanket. For privacy, they rigged a curtain across one corner to give them a space to wash. The room served as their "dining, sitting, writing and bathroom", where they would sit down most nights to their evening meal. "I never want to eat a chicken again, or a cabbage," sighed one of them. "All the chickens undergo the severest drill and physical exercise, and it is most exhausting to try and make a meal of them."[12]

When new patients arrived, it was almost always at two or three a.m. Up to one hundred men would be carried into the hospital yard, having survived an agonizing journey of several days in ox wagons, their injuries jolted at every bump. "Many of the worst wounded died on the way, and those that did arrive were in a terrible condition," recorded Flora.[13] By the time their stretchers were laid in the yard, their uniforms were stiff with congealed blood, their wounds infected, foul-smelling and swollen with pus and the dressings crawling with lice.[14] Exhausted, Flora and the other nurses dragged themselves wearily from their beds to attend to them. Even Emily was shaken by their numbers and condition. "I remember standing appalled as batch after batch of fresh wounded were brought in," she wrote, "wondering how far the very few words of Servian [sic] which I had learnt on the trip out would carry me through."[15]

Working alongside the doctors and male orderlies, the women cut through the men's clothing with knives and scissors and eased off the stinking, encrusted bandages. They cleansed the infected, oozing wounds with lint, working to the outside of the injury with each gentle stroke. Then they treated them with iodine before redressing them with a layer of absorbent cotton wool atop thin gauze, topped by a carefully tied bandage. Where operations were required, the patients were wheeled to the two surgeons who were often forced to work without anaesthetic. "We had to keep it for major cases," explained Emily. For her the work was a turning point. Previously she had looked after a single patient at a time. Now, at last, she had the opportunity to push herself to her very limits. "We had all read the wonderful experiences of Florence Nightingale in Scutari not so very far away but we are privileged, in a small measure, to realize some of them here in Servia [sic]," she wrote with an almost missionary zeal.[16]

All the women grew to respect the courage of their patients, none more so than Flora, for whom there was no greater value than stoicism. "The Serbian soldier prides himself on being able to stand an operation and he will draw himself up proudly, and say '*Ja sam Srbin*' – that means 'I am a Serb' – by which he means to imply that he will go through anything without flinching," she recalled. "They have more endurance than any other race I have ever met."[17] They were also great fun as soon as they began to recover their strength. "A nurse would leave a patient at night going on splendidly, far into the stage of convalescence," reported one journal of their experiences. "Going [on] her rounds the next morning she would hear heart-rending groans from his bed, and see his head buried in the pillow apparently in agonies of pain; at a solicitous inquiry he would spring up with a laugh, and declare himself quite well, whilst the occupants of the surrounding beds shook with laughter at the success of the little jest."[18] The other nurses shared Flora's regard for them. "I cannot find words to express my admiration for them, both as patients and men," wrote twenty-eight-year-old Violet O'Brien in a letter home. "They are simply charming, so grateful for the least attention."[19] It was one of the few things on which they agreed.

The patients the women were nursing were casualties of one of the first battles of the First World War. On 12th August, the day that the Anglo-American Unit sailed from England, two hundred thousand soldiers of the Austro-Hungarian army crossed the rivers that formed the northern and western borders of Serbia. The aim of the invasion was clear from the name given to the campaign by the Austrians, the "Strafexpedition" ("Punitive Expedition").[20] The two sides were well matched but, with the arrogance that came with their position as a great power, the Austro-Hungarians had dismissed the capabilities of the Serbian army. They expected to defeat them in fourteen days.[21]

At the outset of the war, Serbia had a relatively small but disciplined army of four hundred thousand soldiers. Although many of its men were experienced fighters who had fought in the Balkan Wars of 1912 and 1913, the two years of warfare had left the army utterly unprepared for an invasion. The fighting had drained its medical stores. Most of its artillery was outdated, there was little money to re-equip and there were not enough rifles for all the soldiers. More than half the men had to fight in peasant dress for lack of uniforms, and many did not even have boots.[22] But while the invaders had superior equipment and artillery, the Serbian army had strengths of its own. It had able soldiers who were accustomed to hardship and led by experienced commanders. They were also patriotic, unlike the soldiers of Austria-Hungary, many of whom were fellow Slavs who sympathized with the Serbs and disliked the thought of fighting them.

The blue uniforms of the Austro-Hungarian army met the grey-brown uniforms and tattered brown homespuns of the Serbs in mountainous north-west Serbia. To the stunned amazement of the invaders, the highly motivated but poorly armed peasant soldiers fought them to a standstill. The Austrian commander soon reported to his superiors in Vienna that he was suffering "heavy losses" and pleaded with them to send support.[23] Reinforcements reached the Serbs first. In a surprise attack, they drove the Austrians back across the frontier in what became known as the Battle of Cer Mountain. By 24th August the Serbians had won the first Allied victory of the war.[24]

The triumphant Serbians now referred to the punishing army as the "*bestrafte*", the "punished" one, but both sides had suffered greatly. Between six and ten thousand of the invaders were killed, along with three to five thousand Serbian soldiers. "The area between Cer and the River Jadar where this tremendous battle took place was nothing but mass graves and putrefying flesh," commented a French journalist.[25] Forty-five thousand wounded filled the hospitals, both Serbs and Austro-Hungarians.[26] Serbian civilians also suffered heavily. While the Austro-German and Slav soldiers of the Austro-Hungarian army appear to have conducted themselves reasonably well, the campaign was characterized by widespread atrocities by the Hungarian component of the army, who massacred an estimated three to four thousand non-combatants.[27]

The Anglo-American Unit had arrived in Kragujevac a mere five days after the Serbian victory. Although the Serbs had defeated the invaders, throughout September and October bitter trench warfare continued along the northern and western frontiers of Serbia, following a short-lived invasion of Bosnia and southern Hungary by the victorious army.[28] The fighting provided the First Reserve Military Hospital with a continuous stream of casualties, which steadily eroded their limited supplies.

"It took me a month even to learn how to pronounce 'Kraguje-vatz'," recalled Flora. Most of the conversations she had with patients were conducted clumsily through sign language. "Of course we made many ludicrous mistakes at first in consequence," she said.

> I remember finding a man sitting on the operating table one day using the most awful language – I couldn't understand everything he said, of course – and perhaps it was just as well I couldn't, but I was very much surprised at a Serb making so much fuss about the pain, so I went and fetched an interpreter to find out what it was all about, and then I found it was not the pain at all he was fussing about. When he came into the operation, he had hidden, under his shirt, a large lump of sausage, which he was going to take as a refresher when he came to from the chloroform, and this lump of sausage had somehow got knocked down and mixed up with the dirty dressings on the floor, and couldn't be found anywhere, and he was horribly annoyed about it, it wasn't the pain at all he minded.[29]

Emily too fell foul of the inevitable misunderstandings. "Passing through one of the corridors one day, I stopped on seeing a man try to get a better position for his leg which had been terribly smashed," she wrote.

> I moved it a little and was much surprised to hear him say, "Him leg not much good, pretty bad." I asked him if he spoke English and he said, "No, American." He had worked in the mines in Colorado for three

years and had acquired a good amount of "American"... Of course we tried to learn the language, but our efforts at first met with very poor success. I asked one man, as I thought, to open his mouth, but learnt from the shrieks of laughter of the entire ward that I had said "Open your window and put out your tongue".[30]

The long, hard hours of work and struggle to learn Serbian served to take Flora's mind off an event that affected her deeply, the death of her ninety-two-year-old father on 23rd August, only eleven days after she had left for Serbia. From 15th September to 11th October she made no entries in her diary at all, a highly unusual gap from someone who otherwise wrote dutifully. Although it is not clear exactly when and how she was told, she almost certainly received a letter or telegram from home telling her the news. Pragmatic enough to realize that there was little point returning home but wracked with guilt about not being there, she suffered through these weeks with only Emily for support. Reticent about expressing emotion, she occupied herself as best she could. She knew that she would be as busy at Kragujevac as she would anywhere else.

Emily was her sole friend, support and confidante. Although she had an air of earnestness about her that Flora lacked, they shared a keen sense of humour and fun. And both were determined to spend their little spare time away from the hospital, partly to take a break from the conditions but also because their relations with the other nurses were becoming strained to breaking point. By the time they had reached Serbia, the other women had formed another tight-knit group, their cohesion at least partly cemented by their dislike of the high-spirited pair.

While one of the nurses had left to work at another hospital shortly after arrival, the other five quickly rallied around the hospital director, Dr Vučetić. He evidently enjoyed his exalted status among them and would read his "literary" essays on practical medicine aloud to them until late in the evening, his doting wife next to him, her eyes shining with pride.[31] Understandably, Flora chose to spend her free time otherwise. Her diary makes frequent reference to trips with Emily – never any of the others – to the country for walks or rides, to restaurants for dinner, to the casino or theatre and, typically, to go shopping, much to the disapproval of the other nurses. Flora in turn delighted in thinking of unflattering nicknames for them. One became "a touch of mauve", another, the "red-haired mouse".[32]

Neither did Flora think much of Dr Vučetić. She was appalled by the poor standard of management in the hospital. Everything about their work was disorganized, even chaotic, and he could not, she felt, be relied upon to solve the inevitable problems that arose. Worst of all was the standard of cleanliness. Emily too was horrified by what she saw. "I went for a walk one afternoon when I saw a dressing-room orderly emptying waste cans, filled with the pus dressings, in a ditch opposite the main building," she wrote in a report to the American Red Cross. "He answered my question by stating in a surprised voice that they had never burnt them and it seemed unnecessary to start now."[33]

In late September, to their surprise the women were joined at the First Reserve by a young English doctor. Thirty-one-year-old William "Robert" Ridley, from Northumberland, was the eldest of four sons of a Lloyds Bank manager. He had spent his childhood in the picturesque village of Rothbury before attending boarding school in Edinburgh. He was studious and hard-working, and won a place in Edinburgh University's prestigious Medical School in 1901.[34] But the young student struggled through his studies, his health sapped by tuberculosis. In his battle with the disease, it took him nearly ten years to complete his degree. During his final year's examinations, his health collapsed and he was rushed to a sanatorium in Dundee to recover his strength. The Dean eventually gave special dispensation for his degree to be granted, in 1910.[35]

Four years later, Dr Ridley's fortunes were beginning to turn around. He appears to have recovered his health, and had worked as a doctor in Leith, Sunderland and Newcastle. By the outbreak of war, he was also engaged to be married. Driven almost certainly by a combination of patriotism and adventure-seeking, he immediately approached the War Office, hoping for work in Belgium or France. When they refused on the grounds they had no medical vacancies, he contacted the Serbian legation who hired him on the spot. In early September his parents received a call from the War Office offering him a position. By then, it was too late – he had reached Marseilles en route to Serbia.

* * *

By early October the weather was beginning to turn. The hot days of September had been replaced by overcast skies and the cooler days and nights of autumn. The 12th of that month was one such day. The rain, which had begun the day before, continued incessantly, turning the streets of Kragujevac into running rivers of mud and casting a gloom over the chilly wards. That morning, while Flora was at work, she was handed a note from Dr Ridley in which he had scribbled shakily that he was suffering from dysentery. She took it immediately to Dr Vučetić. "Told the Director with the usual results!" she commented disparagingly. As "no one seemed to be getting any move on", she took Emily with her after lunch to visit him at his residence outside of the hospital grounds. Both were worried enough about his condition to stay with him for the rest of the day. Late that evening Flora dashed off through the dark to the hospital to collect a "B.P." (presumably bedpan) for his use, while Emily stayed behind with him. Nurse Violet O'Brien caught her in the act of removing one from the hospital supplies. Any sympathy Violet may have had for Dr Ridley was eroded by her dislike of Flora, and she took umbrage at her breach of hospital regulations. "Met O'B. and had a row with her on the subject," wrote Flora, who had little but contempt for her. Bedpan in hand, she returned to Dr Ridley. Alongside Emily, she stayed with him all night.[36]

The following day, Ridley was still "very bad". Although he required Flora and Emily's constant attention, the other nurses made few allowances. "Americano and I nursed him and did the hospital work too. The Happy Family all furious and won't speak to us. What ho!" jotted Flora sarcastically that evening. With Emily, she began to look after him night and day, in shifts, their exhaustion and resentment increasing as each day passed with no offers of help. Only on one occasion did one of the other nurses – Violet O'Brien, in fact – take a night with him. "Miss O'Brien took night with Ridley!" wrote Flora afterwards in amazement.[37]

On Tuesday 20th October Flora recorded in her diary that, at last, Dr Ridley had had a good night, while Emily wrote his mother a letter. "He's suffering from dysentery," she told her, "but he's much better and hopes to be up in a few days."[38] By Thursday they felt able to spend an evening together at the theatre. But within a few days Ridley's health started to deteriorate again. On 30th October

they were worried enough to call in a doctor. On 1st November
he was worse still. "Moved Dr Ridley up to Hospital at 5 p.m.,"
scratched Flora in her diary. "I took night duty with him. Another
all night," she commented, bitter at the lack of help from all but
Emily. "Dr Ridley better in morning but worse later on," recorded
Flora two days later. Finally, one of the other nurses stepped in to
help. "Mrs Hartney stayed in afternoon, Americano took night.
Called me at 3 a.m. Doctor sinking rapidly. Did all we could but he
died at 5 a.m. No one else there."[39] On 6th November Dr Ridley's
parents received Emily's letter saying that he was better. The following day they received a telegram from Dr Vučetić telling them
that he had died.[40]

At his military funeral two days later the young doctor was
given "music, soldiers, [a] gun salute and all Kragurawatz [sic]
turned out," Flora recorded.[41] Dr Vučetić, his stout figure puffed
further with the importance of the occasion, gave Dr Ridley a
florid tribute.[42] One can only imagine what Flora and Emily must
have felt standing at his grave alongside the other nurses listening
to Dr Vučetić's speech, when they had done so little to help them
keep Dr Ridley alive. A week later, they left the hospital for good.

In the days before their departure they had little time to mourn.
With the hospital already full, new and pressing demands were
placed on it. On 7th November, with winter closing in and the
recalcitrant Serbs still undefeated, Austria-Hungary attacked again
across Serbia's north-western frontier. This time the invaders left
little to chance. They sent an army strong enough in terms of both
manpower and munitions to crush the Serbs. Their initial target
was Valjevo, a town north-west of Kragujevac. They then planned
to move on Kragujevac itself.

The casualties of the fighting were taken in droves to Krague-
vac, quickly overwhelming the limited resources of the town and
its hospitals. Even before the invasion, the First Reserve Military
Hospital had almost run out of medical supplies. "The dressings
began to give out early," explained Emily. "You see, we had not
been able to take much of a consignment with us, and the supply dwindled so that we couldn't dress wounds more than once
in eight or nine days, when all required one fresh dressing a day,
and some two."[43]

Mabel Grouitch had left her Unit a week after arrival to join her husband Slavko in Niš, but kept in close contact with her nurses who told her of the desperate shortage. In a telegram to England begging for supplies, she reported that surgical stores were running short, surgeons were working eighteen hours a day and that her nurses were exhausted from the strain but doing "noble work".[44] However, when the hospital finally ran out of anaesthetic, it became too much for some of them to watch their patients undergo major operations and amputations whilst fully conscious. "[The Serbian soldiers] had to be held down," recalled Mabel. "So indescribably terrible were the sights and sounds that even the nurses couldn't endure it. I remember one day when an experienced Irish nurse [Violet O'Brien], who had seen service in India and many campaigns, fainted during one of these operations. She couldn't stand it."[45]

Along with the medicine and supplies, the First Reserve ran out of clean clothing to replace the filthy uniforms of their patients. Beds were first pushed up against each other in pairs to accommodate three men, the least seriously wounded in the middle. When the beds ran out, the wounded were placed on sacks of straw. Then, when the sacks of straw ran out, beds were improvised from wooden planks placed on iron railings.[46] Food too ran short for both patients and staff.[47] Finally, the hospital could take in no more men. "After the battle of Valjevo," recorded Emily, "we received so many wounded prisoners that, having filled all the houses, we had to improvise beds of boughs along the roadway, and place the wounded there until room could be made on the trains going into the interior. Peasant women helped feed them while they lay there."[48]

Kragujevac alone could not handle the number of wounded. Thousands were evacuated instead to hospital centres farther south like Niš, Skopje and Gevgelija. Some of the patients were sent to hospitals run by other Allied missions, which were now starting to arrive two months after the Anglo-American Unit. Of the British units, many members had been inspired to volunteer for "brave little Serbia" by the stories that had trickled back to Britain in September and October about the "gallant" work of Mabel Grouitch and her "tiny band" of nurses.[49]

The Serbian army was no match for the firepower of the Austrians. The enemy advanced rapidly through the forested and

mountainous country in the direction of Valjevo, with the Serbs
in full retreat before them. When Valjevo fell on 15th November,
the Austrians prepared to move on Kragujevac, only thirty-five
miles away. On hearing the news Dr Vučetić flew into a panic.
He rushed into the room where the five remaining nurses were
eating breakfast to tell them that they had to leave in half an
hour. "It was awful," commented Ada Mann. "We just stuffed
our things together and then went to the patients. For those
who could walk all the clothes were thrown out of the window,
and they put on the first that came to hand. Then the helpless
ones were dressed as far as possible, and put on stretchers, then
in the bullock carts, and off to the station. The last sound we
heard was the knocking down of the beds."[50] All the wounded
who could be moved were sent to hospitals in Niš and Skopje,
well away from the fighting, while the nurses fled south to Niš
by train.

"Saw a dead Austrian. Had tea 400 metres from the Austrian lines.
Drove back under fire… bombardment all night," wrote Flora
excitedly in her diary on 15th November from her room at the
Slavia Hotel in Belgrade. The Slavia was the only hotel still open,
and they had taken the only available room.[51] She had left the First
Reserve with Emily three days earlier, after completing her three-
month contract. With hospital supplies at an end and relations
with their colleagues beyond redemption, they had made up their
minds to leave. They could do more good raising money for the
Serbs at home, they felt, and a short holiday in the capital before
they returned would do them no harm.

Anyone they asked would have told them it was pure folly to
travel to Belgrade just as the Austrians were making their plans
to storm the city, but, for Flora and Emily, the danger was part of
the attraction. After dropping their bags in their hotel room, they
dashed out immediately to visit the newly built and well-equipped
military hospital run by the American Red Cross, a short walk
away.[52] There, Flora and Emily made the acquaintance of its thirty-
year-old head, Edward Ryan, a tall, dark-haired doctor of Irish
descent from Scranton, Pennsylvania. If they were unaware then
of his unrivalled ability to attract hatred, controversy and scandal,
they were to learn of it soon.

For the next two days and nights Flora and Emily became archetypical war tourists. "Looked round town at the ruins," scribbled Flora happily in her diary,[53] while Emily's breathless account of their holiday found its way into the pages of the *New York Times*. "While I was there, shells fell anywhere," she reported. "People were killed in the courtyard of the [American Red Cross] hospital. The Austrian troops were so near that we could see them. They were just across the River Sava. At night they played two big search lights on the city, and if a sign of life appeared anywhere shells were dropped on the spot. No lights were allowed in the city, and it was forbidden to appear on the streets after dark."[54]

When they left the capital for home on 17th November, they left Dr Ryan and the American Red Cross behind to sit out the invasion. The campaign was evidently nearing the end. On 28th November, with his soldiers virtually out of ammunition, General Putnik, the Serbian Chief-of-Staff, took the decision to abandon Belgrade. The Austrians, now certain of victory, paused for three days in their campaign after occupying the capital, to allow their tired soldiers to rest. During this interval a small amount of ammunition arrived for the Serbs from the Allies. It was not much, but it made a limited Serbian counter-offensive possible and, more importantly, it lent them hope. On 2nd December Putnik ordered an attack on the Austrian columns in what he knew would be his final chance to stem their advance.[55]

The attack caught the Austrians entirely by surprise. In the chaos that followed they lost one position after another. Soon they were in full flight, unable to take their weapons or equipment with them over the roads of churned mud. By 15th December Belgrade was back in the hands of the Serbs and the Austrians had been routed. The defeat was catastrophic for Austria-Hungary. Nearly half of its four hundred and fifty thousand soldiers had been killed, wounded, declared missing or taken prisoner. Serbian losses exceeded one hundred and thirty thousand, an immense number in proportion to the size of the army.[56]

The Austrians had left behind a further sixty thousand POWs, bringing the total within Serbia to about seventy-five thousand. While some had been wounded, others had deserted. Czech regiments in particular were reported to have surrendered to the Serbs en masse, complete even with regimental bands.[57] The war had also created five hundred thousand internal refugees.[58] Civilians who lived near the fighting to the north and north-west of the country had fled to the interior, terrified of a recurrence of the atrocities at the hands of the Hungarians which had marred the first invasion.

The Serbs did not have the infrastructure or resources to cope with the scale of the refugee crisis. When winter descended, the towns and villages to the south of the fighting were overflowing with half-starved and ill-housed refugees and prisoners. Across Serbia the incidence of disease started to mount ominously.[59] The British Red Cross, based in Skopje, began to receive patients with diphtheria, enteric, pneumonia and scarlet and relapsing fever, and they were forced to stand by helplessly as several of their patients died agonizingly of tetanus.[60] The rate of illness among the staff also began to rise worryingly. When one of the volunteers contracted smallpox, it sent panic into the ranks of his colleagues. Inevitably, the first deaths from disease soon occurred among the members of the Allied missions. The first British woman to die in Serbia, Miss Nellie Clark, succumbed to septic throat and Grave's disease on Christmas Day, 1914. She had volunteered to work as a nurse with the Lady Paget Mission, also based in Skopje.[61]

Worst affected by the spread of disease and the lack of food and shelter were the Austrian POWs. While there were individual cases of cruelty, the Serbs on the whole treated them reasonably well, employing as many as possible in a range of tasks for a minimal salary or better rations, while families could pay the government to have one as a servant.[62] Many of those who were trained as doctors volunteered for service while others became efficient, hard-working and loyal orderlies in both Allied and Serbian-run hospitals. However, the Serbs simply could not absorb a further sixty thousand into their shattered economy. Many of those who were unable to find work were packed into crowded and filthy former stables, with insufficient food and little by way of sanitary arrangements.[63] Sickness spread rapidly among them.

More help was desperately needed amid the deteriorating situation. New Allied missions continued to arrive, including two more American Red Cross units who were assigned to Gevgelija in the south of the country. In December, Katherine MacPhail was one of five woman doctors to set out for Serbia as part of the First Serbian Unit of the Scottish Women's Hospitals.

Emily realized that conditions in Serbia were ripe for an epidemic. Before she returned home to New York, she wrote anxiously to the American Red Cross, pleading with them to send more help. Shocked at the worsening sanitary conditions, she illustrated her letter with an example of what she had seen happen to used dressings in Skopje on her way home. She was too discreet to name the British Red Cross as the culprits, who had far greater worries than what happened to their dressings and whose eighteen staff were working tirelessly in impossible conditions looking after fifteen hundred patients.[64] "One of their buildings was on a steep hill and the orderly used to empty the dressing cans over the wall where they would blow about in all directions," she wrote. "The Turks [the Muslim population]... used to pick these over, taking the cleanest ones to line their wadded waistcoats. I don't want to be disgusting, but I do want to make you appreciate that this may be the beginning of an epidemic... If any help is coming it must come at once and must be of drastic measure."[65]

CHAPTER 4

TYPHUS

1915

On 12th February 1915, Flora and Emily's ship steamed through the mild green waters of the Aegean, past the towering heights of Mount Olympus, into Salonika's vast harbour. Flora had rushed back to the Greek port after only five weeks at home, gladly leaving behind the damp and chill of an English winter. In the little time she had in England she had launched herself into raising funds for the Serbs. To her "utter astonishment", she managed to collect £2,000 following an appeal for assistance published by the *Daily Mail*.[1] Emily had done equally well. After a nine-day winter Atlantic crossing, she had spent a mere twelve days in New York. So impressed were the American Red Cross by the "courage and fine spirit" shown by "plucky little Miss Simmonds" that they also gave her £2,000.[2] Flora and Emily used the funds to buy a remarkable one hundred and twenty tons of medical supplies, including absorbent wool, gauze, chloroform, Mead's plaster, Phenosol and one X-ray apparatus "with latest attachments".[3] "I did not lose one single package, every one being numbered and the list checked off at Malta, Salonika, Nish and Valjevo," wrote Flora proudly.[4]

They were met in Salonika by a low hum of rumours about conditions in Serbia. Many people were dying of disease; it was foolhardy to go, it was said. Dismissing all such concerns, on 14th February the pair caught a morning train, bringing with them their supplies on five railway trucks.[5] When they boarded, they were taken aback by the ominous smell of disinfectant, so strong that it made their eyes smart, from a formaldehyde-based solution used by the Greek railway authorities to douse the Serbia-bound carriages.[6] A few hours later they caught their first glimpse of the tumbledown Serbian town of Gevgelija, just across the Greek border. As the train rumbled to its final stop, they could not help but notice hundreds upon hundreds of mounds of freshly turned earth in the cemeteries near the railway line.[7]

Waiting on the platform in the pouring rain were members of the American Red Cross, who had been running a hospital in a building by the station. The arrival of the train was the one event each day they looked forward to. It was their only chance to meet other English speakers and swap news of the war, and as many as could be spared had scrambled to be there. As Flora and Emily stepped down onto the wet platform with their bags, the members of the mission rushed forward eagerly to invite them to tour their hospital while they waited for their connecting train north. On their short walk there, the Americans told them hurriedly about their work.

The six doctors and twelve nurses had reached the town on 18th December 1914, and had agreed to take charge of a hospital in an old, rat-infested, former cigarette factory.[8] The four-storey building had no heat, no running water and no sanitary or drainage facilities. On arrival they found the two thousand patients packed tightly together on filthy straw or on the bare floor while men with typhoid, typhus, dysentery and smallpox writhed and shivered among the wounded.[9] By the time of Flora and Emily's visit they had been at work for seven demoralizing weeks. With insufficient food, facilities and medical supplies, they were often forced to stand by helplessly as men with otherwise treatable conditions continued to die.

One of the doctors, forty-year-old James Donnelly, offered to show Flora and Emily around the hospital. The sturdily built doctor, from Brooklyn, New York, had a passion for travel. He had worked in the Far East, Africa and Haiti before becoming one of the first American Red Cross volunteers for Serbia.[10] Flora and Emily took to the "jolly young doctor" immediately. His pride and joy were two "very antediluvian boilers", which, Emily commented wryly, "looked as if they had once upon a time belonged to a locomotive".[11] But they were left aghast by the damp, cold wards, full of sick, wounded and dying men and the news that three of the nurses and one doctor were seriously ill with typhus, a

louse-borne disease which was killing nearly three quarters of those
it infected.[12] The reality of what they were letting themselves in for
now suddenly struck home. If they stuck to their plan to work in a
Serbian hospital, they knew that they would put their lives at risk.

When they waved goodbye from the window of their train, they
both breathed a sigh of relief. The town was a "Godforsaken little
hole", wrote Flora in her diary that evening, as she summed up her
impressions of the day. Three days after their visit Dr Donnelly fell
ill with typhus. On 22nd February he became delirious, seized an
old musket from a Serbian sentry and shot himself in the forehead.
He died almost instantly.[13]

"Typhus raging throughout country. Mortality high. Cholera
feared later," Emily telegraphed the American Red Cross. She was
appalled by what she had seen in Gevgelija and had wasted little
time after arriving in Niš to find a post office from which to send
her wire. She finished her message with a desperate plea. "Help
urgently needed, especially doctors, nurses, with hospital isolation
equipment and disinfectors for clothing. SIMMONDS."[14]

Emily's warning to the Red Cross in 1914 had come to pass. In
November and December, cases of typhus had begun to appear
across Serbia, primarily in hospitals and POW camps. Initially there
was little concern. Sporadic cases were nothing new and, in normal
conditions, the disease could be controlled and cases isolated. But
now conditions in Serbia were anything but normal. The country
had been invaded twice. Although it had emerged victorious, it had
been drained of resources and its soldiers and people were hungry
and exhausted. It could not house or feed its own estimated half
a million internal refugees, let alone seventy-five thousand POWs.
Overcrowding increased the opportunities for transmission and a
disease normally only endemic rapidly became epidemic.

The first major outbreak had occurred in late December 1914 in
the rail and roadway hub of Valjevo. The town of eight thousand
people lay sixty miles south-west of Belgrade along the Kolubara
River, surrounded by hills.[15] Like most Serbian country towns it
had a central marketplace and simple one-storey cottages that
lined broad, roughly cobbled streets. In ordinary circumstances
it was bustling and prosperous.[16] But by late 1914 the horrors of
war were clear to see upon it. The town had been at the centre of

much of the fighting in November and December. Thousands of
grievously sick and wounded men, both Serbian and Austrian,
crowded the filthy hospitals. Long dead horses lay decomposing
in the streets whilst pigs and dogs were sometimes seen feeding
on the human victims of the fighting who had been hastily and
inadequately buried in its vicinity.[17] The town was also crowded
with five and a half thousand POWs who, weakened by hunger
and crawling with lice, were packed together in the storehouses
of the artillery barracks.

The POWs became the epidemic's earliest victims.[18] A handful
of men, initially, began to show symptoms similar to influenza. At
first they were stricken with a severe headache, cough and chills.
Within twenty-four hours they could hardly move, prostrated by
soaring fever and excruciating muscle pain in their legs and back.
Sticky white mucus began to accumulate in their mouths and
throats, coating their tongues thickly. Four or five days later a pink
rash spread from their chests across their bodies and rapidly developed into purplish-red, slightly elevated spots. Often its victims
became delirious or writhed in agony from the wracking pains in
their limbs; many suffered from diarrhoea and became incontinent.
After about a week the high fever dropped away suddenly while its
victims sweated profusely, only to rise and fall two or three times
over subsequent days. Those who survived were often reduced to
near skeletons. The disease raced like wildfire through the barracks
among the lice-covered men who were forced to huddle together
for warmth during the bitter nights. By the time of the first deaths,
hundreds more of the men were showing the early symptoms of
the disease.

In December and January a handful of foreign medical workers
reached Valjevo. The first to arrive, on 11th December, were members of a small Dutch mission, headed by Dr Arius van Tienhoven,
who were returning to the hospital that they had been running before the invasion.[19] Their previously well-managed wards were now
overflowing with sick, dying and dead men. A sole Austrian POW
doctor was attempting to do what he could for the four hundred
patients, but many had not had their dressings changed for twenty
days. The unit arrived to find the floors covered in excrement and
running pus. "But that which made me literally tremble," recalled

Dr van Tienhoven, "was to find two dying men lying in the middle of a pile of bodies."[20]

Next to arrive were Albert Cooke and Barton Cookingham, two American doctors who had become restless while working in the overstaffed American Hospital in Neuilly, France.[21] Cooke was a well-fed police doctor from Whitehall, New York. He looked older than his thirty-seven years, an impression lent by his brown, well-trimmed moustache, round, lined face and carefully side-parted hair. Twenty-five-year-old Cookingham, a young surgeon, was from Red Hook, New York. Pug-nosed, freckled, with unruly sandy hair, he towered over Cooke at nearly 6'2".

The doctors arrived in Valjevo on New Year's Day. Cooke took over the high school, which had been hastily converted into a hospital. Cookingham took over the military hospital, a former hotel. Between them they had four hundred half-starved, wounded men to care for. With few supplies, no drugs and little food, they found it a near hopeless task.[22] "No matter how competent or clever an operator one may be his efforts are more or less in vain in this place," wrote Cookingham desolately. "Our mortality has been high because there has been nothing for the poor beggars to eat post-operative... We have bought eggs and milk for them at times but our salary will not allow us to feed a whole hospital."[23] The doctors found what little respite they could in the companionship of the Dutch mission, who in turn greatly enjoyed the Americans' company. "Cook [sic] was gaiety itself," recollected Dr van Tienhoven. "He amused us all by his American songs and his Negro dances."[24]

During the second half of January, Cooke and Cookingham noticed the sinister signs of fever and spots appearing among the ranks of their wounded patients as the disease spread to their hospitals. They continued their work as black flags denoting death began to appear in the streets of the town, hung ominously above the windows of households. "The only way you can get an idea of the terrible conditions in the town is by reading accounts of some of the great plagues of the Middle Ages," wrote Dr Cookingham later in a letter home.

During the first few months they made some effort to give the victims a decent burial. That was when the deaths were running only fifty to seventy-five a day. Later, when deaths reached 150 a day and when a large part of the population was down with the fever, that was out of the question. They simply stacked the bodies together like logs and hauled them away. The dead wagon made its rounds as often as possible. Bodies were just tossed in and the grim callers passed on to the next house. When the wagon was full, it started for the outskirts of the town. I have seen it pass through the streets with a head or two hanging out behind and arms and legs extended over the sides. The bodies were dumped into a hole outside the city limits and the whole mess hastily covered with earth. Then the wagon and the overworked horse began the rounds again. The misery and the suffering in Valjevo are indescribable.[25]

Despite the growing catastrophe the authorities continued to permit travel to and from the town. Trains continued to arrive and depart, laden with sick and lice-infested passengers. Soldiers on leave and refugees travelled freely on the crowded trains to all corners of Serbia, spreading the disease to villages across the length and breadth of the country.[26]

On 6th February, in the midst of the epidemic, Dr Cookingham wrote to Whitney Warren, a New York architect who had helped fund their trip. "Right at the start I am going to take you by surprise and tell you that owing to an attack of 'Typhus Recurrans' I have not had an opportunity to write before," he apologized.

While writing this I am about two feet away from Cooke, who is on his back with the same malady, and, as he is very weak, he is in no condition to write, much as he wants to. I am at present in what they call the interval, which lasts a varying length of time. At the end of that period, the fever returns again and you have to go through the same thing over again. Twice usually ends it, but it leaves you very weak and thin. I have lost about fourty [sic] pounds already. Poor Cooke's double chin is suffering very much. I am afraid it is lost for ever.[27]

Flora and Emily found Niš even more depressing than they had remembered. They had planned to pass through the shabby, over-crowded town as quickly as possible, but first they needed to receive their assignment from Colonel Subotić, the Vice President of the Serbian Red Cross, and he was proving hard to find. While they

waited impatiently for him to return to his offices, they dropped
off their X-ray machine at the Second Reserve Hospital, which had
been rushed into service in a large municipal building by the train
station. It was also where their former colleagues from the Anglo-
American Unit were at work.[28] They pushed their way through the
entrance, past crowds of "unkempt, unwashed individuals in ragged
uniforms" and through "unspeakably stuffy" corridors lined with
patients. On asking for the women they were directed to a ground-
floor dressing room. They walked into a space that was fifty feet
long and crowded with wounded men, with a long row of tables
placed down the centre to which patients were carried in turn.[29]
There they found three of the five women at work.[30] They looked
exhausted. "Went to hospital and saw Miss O'Brien and 'Scotland',
also the 'Matron' – Mrs Barlow," scratched Flora briefly in her
diary. "Had tea and chatted with the two former... the 'touch of
mauve' and the 'red-haired mouse' also located there," she added,
unable to resist resurrecting her old, uncharitable nicknames.[31]

Dr Abraham of the British Red Cross, more descriptive than
Flora, visited the hospital shortly after they did. Two of the women,
by then, had left for home. He found the other three "very worn
and tired". Little wonder, he remarked. "They had been working
in the same awful atmosphere for months, each day, every day,
with never an open window." They also had six hundred cases of
typhus. "We're not supposed to know," one of the women told him.
"The government is afraid of a panic if the truth were known, so
they're labelled influenza."[32]

Two of the remaining women were planning to leave for home
by the time of his visit. Only Ada Barlow, an untrained nurse from
Manchester who had experience in India and South Africa, was
planning to stay.[33] Dr Abraham asked her why. "I have nothing to
go back for," she replied. "There was nothing more to be said,"
Dr Abraham recalled later. "It was the drab, grey tragedy of the
unwanted woman. She was fat and plain, elderly and rather pasty.
Personally I did not take to her. She was just a piece of flotsam on
the tide of life, but she was an Englishwoman, and the thought of
her made me feel wretched all day. I could hear her saying, 'Remember I shall be all alone.' It was horrible. I hated her for making me
miserable."[34] Two days after Flora's visit to the hospital, the British
Red Cross asked her for a "character" for Mrs Barlow. Although

Flora's response was unlikely to have been positive, Barlow was grudgingly invited to join the British Red Cross Unit in Skopje.[35]

"I'll give you a month to live in that death trap," predicted an American doctor whom Flora and Emily met in a café in Niš, when they told him that they were considering travelling to the heart of the epidemic at the request of Colonel Subotić. The colonel had taken one look at their supplies and paused, turning over in his mind where he should send them. "Would you be willing to go to Valjevo?" he had asked. "I don't like the thought of sending you there but your supplies are badly needed, as are you."[36] Subotić's request was the ultimate test of their nerve. "So we chewed it over together," Flora wrote in her diary that night, "and finally left for Valjevo on the 8 p.m. train."[37]

At three-thirty a.m. on 20th February, in the middle of an epidemic that was killing tens of thousands, Flora and Emily arrived in Valjevo. It had taken them a day and a half on the train to travel the sixty miles from Niš. Emily had made good use of the time. As the train wound slowly through the low hills, she wrote a letter to the Red Cross to follow up her wire. "[My telegram was] not in the least exaggerated," she wrote, her head bent over her note-paper. "If this has not gotten through will you please act on this letter? It is not only for the Serbians we are appealing, but for us all Americans, English, Russian, Austrian. This terrible scourge is not sparing any of us." She was astute enough to tailor her letter to the American political climate. "What care we can give is given alike to Austrians and Serbs, and I feel in making this appeal that this fact should be emphasized, especially to America, where so many are interested in the German-speaking race."[38]

Although Flora and Emily had braced themselves for conditions worse than anything they had ever experienced, they were horrified by what they encountered in Valjevo. "The town is in a fearful state, every place crammed with sick men lying in their clothes in filth and on dirty straw, no beds, nothing, 50 or 60 deaths a day, was much more," Flora wrote in her diary on the day of their arrival.[39] Five thousand lay sick. "Soldiers were lying in their dirty uniforms, straight as they came from the trenches, swarming with vermin, all over the floors of the hospitals, on the floors of the hotels, in the shops, out in the streets, lying on bare boards on a little filthy straw with no blankets in the depth of the rigorous Serbian winter," she recalled later. "There was no one to nurse them, no nursing was being attempted, the only thing that was being done was to sort out the dead from the living in the mornings, and throw the dead into carts and take them out and bury them in shallow trenches, there was no one to make coffins for them and no time to make them." It never crossed their minds to leave. They were needed, there was a job to be done, and that was that. And, as Flora reasoned, "a man can only die once anyhow".[40]

Elsewhere in Serbia, other missions and medical workers were beginning to arrive in number, most notably from Russia, Switzerland, France and Greece. They joined the units who had started work the previous year – the Dutch mission under Dr van Tienhoven in Valjevo, the British Red Cross and Paget Units in Skopje and the American Red Cross in Belgrade and Gevgelija. Other British units too were starting work including the Anglo-Serbian Hospital, which was run by volunteers from the Royal Free Hospital in London and known as the "Berry Unit". Individual "freelancers" also set up base across Serbia, including Mrs Hannah Hankin Hardy, a veteran of the Siege of Ladysmith, who opened and ran a hospital by herself in Kragujevac.[41]

Most noteworthy of all the units to arrive at this time, and the one that would have the most significant presence among the Serbs throughout the duration of the war, was the Scottish Women's Hospitals. The women of the "First Serbian Unit", including Dr Katherine MacPhail, were assigned to Kragujevac at the start of January. Also working in Kragujevac was thirty-six-year-old Dr Elizabeth Ross, from Tain in the Scottish Highlands. Known as "Tibbie" to her friends, Dr Ross had a delicate physique that stood in stark contrast to her steely determination to work as and where she wanted.[42] On her arrival in January 1915 she agreed to take charge of the typhus wards in the First Reserve Hospital, the same hospital where the Anglo-American Unit had been based. "The air was quite indescribable; it was like entering a sewer," wrote a visitor.

I have seen some of the worst slum dwellings one can find in Britain, but never anything to approach these wards in filth and squalor. Men lay crowded together on mattresses. We saw three shivering together on two mattresses. No one washes them; they lie there in the weakness of fever, becoming filthier and filthier. When a man dies the next comer is put straight onto the same dirty mattress, between the same loathsome sheets. The place is full of orderlies certainly, but they crouch apathetically in corners, waiting their own turn to die.[43]

On the day they reached Valjevo, Flora and Emily left their rooms in a private house to meet their new colleagues over lunch at the Fourth Reserve Hospital, known as the "Gymnasium Hospital". They were ushered to the table by their new director, observing that above each seat was a "funeral card". The cards, Flora recorded, had been printed in honour of "the one who sat there before and has just died of typhus". Silently, they each took their place under one of them.[44] During lunch, the tired staff mentioned to Flora and Emily that there were two American doctors, Cooke and Cookingham, lying sick with typhus in a hotel room in the town. The women left that afternoon to find them.

Flora and Emily walked through the ground floor of the doctors' hotel, passing dozens of men huddled together unattended on thin straw, all suffering from typhus. They were directed up the stairs to the doctors' room. As they pushed open the door, they saw only Dr Cookingham, lying alone on a mattress on the floor. Cooke was dead. "[We] found that one doctor had died... and had been taken away," recalled Flora. "At the same time as they carried him out they brought in the coffin for his pal and laid it down beside his bed ready for him."[45]

Cooke had died nine days previously. Although he was seriously ill himself, Dr Cookingham had remained at his bedside for three days and nights as his friend's condition deteriorated. Cooke needed Cookingham's constant attention. On the third night, exhausted and sick, the lanky young doctor fell into a deep sleep. When he awoke, he was horrified to find Cooke lying dead on the floor at his feet. In a bout of delirium he had climbed out of bed and his heart had given out.[46]

Cookingham could hardly believe his eyes when the women approached his bed. "He had given up till he saw us come in," wrote Flora. For the next few days they kept a close watch over him as his health slowly stabilized. He was soon taken to an isolation hospital to which "anyone could go", she noted drily.[47] They also visited the Dutch mission shortly after arrival. They found many of the staff, including its chief, Dr van Tienhoven, suffering from typhus.[48] A few days later, the mission pulled out of Serbia entirely.

Flora and Emily began work on 22nd February. Theirs was the largest hospital in Valjevo, an elegant former school in the centre of town whose many classrooms had been turned into crowded wards for officers, soldiers and POWs. Although it was supposed to be the surgical hospital, most of its patients were suffering from typhus. Several times a day the hospital orderlies made the grim rounds of the wards to sort the dead from the living. They stacked the bodies outside the door, until they could be taken away by ox carts.[49] "Saw 3 dead men lying on stretchers, first thing we saw," recorded Flora. The grounds also contained a muck heap. "It was full of amputated limbs and dirty dressings and smelt to high heaven," she shuddered.[50]

The smell inside, of excrement and rotting flesh, hit them with an almost physical impact.[51] The hospital was intended to take two hundred and fifty men. When Flora and Emily walked round the wards for the first time, they discovered more than eight hundred, of whom seven hundred and fifty were sick and seventy were wounded.[52] Two men had been placed in each bed while the majority had to lie "agonizing" on some putrid straw, the only thing between them and the cold, hard floor.[53] Few had blankets. They lay, uncovered, shivering in their soiled uniforms. Some were so covered with lice that it looked as though "moving grey patches were on [their] dusky skins".[54] Those in the grip of typhus writhed and shouted in delirium. The only doctor still on his feet was the Director. "The hero he was" had been working "day and night" looking after his patients, recollected Flora. He was beside himself with relief at their arrival.

"Took charge of dressing room and did dressings for the whole of Valjevo and countryside. Cleared and cleaned up the dressing room, put the fear of God into the orderlies, scrubbed and sterilized everything," scribbled Flora in her diary on the day they started work. Three orderlies had been assigned to work alongside them. Two were Serbs, Ilia and Uroš.[55] The third was a "Schwabe" – a derogatory but universally used Serbian term equivalent to "Hun", which was applied to Austro-Hungarians. Flora, too, referred to them as "Schwabes", although she observed from the start how hard they worked. Soon, as her esteem for these men grew, she stopped using the term entirely.

Austro-Hungarian POWs were at work in hospitals throughout Serbia. Many were Czech. None were forced to work; however, there was no shortage of volunteers. Most had recovered from typhus and were immune from catching it again. They also reasoned that their living conditions were no worse inside the hospital and, if they worked, their rations would be better. Others simply wanted to help. Throughout Serbia during the epidemic, Austrian POWs who were doctors in peacetime worked side by side with their Serbian counterparts. Some even ran hospitals.[56]

Across Serbia, the staff of the Allied-run hospitals were coping as best they could. In the days and months that followed some threw themselves into rounds of social activity by way of distraction, as one demoralizing day followed another in the wards or operating theatres. Others turned instead to the blackest of humour to get through their work. In the "British Eastern Auxiliary Hospital" run by the British Naval Mission in Belgrade, amputations became a sporting event among its surgeons. One of them, Dr William Sharpe from Brampton, Ontario, was a "rough-spoken and coarse-grained Canadian, addicted to somewhat brutal jokes", one of the orderlies recalled. "I remember his telling us gleefully how he won his bet with a fellow surgeon as to which of them would most rapidly remove all twenty fingers and toes from a pair of frostbitten patients."[57] Even nurses were not immune to becoming blasé. Mildred Farwell, a journalist with the *Chicago Daily Tribune*, was struck when she met an English nurse struggling through her work, alone, in a military hospital. "You ought to see how nicely I take off toes," the nurse told her, while making the motion of chopping. "One whack and they're gone."[58]

Most demoralizing of all was to watch their colleagues fall sick with typhus. The death rate among doctors and medical staff was enormous. Many were too fatigued from the impossible struggle to save the lives of their patients to pay sufficient attention to proper precautions against infected lice. Weakened by exhaustion, they succumbed quickly once infected. By the early spring there was hardly a unit that had not lost a member to the disease.[59] The British missions were particularly badly hit. Two members of the British Red Cross Unit in Skopje died. The staff of the Scottish Women's Hospital, based in Kragujevac, attended funerals on three consecutive Sundays. Two of the funerals were for members of the unit, Louisa Jordan and Margaret "Madge" Neill Fraser. The third was for Dr Elizabeth Ross, who died on 14th February, her thirty-seventh birthday. Since the early 1980s the town of Kragujevac has held a commemoration at her graveside on the anniversary of her death.

Although news had reached Britain about the deaths of previous volunteers, there was no shortage of replacements. In April 1915 the redoubtable Mabel Stobart, whom Flora had known from the FANY and Women's Sick and Wounded Nursing Corps, arrived in Kragujevac with forty-five mainly female staff including Flora's old friend, Nan MacGlade, to set up a hospital entirely under canvas.[60] Units of the British Farmers also set out for Belgrade and Požarevac in northern Serbia, the Wounded Allies sent a small "fever" team to Kragujevac and the British Red Cross sent out a unit to Vrnjačka Banja in the east of the country. One more unit of the Scottish Women's Hospitals also set sail for Serbia, bound for Valjevo.

Flora and Emily soon ditched their starched and formal British nurses' uniforms for something more practical. Before she started work each day, Emily pulled a loose white ankle-length dress over her head and rolled the sleeves up to her elbows. She casually pulled an equally loose white hat over her dark, wavy hair. Flora threw on a grubby white medical coat over a white shirt and dark tie, which she wore with a hat similar to Emily's. She usually had a cigarette trailing between her fingers.

The adversity of the conditions had not troubled them for long. "Getting used to Valjevo sights and smells," Flora jotted in her diary only two days after arrival.[61] Emily too coped admirably, grumbling only about "the lack of soap and not being able to have a good wash".[62] They spent most of their time in the dressing room, which was bare other than for a few tables, chairs and cases of supplies that had been placed on the wooden floorboards. A naked bulb was suspended from the high ceiling by an electric wire. Their window overlooked the section of the hospital grounds where the dead were first taken. "All the coffins were put in a row, and in front of each coffin was a stretcher with a dead man lying, fully dressed, with little wooden crosses at the foot of each with his name and regiment on it," described Emily. "The priest came and chanted the service, and then they were put in coffins and left there for hours."[63]

Within a couple of days they had everything running like clockwork. They expected their orderlies to work as hard as they did, and brooked no nonsense from them. "They seem to bear us no malice though we've done everything but beat them, and we all work quite cheerily doing dressings for dear life," recorded Flora in her diary.[64] But they could do little for certain of their patients. "We stripped [an unconscious patient]," recalled Emily, "and I thought he was wearing a red undershirt. When I looked closer it seemed to me the shirt was rippling. His breast was covered with a sheet of typhus lice... He [later] died."[65] They also struggled to treat those with frostbite and gangrene. "We have two ghastly cases of frostbite in today," described Flora in a graphic letter to her sister Sophia. "One a man with the flesh rotted off his feet and literally nothing but the bones of his toes left. Another, an old man, with his hand coal black and very nearly off! It must be taken off entirely somehow soon..."[66] This was the one dark cloud that hung over the horizon of their work: their "surgical" hospital had no surgeons. They faced watching their patients suffer needlessly and feared that those with gangrene might die for lack of treatment, whose lives could otherwise be saved by amputation. It made Flora and Emily almost sick to see it.

Still, they determined to do what they could for their patients. With so many requiring regular dressings it was essential for them to get through each one as quickly as possible. Flora soon devised a system. She knew that they would do anything for a cigarette. She also knew that she was about the only person in Valjevo with any – she had brought ten thousand with her. "Well I used to stick up a box of cigarettes in a conspicuous place, and tell each man if he was good and didn't make a fuss I'd give him a cigarette when it was all over and they would go through almost anything, and then go off on their stretchers smiling and joking and smoking their cigarettes." Her plan was almost too successful. "I found they were beginning to play me up, and were coming in two or three times in the same day to get their dressings done, they didn't mind a little extra pain for the sake of the extra cigarette, and as we had not time for that, we had to make lists of them, and only do each man every second day."[67]

While overseeing the work in the dressing room they managed to find the time to open an "amateur dispensary" with a medicine chest that had been sent to Flora by an English explorer. With no formal medical training, she began prescribing for patients, with indeterminate results. "Fortunately there was a book of words with it, so I don't think I poisoned anybody," she recalled.[68] They also walked round the wards visiting their Serbian and POW patients whenever they had a spare moment. They had time only to hand out sweets and cigarettes, Flora's universal panacea, but their presence made an enormous difference to the spirits of the men. Their work also lifted the morale of the other members of staff who, faced with fifty to sixty deaths per day, had almost given up. Soon their colleagues began to follow their example. They opened the windows, cleaned the wards, appropriated a bath to use in the hospital and, on Flora's insistence, cleared away the muck heap in the yard.[69]

Within three days of beginning work, the thought of watching men die from gangrene had become too much for Emily, who had specialized as a surgical assistant during her training. "Discussed how soon we should have to begin amputations," wrote Flora tentatively in her diary, as they began to consider what had, until then, been unthinkable.[70] The next day they blew the dust off an old sterilizer they discovered under a bed. Then, rounding up the few surgical knives they could find, they began operating. "It was a case of doing *something* for these men or seeing them die before our eyes without lifting our little finger to help them," Flora later recalled. "So as there was nothing else for it we screwed up our courage and bit by bit we finally ended by doing the operations ourselves. We were very short of anaesthetics, what we had we kept for the worst cases. Besides which, we were so overwhelmed with work that the cases had to be got through without any un-necessary delay."[71]

Emily started first, while Flora stood by with a camera to document the event. "So many of the men here have suppurative parotitis, as a complication of typhus I suppose," wrote the young nurse to the head of the New York chapter of the American Red Cross. "I am sending you a snapshot Miss Sandes took of the very first operation I performed. This man is well now and has joined the firing line again. He hadn't slept for nearly two weeks, and I took nearly half a pint of pus from both sides of his face."[72] Next she began amputating fingers and toes. The watershed for her came when she was faced with a soldier with a gangrenous foot. With no surgeon available, she cut it off herself. After the soldier survived, Emily operated and amputated as she felt necessary, while Flora began to follow her example.[73] Lacking the necessary surgical instruments, she improvised. "Cut off a man's toes with a pair of scissors this afternoon," she cheerfully recorded in her diary.[74] Despite their unorthodox approach to surgery, their treatments appeared to work. "The men had such faith in us because we were English that I really think we cured them more by faith than skill," Flora acknowledged.[75]

True to form, Flora was spending as many evenings as possible "galumphing". She had plenty of willing companions. Emily would join her at the end of each working day for a couple of glasses of rakia, Serbian fruit brandy, while they often met the other members of staff under the funeral cards for dinner. Far from discouraging them from excess, the constant reminder of death led their colleagues to live each day as though it were their last. "They won't let us go to bed early because they say you never know which will be your last night and why waste it in bed when you'll be a long time dead," explained Flora.[76]

There were also the Vinavers, exiled Polish Jews who were running another hospital in the town, who served them tea liberally laced with rum to keep out the cold on their visits.[77] And rarely a day went by without one of them checking on Barton Cookingham as he slowly recovered his strength, although he was still too sick to take part in any galumphing. But Flora's best drinking friend was "Woolly", whom she identified only by the fact that he was Irish.[78] When beer was rumoured to have been found in the town, he was off like a shot to "scour" for it and her diary is littered with references to going drinking with him.

Although the constant round of social visits helped to take her mind off the shadow of death that hung over her, she knew that she had every chance of falling ill. Every slight itch was a cause for concern, and she looked over the seams of her clothes regularly for any sign of infestation by the small, flat, greyish-brown insects.[79] Woolly too was worried. Over a round of drinks one evening they agreed that "whoever got sick first the other should nurse".[80] Five days earlier, on 3rd March, Flora had ended an unusually long diary entry with what was hardly more than a postscript. "Caught my first louse (on me)."

The Serbian government was virtually paralysed by the magnitude of the epidemic and appealed for assistance. Sanitary commissions duly arrived from Britain, the United States, Russia and France. The government agreed to implement whatever measures they deemed necessary.[81] In March, all passenger trains were ordered to stop running for one month, army leave was stopped, hospitals were cleaned from top to bottom and disinfestation bases were set up across Serbia.[82] An educational campaign was also launched to teach the peasant population to fear the louse; however, it was not entirely successful. Many saw measures against typhus as proof of timidity not fitting for a soldiering nation, and took a sort of "gloomy pride" in the ravages of the epidemic.[83]

The sanitary measures virtually quarantined Valjevo. With the stoppage of all rail traffic, few supplies reached the town. Tea, sugar, butter, vegetables and meat soon became unobtainable.[84] The little food available was so expensive that it was beyond the reach of much of the already sick and miserable population. Soon the remaining inhabitants began to look half-starved. Weak from lack of food, they began to fall victim to the epidemic in even greater numbers.[85]

Flora woke on Monday 8th March feeling "seedy". She had been at work in Valjevo for just over a fortnight. The first breath of spring had not yet blown away the rigours of winter and one bleak, wet day indistinguishably merged into another. She spent the morning, as usual, working at the Gymnasium Hospital. She then shivered through the muddy, roughly cobbled streets to visit another hospital in the town. That evening, relieved that the day was over, she met up with Woolly. "The Irishman declared I didn't look very well and dosed me liberally with Sleevovitza [Serbian plum brandy]," recorded Flora. By Wednesday and Thursday she was feeling worse but, undeterred, spent the evenings galumphing with Woolly. Emily too was unwell. Three days earlier, on 5th March, she had put herself to bed complaining of headache and chills. Their director diagnosed recurrent fever, a debilitating but rarely fatal illness.

Both Flora and Emily had suffered bouts of sickness during their time in Serbia. Initially there was no reason to think that, this time, it was anything different. Satisfied that Emily would soon be over the worst, Flora left her in bed to take over the running of the operating room, leaving Milorad, an Austrian POW, to look after her. But Flora's career as chief surgeon lasted a mere seven days. "Had a temperature and couldn't get up. Turned out to be typhus," she managed to scribble in her diary on 12th March. By then there was also no mistaking Emily's diagnosis. The characteristic rash of typhus was spreading across her body.

Flora may have been sick, but she was still as wilful as ever. "Can't stand Milorad," she declared forcefully in her diary. She asked instead for Hayek, another "Schwabe" who had been work-ing as her "batman" – servant – to take his place.[86] Mindful of his promise to her, Woolly also took his place at her bedside, where he could also keep an eye on Emily who lay in the adjoining room. When word of their illness filtered through to a barely recovered Barton Cookingham, he too "crawled up" to visit them.[87] But on 15th March Woolly failed to arrive. "Woolly got sick with typhus, they put him in [the] officers ward of the Gymnasium," wrote Flora who, in the early stages of the disease, was still just about able to scratch a few shaky words in her diary.

The next day she took a dramatic turn for the worse. For a week her life hung in the balance. She lay prostate, wracked with waves of fever and muscle pain, coughing to expel the thick mucus that lined her throat and mouth. Hayek applied cold compress after cold compress to her burning forehead.[88] "Had continual high temperature never less than 41, but Hayek told me afterwards it was always higher than he used to tell me," recalled Flora. Their director also visited them every day, but it was Hayek who struggled to keep her alive. "Hayek is a brick. He lies on the floor at night but never seems to sleep," she continued.

Thought I was going out one night but called Hayek and told him to give me a drink out of the bottle of digitalis the Dr [Director] left by my side, don't know how much you can drink of this stuff but it did the trick that time (afterwards removed it before I poisoned myself). The nights are pretty awful. A[mericano] unable to get up, she has crawled to the door once or twice and looked at me. In spite of the temperature I've never gone off my nut except once for a little while. The Dr told Hayek I'd peg out if temp. didn't come down next day. See no one but the Dr and Hayek, hear Woolly is pretty bad. Have the window wide open and sometimes hear people outside commenting on it. Hayek told me afterwards he was frozen, but he never complained.[89]

On 22nd March, ten days after falling ill, Flora's temperature finally began to drop. Hayek had got her through the worst. Although shorter bouts of fever returned leaving her "fearfully weak" and "unable to eat or smoke", she was again able to write a few short notes in her diary. Emily too had pulled through. Woolly did not survive. He died on Sunday 28th March. Emily attended his funeral the following day. Flora was too weak to go.

Hayek continued to care for Flora and Emily through their convalescence. At a time of near famine in Valjevo, he went to "heroic efforts to cook dainties for them from the only available fare – bully beef, black bread and tea".[90] Emily in turn credited their survival to the altruistic nursing given to them by both Hayek and Milorad. "Being unable to eat, they profited by our 'rations' so that their efforts to help us get well are all the more laudable," she extolled.[91] By early April Flora was able to get out of bed for the first time. She set off on short walks with Hayek, who was ready to catch her if she fell. He picked her spring flowers along the way.[92]

Barton Cookingham was now strong enough to visit them daily. Flora, who was still too weak to leave her room for any length of time, greatly enjoyed his visits. "American[o] cooked prunes, onions, pancakes etc. on the Primus stove and I looked forward all day to our tea party," scribbled Flora from her sickbed. By the middle of April, Cookingham was well enough to stand the long trip home to New York State. Flora dejectedly said goodbye to her friend, who left a minor diplomatic incident in his wake. He had also developed sympathies for the POWs and had agreed to smuggle out letters for them, but was found out by the Serbian authorities and forced to hand them over. "Missed C. very much," wrote Flora sadly in her diary the following day.[93]

Having survived, Flora and Emily were now immune to the disease, but both were seriously weakened by the bouts of fever that they had suffered. Emily returned to work during the first week of April, although she was unable to undertake anything more than light tasks. It would be another fortnight before Flora joined her. By then, only their director and one other member of staff – a "teetotaller", noted Flora with a touch of amazement – were left of the original twelve. The others, without exception, had caught typhus. Most had died.[94]

By the end of April the spring rains had washed the grime from the streets of the town and the sun shone brightly on the simple stucco buildings and cobbled streets as one hot, clear day followed another. With fewer cases of typhus appearing among their patients and their hospital running smoothly, Flora and Emily were able to enjoy the weather. They had survived, and both were determined to make the most of their summer. They spent the mornings doing dressings and checking on their largely convalescent patients, but usually had the afternoons free.

With time on their hands, they volunteered at another hospital. But even this additional work did not keep Flora and Emily as busy as they wished. To pass the time they attended picnics and parties, or walked to a café for beer or slivovitz, in the company of Hayek and sundry others. But as much as they enjoyed these outings, they were not reason enough to stay, and, in early June, there was even less work for them after the Second Serbian Unit of the Scottish Women's Hospitals set up a tented hospital on a hillside near the town, with equipment and supplies for two hundred beds.[95]

With cases of typhus appearing only sporadically and no new wounded coming in, members of the various British units also had time on their hands. By late spring Kragujevac in particular had a surplus of Allied medical teams and dwindling patient numbers, while Serbian-run hospitals in other towns were grossly understaffed. Katherine MacPhail and a colleague, Adeline Campbell, another junior doctor, decided to terminate their contracts with the Scottish Women's Hospitals early and leave for Belgrade, where they felt they could be more useful. They took charge of a large building that housed one hundred and fifty typhus patients, replacing an old Serbian doctor who "looked as if he were dying".[96]

Katherine became one of the last foreign doctors to fall sick with typhus in Serbia. One June evening she was carried by stretcher through the streets of Belgrade by some of her POW orderlies to the nearby military hospital, run by the American Red Cross. She was lucky to survive. She was delirious for days and nearly lost a leg to thrombosis. Almost all of her hair fell out and she also suffered severe, permanent hearing loss.[97] The American Red Cross took care of her for eight weeks, until she was strong enough to return home to Scotland. Katherine had good reason to be grateful to the Red Cross and, in particular, its thirty-year-old director, Dr Ryan, who had also survived typhus. Although she was almost certainly well aware of the rumours that were beginning to fly among the units in Serbia about Dr Ryan and the Red Cross, she was one of the few to keep them to herself.

There were plenty of others willing to pass them on. The favourite topic of conversation among the personnel of the various units was each other. The American Red Cross gave them plenty of ammunition for their gossip. In a series of minor scandals, one of its doctors met a woman on a train and "spent three nights with her", while another was challenged to a duel and had to be smuggled suddenly out of Belgrade.[98] But the very worst of the rumours were about Dr Ryan. By the time the gossip about him had travelled from the capital to the units based across the rest of Serbia, it had been embellished, reworked and retold with salacious pleasure. It was not typhus at all he had had, it was whispered. It was gonorrhoea. He kept his nurses "working like slaves", others said. Over the months that followed, rumours about Dr Ryan continued to grow in force and gather in pace.

After reaching a peak in April, by the summer of 1915 the epidemic was over.[99] Despite the general indifference of the peasant population to infestation, the sanitary measures took effect while the onset of warmer weather reduced the opportunity for the transmission of infected lice. Following on the heels of months of savage fighting, the effect of typhus on Serbia had been devastating. Accurate records could not be kept of the number of dead, but almost certainly one hundred and fifty thousand and possibly as many as two hundred thousand died out of a population of five million.[100] The seventy-five thousand POWs had suffered most. Half died during the epidemic and, in Valjevo alone, only three hundred of fourteen hundred POWs survived.[101] It is estimated that around thirty-five foreign doctors died of typhus, including James Donnelly, Albert Cooke and Elizabeth Ross.[102] Of three hundred and fifty doctors at work in Serbia at the start of the war, one hundred and twenty-six died. One of the latter victims was Flora's friend, Dr Vinaver.[103]

On a hot summer day in mid-June, with new cases of typhus few and far between and work at their hospital "slack", Flora and Emily returned by train to Kragujevac for a visit to the tented hospital run by the Stobart Unit, one of several trips they made around Serbia that summer. They were keen to revisit the town that they had left hurriedly the previous November, but their main aim was to find something more exciting to do. Between them they had decided that what they wanted most was to work for a field hospital – a mobile first-aid station (or "ambulance") attached to the army. If they could pull it off, they would have the chance to work near the front in any future fighting, but there was a problem – women were not as a rule permitted to join, as it meant that they would have to live with the army. That day they received a flat refusal. "Went to [Red Cross] Headquarters, saw Guentitch [Colonel Dr Lazar Genčić of the Serbian Army Medical Service] and another man who said we could not join a Regimental Ambulance," scratched Flora in her diary in annoyance.

She had also travelled to Kragujevac to see how her old friend Nan MacGlade was getting on as Mabel Stobart's chief administrator.[104] She almost certainly found her suffering from the chagrin that was affecting many of the women who had reached Serbia that spring. They had left Britain hot on the heels of reports of the great danger they could face, arriving with heroic visions of battling typhus and rescuing the wounded under fire. But with the epidemic at an end and Serbia's enemies occupied elsewhere, they were crushingly disappointed by what appeared to be little more than a pleasant summer interlude in the Balkans. "Don't worry, there will be lots more opportunities of dying uncomfortably," the doctors of the unit assured them, while Serb authorities begged them to stay.[105] "It's only the lull before the storm," they insisted, in the firm belief their enemies were only biding their time before attacking again.[106]

On their return to Valjevo, still no closer to finding the work they wanted, news reached Flora and Emily that the new director of their hospital, Panajotović, had been given a transfer to a field hospital. Flora lobbied him relentlessly on behalf of both of them. When he finally agreed to take them with him, Emily was equally delighted. "We were very glad to have this wonderful opportunity," she said proudly. "It was the first time that any women had been allowed to go with the army as dressers."[107]

At the end of June, when Flora and Emily left with Panajotović to join the Third Reserve Field Hospital, Hayek came with them. The hospital lay just outside of Osečina, a village in the rolling green countryside north-west of Valjevo, near the Bosnian border. Although the trenches that divided Serbia from Austrian-occupied Bosnia were only a few miles distant, the fighting between the armies that summer was desultory and its staff of a doctor and a few orderlies received a mere trickle of patients.

Before the molten heat of high summer descended upon the hospital, Flora and Emily rose each day in the cool of the early morning. They left their tent on a hill and walked down a steep slope to check on their patients, dress wounds and hand out medicines. Emily was called in to serve as an anaesthetist from time to time, whenever the doctor performed an operation. Otherwise they had the afternoons to themselves. "Nothing ever doing in Hosp. in afternoons, the men asleep," scribbled Flora.[108] With Hayek constantly in tow, they spent the remainder of their days walking in the countryside, reading, horse-riding or bathing in the river to escape the oppressive heat. Hayek continued to do what he could for Flora and Emily. "Hayek got about 3 kilos of strawberries for us," recorded Flora on 12th July. Later that month, he toiled through the heat to cut steps up the hill to their tent. But in reality he was a POW with few rights, and it was Flora and Emily who were now looking after him.

To their regret, with conditions in Serbia gradually returning to normal, the work did not provide the challenge and excitement they craved. "The operations were not very important and were over in August, leaving us with nothing particular to do," recalled Emily.[109] Flora too was disappointed that war had not recommenced. "The advance they talked of does not seem [to be] coming off, all is quiet, no sign of war, so Americano and I have been deciding to go home."[110]

On 30th July they began a slow trip home, stopping en route in Kragujevac. Taking Hayek with her, Flora went to visit Colonel Genčić. She did not make clear her reasons for her visit to him. Perhaps it was a routine visit; perhaps she was trying to make arrangements for the POW who had saved her life. She was not in the least worried about having him with her. He had been permanently by her side since she fell sick with typhus and had been free to go everywhere and do everything with her. But Flora failed to take into account that, since last meeting Genčić, she had defied his refusal to allow her to work in a field hospital. He was now in no mood to make any further accommodations for her. There and then, despite her desperate pleas on his behalf, he sent Hayek to work in a military hospital. She managed to win him a single concession, a promise that he would not be put to work repairing the roads. All she could do the next day was to visit the barracks where Hayek had been sent to beg the captain in charge to look after him.[111] Flora then sadly said goodbye to the loyal, chivalrous Hayek, who at this point disappears from history.

Flora returned home to her family in late August canary-yellow and tired from a bout of hepatitis A she had contracted a few days before leaving.[112] But soon she perked up enough to take a keen interest in the disquieting rumours from the Balkans. Enemy troops were concentrating along the northern frontier of Serbia, she read in the papers.[113] Over the next weeks the news became progressively worse.

On 5th October the Austro-Hungarian and German armies began a savage bombardment of Belgrade and the northern border of Serbia that confirmed the Serbs' belief that they were poised to invade. Also waiting anxiously were the members of three small Allied naval missions who had been sent to bolster the Serbian army, from Britain, France and Russia. Their aim, first and foremost, had been to prevent the Danube waterway from being used by Germany to arm Turkey, which was fighting the Allies in Gallipoli. Now they were expected to help save Serbia from invasion.

The British Naval Mission, under the Command of Rear Admiral Ernest Troubridge, had arrived in Serbia in early 1915.[114] Although it was tiny, only seventy men, the Serbs put their faith in them and the even smaller French and Russian Missions to defend their northern border, and transferred the greater part of their thin forces to the east to face the Bulgarians, who were said to be mobilizing. They also maintained some troops in Serbian Macedonia to the south.

After two days of bombardment, the invasion began. Three hundred thousand Austro-Hungarian and German troops attacked from the north. The Serbian army, only two hundred and fifty thousand strong, was overwhelmingly outgunned and outnumbered, while the Naval Missions were too weak and ill equipped to help stem the attack. Soon after the start of the assault they were forced into retreat. Two days after the fall of Belgrade on 9th October, three hundred and fifty thousand men of the Bulgarian army attacked along the eastern frontier of Serbia, with the sole ambition of achieving the country's long-standing territorial ambitions in Macedonia.

The defeat of Serbia was strategically vital to Germany and Austria-Hungary. At a stroke it would allow them to deliver supplies via the Danube to Turkey and diminish the threat to the territorial integrity of Austria-Hungary from its restless Slav population. They also hoped that decisive success would bring neutral Romania into their orbit. Germany took charge of planning the attack. Following two bungled invasions of Serbia, it had no intention of tolerating any further Austro-Hungarian military incompetence.

Despite the crushing odds against them the Serbs maintained their unshakable faith that the Allies would come to their rescue. On 5th October the first troops of the Franco-British Expeditionary Force landed in Salonika. Soon after their arrival, the French pushed north into Serbia, joined a couple of weeks later by the British, whose support for the new campaign was lukewarm at best. The Serbs were joyous at the news. Rumours, founded only

in hope, grew about the collapse of the enemy. Niš and all the surrounding villages were expensively decorated with flowers, gaily
coloured bunting and Allied flags to welcome the troops. Crowds
flocked to the station to welcome them. They never came. None
of the stories were true.[115] By the time the Allies had chosen to act,
it was too late to save the Serbs.

Worried sick about missing the action, Flora cut her holiday
short. She wrote a few hurried lines to Emily in New York to tell
her she was returning to their old hospital in Valjevo, asking her
to join her there.[116] Then she threw together a few things and
raced by train through the cool, autumnal French countryside
to Marseilles. There she boarded the *Mossoul*, an old cargo
steamer. It was packed, not just with blue-uniformed French
soldiers, but with munitions smuggled alongside the bags of flour
in the hold.[117] At six a.m. on 21st October she joined the other
passengers on the deck as it steamed slowly out of the harbour,
past the Indian camps that lined the shore. Among the many
passengers standing alongside her, watching as the distant hills,
white houses and great cathedral of Marseilles faded into the
thick morning mist, were the members of a number of women's
units heading east. The majority were travelling to Serbia. Most
were with the Girton and Newnham Unit, the latest sent out
by the Scottish Women's Hospitals, but there were also a few
"freelancers" who, like Flora, were returning to Serbia on hearing the news of war.

The other women eyed Flora curiously. To those nervously leaving for Serbia for the first time she was an imposing figure. Not
only had she more wartime nursing experience than anyone else,
she had survived typhus and could speak some Serbian. She was
outgoing, plain-spoken and confident enough to do precisely what
she liked, including smoking, which was considered daring and
anything but ladylike. Many also looked enviously at her short
hair. Soon, the more rebellious followed suit, in a "craze" that
swept up the women of the Scottish Women's Hospitals.[118] "Flora
Sandes on board," scribbled Dr Isabel Emslie after catching sight
of her. "[She is] a tall, handsome woman with short grey hair and
a faultless khaki coat and skirt."[119]

* * *

The ship headed south-east on its long voyage, passing first through
the Straits of Bonifacio dividing the rocky coasts of Corsica
and Sardinia. The weather was beautiful. "Lovely day, calm as
glass," recorded Flora in her diary two days into the trip as they
passed the lights of the African coast.[120] Despite the apparent
tranquillity, its passengers were all too aware that, beneath the
dark waters of the Mediterranean, floating mines lurked and
German submarines were on the prowl.[121] Neither did the captain let them forget the danger. He put them repeatedly through
lifeboat drill, ordered them not to lose sight of their life vests
and made them sleep in their outdoor clothing. Above all, they
were warned never to show the faintest light on deck at night.
Even cigarettes were forbidden, to Flora's dismay. "Captain Pym
scared a couple of the girls to death with his talk of ammunition and submarines," recorded a fellow passenger.[122] For Flora
it was all part of the adventure. She nonchalantly reported their
first scare in her diary. "Great excitement; was it the enemy!!"
she scribbled brightly.[123] When the *Mossoul* left for Salonika on
the final stage of its long voyage, submarines were once again
reported to be in the vicinity.

"Arrived Salonique 6 a.m. after a very strenuous night dodging
submarines and nearly running down a destroyer. Whistles blowing and Captain cursing all night, and everyone getting up and
admiring scenery at dawn!" wrote Flora from her room at the
Bristol Hotel.[124] It had taken them fourteen days to travel from
Marseilles, a trip that in peacetime normally took less than a
week.[125]

News had filtered through to her and the other passengers
during the voyage that the situation facing the Serbian army
was increasingly grim. By the time they reached Salonika on 3rd
November, they all knew that the Austro-Hungarian and German
armies in the north had made slow but steady progress while the
Bulgarians had quickly overrun the south of the country. The
news, bad as it was, made Flora's heart race with excitement.
Her worst fear had been that the fighting would be over before
she arrived and that she would miss the chance to work near
the front. She had also been turning over an idea in her mind
ever since, the year before, she had been out riding alongside

a Serbian soldier in Kragujevac. "What do you want to be a
nurse for?" he had asked her, impressed with her horsemanship.
"Your skills are wasted in the hospital wards. Why don't you
join the army instead?" For the first time, his suggestion made
her realize that, as a woman, it might just be possible for her
to become a soldier, if she really wanted.[126] By the time she
reached Salonika, there was nothing she wanted more. "I've
always wished to be a soldier and fight," she confided to Dr
Isabel Emslie on the voyage.[127]

CHAPTER 5

INVASION

1915

From the window of her room at the Slavia Hotel in Prilep, Flora looked out onto a stable yard full of donkeys, pigs and "the most villainous-looking Turks [Muslims] squatting about at their supper". "These," she wrote in her diary, "are the ones who will come in and cut my throat if Prilip [sic] is taken tonight." The town was only five miles south of the fighting between the Serbian and Bulgarian armies in the Babuna mountain range, in Serbian Macedonia. The Babuna Pass controlled the entrance to the plain below. If it fell to the Bulgarians they would be able to advance unopposed, first on Prilep and then Monastir, the capital of Serbian Macedonia. The fate of the towns lay in the balance. Although the Serbians were resisting doggedly, they were now barely holding on to the Pass. They were running out of ammunition, they had no big guns to respond to Bulgarian artillery fire and they were far outnumbered by the incomparably better-equipped Bulgarian army.

Through the bare floorboards Flora could hear the singing of the Serbian soldiers who crowded the café below. Even this chorus did not drown out a heated quarrel that was taking place just outside her room. Someone was making a violent effort to break the lock on her door, and Flora could hear the boy attendant arguing with him. She did her best to take her mind off the inauspicious surroundings by writing in her diary, while smoking one cigarette after another. With her in the sparsely furnished room were her campbed, sleeping bag and tea basket. She also had her revolver. Before she went to bed she reassured herself by thinking, "If I live through the night, things will probably look more cheery in the morning." To improve her chances she tucked the revolver under her pillow.

In the middle of the night she was suddenly awakened by the sound of shouting and banging. She grabbed her torch, fumbled for her revolver and sat bolt upright in bed. "That's done it," said Flora to herself. "It's like my rotten luck that the Bulgars should pitch on tonight to come in and sack the town." As she sat motionless, the revolver gripped tightly in her hand, the noise moved away from her door. With a sudden rush of irritation she realized that it was only two drunks staggering along the corridor to bed. Telling herself not to be "more of a fool than nature intended", she turned over and went back to sleep.[1]

Flora had arrived in Salonika only the week before, her plans in disarray. She had been told on arrival that not only would she have to abandon her hope of returning to Valjevo, she would have to give up all thoughts of working in Serbia.[2] For a few disheartening hours, she "generally foraged round trying to find a way up to Serbia" by wandering the narrow, cobbled streets and busy cafés in search of anyone who might know how to get there.[3] At last, she saw a glimmer of hope. "You can't travel directly north," she was told, "but the trains are still running to Monastir." The town, to the north-west of Salonika, was only thirty miles from the fighting.

Two days later, on 5th November, Flora had jumped on the early morning train brimming with excitement. With her travelled a handful of others who had also found themselves stranded in Salonika. Among them was Elia Lindon, one of the rebels with cropped hair who had sailed with Flora on the *Mossoul*, who had been hoping to return to Serbia, where she had worked in the spring of 1915.[4] By the time they stepped wearily down onto the platform of the dark station in Monastir eleven hours later, they had agreed to work together as close to the fighting as possible.

Early the next morning Flora rose from her bed in a room on the outskirts of town and pulled on a Serbian uniform.[5] Although she as yet had nothing but a faint hope that she might find a way to join the army, she liked how it looked and saw no reason why she should not wear it if she wanted to. That afternoon she walked along Monastir's wide central boulevard and down a narrow side street to seek advice from Charles Greig, the British consul, at his residence in a simple, two-storey stucco building.

Greig was thirty-five years old, educated at Harrow, Oxford and Cambridge, and conscientious to a fault about his duty to ensure the safety of his British subjects. Flora was equally determined that he would help her get closer to the front. "Could you help Elia and me get to Prilep?" she asked. "The town's still in Serbian hands," he replied, "but there's not much point you going as they're expecting to have to evacuate any minute. It's only a few miles from the fighting and the road there is threatened by Bulgarian comitadjis [irregular forces]." He paused thoughtfully, then told her that he had to accompany a small British party there in two days' time. "You can come if you're absolutely sure you want to," he told her. "We'll see if you're needed in the hospital." Two days later Flora threw her knapsack, campbed and rug into a lorry and clambered on board alongside an escort of three or four soldiers for the twenty-five-mile journey north. They were "armed to the teeth", she noted with a shiver of anticipation as the lorry rumbled slowly north behind a car carrying Elia and Greig. That afternoon they reached the town safely.[6]

Flora could sense the prospect of war in the air. Prilep's cafés, small hotels and tree-lined streets were thronged with soldiers, winter was closing in, food was getting increasingly expensive and the Serbian population were readying themselves for sudden flight. Desperate to get the excuse she needed to stay, she approached the hospital that afternoon. Its director was far from happy about taking on the responsibility for a British national. "Not a very enthusiastic reception," she recorded. Nonetheless, he "accepted the inevitable with a very good grace" when he realized that she was not going to take no for an answer.[7]

Pleased as she was that she had managed to "gradually edge" her way to the front, it came as a shock when Greig returned to Monastir that evening, taking the British party with him.[8] Elia too had decided to leave. "After the first satisfaction of getting my own way in spite of hell and high water," scribbled Flora that evening in her dismal hotel room in Prilep, "when I waved the cars goodbye I felt the loneliest thing on earth."[9] A week later, safely away from the fighting, Elia arrived in the small town of Gevgelija near the Greek border, where the Girton and Newnham Unit of the Scottish Women's Hospitals had set up base. She explained to the women of the unit that she had been evacuated as the Babuna Pass was on the brink of falling to the Bulgarians, but that Flora had refused to leave.[10]

"Woke up about 6.30, very much surprised to find myself still alive," scratched Flora in her diary the morning after her arrival in Prilep. She brewed herself a quick cup of tea and then dashed down to the military hospital to start work, hoping that she would find it sufficiently disorganized to give her the justification to stay. She was not disappointed. The staff of four or five doctors and "2 nondescript females who hinder in the hospital" were barely coping. They were also running worryingly short of beds, bedding, medicine and equipment. Although very few of their patients were wounded, their wards were crowded to capacity with about one hundred and fifty men, most of whom were sick with dysentery. Flora threw on her grubby white overcoat and set to work. "Dressed a few wounded in dressing room, usual Serbian style, half a dozen incompetent people falling over each other," she jotted scathingly in her diary later that day. "Then went round the rooms, and, as I expected, found plenty to do." Two days later she reported that they could take no more patients and were having to turn men away.[11]

Although by then there was enough for "a dozen nurses" to do, she knew that she would be evacuated to Salonika along with the other members of staff when Serbian positions on Babuna fell.[12] Her one chance of staying, she knew, was if she could find work with the army. She had worked for a military ambulance briefly with Emily in Osečina, and she saw no reason why she should not join one again. The closest one, a few miles to the north of Prilep, belonged to the Second Regiment. When she heard that her hospital director was travelling back to Monastir, she asked if he would secure the official approval she needed to join it. He arrived back the next day with her papers. During the late afternoon of 13th November, she packed her things and left the hospital. She had been there less than a week.

While Flora was sitting in her hotel room contemplating the wisdom of her actions, the German, Austro-Hungarian and Bulgarian armies were continuing to make relentless progress through Serbia, despite grimly determined resistance from the Serbian army. Initially the Serbs were driven by the belief that they only needed to hold the enemy at bay for long enough for the Allies to come to their rescue. But when the half-hearted Allied response failed to save them, the Serbs fought desperately to slow the advance and prevent being encircled. It was impossible for them to take the offensive. Every man was at the front, there were no reserves, and their lines were so thin that they were forced to rush troops from one crisis to another to prevent their flanks from being turned.[13]

Civil administration in Serbia began to collapse. Telephones stopped working, the postal service ground to a halt and the publication of newspapers ceased. Banks closed and Serbian money began to lose its value. Transportation and communication links were destroyed, making it more and more difficult to deliver food, which became increasingly scarce for both humans and animals. As one town after another fell to the invading armies, a mass of terrified refugees fled before the onslaught.

The largely female British missions within Serbia were faced with a stark choice. They could remain with their patients and be taken prisoner, or they could join the throng of refugees. Most heads of units gave their members the choice. With a handful of exceptions, the few men of British nationality – who faced the possibility of being interned for the duration of the war – joined the retreat. Of the women, about half chose to stay. None of them knew what would happen to them when they fell into enemy hands. Those who decided to leave joined the endless processions of ragged and hungry refugees. Jumbled among them were automobiles, Serbian field hospitals, foreign diplomats, ox carts, packhorses and farm animals, alongside columns of troops, artillery and cavalry, all moving at the same slow pace. With them came two groups whose suffering was especially pitiable: roughly twenty-seven thousand schoolboys aged between twelve and eighteen who had been ordered by the government to flee to save them from internment or from being forced to join an enemy army, and the thirty-five thousand Austro-Hungarian POWs who had survived the typhus epidemic of the spring. Flora's friend Hayek almost certainly would have been among them.

When the sole railway running from north to south was cut by the Bulgarians, it severed the refugees' only means of escape south, to Salonika and Greece. They were forced back on their tracks into a smaller and smaller section of territory, towards Kosovo. First, the oxen, horses and pack animals began to starve. With no forage left, they were driven on until, exhausted and emaciated, they collapsed and died by the roadside.[14] The refugees too began to starve, unable to pay for the little food available. Their condition worsened with the weather. They had no shelter in the open from the relentless rain that fell throughout much of late October.

The weather deteriorated further on the morning of 17th November. The temperature plunged rapidly and it began to rain in torrents upon the already exhausted soldiers and ill-clad refugees huddled out in the open. Then the rain turned to driving snow. Throughout the day it continued to grow colder. The members of the Allied units began to witness the deaths of the oxen and horses that were already on the brink of starvation.[15] Soon they began to witness the deaths of refugees. "On all sides were dead horses and oxen, singly and in heaps, half buried in snow, with swarms of carrion crows whirling and croaking overhead," said a British war correspondent of the apocalyptic scene. "It was a realization of the retreat from Moscow such as I never expected to see. The gaunt, half-starved faces of the passing soldiers did nothing to destroy the illusion."[16]

The ambulance of the Second Regiment was engaged in treating the men of the Second and Fourteenth Regiments of the Morava Division, who had been injured in the fighting at the Babuna Pass or taken ill. Although the battle was ferocious, only a handful of its patients were seriously injured. Most had straggled down unaided from the Pass to the ambulance. The regimental stretcher-bearers were only able to carry a lucky few of the badly wounded men down the steep mountainsides. The others died unattended where they fell.

The ambulance was camped on some rocky and treeless ground to the side of a rough and isolated track, well within earshot of the boom of the guns. To the north and east rose the wooded heights of the Babuna mountains, just over a mile away. It was intentionally lightly equipped so that it could follow the Second Regiment at short notice and comprised little more than two or three covered ox wagons, a dozen small bivouac tents and one large bell tent lined

with straw. It had just enough capacity to give first aid to twenty
injured or sick men at a time, until they could be evacuated by
ox wagon to one of the base hospitals.[17] They were cared for by
a staff of roughly fifty, including a Greek doctor, several medical
orderlies and a Serbian girl, about seventeen years old, who lived
and worked with the men. The numbers were made up by a guard
of heavily armed soldiers.

It was pitch black when Flora arrived at the ambulance on the
cold night in mid-November. She was welcomed by its Greek doctor and many of the men, who "were as amiable as only Serbians
can be when you rouse them out in the middle of the night and
turn everything upside down".[18] In the grey dawn she crawled out
of her bivouac tent to get her first good look at the camp. She was
struck first by the quantity of weaponry carried by the ambulance.
It was a world away from the gentle civility of the British Red Cross.
"The entire [Serbian] Red Cross go armed to the teeth," she wrote
admiringly in a letter to her sister.[19] She also met her remaining
colleagues. "Made acquaintance with the Serbian girl, queer little
cuss, more like a soldier, and wears soldier's clothes sometimes,"
commented Flora in her diary that day.[20] She had never before come
face to face with one of the handful of women in the ranks of the
Serbian army and was both impressed and reassured. If the girl
could live and work with the army, Flora reasoned, so could she.

The girl helped her settle into her work. "She gave me lots of
tips," Flora recalled later. "Though I had been under the impression that I knew something about camping out and roughing it,
having done so in various parts of the world, she could walk rings
around me in that respect."[21] She could also speak German with
Flora, who was still struggling to learn Serbian. Many of the British women who worked in Serbia during the war, like her, found
it bewildering at first. One complained bitterly that it had seven
cases, two aspects of the verb (perfective and imperfective) and the
dual as well as the plural, and that it even contained six different
words for sister-in-law.[22]

Flora spent her first morning with the ambulance hurriedly
working alongside two of its orderlies, washing, disinfecting and
dressing the wounds of the injured who were carried to them on the
ground outside the tents. During the course of the day a handful
of new casualties trickled in. The Greek doctor took charge of the

sick, while Flora and the orderlies quickly bandaged the wounds of the injured, ahead of their evacuation. But as they waited anxiously, only two or three ox wagons arrived that afternoon to remove their patients to the nearest base hospital. There were only enough places for the very worst cases. The others – some of whom were "so sick that they could hardly crawl" – faced a walk of several miles to escape the Bulgarians. "One man protested that he would never do it," wrote Flora, who interceded on his behalf. "However, the ambulance men, who were well up to their work, explained that it was absolutely imperative that all should get off into safety." If they fell into the hands of the Bulgarians, they told her, they would simply be killed. "Go, brother," they told him kindly. "*Idi polako, polako*" ("Go slowly, slowly"). Fortified with cognac from the orderlies and a handful of cigarettes from Flora, he limped off with the others.[23]

"Sleep in your clothes tonight," the Greek doctor warned Flora when she returned to her tent for the night. "Don't even take off your boots."[24] She was fast asleep at one a.m. when a messenger woke her with an urgent wire from Greig asking her to return to Prilep immediately. Flora studied it closely. She decided that, while it was admittedly strong advice to go back, it was not quite an "*order*".[25] Armed with this semantic nuance, the following morning she suggested uncertainly to her new colleagues that she would like to "stick it out" with them. "I wasn't sure, you see, whether I'd only be a nuisance and anxiety, but they all seemed fearfully bucked," she wrote to her sister, "and they seem to think I've done something wonderful."[26]

   That evening, grim-faced, they received the news that Serbian positions on the Babuna Pass had fallen and that the Bulgarians were marching on Prilep. The ambulance lay directly in their line of advance. Flora and the girl worked frantically alongside the men packing up equipment and supplies, taking down the tents and helping the sick and wounded men into ox wagons.[27] At eleven p.m. they clambered out of the rain and mud into a covered horse-drawn wagon that lumbered slowly south into the darkness. None of them knew if they had left in time to escape the Bulgarians.[28]

* * *

The fall of the Babuna Pass was a devastating blow to the Serbs. The Pass was the last link between the forces in Serbian Macedonia and the rest of the army to their north. Those in Serbian Macedonia, including the Second Regiment, were only a small segment of the army. Most of its soldiers, to the north, were hemmed in on the Kosovo Plain, surrounded by the invading armies to the north, east and south, having been driven from the rest of the country by the enemy. With them were tens of thousands of refugees and dozens of men and women of the Allied missions. To the west, their passage was blocked by the wall of snow-covered and forbidding mountains that marked the Serbian border with Albania and Montenegro.

When a final, doomed attempt failed to break through to the French and British to the south, the Serbian Chief-of-Staff, General Putnik, knew that only two options lay open to him. He could surrender unconditionally to the enemy or order his men to retreat over the frozen mountain passes of Albania and Montenegro in an attempt to reach safety along the Adriatic coast. On 21st November he chose the latter. For the French and British there was no longer any possibility of breaking through to the Serbian army. The French fell back towards Salonika, joined shortly thereafter by the British. By 13th December the Franco-British Expeditionary Force was back where it started, in Greece, having failed in its primary task of preventing Serbia from ruin.

"It was a lively experience," scribbled Flora happily in a letter to Sophia describing her narrow escape from the Bulgarians with the ambulance. "I have a hand grenade which a Serbian woman gave to me and which I know how to use, and a revolver," she boasted to her sister, who likely felt anything but reassured. "We came through Prilep," she continued. "Our rear men looted the town and set fire to a part of the Bulgarian quarter as we went through, but they didn't find much to loot. One man told me he broke open three shops to find a pair of boots, and couldn't get one."[29]

The ambulance had fled south through the pitch dark, where it had joined other Serbian units along the road. It was "a most unpleasant night", wrote Flora, "rumbling along in the dark, not knowing whether the Bulgars had got there first and cut the road in front of us". At sunrise they stopped a few miles from Monastir to await the arrival of Colonel Milić, the Commandant of the Second Regiment of the Morava Division.

Milić had already heard of the presence of an Englishwoman travelling with the army. When he rode up with his headquarters staff he found her standing around a blazing fire with the men of the ambulance. He was fascinated by the khaki-clad thirty-nine-year-old nurse who stood before him in boots and breeches and who spoke to him as if she was every bit his equal. He was impressed too by her plain-spoken and direct manner, her obvious enthusiasm for working near the battlefront and her apparent fearlessness. She was far from what he had expected.

Flora too was curious to meet the middle-aged, lean commandant. Although his well-kept uniform, polished boots and trimmed moustache lent him an air of authority, he entirely failed to intimidate her. He was "a perfect old dear", she wrote to her sister.[30] Like Flora, he could speak German. She was pleased more than anything to find another person with whom she could easily communicate. "We… had a great powwow," she recalled of their meeting. "My first impression of him was that he was a real sport, and later on, when I got to know him very well and had the privilege of being a soldier in his regiment, I found out that not only was he a sport, but one of the bravest and most chivalrous gentlemen anyone ever served under."[31]

Milić could see that his men took comfort from the fact that a British woman had chosen to stand by them at a time when they were on the verge of defeat. More than that, Flora's company provided a much needed respite for him from the near impossible task he had on his hands. Although his Second Regiment had been ordered to act as a "rearguard" in an attempt to keep the Bulgarians at bay, he had no big guns to answer the enemy's artillery, his soldiers were outnumbered four to one, and the Serbian front lines were so thinly manned that the Bulgarians could simply walk round them. All he could do was to rush men from one point to the next in a doomed attempt to stem the advance. At night, to get his mind off his troubles, he would stay up playing chess with Flora. "The Commandant and I were very evenly matched," she wrote. "We used to have some tremendous battles, sometimes long after everyone else was asleep, and always kept a careful record of who won."[32]

Milić became Flora's protector, mentor and friend. Three days
after they met, he invited her to remain at his regimental headquarters, on the premise that she could work for the small field ambulance attached to it. "As it is closer to the front," explained Flora
in the letter to her sister, "I accepted and behold me now installed
afresh."[33] Next, he assigned her an orderly, Vliaho. Having grown
up with servants, his appointment hardly merited a comment in
her diary. Vliaho brought her supper each night, ensured she had a
place to sleep and, most importantly, helped with her belongings.
"I hadn't very much [luggage]," wrote Flora, who nevertheless had
considerably more than anyone else.[34] Her new Serbian colleagues,
no doubt assuming that all Englishwomen travelled thus, took
her and her luggage in their stride. But she was less happy when
Milić assigned a guard to the wagon she had been given to live and
sleep in. He "spat and hawked violently all night" she grumbled
irritably in her diary.[35]

The guard aside, Milić did not attempt to coddle Flora. Once he
learnt of her keen interest in the progress of the battle, he lent her
his second horse, a white half-Arab called Diana who could gallop
"like the wind", so that she could join him on his visits to the shallow Serbian trenches in the hills.[36] Milić was greatly impressed by
her riding skills. "The Commandant seems awfully bucked that I
can ride, and declares they have a small cavalry detachment of 30 of
the best riders in the Reg. and that I'd better belong to that," wrote
Flora excitedly in her diary. "They seem bent on turning me into a
soldier, and I expect I'll find myself in the trenches next battle!"[37]

On 22nd November Flora arrived in the village of Topolchani in
the company of Milić, his staff and the regimental field ambulance.
In the three days since she had joined them she had travelled with
them as they had slowly retreated south towards Monastir, losing
one position after another to the Bulgarians. It was "heartbreak-
ing" for Milić, Flora could see, to be forced to abandon more and
more territory to the enemy. Still, he steadfastly refused to throw
his men's lives away on battles they had no prospect of winning.[38]

She was there with Colonel Milić, his staff and a Greek doctor when the Bulgarians attacked through the cover of a driving
blizzard the following morning. From the doorway of a house by
the roadside, she listened as the muffled crack of rifles shattered

the grey calm. "There we stood about in the snow and listened to a battle which was apparently going on quite close," described Flora. "Although we strained our eyes we could see nothing – there was such a frightful blizzard. A company of reinforcements passed us and floundered off through the deep snowdrifts across the fields in the direction of the firing." Suddenly, her pulse racing, she heard the Bulgarians storm the Serbian positions. "The crackle of rifles got nearer and nearer and at last, about midday, [we] could hear the 'Hurrahs, hurrahs' of the Bulgarians quite close as they charged."

The doctor shared none of her composure. "[He] charged past me in a great hurry, and promptly fell over his horse's head when it stumbled in the snow," she noted contemptuously in her diary. "The Ambulance was ahead on the move, I wanted to wait until [Milić] went, but the doctor shrieked we must go." Flora grudgingly set off with him on Diana to rejoin the men of the ambulance. Although they were camped a mere two miles away, it took an hour to reach them, through the snow and penetrating cold.

Flora was at work in the bleak twilight of the late afternoon carefully dressing the wounds of injured men when the sudden crack of Bulgarian guns threw the doctor into a renewed state of panic. "[He] got into an awful state because he had had no order to move and the guns were banging away, the flashes showing on the snow," she wrote acerbically. This time, when the doctor and the men of the ambulance prepared to retreat, Flora insisted on staying behind. "I'll wait for Militch and follow later," she told them emphatically. The day's events had been too much for the Greek doctor. Soon after, to the scorn of Flora and the men, he abandoned the ambulance for good.[39]

To be in the thick of the battle was something that Flora had long dreamt of, ever since as a child she had read and reread 'The Charge of the Light Brigade' and spent hours imagining herself as the central character in Kipling's tales of heroism and adventure. She had high hopes for the climax of the Bulgarian attack. "I had great visions of a gallop with [Milić] with the Bulgarians hotly pursuing us, as he always waits till the last minute," she explained.[40] But her hopes of a dramatic chase were dashed.[41] When Milić finally arrived, at nine p.m., they set off together on horseback for the village of Mogila, a couple of hours south on the road towards Monastir. "Instead of the wild cinema gallop," wrote Flora,

> we had one of the slowest, coldest rides you can imagine. There was a piercing blizzard blowing across the snowy waste, blinding our eyes and filling our ears with snow; our hands were numbed, and our feet so cold and wet we could hardly feel the stirrups. We proceeded in dead silence, no one feeling disposed to talk, and slowly threaded our way through crowds of soldiers tramping along, with bent heads, as silently as phantoms, the sound of their feet muffled by the snow. I pitied the poor fellows from the bottom of my heart – they were so much colder and wearier than I was myself, and I wondered where the "glory" of war came in. It was exactly like a nightmare from which one might presently wake up.[42]

They were chilled to the very bone when they finally reached a tiny village of roughcast stone houses where they found shelter in a loft. The next evening, with the Bulgarians close on their heels, Flora, Milić and the officers were forced to retreat again, this time towards Orizari, a village on the outskirts of Monastir.

Flora was now the only woman with the regimental ambulance. The Serbian girl had taken the opportunity, as they neared Monastir, to visit the town to pick up some winter clothes. Although she understood that she had intended to return to them, Flora never saw her again.[43] As the sole female, Flora's one complaint about life with the regimental ambulance was the lack of all privacy. "Found lavatory and washing arrangements extremely difficult under the circs," she commented shortly after joining them. The best that she could do was position her wagon strategically so that it was "not quite so public".[44] She remained otherwise silent about how she coped with sanitary matters at the front. Most likely, the men of her regiment arranged for her to be given the privacy of a tent or shelter where they could, and turned a courteous blind eye where they could not.

The thing she missed most was having a good bath. In the two weeks she had spent with the Second Regiment everyone she had spoken to had assured her that it was impossible to have a bath in wartime. "War with the Serbians having lasted now 500 years.

Off and on, I don't suppose many of the present generation have had one," she commented wryly to her sister.[45] Finally, she got her chance in Orizari. Her orderly Vliaho, who likewise thought it incomprehensible that anyone could possibly feel the need for a bath, procured a filthy "sort of stable" for her, set up her rubber bath, filled it with hot water and stood guard outside.

Cleanliness was not Flora's only concern. Her clothes were also by now infested with lice – or "a certain kind of livestock" as she called them more delicately in print. After her bath she set to work dealing with their proliferation. "I burned a hole in my vest cremating some of them," she wrote, "but judging by the look of my bathroom, where the soldiers had been sleeping, I am not at all sure that I did not carry more away with me than I got rid of."[46] Flora's hunt for lice was interrupted by the sudden arrival of Charles Greig. The dutiful young consul was determinedly trying to get the remaining British nationals around Monastir to safety, and he had not yet given up on Flora. His arrival was announced to her by Vliaho. Flora threw on her clothes and went out to see him. "I've got the car to take you to Salonika today if you've had enough," he told her. "I'm not going to leave for anything," she replied.[47]

Greig could see that there was little point pursuing the matter further. "You're quite right to stop," he told her graciously, before driving her to Monastir and back so that she could collect a large case of cigarettes and her well-travelled violin. Before he left, he handed her jam and balaclavas to give to the soldiers of her regiment and they parted "warm friends".[48] A week later, just before Monastir fell to the Bulgarians, Greig hastily married a local girl, Emily Vladica.[49] When he left for Salonika, still in wedding dress, he carried with him the letter from Flora to her sister Sophia. "I'm having the time of my life with the 2nd regiment (Serbian) making a last desperate stand against [the] Bulgarians," she told her.[50]

The evening after Greig's visit, Flora joined Milić in a visit to a soldiers' camp outside Orizari. She brought with her the supplies that Greig had given her, along with some of her cigarettes. She was introduced to the officers and given an enthusiastic welcome by the men, who took real pleasure in the small gifts. "It turned out to be the Fourth Company of the First Battalion [of the Second

Regiment, Morava Division of the Army of the New Territories],
strange to say, the very company that I afterwards joined, although
I didn't guess that at the time," wrote Flora. "It was a most picturesque scene with the little tents all crowded together, and dozens
of campfires blazing in the snow with soldiers sitting round them;
they all seemed very cheery in spite of the bitter cold."[51]

The next day, 28th November, was Flora's last in Orizari. At
nine p.m. she joined Milić and his regimental-headquarters staff
on horseback as they rode slowly down the dark, icy road into
Monastir. Milić had brought her with him to visit the divisional
commander, General Miloš Vasić. Among the matters that he
needed to discuss was Flora. Her position with the army hung in
the balance, as both Milić and Flora knew all too well. By now
she realized that there was little point pretending she could be
useful as a nurse in such conditions. Desperate not to be sent
back to Salonika, she rested all her hopes on being accepted into
the ranks of the army as soldier. A few days previously she had
removed the Red Cross insignia from her arm. Bracing herself
for the rejection that she thought would follow, she told Milić
half-jokingly that she would instead join the Second Regiment
as a private. Instead of the refusal she so feared, he "laughingly
took the little brass figure '2' off his own epaulettes and fastened
them on the shoulder straps of his 'new recruit', as he called me,"
recalled Flora.[52]

But Milić knew that his unusual soldier needed General Vasić's
final approval. Although the general gave Flora a friendly reception, she remained sick with worry, fully expecting that she would
be "ignominiously packed back to Salonique as a female encum-
brance". Awaiting sanction too was a young Greek eager to join
the Serbian army. As the two potential recruits stood nervously
before him, Vasić turned first to him. "I can have no foreigners
in the army," he told him, cutting short the pleas of the disappointed man.[53]

Vasić then turned to Flora. "If you remain with the army, you
will have to go with them through Albania. The trip will be terrible, like nothing you have ever experienced," he warned. "The
last train goes down to Salonika tonight, and if you want to go you
must go at once." "Will I be a burden?" she asked bluntly. "Quite
the reverse," he replied genially. "It would be better for us if you

stopped, as your presence will encourage the soldiers. You represent the whole of England to them." Flora had already made up her mind. "I'll stay, in that case," she answered, to the indignation of the Greek, who had just witnessed the enlistment of a grey-haired thirty-nine-year-old Englishwoman.[54]

For Flora it was almost too good to be true. She was now, officially, a private in the Serbian army. She had not only realized her long-standing dream, but also achieved unique status. At a stroke, she became the only Western woman to enlist in a regular army during the First World War.

PART TWO

CHAPTER 6

RETREAT

1915

The black, snow-peaked mountains marking the border between Serbian Macedonia and Albania rose menacingly in the distance ahead of the soldiers of Flora's new Second Regiment. Long columns of hungry, lice-covered, bedraggled men made their way slowly along the rough road, dragging their sore feet westwards towards the heights. Strings of starving pack animals lumbered slowly alongside them, the weight of their heavy loads cutting into their flesh.

Flora had joined the miserable procession at midnight on the night she had been accepted into the army as a private, in the company of Milić and his regimental headquarters. She had stoically endured a series of punishing nocturnal treks on horseback that took them along the gradually ascending, serpentine roads that led through the stunted foliage covering the region. "The roads were really fearful, one solid sheet of ice," she later recalled. "Occasionally we all used to get down and walk for a bit to warm our feet, which became like blocks of ice, but the going was so hard we were glad to mount again."[1] Ominously, the road was also lined with the bodies of emaciated animals. "Every few yards we passed the horrible-looking corpses of bullocks, donkeys, etc. with the flesh half stripped from them, whether by birds or what I don't know," she shuddered.[2] The only available shelter from the bitter wind along the isolated route was the occasional white blockhouse, each of which was packed with soldiers and filthy beyond all imagination.[3]

* * *

Flora now took her part in the great "retreat" of the Serbian army across the ice- and snow-covered mountains of Albania and Montenegro, where its men hoped to find sanctuary and safety on the Adriatic coast. There, they believed, their British, French and Italian allies would come to their rescue. At the outset, there were estimated to be two hundred and fifty thousand Serbian soldiers, thirty-five thousand POWs, twenty-seven thousand Serbian boys and tens of thousands of civilian refugees.[4] Dozens of men and women of Allied military and medical missions joined them.

The retreat had started well before the Serbs were driven into the mountains. For those who had been driven relentlessly across the country by the force of the enemy onslaught, it had begun not just weeks but hundreds of miles before. By the time it reached the mountains, the army had already undergone appalling privations. It had been fighting without rest for approaching seven weeks. The men were exhausted, hungry and ragged. Some were wounded. Others were afflicted with dysentery and other illnesses. Although the Adriatic was ninety miles away, in practice the distance they had to traverse was easily twice this, as the tracks were not direct but twisted and turned over icy mountain passes up to five thousand feet high.[5]

The army travelled by four routes. The northernmost was through Montenegro to Scutari (now Shkodër). The next two routes farther south were through Albania; one led to Scutari, the other to the coast near Durazzo (now Durrës). The southernmost track was the one taken by Flora and the Army of the New Territories. They travelled from Monastir, past Resna and Lake Struga to Elbasan, Kavaja and to the Durazzo coast.[6]

Irrespective of their route, the soldiers faced the combined threats of starvation, exposure, disease and exhaustion. Those travelling through Albania faced a further threat – the bitter hostility of the inhabitants. Although this animosity stemmed partly from fear of the strain that the starving Serbs would place on the limited resources of the region, it went far deeper than that. In 1912 and 1913, following the collapse of Ottoman rule, the Serbs had marched a heavily armed and well-organized army through Albania in an attempt to seize an Adriatic port. They had shown little mercy to the population during their ultimately unsuccessful invasion. The Albanians now seized the opportunity to show the Serbs none at all.

At best, the Albanians exploited them commercially. There was so little food available that they could charge whatever they wanted. Refugees, POWs and soldiers without gold were forced to barter with their clothing. Many were so desperate for food that they exchanged their coats and boots, in midwinter, for small pieces of bread. The Albanians also massacred the Serbs in their thousands. They targeted those who could not retaliate, in particular the boys, civilian refugees and stragglers. Soldiers were also shot as they passed through narrow mountain passes with no avenue of escape.[7]

Milić had more than just the Albanians to worry about. He needed little reminding of the proximity of the Bulgarian enemy – the constant boom of enemy artillery that resounded across the hills around them saw to that. Although he grew tired and pale from the strain and lack of sleep, he remained ready with a word of encouragement for his men. At every halt Flora saw him issue orders, rig up field telephones, pore over maps and greet dispatch riders who brought news, never good, from the battlefront.[8]

The Bulgarians continued to drive Milić and his Second Regiment closer and closer towards Albania. The border was intensely symbolic to the men. "In the bitterly cold grey dawn we stood around in black, churned-up mud, shivering, hungry and miserable," recorded Flora in her diary on 8th December. "The discouraged soldiers trailed along the road, in the half-light of a winter morning, and altogether we looked the most hopelessly forlorn army imaginable, setting our faces towards the dark, hard-looking range of snow-capped mountains which separate their beloved Serbia from Albania." Three days later they arrived at the top of the hill that marked the frontier. "We halted for a few minutes, and sort of said goodbye to Serbia, and then rode on in silence into the Albanian valley."[9]

Although Flora was near the heart of the action, the war was still little more than a curiosity and novelty to her. She took the occasional solitary stroll at various stops en route, much as a tourist would, to get a better look at her surroundings. "Coming back I was stopped and closely questioned by an officer," she recalled after one such walk. "He did not know who I was, and was evidently puzzled. He wanted to know where I had been and why, and seemed to think that I might have been paying a visit to the Bulgarians." Milić was "very much amused" when she later told him what had happened. "Don't go and get shot in mistake for a spy," he cheerfully told her.[10]

Milić had looked after Flora well. His paternal eye and the relatively privileged orbit of regimental headquarters had left her, so far, largely unaware of the extent of the suffering that affected much of the army and, in particular, the thousands of POWs and schoolboys who accompanied them. Although the POWs had been given little choice in the matter – the Serbs were not about to permit them to be absorbed again into enemy ranks – many did not have any heart for the war and retreated voluntarily, little knowing that virtually no food could be made available for them.[11] The boys followed ill-conceived and ill-executed orders by their government to leave, along the more northerly routes. They were given little supervision or protection and did not have the strength, endurance or advantages of their older brothers in the army in getting shelter and food. Early on, members of Allied medical and military missions began to see them en route, huddled together, crying from hunger and homesickness.[12]

The horrifying reality of what the retreat meant to the POWs was brought home to Flora with a sickening jolt. During one of her hillside jaunts she had approached a little hut and peered inside the dark doorway. In front of her lay "9 dead Austrians, a horrible sight, the poor devils lay just as they died, from sickness and starvation, unable to go any farther," she scribbled in an angry diary entry. She was aghast at what she had seen, her friend Hayek's face almost certainly flashing before her eyes as she contemplated his fate. "There doesn't seem to be much 'glory' about this war and if there is I've never come across it," she wrote in a rare diary entry critical of the conflict.[13]

By the time that Flora crossed into Albania with the men of the Second Regiment, the British medical staff who had remained behind in Serbia had been prisoners of the Germans, Austrians and Bulgarians for up to seven weeks. The first to be captured were the Lady Paget Unit in Skopje, who were taken prisoner by the Bulgarians on 22nd October. Next, on 7th November, the remains of the Lazarevac and Kragujevac units of the Scottish Women's Hospitals were captured by the Germans in Kruševac, a town on the main railway line south from Belgrade. Three days later, their colleagues from the Valjevo unit were taken prisoner by the Austro-Hungarians in the nearby spa town of Vrnjačka Banja. Other missions were also captured in Vrnjačka Banja, including the Berry Unit, the Wounded Allies, British Red Cross and the Farmers.

The occupiers uniformly allowed the units to continue their work until arrangements could be made for them to be repatriated, although their treatment of them varied considerably. The Austro-Hungarians in Vrnjačka Banja treated their British prisoners with remarkable courtesy. They made it clear from the outset that they had no intention of interfering with their work and, though they looked "half-starved" themselves, ensured that the units were supplied with daily rations.[14] Lady Paget too developed a good working relationship with the Bulgarians who took her staff prisoner in Skopje. They supplied her generously with food and basic medical supplies while allowing her to continue to run her hospital more or less as she chose. One month later over a thousand Germans arrived. They seized the unit's horses, burned their firewood and exhausted their water supply, while treating their supposed Bulgarian allies with utter contempt. So hostile were the relations between the Germans and Bulgarians that the latter began to collaborate with their British prisoners to get the better of them. When the Germans attempted to take control of the hospital building, the Bulgarians flew their national flag over the hospital to deny it to them.[15]

The women of the Scottish Women's Hospitals in Kruševac were similarly permitted by their "brusque" German captors to continue working at the Serbian military hospital in the town, but their movements were closely controlled and almost all of their equipment was requisitioned, leaving them with almost nothing to treat their twelve hundred patients.[16] After only three weeks the women were sent to a POW camp in Kevavara on the edge of the Hungarian plain, where they were joined by their colleagues from Vrnjačka Banja. All thirty-two, as well as a number of strays from other units, were quartered in two small rooms, but they were not otherwise ill treated.[17]

The American Red Cross Unit under the charge of Dr Edward Ryan remained in Belgrade. As nationals from a then neutral country, they did not expect to be taken prisoner or mistreated by the invaders and they accordingly agreed to accept the patients of two British units, the Farmers and the British Eastern Auxiliary Hospital, when they hurriedly evacuated the besieged capital.[18] Before Ryan's unit left Serbia in early November, its eighteen staff had worked to the point of exhaustion in treating some of the thousands of victims of the fighting.

One of the dozens of British women taken prisoner was Flora and Emily's former colleague from the Anglo-American Unit, Ada Barlow. She had remained behind in Skopje after the British Red Cross Unit that had so begrudgingly agreed to take on the "fat and plain, elderly and rather pasty" nurse returned home. Lady Paget discovered her there in October, at the time of the invasion. "In the hospital at the Citadel, commonly known as the 'Grad', there were more than a hundred severely wounded cases," she recalled.

The Serbian hospital staff had already left, the only occupant of the huge, rambling buildings being Mrs Barlow, an Englishwoman, who had refused, when the order for evacuation came, to leave her patients. Many of these men had not been undressed since their arrival several days before, and were lying on mattresses on the floor, gaunt, waxen effigies in their bloodstained uniforms; some in a raging fever, others dying of hideous, septic wounds, all entirely dependent for nursing on Mrs Barlow, aided by two or three Serbian women from the town.

Only when the last of her patients were evacuated to the hospital run by Lady Paget did Mrs Barlow agree to leave. She joined the staff of Lady Paget's Unit where, at last, her remarkable courage and dedication to her patients appears to have been recognized.[19]

Flora's association with Milić and his regimental headquarters had given her considerable privileges. She had educated company, an orderly, a bed for the night and a horse to ride. More importantly she was able to share their food instead of having to rely on the worryingly irregular rations given to the ordinary soldiers. But she also realized that being attached to them had one fundamental drawback – it would deny her the opportunity of experiencing the ultimate excitement, that of risking her life on the battlefront – which by now she wanted more than anything else. Although Flora was a private in the Second Regiment, she did not yet belong to a particular company and, while Milić had continued to take her on his inspections of frontline positions at every opportunity, she was no longer content simply to be a visitor to the front, where greater adventure beckoned. She wanted to be based there. If this meant leaving some of the privileges behind, so be it.

The opportunity that she had been waiting for came her way in mid-December. One morning as she sat idling on a hillside the commander of the First Battalion arrived to see Milić before he left to take up new positions against the Bulgarians with his men. It certainly sounded more exciting than spending the day within the confines – and relative safety – of regimental headquarters. "Might I go with him on Diana?" she asked Milić tentatively. "Yes, all right," he replied indulgently.

That night Flora sent word to Milić that she was going to camp with the men of the First Battalion. They were in turn delighted to see her – she had distributed the jam and balaclavas that Greig had given her to its Fourth Company near Monastir. When they left at three a.m. in torrential rain to take up a position on nearby Mount Chukus, she was asked what she wanted to do. "I'm coming with you," she told them firmly.[20]

It took them until four p.m. the following day to reach the flat, rocky heights atop Mount Chukus. The mountain, at 1,790 metres, was one of several peaks in its range. Like its neighbours, it was covered in a patchwork of small trees, bushes, boulders and bare, brown earth. From the top, it overlooked a wooded plateau below, where the Bulgarians were entrenched. Hardly had they reached the top before the first bullets whistled over their heads. It was Flora's first experience of being under rifle fire.

When the commander rushed the companies of his battalion into the line, Flora made a beeline for the Fourth, which was nearest the Bulgarians. She lay down on her stomach behind one of the boulders that scattered the rough terrain, borrowed a rifle and joined the men aiming in volleys on the woods below to the orders of the platoon sergeant, "*Né shanni palli!*" ("Take aim, fire!") "We lay there and fired at them all that day," wrote Flora, for whom the experience was still much like a holiday adventure.

"I took a lot of photographs which I wanted very much to turn out well; but alas! during the journey through Albania the films… got wet and spoilt."[21]

The Fourth Company was ably led by Lieutenant Janacko Jović. Jović was young, dark-haired and confident, not averse to administering discipline where required, and fiercely proud of leading the two hundred and twenty men of the "smartest company in the smartest regiment".[22] Despite his relative youth, in four years of fighting he had won "every kind of medal for bravery", while his experience and competence had also won him the universal respect of his men.[23]

Jović was impressed enough with Flora's sangfroid under fire and her ability to handle a rifle to enrol her on his books that night as a member of his company. She was overjoyed finally to have her place in the Serbian frontline. Her first night with her new company was one she would remember all her life. "Lieut. Jovitch had a roaring fire of pine logs built in a little hollow," she described wistfully.

> He and I and the other two officers of the company sat round it and had our supper of bread and beans, and after that we spread our blankets on spruce boughs round the fire and rolled up in them. It was a most glorious moonlight night, with the ground covered with white hoar frost, and it looked perfectly lovely with all the campfires twinkling every few yards over the hillside among the pine trees. I lay on my back looking up at the stars, and, when one of them asked me what I was thinking about, I told him that when I was old and decrepit and done for, and had to stay in a house and not go about any more, I should remember my first night with the Fourth Company on the top of Mount Chukus.[24]

The other soldiers accepted Flora without question. She earned instant respect from the fact that she, an Englishwoman, was willing to fight for Serbia and share their hardships. To a degree they were also used to women soldiers. A handful of hardy peasant girls fought in the ranks alongside the men, and there was one, Milunka Savić, in their regiment.[25] The Serbian army was badly short of personnel and needed anyone who could shoot, ride and adapt to the difficult conditions. During her time on Mount Chukus, Flora had proven beyond doubt that she could do all of that. She had

handled a rifle since she was a child, she was among the best riders in the regiment and she was indifferent to the weather. "One
soon gets used to the cold when one is always outdoors," she
commented. Once the novelty of her presence wore off, they saw
her as a fellow soldier, not a woman. "Brother," they began to call
her, their usual term of address.[26]

Flora rose with the men of her new company, shook the early-
morning frost off her blanket, picked up her borrowed rifle and
rejoined them in the line. By the afternoon, she reported cheerily,
the firing had become "very hot", after the Bulgarians had managed to advance up the ridges behind them. Soon their bullets
began to spit across the Serbian positions. That night, when they
were forced down the other side of the mountain, Flora retreated
with them. "We had a few casualties," she stated bluntly, "but not
so very many."
  They now needed to push on towards the Adriatic coast as
quickly as possible. Not only were the Bulgarians at their backs,
if the men did not reach it soon they would starve. The Fourth
Company had long since ceased to receive regular rations and had
finished their last allowance of bread days before. The only thing
left for them to eat were corncobs, which they roasted over their
fires. When water began to run short they melted snow to drink.
With no fodder for their animals, their horses and ponies had also
slowly begun to starve. Flora's immediate concern lay elsewhere.
"We had almost run out of cigarettes and tobacco," she observed
on a worried note. But with every passing day she became increasingly concerned about the men's condition. Although they soon
left the Bulgarians far behind, she could see that they were on the
verge of starvation.
  After being driven from the heights of Mount Chukus they
were ordered to head towards Elbasan, a town of twelve thousand
mostly Albanian inhabitants about fifty miles from the Adriatic.
They arrived on the outskirts at five p.m. the following day. "It
was a filthy little town," Flora commented dismissively. What she
saw of the inhabitants made her livid with rage. "[They] were as
hostile as they dared to be, and used to refuse to sell us anything,"
she wrote furiously. What made her angrier still was the sight of
many of them in Austrian overcoats, which they had taken from the

starving prisoners who had staggered through the town, delirious
with hunger, in exchange for a small piece of bread. Flora knew
that this meant the death of many of them from exposure. She
knew that the Albanians realized it too.[27]

But not all Flora's contact with the Albanians was hostile. A few
days later, on Christmas Eve, after a day of sitting about on one
of the low, bracken-covered hills past Elbasan, she ventured into a
village in the company of Jović – by now her constant companion
on any excursion – where she was welcomed with curiosity rather
than hostility. On Christmas morning, buoyed by the reception
she had been given, Flora suggested to Jović that she try to buy
food for as many of the two hundred and twenty men as possible,
using the money she had left. "We'll send a patrol," he responded.
"And you can also have what money I've got." When the patrol
returned, she was thrilled to hear that they had succeeded. "We
bought a sort of cornmeal for [200 francs], and had it baked into
flat loaves there in the town, and next day when we turned out
for a fresh start we gave each man half of one of my cornmeal
loaves and a couple of cigarettes, telling them it was England's
Christmas box to them."[28]

Although she did not realize it at the time, Flora had been fortunate to be on the southernmost route of retreat. Those who had
travelled by the more northerly routes had suffered an "infinitely
worse" time than her company, she later acknowledged.[29] These
included the men and women of the Allied missions who had
decided to flee Serbia in preference to being taken prisoner. The
women of the Scottish Women's Hospitals who joined the retreat
split into three groups. Two parties of approximately thirty women
each set out across Montenegro for the coastal Albanian town of
Scutari. They had one fatality, nurse Caroline Toughill, who died
agonizingly of head injuries three days after the motor ambulance
she was travelling in went over the edge of a precipice.[30] Another
small group formed the "Second Serbo-English Field Ambulance"
in conjunction with a Serbian director and some orderlies. They
attempted to form temporary hospitals along the line of retreat
until they lost all of their equipment to the Germans.[31] By the time
the three parties finally made it to the Albanian coast, nearly all
the women were suffering from frostbite.[32]

The Stobart Unit split into two before retreating. One half, led by Mabel Stobart, became the field hospital for the Šumadija Division of the Second Army, the "First Serbian-English Field Hospital". She was put in charge of sixty Serbian soldiers and given a temporary rank equal to major by Serbian Army Medical Services. What she saw in the mountains haunted her for the rest of her life. "The track became more and more thickly lined, with the dead bodies of oxen, and of horses, and worse still – of men," she wrote. "Men by the hundred lay dead: dead from the cold and hunger by the roadside, their eyes staring at the irresponsive sky; and no one could stop to bury them. But, worse still, men lay dying by the roadside, dying from cold and hunger, and no one could stay to tend them. The whole scene was a combination of mental and physical misery, difficult to describe in words."[33] More than eleven weeks after leaving Kragujevac, her column finally arrived at the coast after having had to abandon all their medical equipment, which could not be brought over the mountain passes of Montenegro.[34]

The remaining members of Mabel Stobart's Unit, including Flora's friend Nan MacGlade, left three weeks after the field hospital. One of their most harrowing experiences was to encounter one of their former POW orderlies, Nikola, whom they all knew as a cheerful, obliging, "big, round-faced boy". "He was no longer the clean, smart mess orderly in white coat and apron, but was a very sorry-looking figure, lean, haggard and miserable," described the unit's chauffeur.

> Immediately I saw what was the matter. He was starving, literally dying for want of food. I fetched the rations given me that morning for two days and gave them to him, and a dry, hard light glittered in his eyes when he saw the bread. He had become not far removed from an animal, and in his downward journey he had picked up the instinct which no one can explain, which tells a starving dog to eat its food in secret. The expression on his face was hardly human as he turned away.[35]

All members of the Stobart Unit survived their ordeal.[36] No record exists of what happened to Nikola.

Individual members of the other British units – the Wounded Allies, Lady Paget Unit, British Red Cross, Farmers and the Berry Unit – also endured the retreat, as did the British, French and

Russian Naval Missions and medical, diplomatic and military personnel from other Allied countries. A few made it south to Salonika before the roads and railways were cut by the invaders, including Mabel Grouitch who, as the wife of the Under-secretary of Foreign Affairs for Serbia, could not risk being taken prisoner.

After four days at their hilltop camp outside Elbasan, Flora and the Fourth Company began their final push towards the coast. Each day they rose at four a.m., shook their aching limbs and set off as the morning sun rose behind the mountain ranges that they had now left far behind. "Sick or well, the men had to keep on," Flora recalled, the memory of those days burnt deep into her mind. "No one could be carried, and you had got to keep on or die by the roadside."[37] They walked or rode daily for fourteen or fifteen hours, the brown Skumbi River swirling lazily to their left, along a path that slowly descended towards the coast. It was lined with the putrefying corpses of hundreds of dead ponies and horses that filled the air with their sickly, sweet stench.

The march to the coast was now a matter of life and death for the gaunt and exhausted men of the company. Jović pushed them on relentlessly, aware that he could only afford to let them rest briefly en route, sometimes for no more than a few minutes at a time. "Before, when I had been working in the hospitals, and I used to ask the men where it hurt them, I had often been rather puzzled at the general reply of the new arrivals, '*Sve me boli*' ('Everything hurts me')," reflected Flora.

It seemed such a vague description and such a curious malady; but in those days I learnt to understand perfectly what they meant by it, when you seem to be nothing but one pain from the crown of your aching head to the soles of your blistered feet, and I thought it was a very good thing that the next time I was working in a military hospital I should be able to enter into my patient's feelings, and realize that all he felt he wanted was to be let alone to sleep for about a week and only rouse up for his meals.[38]

By the fifth day of their forced march Flora and the men of the Fourth Company heard naval guns, the first sign that they were nearing the Adriatic. At dusk, after they had been travelling for fifteen hours, they finally neared the town of Kavaja, ten miles south-east of Durazzo. Their destination lay a few miles to the other side of the town. "I never saw anything like the mud in Kavaja," described Flora. "It came right above the tops of my top boots, and one could hardly drag one's feet out of it. The road was full of rocks and pits, and every two or three yards there were dead or dying horses which had floundered down to rise no more; and it was pitch dark and very cold."[39]

Flora and the men were on the verge of collapse. Ahead, they could see the light of dozens of campfires of another company twinkling on one of the hills, where they too had been ordered to camp. "We kept pushing on and on, and seemed to be never getting any nearer to them," she remembered. "[I] began to wonder if those really were campfires ahead of us or sort of will-o'-the-wisps getting farther away." It took the Fourth Company three long hours to get from Kavaja to their hillside camp by the sea. "We all turned in dead to the world that night, but very glad to have at last reached the coast," Flora recalled. She had completely forgotten that it was New Year's Eve.[40]

CHAPTER 7

COAST

1916

More than one hundred and fifty thousand skeletal, ragged and ashen-faced Serbs eventually reached the Adriatic coast of Albania.[1] Behind them lay the bodies of nearly one hundred thousand Serbian soldiers and tens of thousands of civilians.[2] By the time the survivors had crossed the mountains and dragged their weary feet through miles of marshland on the approach to the coast, many were near death. "[Outside Durazzo], a figure... staggered up and fell on the threshold of the gate," recalled a member of the British Naval Mission.

> It needed a second glance to recognize in that poor heap of rags, sodden and begrimed with filth, a Serbian soldier... When we lifted him from the stones we saw a face that made the blood run cold at the heart... At first one thought that this was the countenance of an old man, or rather of the mummy of one long dead; and then there came the dreadful conviction that it was the countenance of a youth – a boy of seventeen or eighteen – but so wasted by hunger and suffering that nothing was left there but dry skin drawn like parchment over projecting bones... The lad was all but dead of exhaustion and hunger. He said a word, *hleba* (bread). We gave him a loaf, and he held it in his hand and did not eat. His naked feet were bruised and covered with blood, and he was too feeble to walk farther by himself.[3]

The Serbs had staggered across the mountains of Albania and Montenegro propelled by the belief that British, French and Italian forces would provide them, on arrival, with food and safety. At first they found neither. The Allies had at least agreed on a plan of rescue for the Serbs; where they failed was in carrying it out. The French sent the Mission Militaire Française en Albanie, whose aim was to reorganize the remnants of the Serbian army into units capable of rejoining the fight against Germany and its allies.[4] The British sent another, the British Adriatic Mission, whose aim was to prevent them from dying first from starvation.[5] The Italians, in turn, accepted the responsibility of shipping food and supplies across the relatively short distance from their coastline.

Both Britain and France had sent large quantities of food for the Serbs to Brindisi in southern Italy, a port directly across the Adriatic from Albania where, as agreed, it awaited shipment. But as one day followed another, no ships sailed. "The trip is too dangerous," protested the Italian naval authorities, who had already lost one flotilla to the destroyers of the Austrian navy, as they contemplated the enemy submarines, floating mines and aeroplanes that lay in wait.[6] However, the reasons for their foot-dragging went beyond these risks. Both the Italians and the Serbs had competing territorial ambitions in Albania. Although the Serbs posed no threat whatsoever to their aspirations following the retreat, the Italians deeply resented their presence. In what amounted to a systematic policy of obstruction, not only did they refuse to ship food to them, they attempted to thwart the efforts of relief workers and failed to ensure the proper feeding of the refugees who made it to Italy. Only after repeated interventions by the British and French was enough pressure brought to bear on them to induce them to begin sporadic shipments. By then, it was too late for many thousands of Serbs.

Flora had a talent for turning situations to her own advantage but on many occasions pure luck favoured her. It did so again now. Had she arrived on the coast sixty miles farther north at Scutari as had the majority of military and civilian refugees, she would have faced infinitely worse conditions. By the time she reached the coast near Durazzo with the Fourth Company at the tail end of the retreat, food shipments were becoming more regular and there were enough supplies in the vicinity to keep them from starving to death.[7]

On New Year's Day, Flora and the men of the Fourth Company crawled out of their tents into the warm morning sunshine, rubbed their aching limbs and hobbled as best they could to the top of the hill to get their first look at their surroundings. All around them the tented camps of hundreds of other companies were dotted across the low, rolling hills and along the rough roadsides. To the west, on the far side of a river and stretch of swampland, lay the Adriatic. Although the town of Durazzo was ten miles away, they could see it clearly at the end of a long sweep of yellow sand, nestled against the slopes of a hill. They could also see the distant wrecks of several food ships that had been sunk by the Austrian navy in its harbour, which lent it a desolate and foreboding appearance.

Still, it was a day of celebration. Not only had they all survived the retreat to the coast, it was also Flora's New Year. "Everyone came up and wished me a Happy New Year, our English New Year, that is, as theirs, of course, did not come till thirteen days later," she reported, "and we all hoped that the New Year might prove happier than the old one had been." Flora had also been on Jović's mind that day. He knew that the last food most of the men of his company had eaten during the retreat was that which she had bought for them six days earlier. He also knew that it had almost certainly saved some of their lives. He decided that the best way to reward her for her efforts was to promote her from private to corporal. For Flora, it was to be the start of her rapid ascent through the ranks of the Serbian army.[8]

After a couple of days on the hill overlooking the Adriatic, Flora began to get restless. On 3rd January, hoping "to see the sights", she joined three officers on horseback as they made their way to Durazzo, along a path lined with decomposing horses.[9] The town of jumbled red roofs and pointed, white minarets looked as eastern as its ten thousand largely Albanian and Turkish inhabitants. Its narrow streets were potholed and littered with great rocks. They were also thronged with miserable hordes of Serbian refugees. Among them jostled soldiers in smart grey-green uniforms who were part of the Italian occupying force.[10]

Suddenly, among the grey-green, Flora spotted khaki. "I could hardly believe my eyes, it seemed so long since I had seen an Englishman," she enthused at the sight of a sergeant major of the British Adriatic Mission. "I almost fell on his neck in excitement."[11] The sergeant major was equally astounded at the sight of a grubby Englishwoman in the uniform of a Serbian corporal. No doubt bemused by her story of how she had retreated with the army after having been accepted into its ranks, he took her at once to his headquarters. His fellow officers were equally startled at her appearance. "They looked upon me with more than suspicion at first, thought I was a kind of camp follower I believe," she scribbled in a letter to a friend.[12] Nonetheless, they were at least willing to see that she was well fed on each visit.[13] Flora, who knew a good thing when she saw it, went back to visit them often.

On Monday 24th January Flora was handed a telegram. "Meet me at once in Durazzo. Simmonds." She dropped everything upon receipt of this message from Emily and urged a borrowed horse over the dusty ten-mile track to try to find her. Flora had last written to her in October to tell her she was returning to their old hospital in Valjevo and suggesting they meet first in Salonika. Emily had duly left New York in early December with cases of food, clothing and medicine donated by the American Red Cross.[14] But on arrival in the Greek port, not only was Flora nowhere to be found, Valjevo was under enemy occupation. "I had to look round to find something where I could be of real help," Emily recalled. First, alongside a unit of the Scottish Women's Hospitals and a few Quakers who had been left similarly stranded, she helped establish a large tented refugee camp in the grounds of a hospital in Salonika.[15] Then, when the refugees were about to be evacuated to Corsica and the southern French coast by the French government, she attempted to take her supplies to Albania by boat. "Unfortunately the Italians, [aiming] to keep the Adriatic to themselves and disliking the Serbs whom they consider to stand in their way, interfered a little in our plans," recorded Emily. "[They] stopped the Greek boat and transhipped our supplies to Brindisi where there were a great many refugees."[16]

The refugees who had reached Italy via a handful of returning food ships were barely tolerated, partly due to fear that their poor health would lead to an epidemic. Nonetheless, the Italians did little to alleviate the conditions in which disease could take hold. They were taken to crowded isolation camps surrounded by barbed wire, with little food or water and only a few bare sheds for shelter, paradoxically just the settings likely to lead to an outbreak of typhus or cholera.[17] Emily was shocked by their condition and raced into action. Flora heard later about her work and had nothing but admiration. "Among other little odd jobs she discovered a whole colony of them in Brindisi who had been without food for two days," she praised. "So without any further red tape proceeded to hire carriages, drive round the town and buy up everything in the eatable line which was to be had wherewith to feed them."[18] Before the Italians simply began dumping them over the border into France, she took charge of the rationing of two thousand of them.[19]

Flora's first task on receipt of Emily's telegram was to track her down. Hearing that her friend was about to be presented to Crown Prince Aleksandar, Flora rode to his lodgings, introduced herself and took a seat in his audience chamber to await Emily's arrival.[20] When Emily appeared in the company of Slavko Grouitch, she was taken aback by the sight of Flora in the uniform of a Serbian corporal. She did not approve of her transformation in the least. "Miss Sandes enlisted into the Serbian Army and lives the life of a soldier, which seems to me [a] great waste of a woman – of all the work that only a woman can do," she remarked later.[21] But above all, she was delighted to see her safe, having worried herself sick since hearing that Flora had last been seen heading for Albania with the army.

Twenty-eight-year-old Aleksandar welcomed them shyly but warmly. Olive-skinned, with a thin moustache and a pince-nez perched on his long nose, he had a slightly nervous manner that made him appear more like a student than the commander-in-chief of the Serbian army.[22] Flora and Emily were both shocked by how thin and ill he looked. "He had only been there for two days and is just recovering from an operation [for appendicitis]," wrote Emily in a letter to the American Red Cross. "He still looks very sick."[23] He saw them only briefly, but long enough to tell them both graciously how much he appreciated their work and to decorate them with the Order of St Sava, Fourth Class.[24] Emily reciprocated his gesture as best she could. "His appetite is very poor," his doctor had told her before her royal appointment. "All he fancies is chocolate, which we can't get for him." She had brought with her a case of "comforts" donated by the Red Cross, including chocolate and other luxuries. Half she presented to him. The other half she gave to Flora for her "field hospital" – or so she told the Red Cross, who would not have been pleased to hear that they had made a generous donation to the Serbian army.[25]

Emily had arrived in Durazzo only that morning from Brindisi. She had answered an urgent appeal by the Serbian government to find workers willing to help evacuate Serbian refugees aboard the *Arménie*, a French vessel the American Red Cross had secured for the purpose.[26] Not only were the limited resources of the Albanian coastline grossly insufficient to meet the needs of the throngs of hungry, exhausted civilians, a new and imminent danger had emerged in the form of an Austrian invasion of Albania. The Austrian army, fresh following their victory against Serbia, had marched next against Montenegro. The little kingdom had surrendered with barely a whimper on 17th January. Buoyed by their easy victory, the Austrians continued their drive south through Albania. The only thing that lay between them and the refugees was the Serbian army, who were in no condition to try to stop them.

"Nobody else wanted to go," reported the Red Cross in commenting on Emily's decision to accompany the refugees. Not only were they suffering from all the effects of prolonged privation including lice and tuberculosis, they would have to be crowded together for days on the ships, with virtually non-existent sanitary arrangements and the very real prospect of an on-board outbreak of typhus or cholera. Equally grave were the threats from enemy submarines, floating mines and aeroplanes. Although Emily was well aware of the risks, they did not deter her from going.[27] "Occasionally reports came of Serbian refugees on the coast of Albania, and the trips thither to get them and bring them away Miss Simmonds found even more exciting," reported the Red Cross. "There was nothing dull about them. The prevalence of submarines in those waters did not exactly drive dull care away, but they did prevent the incidence of ennui."[28] What concerned Emily more was that there would be no doctor on board. "I must tell you I felt a little dismayed when I found that I was looked upon as the medical adviser for the whole ship," she wrote.[29] Only one other volunteer could be found to travel with her, John Earnshaw Bellows, a thirty-two-year-old, somewhat earnest Quaker from Gloucester, although two other volunteers, the archaeologist Robert Carr Bosanquet and Emily's old acquaintance Slavko Grouitch, agreed to assist them on the first leg of their journey.

Late that evening Emily brought Flora on board the *Arménie* to help her feed its seventeen hundred men, women and children, many of whom were on the verge of starvation. They slowly navigated their way through its holds and onto its pitch-black decks, handing out bully beef and hard biscuits. The ship was so tightly packed with people that some of the men were unable to lie down. "It was no easy task," recalled Flora.[30] By midnight, they had fed them all. As the dark ship sailed into the black waters of the Adriatic, Flora waved it off from the shoreline before returning to her hotel.

The next morning she rose late and sauntered over to the headquarters of the British Adriatic Mission for breakfast. She had just sat down to a plate of bacon and eggs when suddenly she heard a "most terrific crash, followed by others in quick succession". She pushed her plate aside, stood up and dashed outside to get a better look. Above her in the blue sky were five red-and-white-painted Austrian aeroplanes dropping shiny silver bombs and raining propaganda leaflets on the crowded town. She looked on calmly at the panic all around her. "People were running as hard as they could to get out of the way – at least, the Italians were running, the Serbians always thought it beneath their dignity to do so," she described. "There was a wide subterranean drain leading from the town to the sea, and down this hundreds of Italians crawled, but I think if I were given the choice of crawling down a Durazzo drain in close proximity to some hundreds of the natives of that town or being killed by a bomb I would choose the latter." In all, they dropped about twenty-five bombs, killing about fifty people and wounding many more.[31] "When it was all over I went back again," recalled Flora, "and, finding the headquarters of the British Adriatic Mission still standing, sat down to a fresh lot of bacon and eggs for breakfast, such luxuries not being obtainable every day."[32]

The town of Durazzo was an attractive target. Not only was it crowded with civilian refugees, it was packed to capacity with

Serbian soldiers. The soldiers, one hundred thousand in total, had flocked to the town after having been ordered to march south along the coast to escape being taken prisoner by the Austrian army. Although the Allies had decided to evacuate the civilian refugees to Corsica and the southern French coast following the generous offer by France, the decision on what to do with the men of the Serbian army was far more contentious. Prior to the invasion, the British Adriatic Mission had offered to help feed, reorganize and re-equip the army in situ in Albania, but the Italians, unsurprisingly, were diametrically opposed to this suggestion.[33] They further rejected out of hand the mischievous suggestion by the French that the Serbs be taken to Italy.[34] The logical place to take them was Corfu, which lay alongside the Adriatic coastline to the south. It was only a short distance away. It was also close to the sphere of operations in Macedonia where, after the men of the Serbian army recovered, it was intended that they would take their place alongside the Allies.[35] The one problem with Corfu was that it was Greek. Greece was then walking a tightrope of neutrality, being equally threatened and cajoled by the Allies and the Central Powers, who were both eager to gain a new ally. Impatient with their equivocations, on 12th January the Allies informed the unhappy Greeks as a fait accompli that the remnants of the Serbian army were to be taken there.[36]

The pressing attention of the Allies now turned to getting them to the island before they were overrun by the Austrian army. First, with great reluctance, the Serbian authorities ordered their sick and starving men to march sixty miles south from Scutari to Durazzo, across dank, stagnant marshland.[37] The march took seven days, much of it through pouring rain. British witnesses reported seeing corpses along the track, both human and animal.[38] Upon arrival the men were told the unthinkable – the Allies had been unable to amass enough small ships at Durazzo because the Italians would not lend them suitable vessels. They would have to walk a further seventy-five miles south to the town of Valona, which had a harbour deep enough to accommodate large transport ships and which was sufficiently sheltered from naval attack to win the cooperation of the Italians. On 30th January the difficult task fell to Crown Prince Aleksandar to issue the order to march south.[39]

* * *

Before the town was overwhelmed by the Austrian army, a few small ships had braved the journey to the primitive harbour of San Giovanni di Medua to deliver supplies. The harbour was south of the town of Scutari, where the women of the Allied missions had gathered following the retreat. Empty on their return journey, the ships could at least evacuate them and a privileged few, including members of the Serbian government and diplomatic staff who were taken to Italy around Christmas time. Most women reached home by late December with little more than the clothes they stood up in, healthy but tired, to a flurry of press interest.

The nineteen thousand Austrian POWs who had survived the retreat against all the odds to reach the Albanian coast received no such special treatment. These were all that were left of the seventy-five thousand men who had been taken prisoner in 1914.[40] Many of the starving men had been put to work improving the roads. Near Durazzo Emily had found six hundred of them imprisoned outside the town in a ruined, roofless house, cared for by a solitary Red Cross worker, sanitary engineer Estus Magoon. Many were suffering from cholera and typhus and only one doctor – Dr Zucchi, an Italian – would go near them.[41] "I gave a lot of blankets, rice and milk to Mr Magoon for the Austrian sick," she wrote to the Red Cross.[42] From Durazzo, the prisoners were herded onto ships destined for Sardinia to prevent them from being freed by their compatriots advancing from the north.[43] Hundreds were reported to have died of cholera before the survivors reached the Italian island.[44]

Nearly six of the twenty-seven thousand Serbian boys who had left their homes in Serbia died in the mountains during the retreat.[45] By the time the survivors reached the coast many were barely clinging to life. "In Scutari one night, I saw about 900 boys," described a survivor among their ranks. "They were alone and all sleeping in the mud. There was no food for them, but some soldiers gave them what they had. I do not think many of them could have lived much longer. Some of them ate the bark of the trees, snails and anything they could find in ditches."[46] Before they could be evacuated, a further two thousand had died.[47]

The scale of the emergency had taken not just the Allied military authorities but relief organizations by surprise. Only representatives of two such organizations – the American Red Cross and the Quakers (who were working under the auspices of the Serbian Relief Fund, a British "umbrella" organization which provided the funding for several units) – reached the Adriatic coast in time to be of assistance to the Serbs.[48] The Quakers were the first to arrive, in late November 1915, in the company of the British Adriatic Mission. Two civilian relief workers, Theodore Rigg from Wellington, New Zealand, and Glasgow-born Robert Tatlock, worked largely in and around Scutari in the north of the country before they were driven south to Durazzo by the advance of the Austrian army.

The American Red Cross scrambled to find representatives from among their contacts in the region, including Emily, who brought with her the first Red Cross supplies to reach the Serbs in Durazzo. The Red Cross also enlisted three volunteers from the ranks of the sanitary commission they had sent to Serbia the previous spring to fight typhus, including Estus Magoon. By the end of January the Quakers and the American Red Cross had joined forces in Durazzo to feed the remaining refugees. They finally left Albania with the last of them in early February, having provided food and shelter for thousands of men, women and children, many of whom would otherwise have perished.[49]

Late in the afternoon of 25th January the *Arménie* arrived safely at its first port of call, the town of Gallipoli on the Italian coast. That day the refugees were ushered onto two new ships, one Italian, one Greek, ahead of their long voyage to Corsica. Emily and John Bellows noticed with consternation that the ships' authorities had set aside grossly insufficient food for them, but they put their faith in buying further supplies at their next stop, the beautiful but barren port of Messina at the northern tip of Sicily.[50]

As they prepared to sail, Emily paid a final visit to the holds at noon. What she found made her blood run cold. Three men were suffering from vomiting, diarrhoea and severe cramping, all classic signs of cholera, a highly contagious water-borne disease which could easily kill in two or three days without proper treatment. Although Emily had been inoculated against cholera and Bellows would have been as well, it threatened the lives of anyone else who had been in close contact with them. "This was very serious," she wrote. "The majority of the people were underfed and in a very exhausted condition, and lavatory facilities were wretched." She rushed to tell the captain. Before the ship sailed, he had them carried off the ship to the local hospital.[51]

"We arrived at Messina and the ship was placed in quarantine," recorded Bellows in his diary the next day. "No one was allowed ashore. The people cried out for bread. Miss Simmonds and I went ashore, but were not allowed into the town... they had telegraphed from Gallipoli warning Messina against us. Cases [of cholera] had developed and we were told that one had died." The Italian authorities now did their utmost to see the infected vessels off their shores as quickly as possible. To the horror of Emily and John, they were refused leave to buy food. Worse still, they then discovered that the ships' cooks were selling their remaining supplies of rice and beans with the apparent sanction of the Italian captain. All the while, the captain was under orders to ensure the ships sailed the following day, with or without supplies. Only after the persistent English Quaker reached the offices of the British Consul in an attempt to postpone the voyage did the authorities agree to provide bread to the ships. That day, the resupplied ships sailed for Corsica.[52]

Emily too was at her wits' end. Furious that the captain had permitted such serious abuses to take place in the kitchen, she informed him that from now on she was going to take charge of feeding the refugees. As soon as the ship left dock, she began work. Her endeavours were outlined in the *New York Times*. "Miss Simmonds obtained a large quantity of rice, which she cooked on shipboard for the Serbians," the paper reported. "They were so hungry that one man stuck his hand into a boiling pot and grabbed a handful of rice, which he stuffed into his mouth."[53] She made an immediate difference, wrote John. "Bread, beans and wine were served for the mid-day meal, rice and biscuits for the afternoon meal. The people were much more contented, decks were washed and Serbs put on to clean the holds." But Emily still had her work cut out for her. "The chef could not serve the joint because he had already sold it," John commented as an afterthought.[54]

Although the Serbs had welcomed the news that they were to be taken to Corfu, the fifty thousand men who were already based around Durazzo did not particularly relish the thought of the seventy-five-mile walk south to Valona to catch a transport ship. Neither did Flora. Only a minority, including those declared medically unfit, were to be allowed to embark locally. "Nobody was very anxious for the march if he could go from Durazzo, so one and all declared they had rheumatism or else sore feet," she reported. Flora was given the choice. "I was perfectly fit," she wrote happily, "but, as I was told I might do whichever I liked, I thought I might as well embark at Durazzo." On 3rd February she left the camp for the town and took a room with some of the officers, while they awaited their turn to embark.[55]

A majority of the men, including two thirds of Flora's company, were declared fit enough for the five-day march. The Allies provisioned them as best they could. Each man was given sufficient food and, for once, the road was reasonably good.[56] But although they could insure them against death from starvation, they were unable to protect them from the inhabitants. Although all the men of Flora's company survived, the Albanians repeatedly ambushed the columns, targeting the supply trains in particular.[57] In early February the first men of the Serbian army embarked from Valona for the short trip down the rugged Albanian coast to Corfu.

After nearly three months in captivity, the first of the British women who had been taken prisoner in Serbia were on their way home. Thirty-two women of the Scottish Women's Hospitals and a handful of strays who had been interned in Kevavara in Hungary were released on 4th February and sent home by way of Budapest, Vienna and Switzerland.[58] The British Farmers left Vrnjačka Banja on 10th February. They were sent home via much the same route, in "comfortable railway carriages with good food", with guards chosen for their ability to speak English.[59] Eight days later the Berry Unit were also sent home from the town, with two similarly selected guards who evidently took great pride in the fact that they had been picked to accompany them. In Vienna, its members were generously given freedom to visit the city. Many took the opportunity to go shopping. "Some of our party saw in a shop some 'Gott strafe England' [God punish England] brooches which they wished to buy as curiosities," wrote Dr Berry. "The shop people were much embarrassed and refused to sell them, saying, 'Those are German, not Austrian, you cannot buy them.'"[60]

The last of the women to be repatriated were those of the Lady
Paget Unit who left Skopje for Bulgaria on 17th February. They
were interned "comfortably" for a month in Sofia, where they were
cared for by the Bulgarian Red Cross. Ada Barlow travelled with
them, through Petrograd to Scandinavia. They eventually reached
Newcastle in late March.[61]

Emily and John's refugee ships arrived in Corsica on 13th February,
after a trip of nearly three long weeks.[62] "We have had an awful time
here," Emily wrote. "Really we have suffered tortures from vermin
on this trip."[63] Not only had they been forced to spend nearly
two weeks in the prison-like confines of the barren, quarantine
island of Frioul off the southern French coast, they had suffered
two deaths. One, a woman on the Greek ship, had succumbed to
tuberculosis, while the other, a man on their Italian vessel, suffered
fatal injuries when he fell from the top deck into the front hold.[64]
Many of the grateful passengers wrote Emily letters afterwards to
thank her for seeing them to safety. A Serbian offered to translate
them for her. "The work is very slow," he told a journalist. "You
see, they make me cry."[65]

Following four long days in crowded, unsanitary Durazzo, Flora
and Jović arrived at the harbour ahead of their evacuation to
Corfu. There, under the hot, mid-morning sun, they took their
place on a barge packed with Serbian soldiers, which a tug towed
slowly towards one of three Italian steamers anchored in the harbour. All of a sudden they began to hear a faint hum, then the
ominous throb of engines above them. "We had just got alongside the steamer when an aeroplane came exactly overhead,"
she recalled. "It passed over us three times, dropping bombs all
around as if they were shelling peas. Backwards and forwards it
came, columns of water shooting up, now 50 yards to the right,
now a little to the left, showing where the bombs hit the water
harmlessly." Flora held her breath. "Every moment it seemed as
if the next one must drop in the middle of our barge, but we were
pretty well seasoned to anything by now, and... we sat still and
stolidly watched sudden death hovering over our heads in the blue
sky, but it didn't seem somehow like playing the game when we
couldn't retaliate at all."

The captain of the Italian steamer lacked the composure of his Serbian charges. "Sheer off!" he roared at them. "I'm not having my steamer sunk for you miserable lot. I'll be damned if you're coming aboard." As the aeroplane turned tail and headed home, the little tug pulled the barge back to shore until another steamer could be found to take them south to Valona. In the chaos of the embarkation, Flora and Jović became separated from the rest of their company and their possessions. They arrived in Valona with little more than what they were wearing. The following day, still without luggage, they sailed for Corfu. It was an inauspicious start.[66]

CHAPTER 8

CORFU

1916

The ship carrying Flora steamed south into the night, past the black-shadowed mountains of Albania, towards Corfu. After her long, uncomfortable journey, Flora was full of enthusiasm to see a place that she remembered as "a land flowing with milk and honey" from her brief midsummer stopover there with the members of the Anglo-American Unit in 1914. Instead, when she stepped gingerly onto a cold, muddy, dimly lit quayside at the remote port of Gouvia, she looked around in dismay. In the company of Jović and one other officer she spent a miserable night huddled on a packing case by the sentry's fire in a borrowed coat, while she waited for a morning that could not come soon enough. "There was one of the most beautiful sunrises I have ever seen," she wrote later, "but under some circumstances you feel you would most willingly barter the most gorgeous panorama of scenery for a cup of hot tea."[1]

As the warm morning sun slowly chased the bitter chill from the air, the three of them set off on foot to find the camp where sixty-eight men of their company had already been sent. After a weary eight-mile walk they reached their low bivouac tents, brushed the dust from their clothes and joined their comrades as they waited expectantly for food and provisions to be delivered. That night they all went to bed hungry. The following day Flora and Jović were told that, due to a "hitch", the existence of their camp had not yet been registered with the authorities. Until it was, there would be no food for them. With Jović's help she scraped together sixty francs, sufficient only to buy each man a third of a loaf of bread. "The Greeks know how to charge starving men," she fumed later.

With not so much as another franc between them, Flora knew that the authorities had to be forced into action lest the men sicken or starve. "Would you let me go into the town? I might be able to organize something," she asked Jović. "All right, Corporal," he responded. "Go along and see what you can do."[2]

The next morning she spotted her chance in the form of a British Army Service Corps motor lorry slowly rumbling along the road near the camp. Hurriedly telling the men that she would return that evening with food for them all, she dashed through pouring rain to hitch a lift to the town of Corfu, fifteen miles away. She traipsed through the narrow and winding streets only to be dismissed by the British, French and Italian authorities in succession. By the end of the day she was wet through, cold, hungry and miserable. "I was beginning to despair," she recalled, "when I thought I would have one more try with the French authorities." Standing bedraggled before an official, she launched into her long tale of woe, pulled out her handkerchief, sniffed loudly for added effect and "made the biggest bluff at crying I could screw up on the spur of the moment". He rushed to comfort her. "We'll give you what you want," he told her hurriedly. "But you mustn't make a precedent of doing business this way." She nodded, sniffed again, wiped her eyes, and thanked him. That evening, having secured the promise of the delivery of regular rations, she returned exultantly by carriage to the camp with two sacks of bread, another of bully beef and a barrel of wine. Jović patted her on the back. "You've been a pretty good corporal," he told her.[3]

Flora had done well by them. Most companies had had no such luck. The French authorities had taken charge of the immense task of feeding the one hundred and fifty thousand Serbs on Corfu, many of whom were sick and emaciated. One problem after another beset their efforts. For the first six weeks the rain, wind and hail that lashed the island turned the roads into quagmires, creating immense transportation headaches. Such logistical difficulties were exacerbated by problems which would have verged on comical had their consequences not been so catastrophic. The French had shipped across large quantities of Australian frozen meat, which they distributed across the island to the Serbian camps. The Serbs, who had never seen frozen meat before, simply threw it straight into boiling water. Until it was explained to them that it had to be defrosted first, the results had the consistency and edibility of a "pneumatic tyre".[4] Yet another culinary miscalculation was made by a philanthropic American who inexplicably sent the Serbs large quantities of tinned pumpkin. "All the tricks and chicanery of the kitchen" would not induce them to eat it.[5]

Others fell ill or died after being fed food that was too solid or rich for their systems. "The incessant wet, combined with the effects of bully beef, on men whose stomachs were absolutely destroyed by months of semi-starvation was largely responsible for the terrible amount of sickness and very high mortality among the troops during the first month of our stay here," noted Flora. "This was especially the case among the boys and young recruits, who, less hardy than the trained soldiers, were completely broken down by their late hardships and died by thousands."[6]

Neither were adequate medical arrangements in place to deal with the thousands who needed treatment. The numbers at first overwhelmed the few Serbian and French doctors on the island, who had little assistance except for a handful of "freelancers", mainly Austrian POW doctors and local nuns. Starvation continued to take its toll, while typhus, typhoid, cholera and dysentery reappeared among the ranks. The sickest were taken to two small islands off the coast of Corfu. One, Lazareto, was used to quarantine those with infectious diseases.[7] The other, the barren island of Vido, was used for the thousands of men who were expected to die. The "barely living skeletons moving about in tattered uniforms… [were] too weak from hunger to speak, to hear, to think beyond the effort of putting one foot before another," recorded the American archaeologist Harriet Boyd Hawes, the sole relief worker to aid the French and Serbian medical staff on the island in the early weeks. "They could not be treated like human beings. Only violent tones and gestures could reach their stricken senses. So though our hearts were breaking for them, we must scold to get them into line, to insist on fairness in feeding. In the first days they ate to their destruction anything they could lay [their] hands on and cried like babies when denied."[8]

Throughout February and March, around one hundred men died daily on the island. Their bodies were stacked "like a woodpile" behind a screen at the small harbour. At intervals during the day and night, they were taken offshore by boat, weighed down and thrown into the sea.[9] Altogether, around five and a half thousand men died on Vido, which is now a site of pilgrimage for many Serbs.[10]

After a few long, cold days at the wet and uncomfortable camp, Flora had had more than enough of lounging about in the incessant rain with nothing to do. "I simply can't sit and twiddle my thumbs as they do," she once wrote impatiently of her Serbian companions.[11] The monotony was broken only briefly when she was transferred with her company to a permanent site near the coastal village of Ipsos, where the rest of the Morava Division were based. But although the new camp was set in a picturesque part of the island among hills, glades and trees, she soon grumbled that they were now "very far from anywhere".[12] Restless, bored and in search of the constant stimulation she required, she began to use the lorries which delivered the company's bread as a sort of bus service to get around the island.

In mid-February Flora met Robert Carr Bosanquet, an Eton-educated archaeologist who was one of four overworked representatives of the Serbian Relief Fund then on the island.[13] "She is an adventurous English nurse, who has attached herself to a Serbian cavalry regiment, holds the rank of corporal, roughs it with the toughest of them, sleeps on the ground, under a little bivouac tent, without even a groundsheet, and dresses like a man," he described in a letter home to his wife. But what interested him most were her linguistic skills. "[She is] about 40, white hair, tanned, round-faced and cheery. We want her to help us as [a] Serbian interpreter," he added. Flora too had taken great interest in his work along the quayside, unloading and sorting supplies. When he asked her if she would consider helping them, she leapt at his offer. Above all, she was keen to find something that would both keep her occupied and give her an excuse to escape her remote camp for the relative excitement of the town.

The Fund set her to work overseeing gangs of Serbian soldiers at the crowded harbour who were tasked with unloading shiploads of supplies and transferring them to one of two storehouses for sorting. Early each morning she walked over the polished stone streets to the quayside, climbed down the stairs to the waterfront and picked her way through the mountains of crates piled high against the stone walls that divided the shore from the streets of the town above. There she joined a crush of men and horses working furiously to unload and shift supplies, overlooked by curious locals watching the action from the railings above. "The quay was a most interesting place," recollected Flora, "though I should have enjoyed the work more if it had not poured steadily all day and every day."[14]

Apart from the weather, the job suited Flora to the ground. The atmosphere was hectic and chaotic, never dull, with English, French and Serbians jostling for transport and labour. She was a good manager with a distinctive and highly effective technique, which combined scheduled breaks with the willingness to use gentle psychological manipulation if her men required further incentive. She was also one of the few conversant in the three languages spoken at the quay. The officers and men of her company had gone to great lengths over the past months to help her learn Serbian. She could now speak the language fairly well, although there were still moments when it failed her. "One day I told my orderly to go and fetch my thick coat, which he would find on a chair in my room, and bring it to me," she recalled. "He duly arrived back about an hour afterwards with the coat *and* the chair, which he had carried all through the town, and was much discomfited at the howls of laughter with which we all greeted him. I asked him what the landlady had said to his removing her furniture like that, and he confessed that she had made a few remarks, but, as she spoke nothing but Italian and he nothing but Serbian, they passed lightly over his head."[15]

But her Serbian was still good enough to be of use at the quay and, once others learnt of her linguistic abilities, she was in great demand as an interpreter. "It was quite a usual thing to find an Englishman, who could not speak French, trying to explain to a French official that he wanted a fatigue party of Serbian soldiers to unload a certain lighter, and neither of them being able to explain to the said fatigue party, when they had got them, what it was they wanted them to do," she wrote, pleased to be of use.[16]

Flora was confident before starting work that she would work well alongside her new Serbian colleagues. What worried her was how she would be treated by the British. The officers of the British Adriatic Mission in Durazzo had treated her with suspicion at first, and she was concerned, rightly, that the ordinary British Tommies would do likewise. "I can't say I was struck by the friendliness of my fellow countrymen in Corfu," she wrote in a frank letter to a friend from home.[17] With time, her aptitude for hard physical work in the wind and rain, her linguistic competence and obvious managerial ability won most of them over entirely. In print she glossed over her initial problems with them. "I was rather afraid of the British Tommies at first," she wrote. "But, on the contrary there was nothing they would not do to help me, and the French soldiers were just the same."[18]

Within days of starting work for the Serbian Relief Fund, Flora began to see familiar faces in Corfu town. A few of the women that she had known from Serbia had begun to arrive both singly and as members of reorganized relief units. Although the relief effort had got under way slowly, by April it had started to gather momentum. Provisions began to arrive in volume from Britain, America and France, but the number of volunteers remained relatively small. Only two British organizations were represented – the Wounded Allies and the Serbian Relief Fund – on an island with tens of thousands of sick or wounded Serbs.[19] The former sent out a unit of only five members at the end of March to set up a hospital in a private villa at Benitses, thirteen miles south of Corfu town.[20] Over the following weeks and months they sent additional staff from Britain and generous supplies of hospital stores, food and clothing. By midsummer they were running a hospital for over one hundred and fifty "poor broken-down men".[21] "Many are quite incurable," wrote one of their doctors, despairing of the task she faced. "[They] must slowly die of inanition because they can never digest the simplest food. An overdose of morphia would be the kindest treatment for them."[22]

In mid-March the Serbian Relief Fund established a hospital in wooden barracks and under tents five miles from town. Initially twenty-four strong, its members included Flora's friend Nan MacGlade, who put her formidable organizational skills to work at its secretary. Not only did its members look after two hundred "gaunt skeletons" of patients, they agreed with the Serbian authorities to visit two "colonies" of sick and neglected Serbian boys, all survivors of the retreat.[23] One such colony was based at the village

of Paiteti, south of Corfu town. The other was two miles west of
the town, at Potamos, a picturesque village of two-storey houses
dominated by an ancient clock tower.[24]

By April, the colony in Potamos had finally received its first permanent worker in the form of Emily. Having seen her shipload of
refugees to safety, she had returned to work in a French-run cholera
camp on the island before transferring to the village at the behest of
the Serbian Relief Fund to take care of its three hundred and fifty
boys, all of whom were "in a very bad way". Within days she had
established a hospital for them, consisting of "four walls, a roof, a
rickety table, a broken chair, two windows and a hole in the wall".[25]

Hardly had the boys started to "perk up" under her care when
Emily was faced with another emergency. She was horrified to be
told that the army were about to send hundreds of men to the village who had been released prematurely from hospital. Most were
too old, ill or maimed to remain with the ranks.[26] Although the
Serbian Relief Fund sent two British Quaker volunteers to help her
ahead of their arrival, she had no shelter for the men, no latrines,
no adequate kitchen facilities or rationing, no laundry and only
her tumbledown hospital to deal with their medical requirements.
In the pouring rain on 26th April, thirty ageing, weather-beaten
men limped into camp. Thankful that the numbers were manage-
able and all the men had their own small tents, Emily and the two
Quakers, Ernest Gallimore and Anthony Dell, fed them and helped
them get settled in a camp outside the village.

At six p.m., just as they were congratulating each other that the
crisis had not been as bad as they at first had feared, a further
sixty men suddenly arrived. While Dell and Gallimore rushed off
through the wind and rain to try to find food for the camp, Emily
remained behind to secure what accommodation she could. No
sooner had she found space in some empty houses when a further one hundred and forty arrived. Several were seriously ill. She
brought the sick to her hospital and scrambled to find space for
the others in the village. By nightfall, she had them all sheltered
in houses or barns.

The following morning they began work at first light. They obtained straw for the men to sleep on, erected three large tents they
had begged from the British military authorities, bought wood and

drew rations from the town of Corfu, erected a temporary kitchen with four hastily built fireplaces and transferred the men to the tents from their barns and houses. That afternoon they were sent a further sixty-eight men, all of whom they eventually managed to feed and shelter. By the end of that second day, the Quakers had nothing but admiration for Emily's work. "We both wish to express our great debt to Miss Simmonds," wrote Dell and Gallimore in their weekly report to the Serbian Relief Fund, "for the great assistance she gave us during what was for one or two days a rather acute emergency."[27]

Day after day, rain and bitter wind continued to whip the island. So great had been the pressure on the French authorities to feed the Serbs that the question of their clothing had at first been entirely neglected, despite the appalling weather. Weeks after they had arrived, many were still dressed in the same ragged, filthy and lice-infested uniforms that they had worn across the mountains of Albania and Montenegro. Others were even worse off. "It's quite common to find a Serb with nothing under his worn tunic," wrote Robert Carr Bosanquet in a letter home.[28] Although ships had steamed into the harbour carrying bales of clothing, not all of it was appropriate to the needs of men, and one had even brought with it a cargo of women's garments, although all the female refugees had been taken to Corsica. "We were so badly off for clean clothes for our... men," wrote one of the Serbian Relief Fund doctors, "that we just had to use the female garments, some of which were garish evening dresses!" It was nothing short of extraordinary, she added, to see six-foot Serbian soldiers "clad in female silks and satins wrapped around them with string".[29]

The companies of soldiers assigned to work at the harbour in Corfu town were also insufficiently dressed. "All these poor fellows working down on the quay had had their uniforms taken away from them and burnt, and had been provided with a blue corduroy suit for working in," recalled Flora. "Their old ones, though dirty, were warm, and their new ones were very thin, and in most cases they had hardly any underclothes." When she heard that a shipment of British uniforms had arrived for the Serbs but that the French authorities were refusing to distribute them without the underclothes to go with them, she raced into action. In the belief that all she needed to do was secure the underclothes, she went to see the Serbian Relief Fund, who readily promised to supply her with them. "Then my troubles began," she recalled. "First I had to get a paper signed by the English saying they would give them if the French approved; then another, signed by the French, that they did approve and would give the uniforms; then one signed by the Serbian Minister of War; then back to the French again to be countersigned; then back to the Minister of War; then to the Serbian warehouse, who refused to give them because I hadn't got somebody else's signature, and so on and so on." After three long days of traipsing over the slippery stone streets in the rain to get the necessary papers signed, she proudly took possession of the clothing. Single-handedly she managed to supply over three thousand sets of uniforms and underclothes to her regiment. "We had the proud distinction," she remembered, "of being the first regiment to be fitted out in new, clean English khaki uniforms."[30]

Each weekend, until a severe chill brought on by the inclement weather forced her to stop work at the quay, Flora hitched a lift back to Ipsos to visit the men of her company. Without fail, she carried with her either supplies for the divisional ambulance or small luxuries for the men, who took considerable pride in their Englishwoman corporal. Not only did her presence set them apart from all other companies, to them she was by now their rescuer, champion and saviour. She had bought them food in Albania, prevented them from starving during their first days in Corfu and had fitted them out with new uniforms. Full of gratitude and anxious to do something for her in return, they formed a committee and spent long hours discussing how best to thank her. On Flora's return one weekend, they shyly presented her with a letter of appreciation. It meant more to her than a "string of medals", she wrote later.

Esteemed Miss Sandes!
Soldiers of the Fourth Company, 1st Battalion, 2nd Inf. Rgmt., "Knjaza Michaila", Moravian Division, 1st (Call) Reserves; touched with your nobleness, wish with this letter to pay their respects – and thankfulness to you; have chosen a committee to hand you this letter of thankfulness.

Miss Sandes

Serbian soldier is proud because in his midst he sees a noble daughter of England, whose people is an old Serbian friend, and today their armies are arm-in-arm fighting for common idea, and you Miss Sandes should be proud that you are in position to do a good, to help a Serbian soldier – Serbian soldier will always respect acts of your kindness and deep down in his heart will write you kind acts and remember them for ever.

Few months have passed since you came among us, and you shared good and bad with us. During this time you have often helped us to pass through hardships, buying food for us, and financially.

Thanking you in the name of all the soldiers, we are greeting you with exclamation:

Long life to our ally England,

Long life to Serbia,

Long life to their heroic Armies,

Long life to noble Miss Sandes!…

[signed by the men of the company, to which its commander added his sentiments:]

To Miss Sandes, Corporal, volunteer of this Comp.

Please receive this little, but from heart of my soldiers, declaration of thankfulness for all (for help) that you have done for them until now, and in time, when they are far away from dear ones and loving ones at home.

To their wishes and declaration I am adding mine…

Commander of the Company,

Janachko A. Jovitch[31]

For two weeks groups of discharged soldiers continued to hobble into Potamos. As the men arrived they were stripped, washed and given new clothing, while Emily took charge of the sick. Dell in turn ensured the men were occupied. By June several were engaged in laying out gardens in the camp while others were busy sewing clothes, weaving baskets and making straw hats, hammocks and artificial flowers. The project was a great commercial success. The goods were "being sold as fast as they could be turned out," he reported to the Serbian Relief Fund, proudly adding that the health of the men was beginning to improve.[32]

   Once the health of the boys and discharged soldiers had stabilized sufficiently, the French authorities began shipping them to
the southern French coast around Marseilles. That summer Emily
took charge of two shiploads. First she accompanied the anxious,
forlorn men on the long voyage. Then she returned to accompany
the boys, many of whom had been under her care for months.
"Before parting with them they gave me a dear letter of thanks to
which they had affixed their 700 signatures," she recollected. When
her transport sailed for Corfu, five hundred Serbians came down
to the dock to see her off.[33] From the crowd, four brothers stepped
forward to present her with a rug made by their mother, whom
they had last seen months ago when they fled Valjevo to join the
retreat. It was their only possession from home. "She declined and
they insisted," recorded the Red Cross. "Finally she offered to buy
it. No money could buy it, they declared. They had slept under it
and gone hungry rather than sell it, but now it was hers. The boys
were firm; she had to take it. She had cared for them on the ship
and in the camp; that was all." Emily choked a thank you as they
placed it in her hands. To the shouts of *"Spogum!"* ("Farewell!")
from the hundreds at the harbour, she wiped her eyes, said her
goodbyes and boarded her ship.[34]

With the onset of spring the problems that had besieged the Serbs'
first weeks on the island – inadequate food, clothing, shelter and
medical facilities – receded. As the cold and rain gave way to clear
blue skies and warm sun, men who had been hardly more than
skeletons began to regain their strength and morale. Those based
in Corfu town filled the cafés and restaurants.[35] Each division set up
its own theatre. Regimental bands began to reform, supplied with
instruments donated to them by the islanders to replace those lost
during the retreat. In April, the first edition of the *Serbian News*
was printed and distributed while the Serbian government-in-exile
began feuding with renewed vigour in premises on the island.
   French plans were also well under way to reorganize, re-equip
and retrain the army. The weapons the men had lost, sold or dis-
carded during the retreat were replaced. Military discipline was
reintroduced and the men were drilled, exercised, paraded and
marched in their new British khaki uniforms, blue French overcoats,
American boots and traditional Serbian field caps of thick khaki.[36]

Within weeks, under the oversight of the French, six new strong divisions had been formed from the twelve shattered ones that had arrived on the island in February.[37] At the start of April, the men were overjoyed to hear that they were to be taken one step closer to home, to Salonika to join their French and British Allies at the front. Over six weeks one hundred and twelve thousand soldiers were gradually transported by sea to their new camps around the Greek harbour, where they continued their rigorous training and rehabilitation.[38]

On 22nd April, while they waited to be taken by ship to Salonika, Flora and the men of her regiment celebrated their annual "Slava" in honour of their regimental patron saint. Part religious ceremony, part feast and gala, this time the festivities also marked a transformation that was nothing short of astonishing given the mere eleven weeks they had spent on the island. "You would never have guessed that they were the same men who had gone through that terrible retreat in the Albanian mountains and arrived at Corfu in such deplorable condition two months before," remarked Flora in wonder.

Flora's old friend Colonel Milić was in attendance. He too wished to honour the near-miraculous transformation of the men of his regiment, but he also wanted to commend Flora publicly for her work and devotion to them. "Where's the Fourth?" he asked her as he gestured towards the assembled companies. "Just behind the Third," she responded, pointing to the rows of immaculately uniformed men. "Well, come over there with me, I want to speak to them," he told her. As they approached, the men sprung to attention. While Flora looked on with a mixture of embarrassment, pride and uncharacteristic shyness, he launched into a long speech. "On this great Regimental Slava Day, I take great pleasure in promoting Miss Sandes to sergeant," he finished by telling them. "*Zivio! Zivio! Zivio!*" ("Hurrah! Hurrah! Hurrah!") shouted the men at the end of the speech. "I have never in my life had so much handshaking and patting on the back," she remembered proudly.

Early the next morning, Flora and her regiment sailed from Corfu. On a balmy Easter Sunday, when their ship moored safely at Salonika harbour, they were one step closer to rejoining the fight to liberate their homeland.[39]

* * *

The Serbian forces who arrived in Salonika were a world away from the disordered group of men who had stumbled and straggled across the mountains to the Adriatic coast a few months before. But instead of seeing an army of hardy survivors, their British and French Allies looked askance at the ageing, weather-worn veterans who marched slowly, slouching as they walked, armed with rifles handed down by the French and dressed in a mishmash of uniforms.[40] It was with considerable scepticism that they heard the news that they were being sent for further training in camps around Salonika. It would take more than that, they thought, to make the Serbs fit to fight alongside them.

The men of Flora's Morava Division were sent to a camp about seventeen miles from the harbour, in the hills. "It was a lovely place," recalled Flora.[41] She spent the rest of April and May with them, in increasingly uncomfortable heat, before she was granted two months' leave to return home. She spent the rest of the summer in England on a mad rush of social visits, all the while trying to find the time to write her first book, the hastily penned *An English Woman Sergeant in the Serbian Army*, by which she hoped to raise awareness and sympathy for the Serbian cause. After one final rushed holiday to Ireland, she returned to Salonika at the start of August to rejoin her company.

Flora's autobiography was published that autumn, one of many such books relaying personal experiences to be printed during the war years. Although its publication received both positive and relatively widespread press coverage – all of which she clipped, saved and pasted into a scrapbook – it failed to catapult her into the public eye as Britain's only serving woman soldier.[42] After two years of war, it took far more to grab the attention, let alone imagination, of the public. Flora's adventures over the following months would do just that.

CHAPTER 9

MONASTIR

1916

In the heavy, still heat of a late summer afternoon, Flora advanced warily with the Fourth Company on the plain below the windswept Macedonian village of Gornicevo. Their orders were to seize and hold a small, wooded hollow that had only just been evacuated hurriedly by the Bulgarians after days of determined Serbian shelling. As they stepped quietly into the shade of the trees, all was silent over the soft tread of their boots and the lazy buzzing of flies. Suddenly the putrid, sweet stench of death hit the back of their throats. Scattered all around them, between the ruins of several rough stone huts, were decomposing corpses, body parts and scraps of brown Bulgarian uniform. "The Bulgars had been there for 25 days," Flora scribbled in her diary in disgust. "They had never troubled to build dugouts, nor even to bury their dead."[1]

Her company had left for the mountain village that morning, 12th September, to join the other companies of the Morava Division ahead of the impending assault on the ridge on which it lay. Flora was pleased to be on the move, having spent much of the preceding month some distance from the fighting "messing about" and gambling over cards with Jović and the men of her company. But while other companies hurried to take their positions ahead of the attack, the Fourth were ordered to remain in the hollow in reserve. Flora sat down heavily in disappointment beside Jović behind the shelter of a wall and did her best to shut out the smell of the bodies. She waited impatiently for the order to advance, eager for what she termed "sport".[2]

* * *

Gornicevo ridge marked the southernmost point of the crescent of mountains and foothills that circled the town of Monastir to its east. Near the top was the village. The strike was to be the test of a new Allied military strategy, to attack the Bulgarians on these heights. If the Allies could succeed in driving them back, they would be able to bypass the heavily defended enemy trenches south of Monastir, which they had previously failed to take in a series of near-suicidal attacks. The battle was also a test of Serbian resolve. The Serbs, with French artillery in support, had been chosen to lead the attack. It was an open question how an army of the survivors of the retreat would perform. All Allied eyes in the Balkans were upon them.

As darkness fell over the bare, grey hills, the Serbs moved quietly into their positions lower down the ridge, lying flat on their stomachs in the shallow ruts that they had scraped from the hard earth, the moon bright above them. Only occasionally that night did the sound of distant artillery fire break the eerie silence. Then, without warning, as dawn approached, the roar of heavy guns ripped through the air, followed by explosions that shook the earth for miles around as French artillery went into action. The shells burst on the hard ground, illuminating the crest and sides of the ridge with continuous flashes and exploding earth and rock in every direction, while deafening echoes reverberated from mountain peak to mountain peak.

After half an hour of bombardment, as Allied observers watched intently through field glasses from the safety of hills to the south, the Serbs were ordered to attack. With white, green and yellow star shells bursting like fireworks over their heads, they clambered out of their shelters and began to advance up the steep sides of the ridge towards the village, to the added crack of rifle fire and spit of machine guns. The observers could see men fall as they scrambled up the exposed slopes under the moonlight, only to be replaced by others who passed their crumpled bodies during their advance. The Serbs pressed on ever higher, while the heavy guns opened fire again on the ridge, only to be replaced by the sound of rifle fire from the far left. All of a sudden, a red star shell soared over the summit, followed instantly by a storm of sound just below, as they used every gun, rifle and bomb at their disposal in an attempt to break through the thick barbed wire that protected the Bulgarian trenches atop the crest. The Allied observers held their breath. When the attack finally died down, the ridge was in Serbian hands.[3]

At four a.m. the boom of artillery from the fighting at Gornicevo had shattered the sleep of the women of the "American Unit" of the Scottish Women's Hospitals.[4] The unit was based near the town of Ostrovo (now Arnissa, in northern Greece), a few miles from the fighting. Sixty women under the capable charge of the Australian-born New Zealander Dr Agnes Bennett had arrived on site in early September, attached to the Serbian Third Army. By mid-September they had nearly finished setting up a two-hundred-bed tented hospital on a stretch of level ground under the shade of ancient elm trees, a short walk from Lake Ostrovo. To the north rose the heights of Kajmakcalan, a vast, twin-peaked, snow-crowned mountain that dominated the region for miles around. Due west lay Gornicevo ridge.

As the Serbs had prepared to launch near-simultaneous attacks on Bulgarian positions atop both Gornicevo and Kajmakcalan, the grey-, white- or khaki-uniformed women rushed about making the final preparations to their wards, the thunder of the guns lending added urgency to their work. Theirs was the only hospital near the front and they knew they would be expected to treat the most dangerously injured men.

A few days later the women chauffeurs of the Scottish Women's Hospital's Transport Column delivered their first patients in their five Ford ambulances. This unit, which operated independently of Dr Bennett's, was under the charge of sixty-one-year-old Katherine Harley, the sister of Sir John French, the British Commander-in-Chief at the start of the war. Its eighteen women, almost all of whom came from wealthy car-owning families, had been selected for their ability to drive and do their own repairs. Many had not worked a day in their lives before the war.

Each morning at first light they pulled flannel shirts over their bobbed hair, stepped unhappily into khaki skirts (having been banned from wearing breeches) and laced up heavy army boots before grinding the first cigarette of the day under their heels. After cranking their engines, they set out for the dressing stations. One was situated at the base of Kajmakcalan. The other lay five thousand feet up. To reach it, the women had to drive up a mountain track strewn with boulders, to one side of which lay a precipice, competing all the while for space with horses, mules, soldiers and motorized transport. On arrival two or three severely injured men were loaded into the back before they turned their ambulances around ahead of the perilously steep descent. When the women eventually reached the hospital they would sometimes make the horrifying discovery that one of the men had died during the journey. So distressing was this to the drivers and hospital staff that Dr Bennett travelled to the dressing stations to beg them not to send them the "hopeless cases".[5]

At three a.m. on 13th September, ahead of the victory on Gornicevo, the Fourth Company was ordered forward in pursuit of the retreating Bulgarians. Flora was only too anxious to leave the shelter of the hollow. Not only was it "very cold and smelly", during the attack a shell had burst just six yards from where she had been sitting and she had been lucky to escape unscathed. "Chased Bulgars all day over the most awful hills and stones, I don't know how many miles," she scribbled during quieter moments. "Had a great shooting match at long range. I used up all my ammunition. Saw Vukoje [her platoon officer] bring one down with my carbine at 1,000 yards."

Over the following days they continued their gruelling march north. Although Flora carried very little – only a cartridge belt, her carbine and revolver, a water bottle and a square of canvas tenting – the advance was pushing her to her physical limits. Hardened to the outdoors though she was, as she had dragged her aching limbs and bleeding feet over the hills she had at times wondered if she could "stick it".[6] It was also highly dangerous. With the men, she was shot at and shelled repeatedly, a matter-of-fact account of which she duly recorded in her diary.

On the occasions she had a particularly narrow escape she would be whisked off to lunch or dinner by Major Pešić, the Commandant of her battalion. Flora was only too glad to accept the invitations from the middle-aged "old soldier" who wore a row of medals across his chest, walked with a swagger stick and kept his dark hair neatly trimmed and his moustache turned up at the ends.[7] She had come to think highly of him. He "seemed to know the name and family history of pretty well every man in the regiment," Flora recalled, "and had a laugh and joke for everyone, even under the most trying circumstances."[8]

Her old friend Colonel Milić, the Commandant of the Second Regiment, also kept a protective eye on her insofar as she would let him, despite his heavy responsibilities. "Nothing could have exceeded the Colonel's kindness to me," she recalled. "After any big engagement he would send an orderly right up to the line to find out if I was all right; generally with a present of two or three packets of cigarettes, a bottle of wine or a tin of sardines; the latter a much prized luxury." Like Pešić, Milić treated Flora as his equal on her visits to his headquarters, to the scowling disapproval of his servant. "He used to be greatly scandalized when the Colonel told him to hand me the coffee first; a mere sergeant, and a woman at that," she commented. "The Colonel used always to laugh and ask him why he didn't, whereupon he would shake his head and say he couldn't possibly, it wasn't right."[9]

Flora's other great friendship during this time was with Jović. Over the course of the ten months they had known each other, an intense bond of affection and common cause had arisen between them from their close collaboration in ensuring the survival of the men of the company. Although their relationship has been portrayed as a romantic one, there is no proof whatsoever of this, and it is unlikely that Flora would have been willing to compromise her status as a combatant and "honorary man" in this manner.[10] Nevertheless, they were together constantly, playing cards, drinking, eating and arguing. So familiar had they become with each other that, to Flora's annoyance, he began to lecture her about what he saw as her transgressions. "Janachko... jawed me like the devil for gambling!" jotted Flora crossly in her diary, after she lost money playing cards.[11] But spats and bickering were soon followed by reconciliation. Despite his fondness for her, Jović understood her determination to fight on equal terms alongside the men of the company. He accordingly made no attempt to protect her by trying to send her away to battalion or regimental headquarters.

The men of her company had no difficulty in having a woman among them at the front. Flora by now had been with them for nearly a year and had proved time and again that she could hold her own. "They are all awfully good to me, and treat me like a kind of mascot," she wrote. "I'm always in the front line with them, and they are terribly worried that I may get killed."[12] They were even more afraid that she might be captured. Her "great pal" Sergeant Miladin, who at 6'4" towered over most of the men in the company, tried to take on a role akin to her personal bodyguard in battle. "Whatever happens, stick close to me," he told her urgently. "As long as I'm alive I'll never let the Bulgarians take you prisoner."[13] But in other respects she was an old comrade. They accepted unquestioningly that she would fight alongside them in any "scrap" and they called her "brother", as they did with each other. The men also found her presence reassuring, not only as a symbol of British support, but also on a more fundamental, practical level. If they were injured they knew that Flora would be on hand to bind them up. Although she had in the past resisted being forced back into her old role, she was now confident enough in her abilities as a soldier – and in her colleagues' acceptance of her as such – to be willing to act, on occasion, as nurse.

The Fourth Company were sent into reserve a few days after the successful attack on Gornicevo. After ten days of sitting around, gambling and helping anyone with a supply of wine get through it, Flora was getting restless. Paying a visit to the Scottish Women in nearby Ostrovo, she thought, would at least help pass the time. Her request for a day's leave reached the ears of General Miloš Vasić, Commander of the Third Army. Vasić, who in his earlier capacity as Commander of the Morava Division had approved Flora's enlistment at the outset of the retreat, was all too happy to oblige. To her delight, he offered to accompany her personally on a visit to their camp. Early in the morning on 29th September Flora set out with the red-overcoated colonel, his gold epaulettes glinting regally in the sun, in one of the divisional motor cars.[14] After a dusty two-hour trip, they reached their camp. "Went to Scottish Women, met little Harley [Edith Harley, Mrs Harley's daughter] and went back with her to lunch with Mrs Harley's unit," summarized Flora briefly in her diary.[15]

Within days Dr Bennett was regretting Flora's visit. Even before the hospital had opened its doors, she was struggling to maintain order among the more rebellious elements in her unit. Far from disapproving of unconventionality, many women of the American

Unit were busy seizing the opportunity to embrace it, in the comparative freedom that being so far away from home gave them. The girls of the nearby Transport Column were already providing what she considered a bad example. "It has been awfully hard having the Harley lot always in view," she complained in the pages of her diary. "They are absolutely undisciplined and I think the results are being seen now... Some of them are nice girls and I should like to have them, but Mrs H. is too old and won't see where their want of discipline is leading... I am worried; these girls will smoke so much, but I don't think it is wise to interfere at present: some are even, out of mere bravado, smoking cigars."[16] At least the women were "quite free from any trace of what we call 'nonsense' where men are concerned," reported a commissioner from the Scottish Women's Hospitals on a visit to the two units later that year, apparently entirely oblivious to the fact that a number of the women were by inclination more interested in each other.[17]

Flora's appearance, in the uniform of a Serbian sergeant, sent ripples of excitement through the units. She was just the sort of example that they could seize upon: a British woman doing precisely what she wanted, all the while ignoring social convention with apparent impunity. "She is quite tall with brown eyes and a strong, yet pretty face," wrote a cook with the American Unit in enthusiasm after having met her. "She is a sergeant in the 4th Company and talked to us for a long time about her experiences, and the fierce fighting she and the men of her company had to face. We felt so proud of her and her bravery."[18]

Two weeks later Dr Bennett bemoaned in a letter the "most undesirable" temptation that joining the Serbian army was presenting to the women of the Scottish Women's Hospitals. Three ex-employees had already succeeded in joining the Serbian Army Medical Service as drivers and Flora's visit only served to encourage the others.[19] Not long after, more women of her unit tried to follow her example. One, "a woman with two little children at home, has tried to enlist in the Serbian Army like Miss Sandes," wrote the scandalized Commissioner. "She was not accepted because I was consulted and said I strongly disapproved." So worried were the Executive Committee of the Scottish Women's Hospitals about future defections to the army that they inserted a new term into their contracts, to the effect that anyone leaving their organization needed to travel directly home and report immediately to headquarters.[20]

In early October the Fourth Company were ordered back into the thick of the action in a Serbian offensive that, over subsequent days, succeeded in driving the Bulgarians nearly seven miles north, from peak to peak in the cold, barren mountains. By 8th October they had reached Slivica, a desolate jumble of low, stone houses set below hills bristling with great, jagged stones. Flora had enjoyed every moment. Although she had again become footsore and had suffered with the rest of her company in the extremes of heat during the day and bitter cold at night, there had been plenty of excitement to make up for it. She had watched villages being shelled, Bulgarian prisoners taken, and had spent moonlit evenings with Jović and the men of battalion headquarters. She met the news with disappointment the following day that her company were being sent back into reserve so soon after they had left it last. "We have nothing to do all day but sit on a rock while they shell all around," she grumbled sulkily.[21]

Leaving the rest of her company to settle into their dugouts, Flora irritably clomped off to explore the surrounding area. She picked her way nonchalantly over the rocky ground towards the Crna River, then looked up at the noise of a commotion nearby. To the sound of a torrent of curses, she approached a knot of Serbs gathered idly in a circle around a young, badly wounded Bulgarian soldier. Flora stood for a moment taking in the scene in front of her. The man was lying on the ground in the hot sun, unable to move, just out of reach of a pool of water. "No one was doing anything for him," she wrote. "I took to this chap because he had such spirit, and wouldn't kowtow to anyone. Though he was badly shot through both thighs and couldn't move, and expecting every moment to be treated as they treat the Serbs, he lay there hurling abuse at everyone, and said if he had a rifle he would shoot us yet, and he was just a lad."

As her admiration for the courage of the Bulgarian grew, she felt a rising tide of anger with the soldiers surrounding him. "Why aren't you doing anything to help?" she snapped, before ordering them imperiously to fetch bandages, iodine, bread, water and brandy. She knelt beside him to clean and dress his wounds. All the while the Bulgarian watched her suspiciously through narrowed eyes.

He "refused [the water and brandy] at first under the impression that it was *poison!*" commented Flora incredulously. He was beside himself with gratitude when he finally accepted that she meant him no harm. "The poor chap was quite grateful... and said I was a '*silna brat*' ['fine brother']," she crowed proudly.

Flora's next task was to see that he received proper medical attention. Hesitantly, she approached Pešić. As she suspected, he was anything but happy about her rescue mission. "What on earth do you think you're doing, Sandes?" he responded furiously while she stood silently before him. "I can't even get my own men off to the ambulance! And what business was it of yours wandering around when they're shelling? You were lucky not to get yourself killed." That evening Pešić gave orders for the Bulgarian to be sent to the nearest field ambulance. "His bark is always much worse than his bite," she observed later, pleased to have got her own way. "They think a lot of my opinion, and would even let me keep a pet Bulgar, I believe, if I wanted to," she finished smugly.[22]

To Flora war was still little more than a glorified game, played on a grand scale, where courage combined with the rules and virtues of the cricket pitch applied – self-control, willingness to follow the rules, the desire to compete with honour and, above all, the necessity of upholding fair play. Killing the wounded and defenceless was not sporting, and neither was leaving them to die in agony. It made no difference to her, when faced with the wounded Bulgarian, that "the *least* the Bulgars do to our wounded and prisoners is to cut their throats".[23]

War was the most exciting "sport" that Flora could experience, far greater than racing her Sizaire-Naudin at Brooklands, travelling across America by goods van, hunting deer or even heading straight into the middle of a typhus epidemic in full knowledge of the danger. She littered her diary with sporting references. "Had a great shooting match at long range," she jotted in her diary following the attack on Gornicevo. "Janachko got some fine shooting," she commented enviously after another eventful skirmish. So too did she believe that a day's merit could be evaluated according to whether it was "sport" or not.[24] "There's no sport at all in climbing a mountain all night in pouring rain, or sitting behind a rock till you have cramp," she complained.[25]

But there was plenty to make up for the moments of adversity. It was a life of "incessant fighting, weariness indescribable" that went "hand-in-hand with romance, adventure and comradeship, which more than made up for everything". It was everything she loved to do. She was out in the fresh air, pitting her wits against others and pushing herself to overcome severe hardship. It was also a life without pretence or affectation, airs or graces. War was quite the most exciting thing she had ever experienced. "I'm sure when I do get home, except for sunburn, no one will believe I've been through anything at all, as I seem to thrive and grow fat on it," she scrawled happily in a letter.[26]

Flora had also adapted extraordinarily well to being under fire. It was all part of the game. Even though she had seen men around her "catch it", she never appeared to doubt for a moment that her luck would hold. In print she passed lightly over the problems she encountered during her first weeks in the field. "I seemed to take to soldiering like a duck to water (perhaps I may have been one in some previous life)," she wrote. In reality she had at times been shocked, albeit briefly, by the conditions she was expected to endure. "Where are we going to sleep?" she had yawned to Vukoje at the end of a long day at the start of the campaign. "Why here of course," he responded. "I looked down at the squelchy, black mud, and sat down gingerly beside him, without further comment," she recalled. She had also faced a considerable physical challenge. "You can't call it marching, over these mountains," she grumbled to a friend. "It's the most devilish country, bare hills covered with big rocks, loose rolling stones, and no water. The Serbs are used to that sort of thing, and think nothing of going miles over these hills at a good stiff pace."[27] Nothing short of grim determination and sheer willpower had got her through the first days of the campaign and, although she soon became "more seasoned", she often trailed behind the men during their advances.[28] "Sometimes I would be so tired after some long climb that when the critical moment came to run across the last stretch of open ground, fling ourselves down and open fire, I simply could *not* run," she commented later. And so, she summarized modestly, she acquired "a quite fictitious reputation for bravery and coolness".[29]

* * *

With Slivica firmly in Serbian hands, the army began its advance on Polog, a village of similar size three miles due north, over barren, broken and mountainous country. The advance, over the following weeks, was characterized by quiet intervals punctuated by vicious attacks and counter-attacks that gradually decimated the ranks of both armies. "Ours was an entirely different sort of warfare to that on the Western Front," wrote Flora. "Anything more unlike the engagements one sees in pictures, and on the cinema, it would be hard to imagine. There was no 'going over the top', there being no trenches; getting *to* the top of one mountain after another, where the Bulgars were snugly ensconced, was always our objective."[30]

The Bulgarians put up ferocious resistance, in the full knowledge that if the Serbs continued to make ground against them through the mountains east of Monastir they would be forced to abandon the prized town. With the Fourth Company, Flora continued to play her full part in the cycle of stop and start, attack and counter-attack, failure and success that typified the fighting that month. In the midst of such warfare, the relative abilities of their commanders soon became apparent. Flora sprinkled her diary with both praise and criticism. "Avram drunk in afternoon. Ordered us ahead, no lines of communication, no officers to give orders, our whole Company bunked... 4 of our men wounded," she scribbled furiously after one disastrous attack.[31] Only one man received consistent praise from her, Dodić, a "very small" lieutenant.[32] He would soon prove himself beyond doubt to be one of the bravest men in her company.

By mid-October the weather was beginning to turn. The fine, hot days of a Macedonian autumn had gradually been replaced by grey, overcast skies, while the clear, pleasant moonlit nights had given way to biting cold. With winter in the air and the loss of so many of their old comrades weighing heavily upon them, Flora reported moments of discouragement among the men of her battalion. Their morale worsened further following the deaths of several of their commanders. The Third Company had been particularly hard hit, losing three in as many days. On 17th October Jović was sent to replace the last one killed.

Three days later Flora's faith in the seemingly blessed existence of her closest circle of friends was shattered. She woke early with the Fourth Company behind a position they called simply the "big rock", a natural fortification on high ground between the villages of Slivica and Polog. They had been on guard throughout the night and into the dismal, grey hours of the early morning, knowing full well that the Bulgarians were planning a counter-attack. Just before daybreak, in the pouring rain, it came. Its violence took them all by surprise. Flora first heard the sudden war cries of the Bulgarians – *Hourra! Hourra!* – as they hurled themselves towards the Third Company, on her left. With her nerves "strained to breaking point", she knelt on the sodden ground, raised her rifle to her shoulder, tightened her grip, placed her finger on the trigger and blinked her eyes rapidly through the sheets of rain, readying to fire at the first sight of Bulgarian khaki. Instead, to her dismay she saw the blue-uniformed Third Company rushing back towards them in disarray, the Bulgarians in hot pursuit. "The man lying beside me collapsed with a grunt, shot through the heart [and] several were wounded," she wrote breathlessly of the events that followed.[33]

The panic spread to the Fourth Company. They leapt up en masse and ran with the men of the Third to the inadequate shelter of a ravine. Flora too had to run for her life, bullets flying all around her. By late afternoon she was lying flat on the ground behind a small rock with Bulgarian bullets humming in the air over her head, having had nothing to eat for nearly twenty-four hours and soaked through to the skin in the continuous downpour. Every bitter blast of wind ripped through her wet uniform, chilling her further, while the ground on which she lay was "rapidly turning into a very squishy bog". "The only thing I could think of to keep up my spirits and while away the time, was to repeat the 'Charge of the Light Brigade', which, as a child, I thought the most wonderful poem in the world. Over and over at intervals I repeated it to myself, though excepting for the fact of being 'in the mouth of hell' there wasn't much in the poem that would fit our case."[34]

Flora straggled back to battalion headquarters that evening, taking what little consolation she could from the fact that the Serbs had finally rallied to seize the big rock from the Bulgarians. She was exhausted, wet and hungry, and covered in mud and blood from the wounds of a couple of men she had dressed under fire. She knew at a glance from the solemn faces of the Commandant and the Battalion Staff that something was seriously wrong. "Janatchko was killed by a bullet in the morning," she wrote tersely in her diary after she left them, her hand shaking as she forced herself to write a few words. "He had been Commander 1st Co. 3rd Battn. 3 days. I heard it from Comm. [Pešić] in the evening."[35]

His death struck her to the very core. In a stroke she had lost her constant companion, best friend and confidant, someone for whom she had endless admiration and affection. Jović had overseen her enlistment as a private into the army, had struggled alongside her during the retreat to keep the men of the Fourth Company alive and had been her steadfast supporter. Now the reality of war was brought home to her with a shock and, for the first time, she questioned her perception of war as sport. There had been nothing sporting in his death or in her feeling of bereavement. She wrote furiously in a letter to a friend the following day that she had changed her "mind about 'sport', and loathe[d] war and everything to do with it with [her] my heart…" A few days later, the bitterness and anger at his loss as fresh as ever, she wrote another otherwise uncharacteristically cynical description of the war. "If anyone in Croydon begins to ask me to describe the war I shall tell them to go into their back garden and dig a hole and sit there for anything from three days and nights to a month, in November, without anything to read or do, and they can judge for themselves, minus the chance of being killed of course."[36]

Flora struggled through the next days. The section of the front assigned to her company once again returned to a state of relative quiet and inactivity. It gave her none of the excitement she needed to get her mind off Jović's death. The bleak, wet weather did nothing to lift her mood, and she wrote forlornly in her diary that she was having problems sleeping. Her friends in the company rallied round her as best they could, although Flora would have done her utmost to keep her emotions in check. Pešić too continued to keep an eye on her. He was "awfully good to me", she recorded after he had tried to cheer her up over lunch two days later.[37]

A fortnight following Jović's death, she visited his grave whilst back in reserve. "I still feel as if I had dreamt it, that it can't be true," she noted.[38] In her 1927 autobiography, the grief of his death still evident, she wrote him a restrained epitaph. "Our company had changed hands, and our old [commander], Lieutenant Jović, who had taken such care of us all through Albania, and to whom

the men were devoted, was with the unlucky Third Company...
He had fought through the Turkish and Bulgarian Wars; had every
kind of medal for bravery, and had, in two years, risen from private
to [commander]; almost a record in that army."[39]

On 13th November the Serbs made their final preparations to seize
the village of Polog. Flora's Morava Division, with French artillery
once again in support, were ordered to lead the attack. An Allied
journalist watched from a nearby summit as the Serbs readied
themselves for the advance. "Every gun the Bulgarians could bring
to bear was trained on the advancing troops," he observed. "But
the Serbs are past-masters of mountain fighting and know how to
take advantage of every scrap of cover. We could see them crawling
through the ravines, working their way along the dry watercourses,
in and out of the boulders and trees, everywhere that nature had
provided barriers against the bullets and shrapnel of the enemy."
That afternoon they retook the village from the Bulgarians while,
that night, they captured the mountain crest above.[40] Only two
Bulgarian strongholds remained to be taken, Hill 1212 and Hill
1378. The odds could not have been higher. If the Serbs could seize
both peaks, the Bulgarians would be forced to abandon Monastir in
the valley below. Both armies were ordered to fight to the last man.

While other units of the Morava Division took part in the attack
on Polog, the Fourth Company were sent on extended reserve that
lasted well into November. Near the middle of the month, fed up
with forced inactivity, she asked Colonel Milić for two or three
days' leave to visit the Scottish Women's Hospital and Transport
Column near Ostrovo. But hardly had she returned to camp, his
agreement secured, when the Fourth Company received their orders to return to the front. "So much for the visit," thought Flora
to herself.[41]

As she was having lunch with her company en route to the front
the next day, Milić spotted her. Over coffee, he spoke to her as usual
in German, their only shared language at the time they had first
met. "I thought you wanted to go to Ostrovo, Sandes," he said.
"Why don't you go?" "But we are going to the front," she replied.
"Oh, we're only going to hold some lines of communication near
another reserve," he responded genially. "We'll not be near any
fighting. You have plenty of time to stay away for several days, and

I'll give you a horse to start now, if you like." Then he turned and spoke to a colleague in Serbian. "You know we are going right into the thick of it. It would be such a pity for her to get killed. I'd like to keep her out of it." They all laughed with embarrassment when she responded in Serbian. "Thank you for your thoughtfulness," she replied hesitantly, "but I would like to stay with my company."[42]

On the bitterly cold, snowy night of 15th November, Flora crept into place on the slopes of Hill 1212. With her were the five hundred remaining men of her regiment, which had been two thousand strong only three months before.[43] She must have known that she faced a grave risk of being injured or killed but put such thoughts to the back of her mind, trusting luck once again to see her through. At the break of dawn the following morning, the Bulgarians used the shroud of fog that covered the peak to launch a devastating pre-emptive surprise attack on Serbian positions below. The brunt of it fell on the Fourth Company.

What happened next was widely reported in papers around the world. Most contained Flora's description of the attack:

The fighting was a sight that day, but, unfortunately, I only saw the start of it. There was deep snow on the ground, the bugle was blowing the charge, and we were going up the steep hillside while the Bulgars, hidden by the early-morning mist at the top, were firing down on us. The Bulgars had counter-attacked at dawn and driven our men back, and everybody was mixed up. There were no trenches or anything like that.

My company was peacefully sleeping in the snow behind a rock, as we were battalion reserve that night, when we were called up at dawn as re-enforcements. Battalion reserve is a rotten job. You get all the shellfire that's going, and you never know what's going on in front until you are suddenly roused out and plunged into the thick of it, as you're only a few hundred yards back and you sleep with your rifle in your hand.

There's first a shout of "Company forward", and everyone's off like a streak. When we arrived on the scene the men were rallying for a counter-attack. The bugler had got "cold feet" and an officer had taken the bugle and was standing up against the skyline, where everyone could see him, a mark for every bullet, blowing for all he was worth. He wasn't blowing a bit the right notes, but everyone knew what it meant.

We knew the position had to be retaken at any cost, as it meant the fall
of Monastir if we could.

   We went anyhow we liked, taking cover as we could. An officer and
about a dozen men and myself got to the top, when some bombers
dodged behind the rocks and hurled bombs at us at close range and
scattered us.[44]

"I immediately had a feeling as though a house had fallen bodily
on the top of me with a crash. Everything went dark, but I was not
unconscious for I was acutely aware that our platoon was falling
back," wrote Flora later. "It was exactly as though I had gone blind,
but I felt the tail of an overcoat sweep across my face. Instinctively
I clutched it with my left hand, and must have held on for two or
three yards before I fainted."

Unconscious, Flora lay bleeding into the snow. Shrapnel had
shredded the flesh of her back and the right side of her body from
shoulder to knee. Her right arm had been both broken and badly
lacerated by the blast. The other members of her platoon had
run for cover to the nearest rock. Among them was little Lieutenant Dodić. He darted a glance out from behind his shelter in the
direction of the enemy. Ahead, he saw Flora lying motionless on
the reddening snow. Under the "very noses" of the Bulgars, he
inched round the side of the rock and crawled out on his stomach
towards her. "Stretch out your arm," he pleaded in a low whisper
as he neared her. "Stretch it out!" Flora lay unresponsive in front
of him. Not knowing whether she were alive or dead, he edged out
further, grabbed the wrist of her broken right arm and shuffled
backwards, dragging her with him. Two men waited anxiously
behind the rock for him to return. As he came within reach, they
yanked them both to safety.

Hurriedly, they wrapped Flora up in a piece of tenting. Then,
while she slowly regained consciousness, they bundled her down
the hillside "like a rabbit flung into a poacher's bag". Three or
four other men had by now joined the attempt to get her to safety.
They darted anxious glances around them through the falling snow,
fearing a further Bulgarian advance. If they were taken prisoner,
they all knew that they would almost certainly be killed forthwith.
"Don't all get taken on my account," she whispered to them. "We're
not going unless we can take you with us," they replied firmly.

When the stretcher-bearers arrived, one of them dropped down next to Flora and pulled out a knife. He sliced through her clothing and bandaged her up as best he could. Then he poured half a bottle of brandy down her throat and put a cigarette in her mouth. "It takes a lot to kill me," she assured one of the men who had been watching her, his eyes full of tears. "Wait and see, I'll be back again in ten days." To the worried glances of the men, they laid her on a stretcher, picked her up off the ground and set off down the mountain into a raging blizzard.

The next day, after the Serbs had finally captured the Bulgarian positions on Hill 1212, they found the bodies of ten Serbians who had been taken prisoner lying in a row, near the spot where Flora was wounded. They had had their throats cut from ear to ear. For risking his life to save Flora from a similar fate, Lieutenant Dodić was awarded the highest decoration for bravery, the Karađorđe [Karageorge] Star (Officer's).[45]

Two days later, the Serbs took the town of Monastir.

CHAPTER 10

WOUNDED

1916–17

"Is she alive?" demanded Colonel Milić when the doctor of the First Dressing Station answered the field telephone. He had called the moment the reports reached him of Flora's injuries. "We've not seen her, sir," the doctor replied. "Well, send out a patrol. She must be out there somewhere," Milić responded curtly. Hardly had the doctor sent out a search party into the snow-shrouded landscape when Milić telephoned again. "Have you found her?" he asked. "Not yet," replied the doctor. "Then send out another patrol," he insisted. A few minutes later, he interrupted the busy doctor again. "Well?" he queried abruptly. "I'm sorry, sir, she's nowhere to be found," answered the doctor despondently. "I've already sent out two patrols. I simply can't spare any more men." "Are you waiting for me to come and join the search?" snapped the furious colonel. "I don't care what it takes. I want you to send out every last man until she's found."[1]

The stretcher-bearers had carried Flora off into the blizzard towards the dressing station, by coincidence the same one that she had joined near Prilep almost a year ago to the day. They stumbled though the snow, straining their eyes through the storm in an attempt to spot any landmarks that could lead them there. The trip should have taken them half an hour. Instead, they missed the station. As they walked grimly in circles carrying Flora, their faces whipped painfully by the snow and biting wind, her blood began to seep through her dressings, through the thick fabric of the stretcher, onto the snow. She remained conscious all the while, shivering and shuddering from the agony of her wounds, the loss of blood and the cold. "I was just about at the end of my tether," she recalled. It took the exhausted men nearly two hours to spot the small tents of the station.

The harried doctor met Flora's arrival with a surge of relief. First he issued instructions for her to be laid carefully in the operating tent. Then, while he placed a call to Milić, he ordered her to be given hot drinks. On his return she was lifted gently from her stretcher onto the operating table in the centre of the tent.[2] Even if they had had anaesthetic available, they had so many wounded that they would have lacked the time to use it. Telling her to grit her teeth, he stood at her head while another doctor began to probe her wounds for shrapnel. Flora was by now so distraught that her usual nerve and stoicism momentarily left her. "I buried my nose in the broad chest of [the doctor]... and frankly yowled for the first time," she confessed. The doctor knew exactly how to deal with her. "Shut up and remember you're a soldier," he barked as he lit a cigarette and shoved it between her lips. "[His words] had far more effect than any amount of petting would have done," she remarked later.[3]

Flora had been seriously but not dangerously wounded. By the time the doctors had placed her on the ground to make room for the next victim of the fighting, they had removed what they could of the shrapnel from her right side and had bandaged her shattered right arm. They knew that she would require further operations to remove many of the smaller splinters, once she could be evacuated to hospital in Salonika.

Milić's intervention on Flora's behalf was one of his last. The "gallant, jolly, little colonel" who had looked after Flora so well, treated her as his equal and tried so hard to save her life was killed later that month when a stray shell landed on his tent.[4]

That evening Flora was taken by stretcher to the divisional ambulance at Dobroveni, near where Jović was buried. She arrived at two a.m. "They wrung me warmly by the hand, and congratulated me on being wounded; for in those days it was considered an honour to be wounded in the defence of your country," she recalled.[5] That day the first of a series of journalists arrived to visit her. "The Englishwoman sergeant had a tent to herself," wrote Herbert Corey, an American journalist for the Associated Press.

She was lying on a litter, covered with some rough blankets, when we entered. We saw a wholesome, fresh-faced woman, who might be something less than forty and looks thirty years old. She smiled pleasantly at us. "Badly wounded?" "Rather painful," said she. There was some desultory conversation. The picture of that… journey down the mountainside, in the darkness and snow-charged rain, suffering from shrapnel wounds, persisted in my mind. I asked about it. "Rather bad," said she. That was all… She is at once a good soldier and womanly woman. Most woman soldiers – it is only here in the Near East there are woman soldiers – are either freaks or harridans. Miss Sands [sic] is neither. "Why did a woman like that go in for soldiering?" I asked a friend. The friend is an English officer. He considered for a time. Then – "Um," said he. "Did you ever live in Croydon?"[6]

"Will she live?" Flora's stretcher-bearers were asked time and again as they passed strings of mules carrying other wounded. "It looks like she will," they replied brightly. She had spent one night at Dobroveni before her stretcher was hung from the axles of a two-wheeled handcart. She had then been handed over to the three men who were charged with wheeling her to the next dressing station, several miles farther south on a low hill above the village of Krušograd.[7] It took them much of the day to get her to the Third Danube Field Ambulance, which was virtually adjacent to the mobile Scottish Women's Hospital's Transport Column. One of the chauffeurs, Elsie Corbett, went to see her. "I… found her lying on straw in a corner, her wounds already dressed, but with more wounded being carried in and piled more or less on top of her." After her doctor reassured her that he would take no offence, Flora agreed at the request of the women to transfer to their tented camp. "She seemed to be wounded absolutely all over," wrote Elsie, who regarded her with the same awe as the other women of her Column, "but said we moved her much better than the Serbs did, which we felt was a tremendous compliment from her."[8]

Flora spent one night with the Scottish Women. The following morning they drove her to Sorović (now Amindeon), a village that lay close to the southern tip of Lake Ostrovo where the Serbian Relief Fund had just finished erecting a tented hospital.[9] One of the only hospitals in the region to take civilians, it was run mainly by women. "These girls… dressed in short skirts and trench boots,

smoked like the deuce, and some of them were pretty good swear-
ers... and all of them were about as efficient as it was possible to
be," wrote Major Cecil Alport of the Royal Army Medical Corps.[10]
Hardly had Flora been welcomed as one of their first patients when
the demands started to arrive from the Serbian military authorities.
"I got to know about [her] because of a wire sent from the Serbian
headquarters enquiring whether she was in the [No. 33] Stationary
Hospital," recalled Alport.

> They were in a terrible state of mind, fearing she had been killed and
> not knowing what had become of her... Naturally, when I heard she
> was a casualty in the hospital next door, I called to see her, expecting
> to find an Amazon – one of the Spartan sisterhood. Instead, I found a
> sweet-faced woman, bordering on middle age, with short grey hair and a
> pleasant voice... She told me that before she was wounded she had been
> in the trenches for thirty days without being relieved, and when I add
> that the weather during that time had been extremely cold and wet, it
> will be readily appreciated how greatly she must have suffered and how
> extraordinary her courage and powers of endurance must have been.[11]

On 21st November, five days after being wounded, Flora was lifted
onto a hospital train – in reality, nothing more than a series of
modified cattle trucks – for the journey from Sorović to Salonika.
Sixteen hours later she arrived at the 41st General Hospital.[12] The
hospital, at Samlis, was just over seven miles from Salonika along
the road to Monastir. One of several based in or around the town,
it had been opened only three months previously, in August 1916,
as part of a commitment by the British and French to provide seven
thousands beds each for the Serbs who had no hospitals of their
own.[13] The Girton and Newnham Unit of the Scottish Women's
Hospitals had also set up a tented hospital at Salonika's harbour,
having had their plans to work in Serbia thrown into chaos by the
invasion the year before. Other hospitals were run, staffed and
equipped by the French, Italians and Canadians, to handle what
would amount to two hundred thousand admittances during the
course of 1917 alone, the vast majority for malaria, which was
tearing strips out of the ranks of the Allied armies.[14]
    Such hospitals became virtual "townships of canvas", where
cooking, laundry, medical treatment and administration were

carried out on a near industrial scale under mostly tented accommodation.[15] So too did they become centres of entertainment, in
an effort by the hospital authorities to keep their charges occupied.
Most famous of all for the quality of its concerts was the British-
run hospital for venereal diseases, which was tucked away along a
dusty road on the outskirts of Salonika. "Transport some hundreds
of thousands of British men between the ages of eighteen and forty
odd to a more or less glamorous East, hot sun, cheap and fiery
liquors, moonlight, dark-eyed houris of the night and 'What have
you'," wrote one pragmatic commentator. "The result is the presence of a VD hospital on the outskirts of Salonika… The concerts
given at that particular hospital were famous for their excellence…
perhaps it was due to the fact that the audience being exclusively
of the male sex, and the atmosphere being in some way conducive
to the broadest form of humour…"[16]

"Good God, another of them!" exclaimed the second matron
when she was told of Flora's arrival.[17] She already had one woman
soldier, Milunka Savić, on her hands. The last thing she wanted
was another. Twenty-eight-year-old Milunka looked more like a
chubby, fierce boy than a girl. From a village near Novi Pazar in
south-west Serbia, she had been fighting with the Serbian army for
years, having first enlisted during the Balkan Wars. She belonged to
the same regiment as Flora and had been brought to the hospital
after being shot in the thigh. This was the fifth time she had been
wounded.[18]

Although Milunka already had a fearsome reputation for bravery, she was also renowned among the hospital staff for a series of
misdemeanours. "Long before she was able to walk properly she
got out of bed," wrote Flora, who came to relish the tales of her
many transgressions.

[She] hobbled out of hospital on crutches and went down town without
leave. When she reappeared next day, having been absent for twenty-
four hours, the colonel [Colonel Brackenridge, the hospital director]
put her by herself in a small tent, as a punishment. She solved the
problem by immediately setting fire to the tent. As soon as her leg was
strong enough she repeated the performance, and stayed away for three
days. On her return the exasperated colonel put her under arrest in a

small tent, with a sentry at the door; but she completely flabbergasted
the sentry by walking out under his nose. "What could I do?" said the
Tommy, ruefully. "She just laughed at me when I tried to stop her, and
I couldn't shoot a woman in cold blood."[19]

The second matron found her new patient in no mood for friendly
preambles. Flora had been "dumped" into bed the night before by
a self-important sister, who handed her an aspirin, berated her for
smoking and ordered her to go to sleep. Racked with pain, she had
spent a sleepless night. "Matron, I've got a packet of cigarettes
under my pillow, and sister says you are going to take them away
from me," she stated irritably. To her surprise, the matron gave
her a grin. "Smoke as much as you like," she replied amiably, "so
long as you don't set the tent on fire." She was "an Irishwoman
like myself", concluded Flora approvingly later.[20]

Monastir had finally been wrestled from the Bulgarians by the
Franco-Serbian offensive on 19th November. For the first few days
after the fall of the town the Serbs and their allies had continued
to skirmish half-heartedly with the Bulgarians who had fled north
towards Prilep. But by 11th December all operations had ceased.[21]
With winter virtually upon them, the soldiers who had survived
weeks of fighting against all the odds were at the limit of their
endurance. The Allied armies had no reserves of men to exploit
the victory, while the ranks of the Serbian army, who had borne
the brunt of the fighting, had been decimated. Of, for example,
the six thousand men of the Morava Division who had fought at
Hill 1212, only eighteen hundred were left standing after the battle.[22] Although the recapture of the town was of great political
significance for the Serbs, it had little strategic value in and of itself.
With the suspension of Allied operations the Bulgarians were able
to regroup and return to the mountain heights that overlooked
Monastir from the north, positions that were as strong as those
they had held before the onset of hostilities. They were also close
enough to the town to be able to shell it at will.

The war had created a refugee crisis throughout Macedonia at
the outset of winter, as villagers fled before the fighting and townspeople, many Jewish, abandoned Monastir in their thousands to
escape the rain of deadly Bulgarian shellfire. Even during times

of peace, many of them had led a hand-to-mouth existence. They now flooded towns and villages with little more than what they were wearing. With insufficient access to decent sanitation, food, clean water or fuel for heating or cooking, the incidence of intestinal problems and diseases such as tuberculosis and rheumatism began to rise ominously among them, as did the threat of typhus.[23] Although the Allied armies across the region saved them from outright starvation by providing food as and when they could, for months there was no central organization and no coordinated relief effort to provide them with other basic necessities.[24]

Emily was one of the first to begin work among them. After her work had finished in Corfu in the autumn, she had transferred to Salonika. By early October she was inspecting hospitals and refugee camps across the region on behalf of the Serbian Relief Committee of America, in partnership with forty-three-year-old Ruth Farnam from Long Island, who had a marked talent for self-aggrandizement, to the irritation of most of those who spent any time in her company.

When Emily left Farnam's company – whether by volition or luck is unclear – to look after thirty-four orphaned children in the coastal resort of New Phaleron near Athens,[25] Farnam continued the visits of inspection throughout the region. One of them was to the American Unit of the Scottish Woman's Hospitals, to the utter dismay of its competent and modest director, Dr Agnes Bennett. "She always referred to all the royalties of the Balkans by their Christian names," Dr Bennett wrote in disgust. "And when she departed told me if I wanted to see her to be sure and search for her in the social columns of the New York Press and I should know at once where she was to be found!" Worse still for Dr Bennett, on Farnam's return to the States she informed "all and sundry" that the unit were giving no credit to the Americans for the money that supported them and that they were not flying the American flag. Dr Bennett was forced in response to this allegation to write to the Committee of the Scottish Women's Hospitals to explain that the Geneva Convention did not permit them to fly it. By then, however, the damage to fund-raising efforts in the States had already been done.[26]

Farnam left her unfortunate hosts in the American Unit to accept an invitation graciously extended to her by the Serbs to visit an observation post near the frontline. She was taken around 9th October to see the battle for the village of Brod. She later proclaimed in print that she was the "first woman of any nationality to enter reconquered Serbian territory", disingenuously ignoring Flora's presence, of which she would have been all too aware. For the duration of the war she capitalized on her visit to the front by giving fund-raising talks in the States under the guise of "Sergeant" Ruth Farnam, dressed in Serbian uniform, in which she stated that she was the "only American woman soldier of the war".[27] She was no such thing.

By the end of the month, with Farnam on her way home, Emily had been asked by the Serbian authorities to undertake relief work among the refugees. She agreed at the request of the American consul in Salonika to accept forty-four-year-old Amelia Peabody Tileston as her assistant, who, like Farnam, came from a wealthy East Coast family. But unlike Farnam, who was interested only in self-promotion, Amelia soon proved herself to be utterly devoted to the Serb cause, tireless in raising funds and willing to push herself beyond the point of exhaustion in her work. She was also petty, vehemently anti-Semitic and utterly without tact.

Amelia was delighted to be able to work with someone whom she already knew by reputation. "Miss Simmonds has been asked by the Serbian officials to go to the front," she wrote happily in a letter home. "She is the only woman whom they will allow to go there, because she has done such wonderful work for two years for the Serbians that they worship her, and have unbounded confidence in her capabilities."[28] At the start of November Amelia and Emily began work together on the narrow quays of Salonika harbour. They collected and sorted Red Cross supplies that had lain in warehouses for months, while Emily also made arrangements for trucks to deliver the goods to the war-devastated villages across the region, to the admiration of those who saw her at work. "She violated a number of rules and perhaps broke a number of laws," wrote Herbert Corey. "But she got the goods and distributed them where they were most needed."[29]

Flora's time in hospital soon settled into a routine. On clear days she would be carried outside by orderlies to sit in the sun. The surgeon arrived twice a day to dress her injuries, under the watchful

eye of Milunka. "One day, [she] had the curiosity to count my
wounds," recalled Flora. "The count completed, she informed me
that I had twenty-four, and I felt that it was high praise when she
said I could bear pain as well as a Serb. She herself was a perfect
stoic."[30]

Word had spread quickly throughout Salonika of the arrival
of the new patient. On 22nd November, while waiting for news
about the arrival of the trucks, Emily was horrified to hear that
Flora had been brought into hospital, severely wounded, a few
hours earlier. Telling Amelia that she would return in two days,
she dropped everything. She became one of Flora's first visitors,
arriving only hours after she had been carried in. Other wounded
soldiers, often swathed in bandages, began to sneak into the
women's tent to keep her company, only to be chased away by
British nurses who were scandalized by the breach in decorum.
"Let them visit her whenever they want," commented the normally
regulation-bound director, Colonel Brackenridge, when the nurses'
complaints reached his ears.[31]

Word had also reached the Bulgarian wards of Flora's arrival.
One of the patients, by an extraordinary turn of chance, was her
"pet Bulgar", who, by now, was convalescing well. When he heard
that she too had been injured, he "begged and begged" to be carried
to see her, but as a prisoner with few rights he was flatly refused.
To Flora's sorrow and dismay, she was only told much later of his
presence, after he had recovered sufficiently to be sent to a POW
camp. She received little sympathy from her Serbian friends, who
remained deeply antagonistic to their Bulgarian counterparts. His
requests were "too much of a good thing", they told her.[32]

A week after her arrival, Captain Milan Jovičić, the dashing and
handsome half-Serb, half-Scottish aide-de-camp of Crown Prince
Aleksandar, arrived to see her. He was led to her bed outside her
marquee. In the presence of Colonel Brackenridge, her doctor,
the matrons and "as many others as could be collected round
the bed at short notice", he pinned the gold and silver Karađorđe
Star with Swords for non-commissioned officers and men onto
her pyjama jacket.[33] Flora had been given the highest decoration
in the Serbian army for bravery under fire, which carried with it
automatic promotion to sergeant major.[34] A translation of the
order conferring the award, signed by the chief-of-staff of the

Serbian army General Petar Bojović no less, was also presented to her. "Volunteer Sergeant in the 2nd Infantry Regiment Miss Flora Sandes, an Englishwoman, has distinguished herself by her courage and by a rare spirit of self-sacrifice in all combats in which her unit has taken part up to the [16th November 1916], the day on which she was wounded when twenty steps from the Bulgars," stated the order grandly. "[On] the [16th November] at Hill 1212, she served as an example to her company by her bravery."[35]

As the news of Flora's injuries reached the outside world, excited reports of her exploits in the Serbian army hit the British press. "In a clean and comfortable bed, amid comfortable and quiet surroundings, lies a comely motherly-looking little lady. Though her short-cropped hair is grey, her unfurrowed face is young and fresh, with a peachy bloom in the rounded cheeks that tells of perfect health," wrote the special correspondent to the *Daily Express*. "Miss Flora Sands [sic] – that is the little lady's name – is a Scotswoman," he continued, managing simultaneously to patronize his subject and mangle his facts, before describing how she was wounded. Other enthusiastic but often inaccurate reports followed, notable mostly for their varying portrayals of Flora's nationality. Her photo made the picture page of the *Daily Mirror* twice within the space of a week. "British Nurse 'Who Was Always First over the Top' Decorated with the Serbian VC" shouted one headline, to what would have been the despair of Flora, who despised being labelled as anything other than a soldier. Newsflashes followed across the world. "Wounded English Girl Wins Serbian Cross", reported the *New York Times*. Articles appeared in the Australian papers, boasting of Flora's connection to the country through her brother John, a Sydney resident. The Irish too tried to claim Flora as their own. "Kerrywoman Soldier in Serbia", proclaimed the *Irish Independent*, relying on Flora's ancestry to stake a link to the county.[36]

Such publicity turned Flora, for the first time, into a household name. In an era when only men could vote, she provided an example of what women could achieve. She proved so inspirational that British liaison officers attached to the Serbian army grumbled about the amount of time it was taking to reject applications from other women. "Fired by the example of Flora Sandes, who joined

as a private and became a sergeant, we had quite a large number
of applications from British women to join the Serbian Army,"
recalled one such officer.

> The Admiral [the now Vice Admiral Ernest Troubridge, head of the
> liaison staff between the Serbian army and the British government]
> often left to me the unpleasant task of turning them down. In general,
> for obvious reasons, their sex and lack of physical strength rendered
> them unsuitable for service in the infantry, but a sprinkling found jobs
> as transport drivers. I remember particularly one Canadian woman who
> applied. She was annoyed when I asked who would carry her pack on
> the march, and furiously angry when I suggested she would be better
> employed looking after the two young children she had left at home.
> After Flora Sandes was seriously wounded by the explosion of a hand
> grenade, I am convinced we would have raised a regiment of women
> had we been so minded. Their martial spirit was wonderful.[37]

By mid-January Flora was considered well enough to be discharged
from hospital on the condition that she sail for a convalescent camp
for the Serbs in Bizerte, on the north coast of Tunisia. Milunka too
had engineered her own release, to Flora's evident admiration. "The
real joke was when she ran away for the third time," she recalled.

> [She] got the Serb military authorities to give her her papers and return
> to the front, and then came back to hospital to say goodbye to the
> colonel, [Brackenridge] and thank him for all his kindness! She was
> perfectly unconscious of the fact that she had upset him at all, and
> really wanted to express her gratitude for all the care she had received.
> But the second matron, not having the temerity to take her up to the
> colonel's quarters, told her that he was not very well, and that she
> would give him the message when he got better.[38]

"Remember you still have half a blacksmith's shop inside of you,"
the doctor warned Flora as he signed her release papers. "You're
likely to have further trouble on and off." After nearly two months
in hospital, Flora was only too happy to accept the doctor's terms,
in word if not in spirit. She packed the few things she had, bade
farewell to her fellow patients and travelled into Salonika to await
the departure of the French hospital ship. On arrival she was given

the news that the ship would be delayed in sailing. Thinking that this was luck indeed, she put the doctor's warnings to the back of her mind and seized the opportunity to celebrate her discharge in the restaurants and bars of Salonika. So energetically did she enjoy herself that, by the time her ship sailed two days later, she was hardly able to stand. The French doctor on board the vessel took one look at her and sent her to bed forthwith. "So once more, to my disgust, I became a stretcher case," recorded Flora.[39]

In mid-January 1917 Flora's hospital ship travelled south from Salonika harbour, past the heights of Mount Olympus and the scenic Greek islands before sailing through the Sea of Crete to the Mediterranean. There it passed the islands of Malta and Sicily before arriving at Bizerte at the northernmost tip of Tunisia, then the most important French naval base in the southern Mediterranean. As the ship neared the quayside, its more mobile passengers caught their first glimpse of what at first appeared to be little more than a "desolate backwater" of low forts, warehouses, barracks and hotels that lined the waterfront. Behind the town they could see nothing but bare, barren hills.[40] They gazed out over the little Berber villages that lined the shore as the hospital ship turned sharply south to sail down the Bizerte canal to a lake that also bore the name of the town, and which provided a sheltered harbour to passing Allied vessels. All the while Flora lay confined to her hospital bed, following an emergency operation on board. Once the ship anchored she was carried by stretcher to a French-run naval hospital. "There they dug out some more pieces of bomb, and put me to bed for another three weeks, with French sailors to nurse me, by way of a change," she wrote.[41]

In the rush to evacuate the survivors of the retreat from the Albanian coast, French and Italian ships took ten thousand to Bizerte before the Serbian government asked for all transports to be routed instead to Corfu, so that their soldiers could remain as close to Serbia as possible.[42] The government nonetheless had no objection to the continued evacuation to Bizerte of those whose fighting days were clearly over – the shell-shocked, the blind, the epileptics and those missing limbs – and ships continued to arrive throughout the rest of the war from Salonika bearing such damaged men. Their

numbers were further augmented by thousands of recruits of
Serb, Croat, Slovenian, Bosnian or Herzegovinian descent, mostly
from America, as well as by those like Flora who needed extended
convalescence and, in early 1917, members of the ultra-nationalist
Black Hand society who had been purged from the ranks of the
Serbian army.[43]

Although most Serbs lent their support jointly to the ruling
Radical Party and the royal family, those who gave theirs to the
Black Hand were ruthless in their willingness to use any means
necessary to achieve their aim of a single south Slav state under
Serbian leadership, including threats, intimidation and political
assassination.[44] By early 1917, with fighting in Macedonia at a
temporary standstill, its supporters within army ranks began to
agitate and conspire in the face of rumours – likely false – that the
Serbian government was considering signing a separate peace with
the enemy. Even the head of the American Unit in Ostrovo noted
the change in mood. "I'm afraid there is some definite disaffec-
tion in the army (Serb) and a large number of their best fighting
officers have been imprisoned or deported," wrote Dr Bennett in
a prescient entry in her diary. "This place is a hotbed of adverse
currents. I sometimes wonder if they can ever be united. The man
who does it will be a genius."[45]

The Serbian government acted decisively to contain the threat
by ordering what amounted to a purge of Black Hand elements
in the army. One in every thirty officers was suspended, one hundred and eighty were sent to Bizerte where they were imprisoned
by the French in an ancient Arab fort, and three, including their
brutal leader Dragutin Dimitrijević (widely known as "Apis"),
were executed on almost certainly fabricated charges, including
plotting to assassinate Crown Prince Aleksandar. So great was the
infiltration of the Black Hand into the Serbian Third Army that it
was broken up at the end of March and its units divided between
the First and Second Armies.[46]

The majority of Serbian soldiers and Yugoslav recruits were sent
to live at the camp of Nador, which lay three miles outside of the
town atop a featureless hill. It was a "dreary" place of around six
thousand men with no entertainments or social centres, only row
upon row of tents and unlit huts set amid mud and dust. Many

of the men were chronically ill or permanently disabled, but their
many medical needs – which were almost exclusively in the hands
of the French – were ill met by their ally, who was able to devote
little care to their rehabilitation.[47] Instead, a mere handful of British civilian volunteers, their numbers inadequate to meet the vast
need, were struggling against the odds to do what they could for
them. "Some were yellow and withered with dysentery, others were
paralysed after typhus, some lame through frostbite, and others
with all the vital power burnt out of them with the fevers caught
in marshy grounds," wrote one of them despairingly. "There were
blind men and lame men, men without hands or without arms...
There were men, still greater tragedies to themselves and to their
friends, who had become epileptic with head wounds or who, as
a result of shell shock, had lost all nervous control... Never have
I seen such a society of broken people. There they were, indistinguishable one from another in their tattered blue-grey uniforms,
as withered and unwanted and as dismally adrift as leaves on
autumn streams."[48]

While one volunteer set up training workshops, classrooms
and a printing press, another established a blind school to teach
Braille. Yet another, Francesca Wilson, set up "The English Home
for Disabled Serbs" to give one hundred shell-shocked residents
more specialized treatment and care in a series of whitewashed
military huts outside of the town. It was an "interesting experiment," she commented modestly, that combined "Home and
treatment and workshop". "Tremblers strung together pieces of
bamboo and beads to make curtains to keep away the flies, para-
lytics plaited palm mats... epileptics worked in the garden and
blind men made straw hats for them," she wrote proudly of their
accomplishments.[49]

On her release from hospital, Flora had no qualms about pulling
strings to find a room in Bizerte in preference to the dusty and
depressing camp. The town, almost solely Arab in character, was
to her liking. She could wander through its arched passageways,
past its mosques, painted shuttered houses and dark shops open
to the streets, or stroll along the palm-tree-lined promenade by the
sea. An entire industry had developed around the Allied – mainly
French and Serbian – presence, and by the time Flora had arrived

she could saunter to any of a number of cafés, bars and restaurants through its crowded streets, past donkey carts and camels, Arabs and Berbers in traditional flowing dress, who now shared the town with uniformed soldiers and sailors and military vehicles of every sort.[50]

She was soon having a "very jolly time", she reported, surrounded by French and Serbian friends. Should she wish, there were also military reviews, funfairs and amateur concerts on offer, of varying quality.[51] She often played cards into the evening at one of the cafés, or at the Cercle Militaire, a club for officers that she was permitted to attend.[52] She spent other evenings at the Yugoslav Officers' Mess at Nador being entertained by Gypsy musicians over dinner. There were moments of greater excitement too, courtesy of her extensive social connections. "Best of all the Admiral gave the Commandant of the airship and the big aeroplanes... permission to take me up in both, the first fine day," she wrote enthusiastically to her sister Sophia. "I hope to goodness this wind will go down... as they can't go up until it does. It will be topping. I told you I'd plunged in a submarine didn't I?"[53]

Although the rounds of incessant socializing during her three-and-a-half-month stay in the town helped her pass the time, they also made her increasingly aware of her incongruous status. Flora was frequently invited to parties or to dinner by high-ranking Serbian and French officials, but found it difficult to know whether they expected her to behave like a British lady or a Serbian sergeant. "It's a hard world where half the people say you should not dress as a man, and the other half want to punish you for dressing as a woman," she wrote.

Not only was her position ambiguous, so too was her appearance. "Being thin and sunburnt I could often pass as a man, but my voice now and then betrayed me," Flora recalled. It was an ambiguity that she embraced. She liked the fact that she cut a curious figure. It opened doors for her and she relished the attention. She also enjoyed the ability it gave her to be at the centre of practical jokes. One warm night she wandered into the centre of the town with a captain friend, who told her that they were going to a different sort of café than usual, and that she was to keep quiet so that her voice would not give her away. "Three girls came and sat down at our table at once, and he ordered champagne," she described.

Then [the captain] explained that I had only just arrived, and couldn't speak a word of French, and was, besides, too stupid to talk much at all. "He doesn't look so stupid, but he's very shy," said one of them, planting herself on my knee with her arm round my neck. I kept it up for a while, though the captain was almost helpless with laughter. But when she kissed me I could not help turning my head away, and that, of course, made her suspicious. Then she tumbled to it and they were all much amused...[54]

Flora watched jealously as acquaintances, declared fit to fight, were sent back to Salonika at a time when rumours were rife that the Allies were planning to attack again. Both sides had spent the winter recovering from the fighting of the autumn and gradually consolidating their new positions, but the winter had also seen the withdrawal of most German units from the front. With the start of the spring thaw came word of a new offensive, in the knowledge that this withdrawal had also bolstered the prospects of their success.[55] "I loved being with the regiment," she wrote plaintively, "and was desperately afraid that the long-talked-off [sic] offensive would really come off some day, and that I should not be in it. Nor could I bear the men to think I was an '*ambusqué*' [an *embusqué*, a shirker], as we called those who didn't go back when they could."

By May Flora had decided that she was well enough to rejoin her company. She stuck by her conviction, determinedly ignoring any symptoms that hinted otherwise. "The Dr says the nerve in my arm which works my thumb got cut but it's quite unnecessary and doesn't worry me in the least," she commented with more than a hint of bravado. "And my arm is getting quite strong again."[56] Confident that she would not be refused, she applied to the Serbian commandant for permission to leave a town that she now found confining. "You're not yet fit to go," he told her. In steadfast disbelief that his refusal could possibly have been on legitimate health grounds, she pestered him over the following days. Finally, he relented. "All right," he conceded reluctantly. "You can leave shortly."[57]

CHAPTER 11

THE FRONT

1917

It felt good to be back. "It was a glorious moonlight night," Flora remembered. "The mountains looked wild and lovely, and the air was good up there after the relaxing heat of Bizerte. It seemed almost like coming home again, and I was so glad to meet them all once more." The men welcomed her simply but warmly. "Our *vodnik* [their platoon officer, Vukoje] sent his batman with a present of a packet of candles. Perhaps it may not sound a very romantic present, but there, when you could not get the smallest thing, or carry anything more than a knapsack, they were worth their weight in gold."[1]

Flora had also returned to the sad news that her company, the Fourth, no longer existed. "There were only about sixteen of my company left to be transferred anywhere, as we had been so cut up at Hill 1212, and in all the various scraps leading up to it," she reported sadly of the fate of what had once been a proud unit of two hundred and twenty men. The sixteen survivors, including Flora, had been transferred to the First Company, where, at least, they were together again. She took solace that her friend Lieutenant Vukoje "had miraculously come through", as had Second Lieutenant Dodić, who had risked his life to save hers on Hill 1212.[2]

By the time Flora reached her regiment at the end of May, Emily had been hard at work in Macedonia for over five months. At the end of December she had travelled with Amelia Tileston to work at the First Field Hospital of the Morava Division near Vrbeni [now Itea, in northern Greece], "a mournful village of leaky mud hovels".[3] A little later, leaving Amelia behind, she left for Brod, a village just over eight miles north, after she heard rumours that the civilian population were suffering severely from the effects of exposure and starvation. With her came her two Serbian assistants, Jovan Mitrović and Milorad Gligorović.[4] "I was more than a little frightened when I landed in Brod with a Ford car-load of food and two Serbian soldiers, alone in a wilderness of Italian soldiers and Serbian refugees," she recalled. "None spoke English and no other women were here save those I had come to feed."[5]

On her first morning in the village, Emily left her tent on the hills above the town, pulled on her boots and with no further ado made her first proper inspection of her surroundings. "I am not as particular about my morning bath as I was when I left Roosevelt Hospital over three years ago, dressed in my starchy clothes," she commented wryly. Watched closely by the pinched-faced, ragged inhabitants, she picked her way cautiously through the muddy "shambles" of the village, past the crumbled walls of its one hundred and fifty houses, which lay scattered on the foothills of the Chuke mountains.[6]

Conditions were as bad as she had feared. The heavy shelling of the previous autumn had left few homes intact while, in another grim memento of the savage fighting, the frozen, blackened bodies of Bulgarian soldiers lay unburied in the vicinity of the town where they had fallen. Its several hundred suffering inhabitants had been forced to huddle in the least damaged rooms in the heart of winter, with little food or fuel to cook or make fires, few blankets and insufficient clothing. Emily found them near starving, verminous and dirty.[7] She was horrified in particular at the condition of its children. "They were pitiful things, half starved and not even half-clothed," she wrote. "Few of them had shoes or even wrappings on their feet, although it was cold and a raw wind blew from the north."[8]

Using two empty petrol tins as cooking pots, she lit a fire in a stove improvised from boulders and began cooking what would be her mainstay – beans. Soon a "curious audience" composed of Italian soldiers from a nearby transport unit and village children appeared to watch the proceedings. Emily told the children to return in two hours. Half an hour later they were back "with one-hundred-per-cent increase in their ranks". Holding a mug in one hand and a plate in another, Emily dashed across to the transport unit to try to borrow more. The Italians understood her gestures, raided their mess and followed her back to help her serve. That evening, she returned to her improvised kitchen to cook the children supper. Within a few days, she had extended the feeding to their mothers.[9]

A few days later still, the horrors of Valjevo still fresh in her mind, she decided to tackle the matter of sanitation. Handing each of the children a piece of soap, she told them that she would only feed them the following day if they appeared with clean hands and faces. "[The babies] were loaded with lice, carriers of typhus," she wrote. "Having been through one winter of typhus, I did not want another epidemic on my hands." For a short while her plans worked well. "Then the children reported that they had no soap," she recalled. "A little detective work unearthed a scandal: the women had taken my soap and were washing Italian soldiers' shirts in the river with it for pay."[10]

Emily worked in Brod, in the mud, wind, snow and rain, throughout February. The weather was so bad that the rain rotted the mattress of her bed.[11] She also faced raids from German Taubes. "Several times bombs lit close to our camp, but without damage."[12] The days were lonely, hard and comfortless but she drove herself on in the knowledge that a number of the children would almost certainly die without her there to feed them. Word of her pioneering, brave work quickly spread among her fellow medical and relief workers throughout Macedonia, as did reports of her modest appearance. Anyone who met her found her "inconspicuous" in a worn khaki suit. "The little New York nurse... does not even wear her medals," commented one war correspondent of the near-legendary status she had acquired. "When anyone wishes something done or desires to learn something about hospitals it is generally a case of 'Ask Miss Simmonds'." He illustrated his article with an anecdote. "One day in Salonika a relief worker dashed into a restaurant and demanded of friends: 'Where is Miss Simmonds?' The cheerleader of the American Red Cross looked up from his plate of bean soup and replied: 'She's up at Brod, feeding four thousand on seven loaves and a few small fishes.'"[13]

* * *

"This certainly is the most infernal country," commented Flora in a letter home to a friend, written shortly after her return to her company. "It seems queer that they have always waged war for centuries for the possession of Macedonia. To my mind it is the sort of place you would give away with a pound of tea... However there is nothing like getting used to things."[14] There was much for her to get used to, once the initial excitement at being back at the front began to wear off. By the time she arrived at the start of June the relentless sun had driven the last vestiges of moisture from the earth, leaving it dry, cracked and broken by waterless, parched riverbeds. The rocky, harsh terrain was almost entirely barren of green vegetation for miles around. It was also "damned hot", grumbled Flora the day of her arrival, with not so much as a "scrap of shade". And they were beset by "most of the plagues of Egypt", she complained further.[15] But to the west she could lift her eyes to the Chuke mountains, which appeared pale in the shimmering heat of the day. To the south-west lay the Moglena range, dominated by the towering heights of Kajmakcalan.

For the first time Flora was based in a proper trench system, at a position known as the Starovenski Redoubt, where her Morava Division had been sent to relieve a Russian brigade that, as a result of fears about the growing Bolshevik influence following the Russian Revolution, had been deemed no longer reliable and withdrawn.[16] Initially, she revelled in the experience. "This is more like the warfare on the Western Front," she told a friend excitedly.[17] The Redoubt was nearly twenty miles due east of Monastir, north of the village of Grunishta, in hilly terrain between the two mountain ranges. It formed part of the frontline facing the Bulgarians, whose trenches in that region blocked the advance of the Serbs to Prilep and the Babuna Pass. The French and the British held the line east of the Serbs. The Italians held it to the west.[18]

Each evening when the sun descended over the Chuke mountains she left her shelter, walked through a narrow communications trench up a steep and treeless slope and took her place in the frontline trenches over the top of the hillside. Once darkness had fallen she could peer cautiously over the top, past three thick lines of Serbian barbed wire into the eerie quiet of no-man's-land, on the other side of which lay the lines of Bulgarian wire and trenches, anywhere from fifty to five hundred yards away. In front of her were outposts, each manned silently by three men who spent the hours of darkness peering into the land beyond, ready to sound a warning at the first sign of a Bulgarian attack. Snipers too took their place on both sides of the line, day and night, ready to fire at any hint of movement. During moonlit nights, both the Serbs and the Bulgarians could relax, confident that surprise attack was impossible. But when cloud cover drew a pall of darkness over the terrain, they remained alert and uneasy, ears and eyes straining for any unusual sound or sight. On most nights, little broke the quiet except the rare crack of rifle fire or the ringing of picks hitting the hard earth while men worked to deepen the trenches. Very occasionally the scream of a shell shattered the tranquillity. Flora loved the peaceful summer nights, sitting and chatting quietly with the men of her *vod* (platoon). "Lovely nights some of them were up in that sweet mountain air, and worth ten years of ordinary life," she wrote wistfully years later. "A vast panorama stretched before our eyes, veiled in misty moonlight; all the heat and ugliness of the day blotted out... and it didn't seem so very far from heaven."[19]

At sunrise she returned with her company to their dusty encampment, leaving behind a handful of men armed with machine and Lewis guns to watch the lines until the following evening. Shortly afterwards ration-bearers would appear carrying sweet, black tea. Flora would then retreat to her "dugout" – one of a number of rough stone huts – to sleep for five or six hours.[20]

But novel as she first found life in the trenches, her daily existence soon became "regular and monotonous", broken only by the occasional spell in the reserve lines near the village of Grunishta. It was often easy to forget during the warm, still nights or the hot, quiet days that they were at war. When the occasional artillery attack burst upon them, it took them all by stunned surprise. "We had few casualties that summer, so that those we did have were perhaps more deeply felt," wrote Flora. "One man in our vod, Datza, was a great favourite with everybody. He had a genius for getting into trouble, but much was forgiven him on account of his beautiful voice... Even the Bulgars used to keep quiet when, in defiance of all regulations, he would sometimes lift up his voice in the trenches at night... Just as we were finishing our midday meal I heard a single crash, and my batman [her servant, Mitar] ran to tell me that Datza had been killed by a shell a few yards from his own dugout."[21]

Other than the odd, unscheduled burst of shelling, by the time that she took her place at the front, both sides had settled into a comfortable animosity governed by a gentleman's agreement that allowed them to escape the worst of the afternoon sun. They went to sleep at the same time, bombed each other in the late morning, then stopped for lunch and a nap during the hottest hours of the day, before giving each other a final shelling at teatime. Flora approved wholeheartedly of this arrangement. It was both sporting and part of the game of war. "Sometimes, but not very often, they varied these times," she criticized of the occasional ill-mannered Bulgarian breach of the agreement. "We used to feel very indignant if either side did not play the game, and once or twice, when the Bulgars were so unsportsmanlike as to start an unexpected strafe in the middle of dinner, we decided that their rations must have gone astray that day."[22]

It was also a rule of the game that they were fair targets if spotted by the enemy. In practice, this meant that in the daytime Flora and her company were confined to the hillside on which their huts were perched, held down by the risk of sniper fire, with nowhere apart from a dry ravine to walk. Even then, she commented, this arrangement was preferable to that of the previous autumn when all they could do was lie "from dawn to dark with one's nose in the mud".[23] Flora could still play chess during the day, lose money at cards, write in her diary and have a drink with anyone who had any going.

The Bulgarians and Serbs would also contact each other occasionally, almost always for propaganda purposes. "Stop shooting, brothers, and we'll tell you some news," the Bulgarians would shout on occasion over no-man's-land during the night, before calling out the details of recent German victories. "We reply with some tremendous advance of the Allies, sometimes made up on the spur of the moment," wrote Flora eagerly in a letter to a friend.[24]

Although the Serbs and Bulgarians were bitter enemies, both sides appreciated that they were connected by their shared experience at the front. Flora too shared this sentiment. "The friendly little stars twinkled down on us – and the Bulgars," she wrote once.[25] And fraternization of the sort experienced on the Western Front on Christmas Day 1914 had also occurred on at least one occasion between the Serbs and Bulgarians: in December 1916 the two sides had celebrated together and shared food and drink, before the neighbouring French had put an end to the festivities by firing on them. However, by the time Flora took her place in the trenches the authorities had firmly quashed the prospect of any further joint revelry.[26]

When raids across no-man's-land took place, the Serbs and Bulgarians were ready to put any sense of fellow feeling firmly aside. Flora too had no qualms about participating. "I'm going to try out the new rifle bombs with Prebickovic. Do you want to come?" Dodić asked her during one moonlit evening. "Yes, of course," she replied without hesitation, although the suggestion had made her heart race with excitement and trepidation. She waited nervously until darkness had enveloped the land, then climbed silently over the side of the trench alongside the two men. It was her first time in no-man's-land. "We went along cautiously," she recalled, "keeping in shadow as much as we could, and dropping flat on our faces the moment a Verey light [from a flare gun] went up." Quietly, they crept through their lines of barbed wire before inching across what had once been a cornfield towards the enemy. Each sound they made seemed to echo across the land. "Every little bush seemed to have legs, and the dried grasses kept whispering as though trying to tell us that things were creeping through them to pounce on us," wrote Flora. "I devoutly hoped that none of the Bulgars happened to be doing the same thing at the same time, but it seemed more than probable."

Once they had edged as close as they dared to the Bulgarians, Dodić prepared the rifle. "Get ready!" he whispered. Flora and Prebickovic braced themselves for a crack and explosion, then looked at each other in dismay when nothing happened. Dodić shook his head slightly, then gestured to them that he was about to try again. This time he succeeded. "The first was a dud, but the second and third must have fallen right into their trench, for we were rewarded with a tremendous howl, and the next moment a dozen rifles cracked," described Flora. "We lay as still as mice till the hubbub had subsided, and then crawled back, stopping on the way to examine our own barbed wire and see that no one had been cutting it."[27]

Years later, she reflected on how they measured the success of such raids. Although she did not condemn it – it was all part of the game of war, after all – she acknowledged that it appeared savage. "So brutal does one unconsciously become, that when we used to creep out at night on a bombing raid, we always congratulated ourselves on being most successful when the crash of our bomb was followed by a few groans and then silence. Were there a tremendous hullaballoo, we used to say in disgust that in all probability it meant only a few scratches..."[28]

Twenty-five miles to the south-east, Emily was hard at work in Vodena (now Edessa) running a refugee camp alongside Amelia at the request of the American Red Cross, having finally felt able to leave the devastation of Brod behind after two members of the Scottish Women's Hospitals took over her work.[29] The move in March to the picturesque, ancient town that was famous for its many waterfalls came as a relief, as must have the company of another English-speaker. But she must have been reminded soon after she started working again with Amelia that her friend did not share her egalitarian views. "A baby is a baby, so far as its stomach is concerned, whether it comes from a Long Island estate or a Macedonian mountain," stated Emily emphatically.[30] Amelia, by contrast, littered her letters home with anti-Semitic comments. "I went to Vodena to give my services to a camp of... mixed Macedonian refugees (principally Jews) who had been driven out of Monastir. They were an unclean and most exacting lot," she complained.[31]

Happiest when she was busy, Amelia was also dissatisfied by the numbers. Only two hundred refugees, at first, were in need of their assistance. "There is very little to do," she wrote with disappointment during the week of their arrival. "Miss Simmonds has so much experience in dealing with large numbers of refugees that she does it very easily," she praised in a letter home, all the while perhaps feeling somewhat superfluous in Emily's presence.[32] But within days the promised numbers – the majority Jews, but among them Christians, Muslims and Gypsies – began to materialize. With the help of Jovan and Milorad, Amelia set to work alongside Emily

feeding, sheltering and clothing the new arrivals. They arranged for
supplies to be sent from Salonika and accommodated them as best
they could in a monastery, in houses in the town and under tents.
Soon Amelia was able to write home to her mother that she was
at least "very busy" caring for eight hundred refugees, although
as usual she added a barbed note. "As 400 of them are Jews the
work is not as pleasant as it would be otherwise & my dislike of
Jews grows daily greater."[33]

As it had in Brod, the condition of the refugees worried Emily.
Many were sick and suffering from malnutrition after having been
forced to flee their homes months before, and she was deeply concerned that epidemic disease would find hold among them. "Women,
children and old men die for lack of care," she wrote later in a letter
published in America pleading for more women to volunteer for civilian relief work in Macedonia.[34] Although she could provide them
with a degree of medical assistance, she knew that many urgently
needed to see a doctor. Leaving them in the care of Amelia, Jovan
and Milorad, she made the slow and uncomfortable trip to Salonika
to try to find one willing to help. She was turned down flat. "All our
doctors are needed for the army," the authorities told her. "None can
be spared for civilian work." She returned briefly to Vodena, then
left again for Salonika determined to try once more. Again she was
refused. Only on her third trip did her persistence pay off, when she
secured the "temporary" services of a Canadian, Dr Burnham.[35]

In April Dr Edward Ryan also reached Vodena, to organize and
coordinate sanitary and relief work in Macedonia for the American Red Cross. His position as chief distributor of supplies made
him the de-facto head of the refugee camp in the town. Emily
had met him before when, in December 1914, she had toured his
Red Cross hospital in Belgrade. She had sent glowing reports of
his work back to the American papers but now, as he moved to
consolidate control over their mission, she struggled to work with
the difficult, controlling young doctor, while Amelia seethed with
anger. "That loathsome Dr Ryan has come out to be in charge
of all relief work, so I shall leave," she scribbled furiously to her
mother. "It's a shame to send a man like that, who is only out to
get what he can for himself."[36]

Both women left their work at the end of April. After over eighteen months away from home, Emily decided to return to New York

on a fund-raising trip. She left Amelia both supplies and money to
allow her to establish a free "canteen" for Serbian soldiers in the
town, which she moved shortly to the nearby village of Vladova.[37]
Emily gladly left Vodena – and the conflict with Dr Ryan – behind.
She was busy, there was a war on, and she had better things to do
with her time. Amelia, on the other hand, thought of little else.

Throughout the war, although there was often much cooperation
between the volunteers working for the Serbs, there was also some
competition. Its origin was nothing more than territoriality – different units and individuals had "their" projects to protect from
the trespasses of others. In its mildest form, members of one unit
would grouse regularly about those of others in the pages of their
diaries and to each other. But occasionally what was little more
than natural competition would turn into open hostility.[38]

Dr Ryan had a knack for bringing out this hostility in people.
As the head of the American Red Cross Unit in Belgrade, he had
alienated many of his staff. Highly competent, conscientious and
hard-working, he was also supremely confident in his own abilities,
quick-tempered, intolerant of dissent, heavy-handed and authori-
tarian. So harsh was his treatment of his employees that the American Consul in Salonika felt obliged to intervene when the doctor
started subjecting them to military discipline. "He asked the British Marshal to imprison one of them, and feed him on bread and
water," wrote the horrified Consul. "I referred the matter to the
State Department, as a result of which… the [man] was released."[39]

His style of management brought him into inevitable conflict
with his charges, who wished to serve their sick and wounded
patients while exploiting the relative freedom that came from
working in a war zone. On arrival in the Serbian capital, they faced
the threat of invasion, shellfire and epidemic disease, which served
only to encourage a feeling among them that they should seize the
day. And seize the day certain of them did, by conducting affairs,
catching venereal disease, being challenged to duels and, in one
instance, being arrested for theft.[40] When Dr Ryan attempted to
impose his authority, they gained their revenge by spreading rumours about him. By the time he returned to the Balkans in 1917,
many of those working for Allied units had heard the gossip that
he had suffered, not from typhus in 1915, but from gonorrhoea.

Disinclined to cooperate and oblivious to sensitivities, he also trespassed freely and unapologetically into the fields of others on his return. But while most eventually shrugged off their resentment, Amelia's hatred of him came to dominate her almost every waking moment. To someone prone to fits of jealousy, whose social standing gave her a firm sense of entitlement, his attempt to take control of her work was unforgivable. In a public campaign against him, she seized on the rumours and spread them further with a malicious relish. She also heard an allegation that was far more serious, that the unmarried doctor was interested in working in the Balkans for the access it gave him to young girls. It was whispered that he had "ruined" between thirty to forty such girls, all under the age of fourteen, and Amelia passed on every salacious detail.[41]

When Emily returned home to New York in May 1917, Amelia was full of hope that she would take up the battle on her behalf. "I hope Miss Simmonds will do much to clear up the... situation as the Red Cross people are quite unfit for the work they are supposed to do – it's a shame that decent men can't be put in charge," she complained again to her mother.[42] By the summer of 1917 the allegations about Dr Ryan had reached the headquarters of the American Red Cross, although whether it was via Emily is unclear. They were so shocked by what they heard that, at the end of August, they sent out a commission to Salonika to investigate.

The refugees who had flocked to Vodena were representative of the thousands who, in a region of roughly four hundred square miles, had been left almost entirely dependent on ad-hoc handouts from relief organizations and the Allied armies.[43] Many, like those Emily had cared for in Brod and Vodena, were in need of urgent medical treatment. But, by early spring, although there were newly established hospitals aplenty in Salonika and Macedonia, one of the only hospitals willing to admit civilian patients was that run by the Serbian Relief Fund at Sorović, where Flora had been treated after being wounded. Even the main voluntary organization in the region, the Scottish Women's Hospitals, admitted civilian patients only if space permitted.[44] Those run by the Allied armies accepted none at all.

Gradually, voluntary assistance to the stricken population began to trickle in. Although latter efforts were spearheaded across the region by the Serbian Relief Fund, initially the work was conducted by a number of disparate individuals and organizations who focused their early efforts on Monastir. The Bulgarians, from their positions in the mountains to the north, continued to pour a deadly rain of shells on its ancient houses and narrow, cobbled streets. Their fire, which forced its besieged population of women, children and old men into their cellars, made relief efforts in the town perilous work. Initially the victims of the shelling were taken to the sole hospital in the town, which was run by the French Sisters of St Vincent de Paul, who had steadfastly remained at their posts during the fighting of the autumn of 1916.[45] Soon, another tiny hospital was opened by the staff of a Dutch unit.[46]

In January 1917 the elegant but imperious Mrs Harley arrived in Monastir to begin the first programme of civilian relief in the town, after the Scottish Women's Hospitals had refused to renew her contract when they heard she had bullied the Serbian authorities by telling them that she would take her cars home if they did not allow her to work as and where she wanted.[47] In need of a project, she had arrived with her daughter and chauffeur against the wishes of the British authorities, with neither the funding nor access to supplies to make her mission a real success. Soon she was joined in Monastir by two representatives of the Serbian Relief Fund who, by late February, had launched a soup kitchen and clothing-distribution centre. "Were she not her brother's sister [Sir John French, the former British Commander-in-Chief] the Red Cross would have sent her back to England," wrote one of them bitterly.[48]

As the rigours of February gave way to March, the Bulgarians stepped up their shelling of the town. Not only did they subject it to ever more furious bombardments, they began using poison-gas shells, all the while increasingly varying the times of their attacks in an attempt to create terror among the civilian population. One of the first victims of their new strategy was Mrs Harley. She was killed on 7th March by a piece of shrapnel while sitting at the window of her wooden Turkish house.[49] The death of the sixty-one-year-old received widespread press attention across the world. She was given a military funeral on a bitter March day in Zejtinlik Cemetery in Salonika, with thousands in attendance. The acclaim she received in the press was at odds with much of what was said privately. "It was a life thrown away for nothing," concluded one of the doctors of the Scottish Women's Hospitals.[50]

In late July Flora began to suffer from racking stomach pains whilst in reserve. Although she did her best to distract herself by playing cards and writing in her diary, she admitted in its pages that she was feeling miserable. "It's scorching hot weather and not a speck of shade. I'm feeling pretty rotten, hope I'm not getting enteric," she jotted. A visit to the doctor yielded no useful advice whatsoever, to her disgust. "I told the doctor that I couldn't eat, everything made me bad, and all he said was of course I shouldn't eat but ought to be on a milk diet, however he didn't suggest how I was going to keep the cow in the trenches so that was useful," she concluded contemptuously.[51]

That evening, with their stint in reserve at an end, Flora dragged herself back to the trenches with her company. She struggled through the next few days, trying to convince herself that she would get better on her own if only she could tough it out. But days later, feeling washed out, weak and oppressed by the heat, she knew she needed hospital treatment. "Enteritis so bad I applied for leave to go down to Salonique for a few days," she wrote glumly. "If I can get some other food maybe I'll be all right," she continued hopefully, "but I've stuck it for 10 days now, I can't do another spell in the trenches."[52]

Two days later, with Mitar in tow, she reached Salonika. Sick as she was, she headed straight to Floca's, the city's busiest and most fashionable café. Then, fortified by coffee, ice cream and her first dose of civilization in two long months, she set out to find a hospital willing to take her. Having been first rejected by the Scottish Women's Hospitals on the grounds that every one of their beds was taken, she trailed across to the newly opened Crown Prince Aleksandar's Hospital. The doctor who saw her confirmed her self-diagnosis of "acute enteritis" and admitted her as a patient. She was given a room in a wooden bungalow with three of its British nurses: Mrs Hartney – almost certainly the same Mrs Hartney that Flora had worked with in the Anglo-American Unit – Miss Spooner and Isabel MacPhail.

* * *

Isabel's thirty-year-old sister Katherine had first travelled to Serbia in January 1915 as a junior doctor with the First Serbian Unit of the Scottish Women's Hospitals. Hardly five feet tall and barely one hundred pounds, she had "a mass of wavy short hair [and] a touch of melancholy in her Scots voice". Quiet, unassuming and level-headed, she was thought highly of by those who worked alongside her for her professional skill and capacity for hard work.[53]

Katherine also knew Dr Edward Ryan better than most, having spent weeks under his care at his American Red Cross hospital in Belgrade after she had caught typhus in the spring of 1915, losing most of her hair. "I shall never forget their kindness," she commented publicly about her time with them. "[I] owe my recovery in great part to the care & attention of Dr Ryan & his nurses."[54] Impressed with the tall, young, dark-haired doctor, just three years older than she was, she did all she could to keep in touch with him. In May 1916, having spent the first months of the year working in France for the Quakers, she wrote home to her mother after meeting Dr Ryan again briefly in Paris. "It was a great pleasure to see him & hear of all his doings. I hope I shall have the chance of seeing him again sometime," she said. "Of course I may never hear of him again," she scribbled plaintively in a separate letter to her sister.[55]

Still thinking of their meeting, Katherine travelled from Paris to the mountainous French island of Corsica, where she joined the staff of a small tuberculosis hospital for Serbian boys run by the Serbian Relief Fund in the northern town of Bastia. By September she had resigned and was back at work in France, this time at a Quaker-run convalescent home for French mothers and children in Samoëns in Haute-Savoie. There she had spent her days performing minor operations and doing the rounds of the wards, while contending good-naturedly with the head nurse who made it clear that she thought it was a mistake ever to allow women to become doctors. Even the junior staff could see that the work failed to challenge her. "There is a dear Doctor MacPhail who has been to Serbia & is recuperating after typhoid [sic]," commented one in her diary. "[She] is obviously bored stiff."[56]

In early 1917, in search of more challenging work, Katherine had made the treacherous voyage to Salonika to join her sister.

She found work again with the Serbian Relief Fund, first at their
hospital in Sorović, and then in the village of Brod among the
same malnourished and disease-ridden population that Emily had
worked with earlier that winter.[57] There, in May, with the help
of a small team she opened a small hospital of a dozen beds in a
disused stable, vaccinated the four hundred inhabitants and began
travelling to outlying villages in an attempt to immunize as many
as possible. Soon after Dr Ryan's arrival in Macedonia, they met
up again. He must have been as glad to see her as she was him and,
although there is no hint that their relationship ever went beyond
friendship, he stepped in to give her all the help he could. Soon,
under his orders, the American Red Cross had provided her with
a mobile dispensary that her chauffeur could drive from village
to village.[58]

Flora spent two days sitting quietly in the hospital garden among
its wooden and tented barracks, grumbling about the heat and
mosquitoes, sipping castor oil and sending Mitar on various
missions into town. Finally, on the third day, she began to perk
up enough to take a renewed interest in the shops and cafés of
Salonika, and in enlarging her already extensive social connections. One of her first introductions was to Katherine, who was
in the town on a short visit. "I like her very much," Katherine
wrote home after meeting Flora through her sister Isabel, "and
our mutual enthusiasm for the Serbs gives us a lot in common.
She is dressed in Serbian sergeant's uniform which suits her very
well. Yesterday we went into town together to lunch and I helped
her buy a pair of trousers and leggings. The Serbs all love her and
look on her as a sort of mascot."[59]

Flora passed another evening in the company of Amelia Tileston,
who had travelled from Vladova to collect supplies for her canteen.
Helped by Jovan and Milorad, she had spent the summer handing
out free tea, coffee, cigarettes and medicine to Serbian soldiers returning to the front from hospital. Flora listened with great interest
to her description of her work and peppered her with questions.
"I dined last night with Miss Sandes, the Englishwoman sergeant
in the Serbian army," Amelia wrote to her mother the following
day. "She wears of course uniform and I felt as if I were with an
amphibious monster or a mermaid or some other anomaly."[60] Had

Flora known how she would describe her or how utterly tactless she could be, she would almost certainly have been less eager to work with her. As it was, she left her that evening turning over ideas about how best she could help her with her project.

Flora had been thinking for some time about schemes to help Serbian soldiers. With the help of her old friend Bessie Stear, with whom she had travelled through America in 1904, she had already succeeded in getting a small-scale project under way. She had written a letter to her in early June in which she commented that, whilst she got letters and parcels, most of the men in her company had heard nothing from home in occupied Serbia for nearly three years. "We are an entire army of lonely soldiers," she wrote. "I wish people at home... would adopt a few of us... They are so keen on everything English, and prize anything from England so much."[61] Soon, at Bessie's instigation, parcels began to arrive for the men of her company. They received them with the "greatest excitement and delight", recalled Flora. "I was promptly inundated with requests from the recipients to address postcards of thanks for them too. Very funny some of these postcards were, and I used to wonder whether people at home ever made head or tail of them." Such was Bessie's success that Flora started to send her lists of "lonely soldiers" from the most devastated villages in Serbia. Soon, those "most in need of a little cheering up" received their first parcel of the war.[62]

On 15th August Flora was discharged from the hospital to convalesce in Vodena. Three days after she left, fire broke out in the narrow, winding streets of the ancient Turkish quarter on the high hills of Salonika. Pushed by a strong, hot wind that blew a cloud of glowing air ahead of it, it burned its way down the hill, across the Via Egnatia boulevard which divided the old from new sections of the city, to the hotels, restaurants, bars, cinemas and shops that lined the waterfront.

The fire left behind a smouldering heap of ruins that belched smoke for a fortnight. By the time it burned itself out, it had destroyed nearly one square mile of the city. There was little left of the old Turkish quarter, the modern buildings that lined the waterfront had been gutted and it had laid ruin to many historical landmarks including the fifth-century church of St Demetrius. Although loss of life was minimal, the fire destroyed four thousand houses and left around one hundred thousand homeless, whose care was temporarily taken over by the Allied armies.[63] Most hospitals were based on the outskirts of the city, and also escaped destruction.

The Girton and Newnham Unit of the Scottish Women's Hospitals at Salonika harbour had had a lucky escape. As the wind had started to blow great fireballs into their tented camp, the women had armed themselves with sacks soaked in seawater to throw on the flames. Others, holding brooms, perched on the ridge poles of the tents and beat out the sparks as they fell on them.[64] They fought the flames for four exhausting hours before the wind changed direction and began to blow back on itself, sparing the hospital and the parts of the city that had not yet been destroyed.

"It blazed for two days, no one knows how it started, all along the waterfront is burnt and for half a mile inland, and all the old Turkish town," Flora scribbled as she tried to take in the scale of the destruction. "And Floca's," she noted unhappily.[65]

Flora spent a fortnight at Vodena. Away from the doctor's supervision, she charged round the region paying visits, all the while medicating herself liberally with castor oil, alcohol and cigarettes. She rested only when the enteritis got the better of her and when, for three miserable days, she suffered from dengue fever. At the start of September she finally felt fit enough to rejoin her company. "They all seemed glad to see me," she wrote contentedly. "Sat up all night, lovely moonlight night, we are in first-line trenches."[66]

One uneventful hot September day succeeded another until, at the end of the month, less than two months after Flora had left the Crown Prince Aleksandar's Hospital to convalesce from enteric, she was on her way back. After an operation to remove yet more pieces of shrapnel, her doctor confined her to bed. As usual, her diagnosis of the severity of her condition differed substantially from his, and she soon began to push to be discharged to rejoin her company. "You're not fit for the front," he told her. "There's no point even asking. I'm sending you to the [Serb] convalescent camp, where you'll stay put for at least two months." "If I have to convalesce," Flora proposed in reply, "I might as well do it back home in England. Will you at least discharge me for that?" He

thought it over and, securing a half-meant promise that she would
spend her time resting, signed her papers.

  After six weeks in bed Flora was finally released, and arrangements were duly made for Sergeant Major Sandes to return home
on a British transport ship. She looked forward expectantly to
spending her first Christmas with her family in three years. But
when the British authorities caught wind of the fact that their passenger was a woman, they turned her down flat. "The good old
British regulations prohibited women on transports," commented
Flora brusquely. Next, she tried to get passage by hospital ship,
only to be disappointed yet again. "[They] refused also, on the
ground that I was a combatant discharged from hospital." With a
sea voyage effectively blocked, the only other way for her to return
home was via train through Europe. First she had to get to Santa
Quaranta (now Sarandë), a port in south Albania, which lay on the
other side of a range of barren mountains. It was a four-day trip
from Salonika over treacherous and precipitous roads followed by a
short trip across the Adriatic to Italy, but she had no other option.

  She duly visited Serbian General Headquarters, who sent her to
their transport unit to apply for a car. A week later, an increasingly irritable and frustrated Flora was still in Salonika. If she
did not leave immediately, she knew her chances of getting home
for Christmas were minimal. She left it as long as she could bear,
then returned to Headquarters. Brimming with barely suppressed
annoyance, she asked to speak to the Chief-of-Staff, who ushered
her into his office. "May I speak with you as a friend and not a sergeant?" she asked as she stood before him. "Certainly," he nodded.
"I know very well that if ever I'm killed you'll put up a beautiful
tombstone for me as you have for the other Englishwomen," she
stated crossly. "But that's not of the least use to me personally at
this moment as a mark of your affection. My sick leave – which
I need as the result of fighting for *you* – is slipping away. What I
want is a loan of a car *now*, while I'm still alive." "Till the child
howls the mother does not worry," he chuckled in response, quoting a Serb proverb. "Please sit down and don't be angry with me,"
he told her with a smile. As she took a seat, he paused to write
something. "Here you go; take this to the Chief of Transport," he
said, handing her a request for them to give her a car immediately.
Later that day, she was on her way home.[67]

CHAPTER 12

CANTEENS

1917–18

"Would you like me to stand still so that you can get a better look?" snapped Flora to an "old chap" who stood motionless in the middle of the road staring openly at her. She was dressed in uniform, hurrying to catch a train from Croydon to London, and was in no mood whatsoever for anyone to be throwing disapproving looks her way. To her surprise he hurried across the road towards her. "My great wish has been to meet you," he told her as he shook her hand warmly, while she stammered a sheepish apology and made a mental note not to jump so hurriedly to conclusions. "The incident taught me not to be so snappy on such occasions," she wrote later.[1]

Flora was now recognized widely wherever she went. Her arrival back in England was heralded soon after by coverage in the *Daily Mail*, the *Daily Mirror* and the *Daily Express* and she began to use the press interest and her resulting fame to launch an extensive campaign to raise funds.[2] When she had left the front she had only a vague notion of building upon the nascent scheme of sending parcels to Serbian soldiers that her friend Bessie Stear had helped her get under way. By the time she reached home she had resolved to provide winter clothing for as many soldiers as she could, a decision prompted by the refusal of the British Red Cross representative in Salonika (almost certainly Colonel Herbert Fitzpatrick) to give her a dozen pairs of socks for the men of her section. "That's the business of the Serbian Government, not the Red Cross," he told her curtly. "You can't possibly expect to clothe the whole army." The idea of clothing the army had not, until then, crossed her mind. "Why not?" she thought with a flash of anger. "If you want a pig to go straight ahead, you must pull it the other way," she wrote after their meeting, no doubt amused at the analogy at her own expense.[3]

Initially Flora focused her efforts on helping to raise funds for a friend's campaign. The friend – the Hon. Evelina Haverfield – was an experienced fund-raiser who had first arrived in Serbia in April 1915 as an administrator for the Scottish Women's Hospitals in Kragujevac. There she had joined her partner, chauffeur Vera Holme, a former occasional male impersonator who retained her preference for wearing masculine clothing, and whom Evelina had met via their mutual membership of the militant suffragist Women's Social and Political Union (WSPU), presided over by Emmeline and Christabel Pankhurst. Although Flora had developed a rather formal friendship with the delicate-featured, slender fifty-year-old Evelina, not everyone liked her. She was able and efficient, capable of immensely hard work and charming to those she liked. Those she disliked – and there were many – found her cold, proud and distant. Vera, known as "Jack" to her friends, was far more easy-going. In her, Flora had spotted a kindred rebellious spirit: they both took pleasure in disregarding social convention and had a shared sense of fun and adventure. While Evelina remained "Mrs Haverfield" to Flora in correspondence, Flora and Vera soon became "Sausage" and "Jack" to each other.[4]

Evelina's scheme, "The Hon. Mrs Haverfield's Fund (Registered) for Providing Comforts for Serbian Soldiers and Prisoners", appealed strongly to Flora. Directed at military rather than civilian relief, it aimed to provide practical help to men by sending them warm clothing and small gifts. Flora's first appeal on behalf of it hit the papers just before Christmas. "The terrible cold of the Balkans must be endured to be understood," she wrote in a letter published in the *Weekly Dispatch* on 23rd December. "The almost total absence of woollen garments which the men suffer from is likely to render their life in the trenches almost intolerable. Perhaps it may seem an extraordinary thing to appeal on behalf of an entire army, but it must be remembered that the Serbian army depends for its entire sustenance on Allied support." She appealed in particular for unglamorous but desperately needed underclothing, mufflers, socks and gloves.[5]

By early January 1918 Flora's thoughts on future fund-raising were beginning to crystallize. She had kept her conversation with Amelia Tileston at the back of her mind since meeting her the previous August. She had been impressed by her description of her work running canteens for Serbian soldiers, something Amelia herself had copied from Alice Erin Massey, the daughter of a chemical manufacturer from Newcastle, who, equipped with a similar mobile kitchen van, had set up base alongside Serbian ambulances to feed the wounded as they arrived on the train, and whom Amelia had worked alongside in Vrbeni.[6] Flora now began to contemplate doing something similar. By February she had joined forces with Evelina in a shared scheme, the "Sandes-Haverfield Canteen Fund".[7] The Fund aimed to raise money for free canteens for "*cheechas*" – elderly soldiers who would march up to thirty punishing miles daily alongside pack-horses carrying equipment for the army – along with any soldiers facing a long trek back to their regiment after being discharged from hospital. "To have some kind of shanty, however small, on their line of route, where the poor old chaps could have a rest and some refreshment, was what I really aimed at," summarized Flora.[8]

Ahead of her first speaking engagement on behalf of the Fund, Flora stood in the wings of the Alhambra shivering with nerves as she waited for the first half of the afternoon's entertainment to finish. It was Sunday 27th January, and she was scheduled to speak for ten minutes at the music hall in Leicester Square, at a concert arranged by the actress Lilian Braithwaite.[9] She was confident about her ability to raise funds through written appeals in the press, but she was also painfully aware that she had had little experience of public speaking.

In the weeks leading up to the event she had rehearsed a speech until she knew every word by heart. On the day she had dressed smartly in her red-trimmed khaki sergeant major's uniform, onto which she had pinned her row of medals. She had done her best to smooth her short, grey hair under her peaked Serbian officer's cap. Her high black boots had been polished to a shine, and she held her silver-handled swagger stick tightly. But instead of lending her confidence, her appearance worsened her concerns about how her London audience would react to the sight of a woman soldier.

So miserable did she look that a wounded young officer of the Royal Flying Corps, his arm in a sling, came up to try to reassure her. "I can't remember a word I'm supposed to say," she told him wretchedly. "Never mind what you say," he advised her. "Just go on and say anything, they won't hear it anyhow." One star after another – including ballerina Phyllis Bedells, actor Lyn Harding, soprano Amy Evans, contralto Phyllis Lett and comedian Nelson Keys[10] – performed on stage while she fretted and paced. In an attempt to distract her from her worries, the officer continued to chat to her, explaining that he had been wounded in a flying accident. "I'm going back the moment I can," he told her cheerily. Flora was heartened by his words. "If he can be as brave as that, so can I," she resolved to herself. "I'll make my speech or die in the attempt."

When her cue was finally called, she walked shakily to the brightly lit centre of the "enormous, empty stage". Feeling "about the size of a peanut", she looked out over the vast audience and began to speak. "A voice, which did not sound at all like my own made some kind of speech," she recalled. "I have never really had the slightest idea what I did say, but I knew some of the audience were crying, and we got the biggest collection ever taken there at a charity matinee; and my young flying friend patted my shoulder and emptied his pocketbook into my hands."[11]

Flora's success at the Alhambra gave her the confidence she needed to speak in public again. It also lent renewed vigour to her campaign, while her spreading fame gave her the platform she needed to make it a real success. In the days that followed she took to the stage as required, made further appeals through the press, appeared at public events, auctioned souvenirs from the war in Serbia, and raised an astounding £1,235 [the equivalent of around £46,600] following speeches at the London and Leeds Coal Exchanges.[12] "Croydon's Lady Soldier", as she was excitedly christened by a local paper, was even given a triumphant homecoming when she arrived to give a talk to munitions workers.[13] Evelina Haverfield too put her considerable fund-raising experience to use on behalf of the Fund in a series of lectures and visits to girls' schools and colleges. Soon, donations of funds began to flood in from individuals while voluntary societies gave vast quantities of underclothing, shirts and socks.[14]

* * *

Flora predictably had utterly disregarded her doctor's order to rest. This time, however, it did her no apparent harm and she followed her fund-raising efforts in London and Leeds with a trip south to Plymouth. There, she had heard that her seventeen-year-old nephew Dick Sandes, now a midshipman in the Royal Naval Reserve, had arrived in port.

One day whilst in Plymouth harbour a phone message directed to me from the Admiral requested to know whether I had any relations who were soldiers in a foreign army. I said "have you got one there" and he replied "yes, and he won't tell me why he wants to see you." I replied "Good God that must be my aunt." A muffled blurt from the other end of the line and nothing further. A few minutes later Flora arrived under the escort of the Flag Lieutenant, both in full uniform. I did not know whether to kiss or kick my aunt under the circumstances and the Flag Lieutenant would not leave until Flora had been introduced to the First Lieutenant of the ship and arrangements made for her to have lunch on board. The First Lieutenant did the honours in the absence of the Captain. He apparently thought that a few gins would not do any harm – they did not as far as Flora was concerned. She was used to drinking vodka or Rakija [Serbian fruit brandy]… but by lunchtime Jimmy the One had to excuse himself to get back his bearings much to the delight of those present. Incidentally Flora was then only a sergeant major but looked more like a full-blown general in all her finery and behaved like one.[15]

By early 1918, following her high-profile publicity campaign on behalf of the Fund, Flora had little short of celebrity status in England. She was stopped in the streets by policemen and taxi-drivers who would ask after Serbia, and was summoned to a meeting at the War Office to tell them all she knew. "Several years before," she reflected, "[a palmist] had managed to hit the nail on the head, for she had told me I should become notorious in the press; a prognostication which rather alarmed me at the time. It came true, however, and in consequence I spent half my time trying to dodge reporters."[16]

Then, out of the blue, she received a letter from Queen Alexandra's private secretary requesting her attendance at a private royal audience. "What shall I wear?" she replied, worried that

that the Queen would disapprove of women in breeches. "Come as you are," he answered. At noon on Sunday 20th January, Flora presented herself at Marlborough House, dressed once again in full Serbian uniform. Overcome by uncharacteristic shyness, she was escorted into a large, formal reception room. As she entered, the elderly Queen walked towards her and shook her hand. With a practised but genuine concern to put her often nervous guests at ease, she ushered her into a room to show her an oil painting of her husband, King Edward VII; then she asked her to sign her autograph book. "Do you have any photographs of the war in Serbia?" asked the Queen, before poring over the ones that she produced. "I quite forgot to feel shy," Flora wrote of the expression of genuine interest.

At that moment, Princess Victoria peered round the door and walked into the room, curious to see her mother's latest guest. "I wish I could wear those sorts of clothes," she sighed wistfully to Flora when she was introduced to her. "Are you carrying a revolver?" she asked. "Yes, I do always," replied Flora. "Show it to us," asked Queen Alexandra with a mischievous hint of a smile. "Hurry up! Hurry up!" she teased while Flora struggled to undo her holster, which she so rarely fastened. "Supposing someone was attacking me, and you were all that time getting out your revolver." At last, Flora eased it out carefully and pointed out marks left in the metal by the grenade that had wounded her fourteen months before. "Watch out, it's loaded," she warned before she handed it to them. Years later, Flora remembered the visit fondly. She was "such a very lovable old lady", she recalled.[17]

By mid-February 1918 Flora and Evelina had raised sufficient money to make their first contribution to what they hoped would be a network of free soldiers' canteens alongside transportation routes in Macedonia. Their first donation was to Amelia. When Flora's telegram arrived notifying her of the payment, Amelia's opinion of her performed a volte-face. "[Flora] is very capable and a pleasant companion," she wrote about the woman she had first described as an "anomaly". "[Her support] will mean an enlarged field of work, so I'm much pleased."[18]

Amelia had been running her canteen since the previous spring in a "really lovely spot" near Vladova. Although it was just twenty feet above the busy Monastir Road, a running brook a few feet away drowned out the sound of the military lorries that rumbled past. It was a simple affair, with an improvised kitchen, a handful of small tents and a large one for passing soldiers, marked with an American flag proudly flying outside. For company, she had Jovan and Milorad, Emily's former assistants who had now been reassigned to her.

Every day Amelia rose at four a.m. and, with the help of the two Serbs, saw off the soldiers who had spent the night in the large tent. She spent her days cooking soup for new arrivals and handing out tea, coffee, cigarettes and clothing. She had also taken it upon herself to diagnose – not always accurately, as she freely admitted – and treat those with any afflictions who passed her way. She gave quinine to those with malaria and treated the blistered and aching feet of soldiers, while Jovan too took it upon himself to dish out free medical advice. "Of course you have malaria," she overheard him saying once. "You eat plums and then drink cold water; you ought to know better."[19]

Amelia was devoted to the care of the soldiers who passed her way. She also undertook, albeit with far less enthusiasm, to provide some rudimentary medical care to local refugees and villagers, many of whom were suffering from malaria, which was raging unchecked throughout the region. Although she was often their only source of medicine, her bigotry continued to interfere with her work. She did not have sufficient for all, she reasoned, so she might as well save what she had for the more worthy – among which Jews were rarely included.[20]

Her prejudices aside, her work in many respects was remarkable. She often drove herself to the point of exhaustion, working day in and day out in inhospitable conditions. Equally remarkably, she also managed to finance it herself by browbeating her wealthy family, friends and contacts for money, with much success. Her financial independence gave her considerable freedom, as it meant that she had to report to no higher authorities. It also meant that she was able to continue her vitriolic personal campaign against Dr Edward Ryan.

Then, in September, shivering and shuddering from fever, she was hospitalized with a case of severe malaria. The attack was serious and her doctors worried that it might affect her heart. "You must rest," they told her. "If you go back to work too soon, we won't answer for the consequences."[21] Sick and pale though she was, her eyes shone angrily when she was asked about the activities of Dr Ryan by the nine-member "fool commission" who interviewed her at her hospital bed in Salonika in early October. He was arbitrarily supplanting her work and that of others, she accused. He was depriving refugees of their rations and "living in style, not doing much". Worst of all, he was using his work with the Red Cross to "lie low" in the Balkans where he could freely pursue his interest in young girls, she alleged.[22]

In the course of their extensive investigations, the commission held interviews in Salonika, Macedonia, Paris and New York. One of those summoned in Paris was Emily.[23] In early September she had returned to the French capital to await orders from the American Red Cross after spending the summer months in New York appealing on their behalf for funds and volunteers to carry out civilian relief work in Macedonia.[24] The interview put her in an extraordinarily difficult position. Torn by a desire to remain loyal to her friend Amelia but keenly aware of her dependence on the Red Cross for her funding and her papers, she gave little away. She refused to "talk freely" about Dr Ryan and appeared "suspicious" of them, scribbled one member of the commission in his notebook.[25] But others had spoken openly during their interviews, including Colonel Fitzpatrick of the British Red Cross. In a devastating accusation he charged Emily and Amelia with "running about loose". In his opinion, he told the men of the commission, it was they, not Ryan, who should be barred from work in Macedonia.

When the commission submitted its report to Red Cross headquarters, they were unanimous – and almost certainly correct – in their verdict that the charges against Dr Ryan were groundless. The originator of the rumour about gonorrhoea, they reported, appeared to have been a doctor who was working with the unit, Dr Calkins from Oklahoma. "[Dr Calkins] proved to be an undesirable character, contracted gonorrhoea and gonorrhoeal rheumatism and tried to elope with one of the nurses of the Mission," the investigators informed Red Cross headquarters. "Dr Ryan succeeded in stopping this elopement and then called Dr Calkins into his room with the nurse with all the doctors present and told him what he thought of him… The gonorrhoeal part of Calkins's story is made by Dr Ryan's accusers to apply to Ryan."[26] Then, heeding Fitzpatrick's advice, they made a recommendation designed to take revenge on their accusers. Within days of her interview, Emily had been barred, along with all other women, from further work in Macedonia for the organization.[27]

No one from the Red Cross appears to have told Emily of the ban. She waited in Paris in September and into October for word from them of when she would sail for Macedonia, in the not unreasonable expectation that her unrivalled experience and her fluency in the language would mean they would send her back. As days became weeks, to pass the time she began work at Dr Lucas's Children's Hospital for the Repatriated at Évian-les-Bains. The French hospital, on the Swiss border by Lake Geneva, cared for sick French and Belgian children who had been deported from territory occupied by the Germans, who saw them as a drain on their resources. Although the hospital was overstaffed, the head nurse, at least, appreciated her. "We have such an interesting nurse here; she has been three years in Serbia and Macedonia," she wrote. "Miss Simmonds is very enthusiastic over the Serbs; she liked the Russians very much, too; she came into intimate contact with the men of six armies; it was a tremendous experience."[28]

By November Emily had heard rumours of the Red Cross's ruling. "I hear the American Red Cross do not want any more women to go to Serbia," she commented plaintively to a friend. Instead, after only a brief stint at Évian – something that later gave the American Red Cross further ammunition to use against her[29] – she was offered an assignment with their Italian Commission.[30] Desperate for work, she accepted. But before she reached Rome in January 1918, Emily knew for certain that they had blocked her return to Macedonia. After she had spent the previous summer appealing on their behalf for funds, she felt little short of a profound sense of betrayal. "Miss S. writes that owing to Dr R. she has not been sent out here," wrote Amelia upon receiving a letter from her. "It's a shame that her unique knowledge of Serbian isn't utilized," Amelia wrote subsequently. "Truly the ARC is a very badly run affair."[31]

Still, Emily made the best of it. She travelled to Sicily, where she took charge of the distribution of supplies for several thousand refugees before she was transferred to Milan to organize soup kitchens and work rooms. But soon after she started she received a wire from Flora asking her to take charge of one of the canteens. Although the job offer would have provided her with the papers and the funding she needed to return to Macedonia, the young nurse felt obliged to refuse following her acceptance of the position in Italy. But Flora's offer and her appalling treatment at the hands of the Red Cross must have played on her mind constantly. By March, at the end of her two-month contract, she was on a ship home to New York.[32]

After a whirlwind of speaking engagements, press interviews and public appearances that occupied her almost every waking moment, by March Flora's leave was nearly up. A few days before her departure she travelled into London to get her papers stamped at the Serbian legation for her trip back to Salonika. "You can't go back just yet," she was astonished to be told by a waiting official. "You are wanted to go and lecture in the YMCA huts at some of the base camps in France." "But I can't," she replied, as she handed him a document. "My time is up; here is my leave paper." "We are wiring to GHQ [General Headquarters] in Salonique for an extension of leave for you," explained the official. "If you really want to go and help Serbia, and we know you do, then go and lecture as we wish you to."[33]

Although Flora nodded reluctantly, her heart sank at the suggestion. How on earth would they take to a woman soldier, she thought with dismay. They would almost certainly jeer at her as she stood before them in uniform. Even in Britain before the war woman speakers had often been considered inappropriately bold and she would not have forgotten the taunts from the public when she had marched through London streets in uniform as part of the First Aid Nursing Yeomanry. Nor had she forgotten how the British officers she had encountered in Albania and Corfu had dismissed her initially as little more than a camp follower. It was accordingly with a feeling of dread that she began to prepare for her talks.

In late March, just as the first flyers were being distributed announcing the imminent appearance on stage of "Sgt Flora Sands [sic] the Serbian Joan of Arc [sic]", the Germans launched their devastating "Spring Offensive" along the Western Front.[34] With

revolutionary Russia out of the war, they massed all their resources
against the Allies in France in an attempt to secure victory before
America could throw the full weight of her army against them.
On the first day of the battle they overwhelmed British positions
along the Somme. Before nightfall they had advanced over four
miles. Over the days that followed the Allied High Command
were thrown into near panic as one town or village after another
was seized by the enemy. The prospects of Allied victory looked
increasingly bleak.

When Flora stood in front of her first audience, a sea of khaki-
clad, battle-worn British soldiers who were "fighting with [their]
backs to the wall", she began haltingly to tell them of her experiences in Serbia. The "first friendly round of applause" she received
cheered her tremendously. "[It] told me that we were going to be
friends," she remembered. From that moment there was no looking
back. For three weeks she spoke every night and some afternoons
in different YMCA huts along the north coast of France. She had
correctly assumed that her audience were interested only in being
entertained, not educated, and her light-hearted, humorous approach made her appearances a tremendous success. "I used to
put in as many funny incidents as I could think of," she wrote.[35]
Every room she spoke in was packed to overflowing. Even the officers would attend. "I never enjoyed anything so much in my life
as lecturing to the soldiers," she later concluded. "They were the
jolliest and most attentive and enthusiastic audiences it would be
possible to imagine." They were also generous. Although collections were not normally taken at such events, a box was always
put up for those wanting to donate something to their Serbian
counterparts. By the end of Flora's lecture tour the Tommies had
helped her raise enough money to purchase and ship a couple of
Ford cars to the Macedonian Front for the Canteens.[36]

"I am sitting now in a sun shelter made of posts roofed with pine
boughs... in the principal canteen for the Morava Division," described Flora in a letter to Evelina Haverfield from Petalino. The
village lay a few miles south of the Starovenski Redoubt where
her company were based. Five weeks earlier, her lecture tour over,
the "Serbian Infantrywoman" had been given an enthusiastic and
high-profile send-off from London that was even considered worthy

of a mention in the *Times*.[37] In the late spring she had reached Salonika, then hurried west along the congested Monastir Road to visit her new canteens en route to her company.

With the assistance of Amelia, who had taken a mere two months off to recover from malaria, Flora had managed to open canteens for four of the six divisions of the Serbian army. These she placed under the charge of Amelia and her old friend Nan MacGlade.[38] "The outstanding feature is that everything pertaining to them has been made out of nothing," Flora continued in her letter to Evelina, trying to convey how judiciously the funds from their joint venture had been spent. "The net result is three separate places [in and around Petalino] which are always open for the tired, dusty men who pass along the scorching road all day long, to sit and rest in the shade, be welcomed as honoured guests, and provided at once with a cup of tea and a cigarette." It was also a beautiful location. "It was up a hillside, with a lovely view, and neatly arranged with sanded floors, and little baby pine trees planted in front, a grass border, and what will soon be a flower garden," wrote Flora. "The genius of the place is a Serb soldier [Jovan Mitrović] who used to be Miss Simmonds's batman, and who before the war was a café keeper in Belgrade... He is a treasure. The whole is finished off by an elaborate row of large bottles filled with red, then blue, then white mixture, the Serbian colours giving it rather the appearance of a German beer garden!"[39] Amelia was delighted to receive Flora's approbation. "Sergeant Flora Sandes has just been here on her way to the front," she wrote to her sister. "She is much pleased with all I have done. Hurrah!"[40]

After a fleeting visit to the canteens, Flora hurried a few miles north to the Starovenski Redoubt to rejoin the men of her company whom she had not seen for nearly eight months. There she spent a quiet and relatively uneventful summer with them along a front that remained largely static. She spent her days in their dusty collection of huts and her nights in the trenches sitting peacefully under the stars, just as she had the previous year.

By the summer of 1918 the Serbs and Bulgarians had been at war for nearly three years. Both sides were utterly sick of all that it entailed – inactivity, poor food, uncomfortable shelter, being away from home and family and the very real prospect of catching malaria or enteritis, alongside the small but nonetheless continual risk that they might be killed at any moment by a well-aimed shell. But while the Serbs remained fiercely determined to endure whatever hardships necessary to recover their lost country, the foundations of Bulgarian resolve were beginning to crumble. Not only were they tired of taking orders from their German commanders, they were starting to lose faith that Germany would win the war.[41]

The German "Spring Offensive" in the west had slowed, then stalled. When their fortunes worsened still, they began to withdraw further forces from Macedonia in the hope of stemming the pace of their reverses. At a time when German numbers were decreasing, those of the Allies were receiving a twofold boost in the region. Greek neutrality had finally given way under British and French pressure and, in the spring, the soldiers of the Greek army had joined the Macedonian Front in force. The strength of the Serbian army had similarly been augmented by the arrival of roughly eighteen thousand "Yugoslav" volunteers, many of whom were Slav conscripts into the Austro-Hungarian army who had defected to the Russians earlier in the war.[42]

Rumours were rife among the men of Flora's company that the tide in the Balkans had begun to turn in favour of the Allies. By August they knew that they were planning an offensive. As the heat of the summer had increased, so too had the rate of activity all along the front. Labourers toiled under the burning sun to improve the roads and railways and erect telephone and telegraph lines. New training camps and supply depots scarred the landscape and heavy artillery was dragged into place under the cover of darkness.[43]

Flora felt the rising tide of excitement as she watched the pace of work swell to a feverish pitch. At last she had a chance to see "the end of this monotonous trench existence" and experience once again the excitement and "sport" of battle. For the men of her company it was also a chance that they hardly dared hope for – to return to their homes and see their families after so many long, hard years. "The men were extraordinarily optimistic," Flora recalled, "though I do not think the officers were quite so confident; but everything was said and done to encourage the men, who required no encouragement. Not for one moment did they doubt that they were going to march straight back into Serbia; sweep Bulgars,

Germans and Austrians before them like chaff, and, after three years of exile, feel once more the soil of Serbia under their feet."[44]

To her horror, just as she was expectantly awaiting her company to be given their orders to advance, the all-too-familiar waves of pain began to shoot once again through her body. Terrified that she would miss the fighting after all these months of idleness, she dragged herself miserably to a Serbian field hospital in the village of Skochivir with her batman Mitar in tow. "It's only a few short miles away," she consoled herself, planning to escape to the front at the first sign of the attack.

There, Flora had her nineteenth piece of shrapnel removed by a surgeon. He put her to bed in a small tent on her own, with Mitar to keep an eye on her. Within days, boredom and the desire for additional company had driven her to disobey his orders to rest. When she spotted a number of British khaki uniforms some distance from her tent, she limped across to introduce herself. The men belonged to 820 Motor Transport Company, one of several such companies at work for the Serbs, delivering ammunition to their guns in the mountains. She was welcomed by one of the British officers, Lloyd Smellie. "Occasionally she would walk as far as the camp of 820 Company," he recalled, "and I gave permission for her to come to the Officers' Mess to see English newspapers and be given a cup of tea, and the mess servants looked after her accordingly." Even then, after her operation, she was "strong and hearty and could carry a rifle," he remembered.[45]

While Flora was recovering from her operation, she received a letter from General Bojović, now commander of the Serbian First Army, expressing his "heartfelt thanks" to the canteens for all that they had done. Not only had they supplied over one hundred and fifty thousand men with tea, lemonade and cigarettes, they had clothed the whole of the Morava Division, along with thousands of other men.[46] Flora had not quite proven Colonel Fitzpatrick wrong, but she had come close to it. He had refused to give her a dozen pairs of socks; via her canteens, she had supplied the First Army alone with 11,605 pairs.

CHAPTER 13

BREAKTHROUGH

1918

By early September preparations were well under way for an attack spearheaded by the Serbs. The plan, devised by General Živojin Mišić, the Serbian Chief-of-Staff, had first been dismissed by the Allied command as near impossible. He proposed striking the Bulgarians along the Moglena mountain range, a forbidding line of windswept naked peaks east of Monastir, which were at points over seven thousand feet in height. Not only did his plan envisage lifting heavy guns into position on the slopes without the Bulgarians noticing, it relied on driving them out of their mountain-top trenches and concrete gun emplacements.[1]

The key to Mišić's plan was speed and momentum. The Serbs would have to drive the Bulgarians back without giving them the chance to regroup and reform. He would have to push his army to the limits of their endurance. They would have to fight their way across pitiless mountains and dry, scorched plains with little rest and few supplies.[2] Mišić believed that they could do it. So too did his soldiers. By September 1918 he had convinced the Allied command to let him try.

As the "great day" loomed, the men of Flora's company waited anxiously for their chance to advance. "Once back on Serbian ground we don't care if we're killed," the men avowed, as they gazed hard towards the Moglena mountains, on the other side of which lay their beloved country.[3] From her small tent in the hospital grounds Flora sensed that something was about to happen. She packed her things resolutely and told the doctor she was leaving.

"It's been five weeks," she told him. "I've been recuperating quite long enough."

At eight o'clock on the morning of 14th September, from her position on a wooded hillside next to some Serbian batteries, Flora watched as the artillerymen sprang to their guns and opened fire, on a fine but hazy day. *"Prvi top pali, Drugi top pali"* ("First gun fire, Second gun fire"), they shouted while they rained shells on Bulgarian positions atop the heights. Nearby the ground vibrated under Flora's feet and her ears rang with the most "incessant, ear-splitting noise" she had ever experienced, in what was the start of the largest concentration of fire ever seen in the Balkans.[4]

To the north-east of Monastir the Italian and French armies readied themselves to advance while, east of the Vardar River, the British prepared for an assault on their sector of the front around Lake Doiran. These were to be diversionary battles only, designed to prevent the Bulgarians from rushing troops to the focus of the attack. The men of the six Serbian divisions, reinforced by two French Colonial ones, waited for their chance to storm the Moglena heights. They were ordered to capture the peaks of Sokol and Vetrenik, which lay on either side of the Dobropolje ridge.[5]

In the early hours of 15th September the Serbian Second Army and French Colonial divisions began to advance. Flora and the men of the First Army remained impatiently behind. Above them the blue-grey-clad Serbs and French scrambled upwards over the grass and scrub-covered lower slopes, the harsh stutter of machine-gun and rifle fire echoing all around. They hauled themselves up over rock faces and squeezed through gaps in the barbed wire towards the increasingly desperate Bulgarians. By the early afternoon they had stormed the crest of the Vetrenik. Next they seized the length of the Dobropolje ridge. Only the heavily defended Sokol peak remained. After a bloody and savage battle, by nightfall, it too had fallen to the Serbs.[6] Mišić now ordered the Second Army to pursue the Bulgarians through the night without rest.

On 16th September Flora marched off with the First Army through the huge gap in the Bulgarian lines that had been opened by the heroic efforts of the Second Army. For the men the order to advance was as good as being told they were going home. "It would have been no earthly use giving us blankets," she wrote. "We should have thrown them away, as we did everything else that would have impeded our progress, excepting rifle, ammunition, haversack and water bottle."[7]

By the following morning a breach of six miles had been made in Bulgarian lines on a front of twenty. The Second Army pushed them back relentlessly towards Gradsko, a road and rail hub that lay at the junction of the Crna and Vardar rivers. If they could reach it, they would sever the enemy's supply and communications networks and simultaneously divide their army in half.[8] The First Army, Flora's Morava Division among them, took up the chase to the left, across hills, ravines and valleys in the direction of the Crna River. Once across, they were ordered to head towards the town of Veles.

"Turned out before dawn and started 5 a.m.," scribbled Flora in her diary on 18th September. "Still dark. Had the longest and hardest day's march. Roasting hot and the men with their heavy packs were nearly dead and so was I." As the Bulgarians retreated, they set fire to the tinder-dry bushes and scrub, long grasses and woods to create a smokescreen between them and the Serbs. Under the relentless sun, Flora and her company followed in pursuit over the burnt, black grass, skirting shell craters, their clothes grey with soot and their eyes smarting and watering from the acrid smoke and burning heat. "One place we halted in blinding clouds of smoke and hot ashes to sit on, the woods are burning everywhere," she jotted as she looked over the devastated landscape around her.[9]

Over the next few days, under scorching skies and in blistering heat, Flora's First Battalion pressed the Bulgarians back over the desolate rock-strewn hills running parallel to the Crna River. Although other companies in her battalion were facing fierce assaults on the occasions when the German commanders managed to rally their demoralized and war-weary Bulgarian charges, Flora's First Company had escaped lightly. "We all thought we were going straight into battle when we started but after... forced marches we can't catch up with them," complained Flora in disappointment.[10]

Within days of the breakthrough the Serbs had outstripped their food, supplies and artillery. They had also left the Sandes-Haverfield Canteens and the Scottish Women's Hospitals far behind in the

Macedonian hinterland. Nan MacGlade closed the canteens she had been running for Flora and set out behind the army. So too did Amelia Tileston. Of the four Scottish Women's Hospitals units in Macedonia, three prepared to leave. Only the Girton and Newnham Unit in Salonika remained behind.

The Elsie Inglis Unit – named following the death of the founder who had been one of the Serbs' greatest champions during the war (they are "a very charming people", she commented once, "very like the Irish, in almost every way, but much better looking"[11]) – set up base just behind the original frontline at "Dead Horse Camp", so-called due to the half-buried horses that lay all around. The Scottish Women's Hospitals Transport Column had taken to the road with the army to ferry the sick and wounded to hospitals and dressing stations, while the American Unit, under the charge of their new, young Scottish director, Dr Isabel Emslie, made plans to leave Ostrovo for southern Serbia.

Everything about Major Cukavac was precise. The slender, thirty-something commander in charge of Flora's battalion carried himself erectly and took great care over his appearance, from his neatly trimmed moustache to the wire-rimmed glasses that he wore perched on his nose. In character he was a stickler for regulation with a temper to match. "On duty, officers feared his bitter tongue and overbearing manner," Flora recollected.[12]

Cukavac had inherited the thin, hardy, forty-two-year-old Englishwoman from Pešić. He was less inclined than his predecessor to be indulgent – not that Flora particularly expected or wanted him to be – and he insisted that his unusual sergeant major perform her duties no differently from her male counterparts. He reprimanded her for admitting she was tired after a long march, expected her to assist him on tiresome tasks and expended his impatience on her as he did on everyone else. Nonetheless he still took a paternal interest in her and, like Milić and Pešić, also tried to protect her if he thought a situation was dangerous, much to her annoyance.

Flora's initial wariness of him had vanished once she discovered that, off duty, he had a wry sense of humour and was "full of fun".[13] Likewise, he grew to like and admire the woman who dared to treat him as her equal and, on occasion, order him about. Her audacity amused him. "Would you like to turn out and give me your tent for ten minutes?" she demanded of him one evening as she peered through its entrance. "What for?" he queried. "I want to change my clothes," she replied confidently. "Could I also borrow your basin and soap and have some water for a wash?" "Well, of all the nerve!" he exclaimed. "Did anyone ever hear of a sergeant calmly requesting his Commandant Battalion to turn out and give him his tent?" Turning to his batman, he said simply, "Give her anything she wants."[14]

Since her childhood Flora had always enjoyed pushing herself physically. But days upon days of forced marches were far greater a challenge than a morning's icy bath, sleeping outside in the snow or even rowing long distances against dangerous currents, all of which she had done in her relative youth. "Turned out at dawn down the wood and an awful stony hill at a good pace," she scribbled in her diary on the eighth day following the breakthrough. "My feet are cut and blistered and I am dead to the world."[15]

Flora's feet were in an awful state. "I wonder you can walk at all," remarked a Lewis gunner in her company after watching her rub thick machine-gun oil into them during a brief halt. Each morning, she winced as she pulled her boots over her bloodstained socks, before buttoning up a shirt of white flannel – a practical colour in wartime as lice stood out against it. Most days, with the men of her company, she marched off before dawn with little or nothing to eat. They survived only on what they could scavenge en route.[16]

Far worse than bleeding feet, lice and lack of regular food was a shortage of water so serious that, on 21st September, three men of the Second Company died agonizingly of thirst whilst pinned down under enemy fire. "Went the whole day over these infernal hills in the blazing sun, not many kilometres but hills like the side of a house, scorching hot and no water anywhere. The men are dropping with their heavy packs and I am just hanging on by the skin of my teeth," she scratched in a typical diary entry.[17] As they dragged their feet painfully over the broken, stony ground, the stragglers were savagely berated by Major Cukavac. "You're over-hard on the men. They're doing their level best," protested Flora one night. "That might be so, but if a man is really all-in he won't care what I say to him," he explained patiently. "Whilst, if it is only his willpower, and not his legs, that has given out, and if

he can still stand, he will get up and go on, if I cuss hard enough."
He paused as Flora considered his reply, then asked, "How did you
get here? Do you suppose one of those men who fell out was really
as tired as you were? You don't walk on your legs at all. You walk
on your willpower."[18]

It was true, thought Flora, as she briefly lifted her sunburnt face
to look around her on the forced marches. She would see "delicate
lads plugging along" while their seemingly stronger comrades
dropped behind. She bore her commandant's words in mind as she
forced herself up and over the rock-strewn hills, down steep goat
tracks, over hot ash and through the choking clouds of smoke. To
stiffen her determination on the punishing marches, she played the
words of Kipling over and over in her head:

> If you can force your heart and nerve and sinew
> To serve your turn long after they are gone,
> And so hold on when there is nothing in you
> Except the Will which says to them: "Hold on!"

The Serbs could sense victory. "The men are splendid, dead tired,
almost barefoot [and] nothing to eat till nightfall... they are in the
height of spirits," jotted Flora, who, despite her exhaustion, shared
the sense of exhilaration.[19] By 21st September the Bulgarians were
in full, panicked retreat across the entire front, from the hills north
of Monastir in the west to Lake Doiran in the east. As they fled,
they left behind them the wreckage of stations, railway lines and
bridges, destroyed in a desperate attempt to slow the advance of
their pursuers.[20]

On 23rd September French cavalry liberated the sizeable town
of Prilep, the first town of any size to fall to the Allies in the region since the capture of Monastir in 1916. Two days later, when
the Second Army seized Gradsko, the Bulgarians knew they had
lost the war. Thousands laid down their arms.[21] At noon on 30th
September, the day after losing the town of Skopje to the French,
they surrendered unconditionally. Mišić had proved all of his de-
tractors wrong. Not only had the men of his army broken through
Bulgarian positions along a mountain range that had been considered inviolable, they had brought the enemy to their knees only
sixteen days after launching their opening salvo, without regular

rations, supplies or water.[22] For Germany, already on the edge of defeat on the Western Front, the collapse of its Bulgarian ally was a devastating blow. Nevertheless, the German and Austrian armies were still in occupation of much of Serbia. The Serbs continued their relentless progress north, knowing that some of the toughest fighting lay ahead of them.

Flora's bravery and capacity for endurance during the Serbian advance had not gone unnoticed by the military authorities. In particular, she was applauded for her actions on the Ovshe Plain, an expanse of dry, yellow, featureless land north-east of the town of Veles. Although she had done little more than the rest of the men in giving chase after they had been attacked by Bulgarian machine-gun and shellfire, the authorities were keen to heap praise on her. "Volunteer Sergeant Major in this Company, Miss Flora Sandes, has accomplished the following exploits," announced Commander Stojanović of the Second Regiment in his dispatches. She was presented with a painstakingly translated version. "She has stopped the enemies [sic] counter-attack as head of the squadron on the left bank of the Cerna when the enemy counter-attacked the 2nd Company of this Battalion… opening rapid fire against them," he wrote. "On [21st September]… in spite of the greatest difficulties arising from the inequality of the ground and from the want of water, she has supported all day upon the same position all the fatigues of the combat in which she has equalled the soldiers of her company, surpassing them indeed to a certain extent." In his desire to honour the woman who had fought for them for three long years, he ended with a flourish. "On [28th September], she fought very courageously at [Ovshe Plain], outstripping all the company, despite the open ground, and leading by her example as usual the soldiers to accept with joy even the roughest combat."[23]

The news of the Bulgarian armistice came as a bitter disappointment to the men of Flora's company. Proud as they were of their remarkable achievement, most of them wanted to keep fighting, even if it delayed their return home. Flora felt the same. "There we were, stopped by our allies in the full flush of victory we had been through so much to gain, on the borders with Bulgaria, and yet not allowed to go any further," she wrote with a flash of anger. Instead, the French sent their African Colonial troops into Bulgaria as an occupying force. "These, in addition to frightening the women and children, did far worse things in the way of wanton cruelty... than ever the Serbs would have done," commented Flora, who was not otherwise in the habit of using race pejoratively. "If one can believe all one hears," she added, clearly not entirely convinced by the reports.[24]

But the British and French had their rationale. They too had heard the widespread rumours that the regions of Serbia under Bulgarian control had been subjected to harsh requisitioning, summary deportations and public executions by their occupiers. In March 1917 the first reports had emerged that some eight thousand Serbian irregular forces, largely composed of men who had escaped to the mountains and remained in Serbia after the retreat, had risen against their oppressors in the region around Niš and Prokuplje, a village to the south-west. They had heard too that that the revolt had been put down savagely and that there had been mass executions and deportations of families to camps in Bulgaria.[25] The Allies feared that if the Serbs were allowed to enter Bulgaria they would carry out retribution in kind.

Flora thought it incomprehensible that the Serbs could carry out such atrocities. "The idea that [the Serbs] would have revenged themselves by killing women and children... is not to be thought of," she declared. "Though I have sat and listened to the men making blood-curdling threats to the address of the next Bulgar they caught alive, what they actually did do when they found a wounded Bulgar was to give him a cigarette and a drink from their own much cherished water bottle. This I have seen over and over again."[26]

Both the Serbs and Bulgarians firmly believed in each other's capacity for savagery – as did the Allied authorities – and there is indirect evidence that at least some atrocities were committed by both sides.[27] However, they do not appear to have been particularly widespread – with the exception of Bulgarian crimes against the Serbian civilian population in 1917, which were comprehensively documented. And there was little evidence of the Serbian mindset that the British diplomat Aubrey Herbert so famously described: "Accuse the Serb of having put to death 500 Albanians... and the fiery Serb will reply proudly that such is not the case; his gallant countrymen have done better than that: from a thousand to twelve

hundred Albanians have been massacred."[28] When the sinister
Black Hand infiltrated the Serbian Third Army, the authorities
moved decisively to crush it, while Allied personnel attached to
the Serbian army saw or heard little evidence of war crimes having
been committed by the Serbs. In contrast, the Balkan Wars had been
marred by widespread atrocities on all sides, including the Serbs. It
of course remains possible that the Serbs moderated their behaviour
in the presence of Allied nationals, but on the whole there is far
more evidence to indicate that the Serbian army remained for the
most part both disciplined and professional.

"Where's Jovan Simović?" called an old woman waiting patiently
in the rain alongside the muddy road leading north to Niš. She was
one of many eagerly scanning the faces of the passing soldiers.
Like the others she carried a little basket of white bread, eggs and
plums to welcome the son she had not seen for four years. "He's
somewhere behind, with another regiment," replied one of the
soldiers. "Is he really behind?" Flora asked him when they were
out of hearing distance. "How could I tell her he died of hunger
in Albania?" he answered quietly.[29]
  The men of Flora's Second Regiment likewise searched the faces
of the old women, hoping to see a familiar one. Most had been
recruited from the area around Niš and, after three weeks of forced
marches, they were nearly home. They were sick with worry about
what they would find on their return. Those lining the road told
them about the brutal treatment they had suffered at the hands of
the Bulgarians while the sight of ruined cottages and fields empty
of livestock told the same story. "They have lost everything," Flora
jotted in her diary, "stock driven off and everything in the houses,
even their clothes, 'requisitioned' by the Bulgars and Germans...
They say the Germans pay for everything, whatever is asked so I
gather some of them have not done so badly, but the Bulgars just
take everything." But the Serbs also suffered at the greedy hands of
corrupt, unprincipled local officials, she added. "As far as I can
gather some villages seem to have suffered more from their own
'smret' i.e. head man than anyone, he being in with the Bulgars
and requisitioning his neighbours' stock while keeping his own."[30]
  On the occasion that the men of Flora's regiment recognized
someone from their village, they were all too often told that their

parents had died or been killed, or that their cottage had been burnt to the ground and their family interned in camps in Bulgaria. "It seemed, as one man said bitterly," wrote Flora, "as though all the mothers who were left had lost their sons, and all the boys who did come home their mothers." Those who received no news of family pleaded to be allowed to visit their homes. It was rarely granted. "Please, it's only an hour away," they begged Major Cukavac. "I'm sorry," he replied with genuine regret, "I can't let you go. It's orders." Often they "wept outright with disappointment", recorded Flora. Occasionally there was a reunion. "Then there would be hugging and rejoicing," she recollected, "and the whole lot would fall into step with us as we marched on, followed by the wistful eyes of those still patiently waiting."[31]

Flora had marched in the rain with her company to the green, mountainous outskirts of Niš without firing a shot. She had enjoyed neither the inactivity nor the weather. The twisting roads, up and over steep, slippery hills, were in appalling condition. "I feel my enthusiasm for Serbia oozing away in the mud at every step," she grizzled in her diary after a week of virtually continuous rain.[32] It was at least a "triumphal march", she wrote. As they tramped through each newly liberated village, cheering, joyous inhabitants lined every muddy street. They whipped out forbidden hand-sewn patriotic flags from their hiding places and hung them from windows or waved them vigorously to welcome the tired, sodden but victorious army. Rye bread, wine and fruit were pressed on the soldiers from every side. "I'm sorry we have nothing better to give," the inhabitants would apologize, "but the Bulgarians took everything." Flora too was widely fêted. "I looked just like the rest, of course, ragged, thin and sunburnt," she reported, but the men marching in front had generally told the inhabitants about the Englishwoman who had fought bravely alongside them and who had shared their hardships. By the time she arrived, crowds craned their necks to get a look at her. "Before we got through a village I had made everyone's acquaintance," she wrote.[33]

On a dreary, wet 10th October, Flora's company arrived on a hillside overlooking Niš. She had been looking forward to getting back into the thick of the action in the battle for the town, which she had heard that the enemy had been ordered to hold at all costs. Instead, as she looked down over its red roofs, the bulbous dome of its cathedral and the needle-like white spires of its many minarets, the Serbs were already patrolling its potholed, muddy, cobbled streets.[34] "There was street fighting in Nish and great doings and I was out of it to my great disgust. As Mancha [a Lewis gunner in her company] said we had been talking of getting to Nish for the last three years and all we saw of it was a muddy field and pouring rain."[35]

Flora was itching to visit the town. Not that she particularly liked it — she had described it as an "awful hole" after passing through in 1914 — but the prospect of spending a few days on the hilly outskirts resting with her battalion appealed far less. After she successfully begged a horse from her old friend Colonel Pešić, now the regimental commandant, she charged down the hill into the centre. First she dropped in on Emilo Belić, the Chief-of-Staff of the First Army, before spending the afternoon with Cukavac and his family.

That afternoon, Colonel Belić knocked on Cukavac's door to invite Flora to dinner that day with General Mišić, the Serbian Chief-of-Staff. Flora accepted immediately. There was no one more important in the army. He was a veteran of every conflict Serbia had fought in over forty years, a brilliant strategist who was now on the verge of being the author of one of the great victories of the war. That evening she sat down to eat with Belić, a few close members of the inner circle and the lightly built general, the strain of the last years reflected in his lined, worn face. They were in high spirits, flushed with the latest victory, but Mišić suspected that they would not have such an easy time of it in their next battle for the German-held town of Paraćin.[36]

The Serbian victory in the battle for Niš was another military disaster for the Germans. It severed the railway link from Berlin to Constantinople, which isolated Turkey from its chief ally and cut off its supply of war material. By the end of the month Turkey had joined Bulgaria in suing for peace.[37] In the three weeks of fighting leading up to the battle, the Serbs had advanced a remarkable one hundred and seventy miles.[38] Flora had kept up with them, so far, every painful step of the way.

CHAPTER 14

SPANISH INFLUENZA

1918

Flora and her company approached the outskirts of Paraćin cautiously. They had been ordered to hold a position near the railway line that ran to the west of the town. Ahead of them lay the shadowy skeleton of a ruined factory. Beyond lay a dark line of hills, outlined against the purple, evening sky, from which German artillery flashed angrily. Each flash was followed moments later by the dull explosion of a shell striking the town. Hundreds of frightened, miserable refugees clogged the main road south to Niš, carrying whatever household goods they had been able to grab in their panicked flight. The men of Flora's company had flushed with anger at their sight, and murmured threats against the Germans under their breath.

By nightfall they had reached the railway. Keeping their voices low, they crept into position near a low embankment as the German batteries began to sweep their vicinity with their fire. When the first shell slammed into the ground ahead of them with a hot, acrid burst, they pressed themselves into the cold mud behind a low bank. "The Germans know we're here," thought Flora to herself. Each whistle and thudding detonation landed a few feet closer, one a bit to the left, the next a bit to the right, throwing up thick clumps of wet earth in front of them. "We thought they'd get our range every minute," she scribbled. Then a shell landed just short of the bank. Flora pulled her steel helmet down over her ears and held her breath as the next one screamed towards them, certain that it would be a direct hit. Instead it exploded behind them in an empty field. With the immediate danger past, she huddled with the men of her company against the cold of the bank to the sound of the shelling. "There was nothing to do but lie there," she commented. "I went to sleep in the middle of it."[1]

Around midnight Flora was gently awakened. "We're moving forward to the factory," the men whispered to her. She stood up, shook her tired, stiff limbs and picked up her rifle. Under the moonlight she followed them over the broken ground, skirting the fresh shell holes as they picked their way towards the shattered building. They looked grimly about them at the dark, crumpled bodies of the men of their Morava Division, victims of the shelling, who lay scattered across the ground around it. Flora spent a miserable, cold night there with her company. When the grey half-light of dawn brought with it orders to hold a new position, she left the death-strewn surrounds gladly behind. In the stillness of the morning she marched a short distance with her company to a position under a bridge along a river running just south of the town. They spent the following day there sheltering from German shellfire while waiting for the cover of night to fall. "About every half-hour they shelled the bridge, or if anyone went over it, and could distinguish between a soldier and a civvy crossing. Very hot... Never seen worse bombardment than we've had these last two days," jotted Flora. When darkness finally fell they crept to a cold, muddy field, rough with the stalks of its last harvest of maize, to spend the night in the dangerous occupation of "advanced outpost".[2]

By morning Flora was "shivering violently" from fever. "What's wrong, Sandes?" asked Cukavac a touch unsympathetically, from his perch atop a horse. She was sitting by herself on a box in the morning sun by the roadside, looking ill and miserable. "I don't know, but I'm sick," she replied. "I can't walk another step." "All right," he called over his shoulder as he dashed off after his battalion. "You had better go to the ambulance." At that moment, Captain Ljuba, the Regimental Adjutant, rode up. "Ambulance, pooh!" he commented. "What can the ambulance do for you? The Colonel's here [Pešić]; I'll give you a horse and you can ride with us. We'll doctor you better than any ambulance." "I can't," replied Flora. "Can't," scoffed Ljuba. "Now just pull yourself together. We are going to ride through Paraćin and Ćuprija. The people will be expecting to see you and they will be disappointed if they don't, so will the Colonel."[3]

Flora crawled onto a horse that Ljuba secured for her, forced a grateful half-smile and followed him and the rest of the regimental staff through Paraćin. The town had finally been captured, on 23rd October, after fierce fighting and several counter-attacks by the Germans, who were desperate to delay the advance of the First Army.[4] It had been "badly knocked about", she reported, "and there were not many people left in it", but as they came through Ćuprija a few miles farther north she could see the inhabitants ahead crowding exuberantly into the sunny streets. Although her head was throbbing under the hot sun, she braved another wan smile as she entered the town at the front of the procession alongside Pešić and Ljuba, who were keen to show off their Englishwoman sergeant major. They received a rapturous welcome. "All the people cheered and clasped our hands," she wrote, "calling us their saviours."[5] They also placed wreaths and flowers around the necks of their horses. "I... was so smothered... I could hardly see," scrawled Flora in her diary later. "My gee could hardly hold its head up, flags out everywhere and the whole population in the streets, we came in at one end as our cavalry patrols were driving the last of the Germans out of the other end of the town." Still, she wrote, "I didn't feel at all like being 'demonstrated' and was glad when we got through."[6]

The next morning she felt yet worse. When Ljuba and the regimental staff had rushed off early, she was too ill to join them. "Was too bad to stand, nothing for it now but to wait where I am till the ambulance picks me up damn it," she wailed in her diary. "Here's another," commented Dr Boro, the regimental doctor, to his assistant after she had staggered over to the ambulance in the rain when it had finally stopped nearby. "You've got Spanish flu and a high temperature," he advised her. "You'll need to ride back to Ćuprija. A temporary hospital is starting there, but I don't know what it will be like. The doctor is a Greek. If it's too bad get into some private house."[7]

Flora spent two miserable hours on horseback, her face bent against the pouring rain, before she finally rode into the muddy hospital compound. Miloje, the orderly in charge of the horse, had trudged alongside her. With his help she painfully dismounted and walked slowly to the entrance of the low building. Her stomach churned at the stench as she stepped inside. "The hospital was beyond anything I have ever seen," she wrote later. It had been hurriedly evacuated by the Germans, who had left it in an "indescribably filthy condition". The Greek doctor had been "pushed in" with a few orderlies with the sole instruction to do what he could. He had not done much, she thought. "Hundreds of soldiers were lying all over the place, and on the cold, stone floors of the corridor in their wet, muddy uniforms. All down with flu, pneumonia or exhaustion, and the atmosphere was appalling."

Miloje had entered alongside Flora, looked about in disgust, turned on his heels and left, muttering to himself. He returned a few minutes later. "I've found you somewhere else," he told her. "There's a house close by that will take you." On arrival Flora was ushered indoors by two sisters who lived with their elderly mother. Their husbands had both been interned in Bulgaria as prisoners. They dressed her in a shirt belonging to one of the absent men and put her to bed in their best bedroom. "I... then astonished my hostess[es] by sleeping with very little intermission for three days and nights," she recalled. Meanwhile Miloje found himself accommodation in the town and turned himself "from a horse boy into a very efficient nurse and batman". "Evidently," Flora recorded, he had "small faith that any woman would know how to look after me properly."

The day after her arrival she was roused from her sleep by Monsieur Cichot, a French veterinarian attached to her regiment. He had been passing through Ćuprija with the horse transport when he heard that she was in the town, lying sick in bed. "[He] hunted me up," wrote Flora drily, "and prescribed for me as he would have done for a horse. At any rate, that was all the doctoring I received, but it seemed to be pretty effective."[8]

Fortified by the horse medicine, Flora soon began to feel better. Miloje had kept a close eye on her, and had regaled her during her illness with tales of what was going on at the hospital. "The doctor won't take patients in and let one man die on the stretcher outside the door where he had lain all day," he told her. Five days after falling ill she pulled herself out of bed, dressed for the first time and walked shakily down the road to investigate. On the way she met an artilleryman who had been refused admission. "[He] was so sick he could hardly stand," wrote Flora with disgust. "I took his temperature, and it stood at 104." Conditions inside the hospital drove her into a fury. So far as she could see, the doctor had done nothing whatsoever to relieve the suffering of the men who were "dying like flies of flu and pneumonia". Flora rounded on him. "I'm going to report you to the authorities once I get to Belgrade," she raged. "You can do what you like with the hospital," he replied. "It's yours. I'm sick and going to bed." Although he was the only doctor, he stayed there for two weeks, she recalled bitterly.

Tackling the conditions in the hospital may not have offered the excitement of the battlefield, but it was still just the sort of challenge she relished. First she set the four hospital orderlies to work scrubbing the floors and walls with disinfectant, while the head orderly set up a bath at the end of the corridor. "There are also some townswomen here," he told her, "but they've been of little help." Flora found them in a room winding bandages and pasting labels on bottles. "A week ago you pelted us with flowers and called us your 'saviours'," she fumed. "And you're now letting these same men die in front of you on the ground. Has it not occurred to you that these men need a bed?" The following day, they returned with blankets, sheets and clothing. By nightfall she had every man, "unless absolutely dying", bathed and in bed with clean clothes.

With one difficulty solved, Flora tackled the next. The hospital was running short of food and there was little in the town. Although she knew she had only "moral" authority, she wrote out a pass, signed it herself, embossed it with a hospital stamp she had found while rummaging through the doctor's office and handed it to an orderly with instructions to go round the nearby villages. "Beg, borrow or steal it," she told him. The next day he arrived back with a wagonload. There was plenty of food in the villages, he reported, and the inhabitants had been happy to give the hospital what they could. Flora now began writing out passes every second day.[9]

While Flora was hard at work at the hospital, the men of the Serbian army continued their relentless advance northwards, capturing tens of thousands of prisoners as they went, and liberating one town after another. By 25th October the Germans and their

Austro-Hungarian allies, all hope of victory lost, had begun their flight out of Serbia across the Danube and Sava rivers. Three days later Austria requested a general armistice. By 31st October the Serbs had reached the wooded heights of Topčider hill overlooking their capital.[10] The following day, the ragged army, many of its soldiers now barefoot, entered Belgrade in triumph. In less than seven weeks the Serbian army had marched four hundred miles and routed the Bulgarians and Austro-Hungarians. They now pursued the German army across the rivers into Hungarian territory.

Each day Flora watched two or three men die in her wards while the doctor remained determinedly in bed. Many were French Colonial troops. Twice she sent First Army Headquarters an urgent telegraph asking for a doctor and twice she waited expectantly for a response that never came. In desperation, she marched off to the French Battalion Headquarters in the town and asked to see the commandant. "He received me very politely, though I think he must have wondered who this unusual sergeant was," she wrote. Armed by the fact that "the French peg out more easily than the Serbs", she told him that she had a hospital to run but no doctor and that French nationals were dying from lack of care. "All right," he nodded. "I'll arrange for a doctor to visit every day."[11]

As the commandant had promised, from that day forth "a most awfully nice little [French] doctor" arrived to visit the worst cases in hospital, in the company of a young Serbian medical student. Nonetheless, some patients were already "hopeless" cases by the time the doctor examined them, dying of Spanish influenza or the pneumonia that so often followed in its wake. When it swept across the Balkans in the late summer of 1918, the epidemic met not armies of healthy, strong men but men whose systems had been weakened by chronic malaria and the rigours of the rapid advance. "[It] had just struck us like the plague," Flora observed.[12] The first symptom, after a couple of days of incubation, was a persistent cough, followed by numbing exhaustion and high fever. Often its victims suffered from delirium, diarrhoea and sudden nosebleeds. When pneumonia followed, it was "almost as fatal as being heavily gassed with chlorine or phosgene", commented one doctor of the Salonika army. "The lungs filled up with fluid and the patient drowned just as surely, though slowly, as a man drowns in the sea."[13] But not all victims of flu were hard hit. Flora was able to treat such mild cases successfully with a combination of gentle bullying and the horse medicine that had worked so well for her.

Across liberated Serbia medical and relief workers were facing equally appalling conditions as they set up base in the larger towns. By mid-October Amelia Tileston had reached Skopje. There she found two hundred Italian soldiers, former prisoners of the Bulgarians, "in a pitiable state". In the chaos that followed in the wake of the advance, no one had fed or taken care of them. "She bought bread for them," wrote Emily of her work, "which saved the lives of many of them."[14] Also in Skopje were the Elsie Inglis Unit of the Scottish Women's Hospitals who had had moved from their malodorous former base, "Dead Horse Camp", to set up a hospital in a former school. They admitted "mostly overworked and underfed men" suffering from the frequently fatal combination of influenza and malaria.[15]

The American Unit, under the charge of their new, young Scottish director, Dr Isabel Emslie, left Ostrovo to take over a hospital in Vranja, a town of fifteen thousand inhabitants in mountainous southern Serbia. "The operating theatre was ghastly," Isabel shuddered. "A trestle table, covered with the refinement of a brown American cloth, stood in the centre of the room, the wooden floor of which was swimming with blood. A few saws and knives were lying about, and pails full of bits of legs and arms lay round the table and were black with greedy flies. The surgeons [of the Second Drina Dressing Station], with their sleeves rolled up and waterproof aprons black and red with old and new blood, worked steadily and without anaesthetics."[16] The men handed over the hospital to the women against the backdrop of the influenza outbreak. One by one the staff fell ill of flu, disease and overwork. As a blanket of depression and lethargy settled over the devastated country, they struggled daily with orderlies who were disinclined to work and officialdom that had to be nagged and prodded to supply their patients with even minimal rations. "*Samo Serbia spava slava*" ("Serbia only sleeps and feasts"), they joked blackly to each other, in parody of the motto "*Samo Serbia sebi spacella*" ("Serbia alone delivered herself").[17]

Further north still, by 17th October the Scottish Women's Hospitals Transport Column had arrived in Niš, only five days after the Germans had been driven from it. They had spent the month since the breakthrough combing the country for wounded, pushing their cars over the mud-churned roads strewn with debris and across bridgeless streams. Nan MacGlade had also reached Niš, bringing with her all the supplies she could carry for a new Sandes-Haverfield Canteen. What she lacked she bought from the British. It was enough, at least, to allow her to hand out cigarettes, tea, biscuits and "potted meat" – a uniquely British delicacy – to the weary soldiers marching north and give cocoa and milk daily to four hundred men in a nearby hospital. "Poor things!" she wrote in a letter to Flora. "This is the only real nourishment they get."[18] She was joined in the town by members of the Serbian Relief Fund. They were given a building for their use, a former high school that had been used as a hospital by the enemy. The sanitary inspector, Dorothy Newhall, was given the unenviable job of cleaning it up. "The centre of the building looked like a sewage pit," she shivered. "After digging for some time in it we came on human heads and limbs and every kind of filth. Beneath this we discovered a beautiful marble hall and staircase."[19]

When news of the Armistice flashed across the world on 11th November signalling the end of the war, Flora and her Serbian patients met it quietly. "There were no festivities," she recalled.[20] Although Serbia had been liberated, it had also been ravaged. Over half its male population had died during the war, all industry and transportation links had been destroyed, agriculture was in ruins and the country was facing epidemics, not only of influenza, but also of tuberculosis.[21] With so much disease and destruction, few felt much like celebrating. "War, we know, peace, we did know, but Armistice, who can tell?" commented a dispirited woman orderly at work with the Allied troops.[22]

CHAPTER 15

HUNGARY

1918

By 11th November the crisis at the hospital was over. With the "show" running smoothly and the wards emptying, Flora became increasingly anxious to rejoin the men of her regiment. The problem was, she had no idea where they were – although she assumed they had reached Belgrade – and no way of travelling north with the railways nothing but twisted wreckage. She spotted her chance one morning when a staff car passed by the hospital. It belonged to Admiral Troubridge, the former head of the British Naval Mission to Belgrade, who had arrived in the capital charged with looking after the traffic on the Danube. She noticed immediately that it had a seat spare. "Could I get a lift with you?" she asked the obliging chauffeur. At ten o'clock that night she reached Belgrade.

"We all thought you were lost until I got your telegram from Ćuprija," remarked Colonel Belić cheerily when Flora presented herself at First Army Headquarters the following morning. "I sent you two telegrams asking for a doctor," she responded crossly. "Yes, I got them," he replied, "but I hadn't got one handy, and I knew, if you were there, you would get out of the mess somehow. You know you've missed your regiment," he continued. "They left yesterday for the Banat. But don't worry. We'll get you across the river to Pančevo, but you can't leave for two hours. I'll lend you a carriage and we'll then get you across the river by motorboat."[1]

By the time Flora reached Belgrade, her Second Regiment were part of an occupying force that the Serbs had rushed across the Danube. They had been ordered north by the French, who wanted

to show to the world that Hungary had fallen to the enemy, but
the Serbs had their own reasons for wasting no time in staking a
claim to the Banat and the neighbouring Bačka region. Without it
their capital was virtually indefensible, separated from the enemy
by only the width of a river. Romania also laid claim to stretches
of the flat, fertile land. Both countries mounted what was little
more than a land grab, each claiming that the nationality of the
inhabitants gave them the right to the territory.[2]

On 5th November, four days after the liberation of Belgrade, the
Serbs sent across their first units. Over the next few days the First
Army poured over the border, the Second Regiment with them,
with the aim of covering as much of the territory as possible and
driving out the remaining detachments of German troops. They
were under strict orders to behave impeccably, lest they inflame
the simmering ethnic tension. On 9th November they were met
by enthusiastic Serbian crowds in the well-to-do city of Novi Sad
before they continued their advance north, east and west.[3]

Flora could hardly believe her eyes as her boat neared the landing
jetty at Pančevo. It looked to her like "half the town" was crowded
there. There was a band and she could also see several large bouquets of flowers. "Who are they expecting?" she asked an officer
who was travelling with her. "You," he laughed. "They were disappointed at not seeing you with the regiment, so Colonel Belić played
a trick on you by telephoning that you were coming. That's why
he kept you back two hours." With the officer by her side, Flora
stepped off the boat in her well-worn uniform and smoothed down
her windswept hair as the band struck up. "Before I had grasped the
situation they were tying things they call [peshkirs] – long pieces of
thin embroidered white stuff – round my neck and arms and pelting
me with flowers," Flora recalled with a mixture of pleasure and
embarrassment. Then, in the company of the mayor, she was taken
by carriage to a reception in her honour at the town hall. "There
were refreshments and much speechifying," she recalled. After
the speeches were over, she was called on to make one in return.
"Then they put a chair for me to stand on, and I was planted on
that so that the populace would get a better view!" As she stood
over her eager audience, she stammered a few words in Serbian,
her fluency suffering under the pressure of the moment. "Thank

you from the bottom of my heart," she said, thinking fast about how she could conclude quickly. "The mayor will say all I should like if I could." The mayor rose to the challenge of the occasion. "There is nothing the Serbs love so much as making speeches," she recalled drily, "and he made a long one."[4]

Flora caught up with her regiment just as they were about to travel by train to the town of Bečkerek, now known as Zrenjanin, which they had been ordered to occupy. "I shall never forget our triumphal entry," she wrote. Her regiment were the first to arrive in the town of twenty-six thousand inhabitants, roughly one third of whom were Serbian speaking, one third Hungarian and the remainder German. The air hummed with excitement as the blue-grey-uniformed Serbs descended in their hundreds from their carriages onto the bright, sunny platform, met by crowds of townspeople, all eager to get a glimpse of the army they saw as liberators.

She piled into a carriage with Cichot, the French veterinarian whose horse medicine had saved her from the ravages of Spanish influenza, and joined a cavalcade of carts and carriages from the station to the town hall. The Serbian people who lined the streets were ecstatic. "All the youth of the town was on horseback," Flora recorded. "They ranged themselves alongside as outriders, and we galloped along, everyone firing rifles and revolvers into the air." But when they wound their way through the Hungarian part of town, the crowds who lined the streets watched the exuberant procession with silent, sullen faces.

Flora and Cichot's carriage pulled up outside the town hall, a two-storey, white, neo-baroque building that faced a large, grassy square. They stepped out onto the pavement, jostled through its doorway and walked up a set of stairs. There they took their places in a reception room crowded with representatives of both the Serbian army and the town, at the head of which was a Hungarian mayor. He greeted the Serbs graciously, and they responded in kind.

As one "endless, pretty" speech followed another, Cichot began to fidget. He excused himself and wandered out onto the balcony that led off the room. As he leant over it, he looked down onto the massed crowds of people in the street and square below. Then he gazed idly up over the building. There he spotted a sole flag flying. It was Hungarian. He hurried back into the room to Flora's side and whispered angrily in her ear what he had seen. "I'm going to take it down if no one else will," he told her. With Flora egging him on, he marched back to the balcony and yanked down the flag. From below rose a crescendo of angry shouts and protests. Then the crack of a gunshot ripped through the air. In the reception room, looks of confusion and then panic spread across the faces of the dignitaries. Horrified by the dangerously escalating situation, the Serbian commandant consulted anxiously with the major, then issued an order for the Hungarian flag to be flown, but this time alongside a Serbian one. When the red, white and green Hungarian colours once again flapped in the wind, the crowd began to settle. The crisis had been narrowly averted. Flora was unrepentant. Everything about the reception had gone "off smoothly", she concluded, except this "one little, untoward incident". The Serbian authorities were less sanguine. For the rest of the month Flora remained in Bečkerek with her regiment under the watchful eye of a bodyguard that Pešić has assigned to her. Cichot too had been given one. "The colonel of the regiment had become anxious about us," wrote Flora, "as, being the only foreign representatives – especially after the flag episode – he was afraid someone might take it into his head to stick a knife into us."[5]

She was still there when, on 1st December 1918, the announcement was made of the formation of a new country – the Kingdom of Serbs, Croats and Slovenes. The union had been made in great haste, at the behest in particular of the Croats, who wanted protection from the Italian armies who were pouring south to stake a claim to the largely Slav-populated eastern Adriatic.[6] It was a country without established borders, almost all of which were due to go up for discussion at the Paris Peace Conference – and it was one without a constitution to define how power was to be distributed. The Catholic, Western-oriented Croats and Slovenes wanted a federation in which they would be equal partners. The Orthodox, Eastern-oriented Serbs had equally clear aims, to form a centralized state, a "Greater Serbia", in which they held the balance of power.

From Bečkerek, Flora's company was moved north to a village across the Tisza river from Scegedin (now Szeged). It was "not very comfortable", she groused. On 6th January she was allowed to leave early for Belgrade, where her company were about to be posted. The penetrating cold of the capital did not improve her spirits. After years of war, it was a grim, dilapidated and miserable place. It was "a one-eyed city, a city of one-legged men... a city of unrelenting cobblestones and broken houses", wrote one unhappy observer.[7] Few shops or hotels were open. Although the worst of the bomb damage had already been repaired, its houses were decaying, its people looked haggard and ill-fed and its streets were full of homeless, orphaned children.

The medical need both in Belgrade and across Serbia was enormous: of the four hundred and fifty doctors in Serbia at the start of the war, only one hundred returned to practice at its end.[8] The country was full of war-shattered, limbless soldiers and emaciated former prisoners, while the civilian population, who had had little access to medical treatment during the war, suffered widely from a range of untreated diseases. The greatest medical problem by far was tuberculosis, a disease that attacked not only the lungs but the bones and joints, causing severe deformities. By the end of the war, an estimated fifty thousand children were dying annually of the disease across the kingdom.[9]

Emily was one of several "old campaigners" who returned to the capital at the end of the war hoping to help. On 11th November 1918, the headline of the *New York Times* shouted out the news that she had been waiting so long to hear, "Armistice Signed, End of the War!" Days later, she sailed across the Atlantic under the auspices of the Commission Internationale de Ravitaillement.[10] No sooner had she reached Belgrade than she went in search of Flora. She found her living in a room in the city, having turned up her nose in disdain at the "filthily dirty" barracks where her regiment had been temporarily quartered.

With the help of Nan MacGlade and Evelina Haverfield, who had also returned to the capital, they threw themselves into a flurry of activity. In the space of about a week they had opened a canteen for former POWs in an empty building in the town. Soon they were handing out tea, cigarettes, underclothing and soup to an average of nine hundred men per day, many of whom were in a "pitiable condition". "We had good fires always going in two stoves," wrote Flora. "We also managed to get benches and tressle-tables [*sic*], and any soldier could come in and have a mug of hot tea, sit there and play games as long as he liked." In early January the four women began planning a second canteen in Belgrade, this time for the men of Flora's Second Regiment who had since been given permanent accommodation in the ancient stone fortress of Gornji Grad, in the capital's central Kalemegdan Park.[11]

Charitable organizations flocked to the country at the end of the war. Although some were led by veteran workers, many were run and staffed by people who were new to Serbia, had no knowledge of the modus operandi and did not speak the language. With little initial coordination between them, they competed with each other for accommodation and governmental support for their particular project.[12] Even the experienced Serbian-speaking workers found things difficult. Those with no experience found things next to impossible. They received little help from government officials, many of whom were dishonest or shared the air of apathy that hung over the city. The Serbs had a tendency to say yes even when they did not mean it, grumbled one onlooker, partly out of politeness and partly out of laziness.[13] Many relief workers soon left in frustration.

Great as the need was, even some of the most experienced organizations appeared to lose their raison d'être. Among the worst affected were the Scottish Women's Hospitals. While the valuable work of the Vranja Unit continued apace, the other three units still in the region began to show early signs of splintering. Their problems, which stemmed largely from dismal management and vicious infighting between their organizing committees in Britain, were compounded by the dispiriting experience of dealing with Serbian officialdom. By January many members of the Elsie Inglis Unit were on their way home and, in March, most members of the Scottish Women's Hospital Transport Column followed suit. The Girton and Newnham Unit remained behind, but planned to transfer from Salonika to Belgrade.

Other organizations that had been active among the Serbs during the war continued their service, with varying degrees of success and longevity. The Serbian Relief Fund set up hospitals, clinics and dispensaries across central Serbia and a workshop for the disabled at Mount Avala, south of Belgrade.[14] The American Women's Hospitals – in effect an American version of the Scottish Women's

Hospitals – had arrived in Macedonia shortly before the end of the war, where they established hospitals, clinics and dispensaries.[15] The American Red Cross poured in both personnel and resources to conduct medical and general relief work across the country.[16] The American Quakers focused their efforts around Niš and Leskovac in central Serbia and Peć in Kosovo. They placed more emphasis than the other units on reconstruction and, uniquely, built two shared villages in the Kosovan "scrubland" for six hundred homeless Montenegrins and Albanians. They had "some disappointments" in trying to make the nationalities cooperate, commented one Quaker observer.[17]

Still, there were several notable longer-term successes, particularly among the projects run and staffed by the old campaigners. Two such veterans cared for orphans at the Anglo-Serbian Children's Home at Niš. Another, Margaret McFie, set up a blind school. Yet another, Annie Dickinson, the School of Carpentry for Orphan Boys.[18] But of all the successes, the greatest by far was Katherine MacPhail's. She had left Macedonia in the summer of 1918 when her father fell ill with Spanish influenza and had hurried back with the vague idea of opening a children's hospital. With no time to make plans, raise funds or bring supplies, she dashed off with "$100 in her pocket and a bottle of aspirin, which had been given her by a well-wisher as she left for Serbia".[19]

The thirty-one-year-old doctor faced the same daunting series of difficulties in establishing a working charitable enterprise as the other relief workers and one additional one – she had no organization to back her. Nonetheless, she had certain things going for her. She spoke fluent Serbian, she knew people willing to help and she was not fussy. When a well-connected friend offered her the use of an old barracks, Katherine looked round it with dismay but accepted nonetheless. The building had been used as stables by the Austrians and had no water or electricity. Most of its windows were broken, it was full of bugs and it was filthy.

First she went to see Admiral Ernest Troubridge, whom she had first met in Belgrade in 1915. Troubridge did not approve on paper of many of the British women then working in Serbia. "Any woman who has some money and wants to adventure herself had been allowed to arrive in Serbia with what is called a 'unit', which apparently is under no one's control and in very many cases the people are quite undesirable," he complained in a reference that would have encompassed the likes of Flora.[20] In practice however he was kind and helpful to them. When Katherine approached him with her plans for her hospital, true to character, he lent her all the help he could, first sending his marines to her barracks armed, this time, with paint and brushes. "They had only dreadnought-grey," commented Katherine drily.[21]

Next she scrounged a few army beds and supplies from friends in other charitable organizations. Within a week she had one of the few going concerns in Belgrade. Thirty-two starving children – many of them critically ill – were lying in her grey-painted wards. "Seeing that Dr MacPhail meant business everyone who had anything to provide did so," noted one observer. "As Dr MacPhail weighs about 100 pounds and stands about five feet tall, it may furnish some indication of how her energy made popular the sympathy which was accorded to her by various relief organizations."[22] The Serbian government donated wooden beds, the British Red Cross agreed to pay the salaries of two nurses, the American Red Cross gave medicine, dressings and a sterilizer, a British general donated bedding, the Serbian Relief Fund agreed to feed the children, the Scottish Women's Hospitals gave money and volunteers offered their services.

With Troubridge's continued support, Katherine's hospital went from strength to strength. By the end of January her thirty-two children lay comfortably in clean, heated wards, she was beginning to carry out operations with the help of Dr Ibbotson, the marine surgeon, and she had started an out-patients department.[23]

With Sandes-Haverfield Canteens up and running in two locations in Belgrade, Flora and Evelina began to broaden the focus of their fund-raising efforts to take account of conditions in Serbia at the end of the war. Their work continued apace on their Canteen Fund, but now they registered a new charitable society. Through the "Hon. Evelina Haverfield and Sergeant Major Flora Sandes Fund for Disabled Serbian Soldiers" they planned to set up a hostel where men maimed by the war could live and be taught new trades.[24]

While Flora remained behind to run the canteens with Emily and Nan, Evelina returned home to London in early 1919. In February, she oversaw the first of a series of fund-raising events. There was a Fancy Dress and Dance at the Piccadilly Hotel, a meeting at the Royal Automobile Club and talks by prominent speakers. There were even plans to have a "Flag Day" during which little paper flags printed with the name of the Fund and the colours of the Serbian flag would be sold in the streets.[25] But by spring, Flora and Evelina's plans had begun to unravel. After years of war and separation from their families, most disabled men preferred instead to return home. Then, in May 1919, a tersely worded note appeared, tucked away in the columns of the *Times*. "Sergeant Major Flora Sandes is severing her connection with Mrs Haverfield's Fund, as she wishes to work for Serbian soldiers only," it announced. "Mrs Haverfield is doing a certain amount of relief work among the wives and families of disabled men, which she feels it is impossible to drop."[26] In the weeks that followed, Evelina broadened her focus on civilian relief by setting up yet another charity, "The Honourable Evelina Haverfield's Fund for Serbian Children", hoping to raise funds to open an orphanage.

CHAPTER 16

TRAVELS

1919–1920

"How would you like to visit the new kingdom?" suggested Flora's colonel in April. "You ought to go. You'd get a chance to see the territory we liberated from the Austrians, and I'll even arrange for you to be given free passes for all the railways and steamers." Flora agreed with alacrity to take the generous six weeks' leave. Leaving Emily in capable charge of the canteens, she packed a few things and set off happily by train.[1]

By the time Flora set out on her long, tortuous journey from Belgrade to Sarajevo, the worst fears of the non-Serb Slavs about how the Kingdom of Serbs, Croats and Slovenes would be governed were being realized. They had hoped for a confederation, an alliance of equals. Instead, when the dust began to settle it became clear that the Serbs held the upper hand in the machinery of state. Belgrade became the capital. The Serbian King, Petar Karađorđević, became the King of the Croats and Slovenes while the Serbian army became the army of the new kingdom. Posts in both government and army were allocated not by competency and merit, but as prizes for loyal military service, and virtually all were given to Serbs. It soon became clear to the Croats and Slovenes that they had exchanged the politically oppressive but essentially competently run Austro-Hungarian civil service for a politically oppressive, incompetent and dishonest Serbian-run one. The Serbs, far from denying that corruption existed, responded to criticism by stating there was little more they could do when ninety per cent of their university students had been killed during the war. As for the possibility of granting some of the posts to able Croats and Slovenes, they countered that they would not award them to men who had served disloyally with the enemy, in the armies of Austria-Hungary.[2]

"On this trip I looked for no adventures," summarized Flora later, "but I find that if there is one within a hundred miles it comes straight for me." The first such one charged her way when she decided to visit Fiume (now Rijeka) on her way to the Dalmatian coast. She had decided to stop off in the port town of fifty thousand inhabitants after travelling, apparently uneventfully, to the largely Muslim town of Sarajevo, followed by the Catholic Croatian capital of Zagreb. She had visited these towns dressed in full Serbian uniform. She now decided to do the same in Fiume. This was not a good idea.

The Italians had marched into Fiume immediately upon the end of the war. In wilful disregard of the fact that the surrounding countryside was almost exclusively Slav and they could only construct an Italian majority in the town by failing to count a Croat suburb, they claimed loudly and disingenuously that it was theirs by right.[3] It was as though, wrote Flora after she had been forcibly acquainted with the situation, that a district of London populated by one group of immigrants had raised their own flag and proclaimed that they were subject only to the laws of their mother country.[4]

When she arrived in Fiume in April 1919, the question of its future status was so contentious that it had led to the temporary withdrawal of the Italian Prime Minister from the Paris Peace Conference and was enough to bring Italians out into the streets of Rome in a wave of nationalist fervour. The Serb position was just as rigid. If the Italians get it, they said, we will fight. The French too were on the ground in the town, attempting to act as buffers between them. For their efforts, several of their soldiers were lynched by mobs of Italian nationalists.[5] Flora must have been warned that her plans of exploring the Italian-occupied town dressed, as she intended, in the uniform of a Serbian sergeant major, would court disaster. Most likely, she just ignored them. On arrival, to the surprise of no one but herself, she was arrested. "[I was] shut up for half a day by the Italians," she later wrote, "until rescued by an English captain."[6] Seemingly no worse for wear, she brushed herself off and sauntered south down the Dalmatian coast in the direction of Montenegro. Five months after Flora's escape, rogue Italian officers under the leadership of Gabriele D'Annunzio set up the first identifiably Fascist government there, the "Free State of Fiume".[7]

When the war ended it was widely assumed both by Serbs and Montenegrins that the two kingdoms would unite. The Serbs wanted it. So too did a majority of Montenegrins, who shared a common language, religion and many cultural traditions with the Serbs. The unification of Serbia with Montenegro would accordingly have been one of the simplest in history, had it not been for spectacularly inept handling by the Serbs.[8] The Serbs were like "a fighting army that has just come out of the trenches after a long hand-to-hand fight, and thinks it may yet be ambushed," wrote one commentator.[9] Seeing subterfuge where none existed, they moved quickly to force unification upon Montenegro. First they poured their troops over the border. Next, under the mendacious, thuggish and violent nationalist Andrija Radović, they drew up arrangements for the election of deputies to a "Great National Assembly", charged with deciding the future status of Montenegro. The "election", on 19th November 1918, was conducted under the supervision of the Serbian army amid widely reported instances of voting irregularities, arm-twisting and bribery. When the chosen deputies met a week later, they voted unanimously to unite with Serbia. "The election was a ridiculous farce," said one American observer disparagingly. "Not a vote was cast contrary to the wishes of the organizers."[10] On 1st December, when the establishment of the Kingdom of the Serbs, Croats and Slovenes was announced, any reference to Montenegro in the title was noticeably absent. It had been subsumed within Greater Serbia.

Although the majority of Montenegrins had supported unification, the manner in which it had been achieved alienated many.[11] At the start of January 1919 the "Greens" – so-called because they had printed their list of pro-independence candidates on green paper – took up arms against the pro-Serbian "Whites". They were promptly squashed by the Serbian army and White militias. It was simply a "minor local uprising" to the war-seasoned Serbs, commented the American observer, "and the leaders of the sad little

1. Samuel Dickson Sandes,
Flora's father

2. Sophia Julia Sandes,
Flora's mother

3. The Sandes family at Marlesford Rectory, in 1893.
Flora is on the bottom right

4. Flora Sandes, aged
about seventeen

5. Samuel Dickson Sandes, Flora's
brother, in British Columbia
around 1900

6. Flora Sandes in her car *c*.1910

7. Flora Sandes and
her pet dog

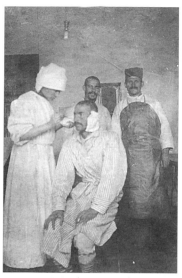

8. Emily Simmonds
operating in Valjevo

9. Emily Simmonds

10. Katherine MacPhail

11. Flora Sandes receiving the Karađorđe Star
in November 1916

12. Amelia Peabody Tileston

13. Samuel Dickson Sandes ("Dick"),
Flora's nephew, in uniform

14. Flora Sandes (front row, second from the left), with officers and men on the eve of the 1918 offensive

15. The Sandes family in uniform in 1918: Victor Newberry (brother-in-law), William (brother), Flora and Dick Sandes

16. Flora Sandes in uniform *c.* 1918

17. Flora and Yurie after their
wedding on 14th May 1927

18. Flora in Bulawayo with Allison
and Richard *c*. August 1945

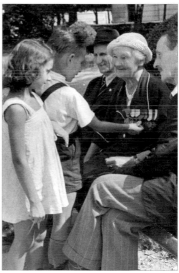

19. Flora during her final visit to
Belgrade, 1954

20. Flora Sandes in June 1956

revolution were thrown in jail."[12] A campaign of terror ensued. The Whites, with the support of the Serbian army, moved to shut down all opposition. They attacked Green villages, looted and burned, stole livestock, took hostages, imprisoned the opposition and, on occasion, executed political prisoners without trial. Armed by the Italians, who wanted to check the territorial ambitions of the Serbs to further their own imperialist aims in the Balkans, the Greens retaliated in kind.[13]

In the wake of years of war, occupation and civil strife, the population began to starve. The Austro-Hungarian invaders had swept the land clean of livestock and food. Nor could the countryside sustain any significant agriculture to help it recover. It was a "wilderness of stones", remarked two unhappy wayfarers. "Imagine a vast sea, storm-tossed into huge waves, and then suddenly solidified into a stony mass."[14] Into a country racked by war and threatened with famine arrived two groups – Allied observers sent to investigate the conditions on the ground at the behest of the Paris Peace Conference and a handful of humanitarian workers. There was also a single tourist – Flora.

At the beginning of 1919 a small unit of the American Red Cross reached the rocky shores of Montenegro, charged with providing much needed emergency relief. In the weeks and months that followed they took over the solitary hospital in the country and set up three more in the major towns. They opened soup kitchens and distributed clothing, ran workshops and sent out district nurses into the villages. The director, Canadian Henry Rushton Fairclough, toadied to Montenegro's Serb governors. Perhaps because he proved himself so uncritical, the Serbs at least allowed his unit to pursue their valuable work, something that they refused to do with other – presumably less accepting – humanitarian organizations, which they unceremoniously ejected from the country.

Unlike Fairclough, the few Allied observers charged with reporting to the Peace Conference were appalled by what they saw. One, Captain James Bruce, the balding, assistant military attaché to the US embassy in Rome, arrived on 1st February. Already in Montenegro was another American, intelligence officer Major Charles Wellington Furlong. From Cambridge, Massachusetts, forty-four-year-old Furlong was clean-shaven and seemingly bookish, an appearance which belied his reputation as a "dashing near-legend", gained from his multifaceted career as an "explorer, writer, painter, soldier, ethnologist and lecturer".[15] Before the war he had led expeditions into Saharan Africa and South America. He was also a champion bull-rider.

Bruce had not met Furlong previously, but he surmised that his remit was much the same as his, "to observe, report and stay alive". "As soon as it was found that I had come to hear both sides of the question obstacles were put in my path," wrote the normally mild-mannered Furlong angrily. In the weeks that followed they were harried, harassed and hounded by Andrija Radović, who was now the Montenegrin premier, and his men. Finally, after clumsy attempts were made on their lives, Bruce fled the country. Furlong remained behind. Other Allied observers, including the official British representative of the Peace Conference, Count de Salis, were treated similarly.[16] Soon their reports reached the ears of the Western press. "The Annihilation of a Nation", shouted one headline, while articles decrying the "Martyrdom of Montenegro" appeared in leading journals.[17]

"To read the English papers one would suppose that the whole of Montenegro is writhing under the oppression of a Serbian Army which has invaded it by force," wrote Flora heatedly in an article, 'A Word for Serbia', intended to contradict what she firmly believed was unwarranted anti-Serbian bias in the press. She had written it after travelling the length of Montenegro in the late spring of 1919, visiting villages and towns en route. By then, most of the insurgents who had led the Green rebellion were dead, imprisoned or taking refuge in the mountains. And she could see that far from everyone was unhappy with the new regime. Large sections of the population, particularly the town-dwellers, were broadly satisfied with the new order. Although she acknowledged that there was still much internal unrest in the country, she put it down to peasant bloody-mindedness. "The fact of the matter is that in some of the outlying villages in Montenegro the peasants... are 'agin the government' on principle, whatever that government may be," she argued. "These *are not* the majority of the population, who, being the same blood as the Serbs, wish to be incorporated with Serbia."[18]

* * *

"My first meeting with Lieut. Flora Sandes was on a troop-laden Serbian army truck in the lonely mountain fastnesses of Montenegro," wrote Charles Furlong.[19] The intelligence officer had been walking down an empty, unpaved road in the grey, rugged mountains above Kotor when he had heard the rumble of army trucks behind him. He had moved over to the side to allow them to pass. "Would you like a lift?" shouted a female voice as the lead truck slowed alongside him. He looked up to see Flora gazing curiously at him out of the truck window.

Earlier that evening she had jumped at the chance to accompany the army on a mission designed to quell a village uprising. She wrote about it later in her article, in an anecdote chosen to argue away the unrest. "One evening when I was staying in a village in Montenegro, I saw a company of *Montenegrin* soldiers in the Serbian Army coming down the road," she recalled. "Where are you going?" she had asked them, in the hope that it was somewhere exciting. "We're off to punish a rebel village which won't lay down their arms," they replied, as Flora's face brightened. When they invited her to join them, she squeezed in alongside them, hoping "to see the fun".

The reddening sun was setting over the violet-shaded mountains by the time they reached the outskirts of the isolated village. Flora, Furlong and three officers walked cautiously towards the cluster of silent, stone houses. Then, in the gloom, they spotted the shadowy faces of a line of men hunched behind the shelter of a low stone wall. On top of the wall rested a line of rifles, pointed directly at them. "Sit down where you are!" barked one of the men. Flora and the men dropped to the ground. "We're unarmed," the officer in charge shouted across to them. "We've come to talk to you." The men whispered a hurried discussion behind the wall. Then they stood up. First they invited the officer to meet the head man. Next they extended the invitation to Flora, Furlong and the other officers. "The entire male population of the village – about twenty – then left their stone wall, and we all shook hands and expressed our mutual pleasure at meeting," wrote Flora incredulously.

The conference began in earnest. "You must put down your arms. You can't defy the whole Serbian army. If you disarm no one will harm you," the officers argued. The villagers shook their heads. "If we do what you say, your army will steal all our cattle," the villagers insisted. At long last, after darkness had descended on the village and Flora's attention had drifted, they reached "some kind of compromise". The villagers handed over their weapons to the Serbian officers, who stacked them in the back of one of the trucks. When the vehicles drove off into the night, Flora and Furlong remained behind in the company of the villagers, two of whom had offered to show them the way through the mountains to Kotor. During their long walk the next day, they confided to them their reason for handing over their weapons. "Tomorrow we'll be given *newer* and *better* ones by the Italians," they said.[20]

In the days that followed Flora charged about Montenegro. She wandered through the narrow, twisting streets of the port town of Kotor. She posed in Serbian uniform for Furlong, an accomplished photographer, and also had her photograph taken in full Montenegrin (male) dress. She attended a ball in Cetinje, the former capital, and was much impressed that the "decorations consisted principally of loaded rifles". When a lorry arrived in the town riddled with bullets, she jumped in alongside the driver – a Montenegrin in the Serbian army, she noted meaningfully – in pursuit of the insurgents who had fired at it. Later she travelled to the southernmost tip of Montenegro to visit Lake Scutari. There, she "came down in a sea plane, which was left a total wreck... whilst a French destroyer and a company of Serbs patrolled sea and land looking for us." When her leave was finally up, she set off back to Belgrade through the heart of Serbia. "I got back from that six weeks' trip," she concluded, "feeling that whatever else life might be, it was never dull."[21]

The Serbia that Flora travelled through on her return from Montenegro was deeply scarred by years of war and occupation. She hitched lifts over muddy, shell-pitted roads, past the skeletal remains of horses, donkeys and oxen, broken trucks and abandoned ammunition.[22] Although a monumental amount of reconstruction remained to be done, there were also signs that conditions were slowly beginning to improve. She saw fields that were green with crops and she was able to travel along the large stretches of the railways that had been mended.

As she had moved through the south of the country, Flora would have also passed barbed-wire-enclosed camps in which some seventy-seven thousand dispirited, war-weary Bulgarians had been interned. After years of war and the brutal treatment of their countrymen by the Bulgarian occupation force, the Serbs were in no mood to treat their former enemy humanely. Instead, they left them to freeze and starve in a country that had sufficient food to feed them.[23]

Throughout the autumn, winter and spring, the sick had been brought in convoys to the Scottish Women's Hospital Unit based in Vranja. With every passing week the prisoners grew weaker. "It often happened that they literally died on the doorstep, in the waiting room or within an hour of coming to us," Dr Emslie added angrily. When she attempted to intercede on their behalf, she was opposed at every turn by Serbian officials. "Gospodica [Miss] Doctor," one told her, "you do not understand how we feel; these Bulgars ought to suffer." "If you do nothing to improve their conditions, you'll have an outbreak of typhus on your hands that will threaten more than just them," she responded angrily.[24]

The first sporadic cases of typhus had appeared, as if on cue, in December 1918. By February the disease was raging through the Bulgarian camps in epidemic proportions: the wards of every hospital across the south of the country were full of delirious patients and cases were appearing in each major town in Serbia. In a smaller-scale repetition of the epidemic of early 1915, the staff of the British units once again began to contract the disease. There was one death, nurse Violet Fraser of the Serbian Relief Fund, who had been attempting to keep Bulgarian prisoners alive by running a soup kitchen for them in the village of Predejane, south-east of Leskovac.[25] By May the epidemic was over. In early June, those still alive in the Bulgarian POW camps were set free to stagger home across the border.[26]

Flora was away on her travels at the end of April when the official list of military promotions was published. It was extensive. Years of war had left the Serbian army bereft of skilled officers while the simmering conflict with Italy and unrest in the new territories meant the country remained on a war footing. In an attempt to fill the many gaps in the ranks, all sergeant majors who had been decorated were automatically promoted to second lieutenants, the first rank of officer class – all except Flora. On her return, her friends broke the news. She did her best to put on a brave face. "That's all right," she told them. "I had never expected it to be." Still, those who knew her well could see how hurt she was by the omission. "It's not fair," they replied adamantly. "You should go to see the commandant."

Bolstered by their support, she booked a meeting with the new battalion commandant, Beli Marković. At the appointed time she duly marched over to his office, stood to attention in front of him, and then let forth a torrent of hurt and grievance. "All my comrades have been promoted while I've been passed over," she told him indignantly as her momentum built. "Either I'm a soldier or not. If I am, then why has a distinction been made? If I'm not, then you might as well demobilize me and let me go home. I've been in the army for nearly four years now. I'm fed up with it anyhow," she told him crossly.

Marković looked at the disgruntled forty-three-year-old English-woman standing before him and stifled a laugh. "An ultimatum, eh!" he replied jovially while holding out a cigarette to her. "Sit down a minute, Sandes, and cool off and let's see what we can do." Flora sat smoking while he leafed through a book of army regulations. "Well, it doesn't say that a woman can't be promoted to commissioned rank," he told her finally. "In fact it doesn't mention women at all. That's in your favour. I'll see what I can do. I will write my own report and opinion of the matter. If no one disagrees, all your reports are good, and Prince Alexander will append his signature, we may possibly have a woman officer in the Serbian army yet."[27]

Flora passed the anxious time waiting for a response by helping in the canteens and on evenings out and about in the restaurants and cafés of Belgrade. She had given up her room in the centre – almost certainly because her funds were running short – in preference for her small, waterproof bivouac tent, which she erected in a small grove of trees near the parade ground of the Grad. The proximity to the canteens meant she only had a short distance to stumble, blurry-eyed, for the six-a.m. start after the latest evening out. And there were nights out aplenty with the men of her regiment and the

English community in Belgrade. Those of the latter who knew Flora only by name took a great interest in her, although her reputation as a fearless, battle-hardened, Boadicea-like figure meant that she was not always quite what they expected when they met her in the flesh. "She is an ordinary, middle-aged female" who was dressed in "full rig and no skirts", wrote one slightly disappointed Red Cross worker after meeting her at a formal reception at Admiral Troubridge's house.[28]

In late June Flora was summoned for a meeting with General Jovanović, the Minister of War. On her arrival at his offices, he wrung her warmly by the hand and congratulated her. She had become the first woman and only foreigner ever to have been commissioned as an officer in the Serbian army. "Don your epaulettes," he told her, as he handed her the shoulder insignia denoting her new rank of second lieutenant. Not only had she been given favourable reports by all the commanders she had served under, Crown Prince Aleksandar had visited the Grad to interview the officers of her regiment about her character. Even then, a special Act of Parliament had had to be enacted to allow a commission to be given to her, which Aleksandar had signed. On her promotion, she was made a "*vodnik*" – platoon officer – and put in charge of around sixty men in the Second Company of the Third Battalion, Second Regiment, Morava Division, First Army.

"I used to think that officers had a soft job," confided one of Flora's fellow second lieutenants, "but I wish now I were a non-com again." Within days of being transferred to the Second Company, she knew exactly what he meant. Every morning bar Sunday the sharp call of the bugle rang out at four a.m., and Flora staggered wearily from her tent, got ready with the help of her batman and, on an empty stomach, joined the rest of her company on the parade ground in the grey dawn. Then, with the other *vodniks*, she either marched her *vod* of around sixty men off to participate in mimic battles or south along the cobbled course to Topčider Park, a brisk hour's walk away. In these verdant surroundings Flora bellowed orders as she wheeled and turned her men in their regulation drills before returning, under the burning summer sun, to the officers' mess in the Gornji Grad. After a noon lunch, she retreated to her shaded tent for a brief siesta. At two thirty p.m.

the bugle sounded again. She emerged blinking into the bright sun and, for three further hours, put her *vod* through a different set of drills, this time within the confines of the Grad. At six she joined everyone on the parade ground for evening prayers before she set out, every third night, as head of a patrol through the silent streets of Belgrade checking on isolated sentries. It meant a dreary, dark three-hour walk and a midnight finish, before the day began again at dawn.

Flora had found her new role daunting at first. Her fame, which she normally enjoyed, this time only served to add to the already great pressure on her. It meant that every officer who happened to be passing while she was drilling her men would stop and watch. "Woe betide me if I made a slip at morning drill," she bemoaned, "for directly I showed my face in the mess room for dinner I would be greeted by a perfect hail of good-natured chaff." Her role was made harder still by the fact that she was not a native Serbian speaker. "Though I could talk it fairly fluently," she explained, "I had to learn so many words of command, and the exact tone in which to give them."[29]

With the assistance of a sergeant major, she learnt fast. She quickly became a familiar sight on the streets of Belgrade, much to the delight of the English staff of the various missions, including Dr Isabel Emslie of the Scottish Women's Hospitals. "Flora Sandes… had a platoon of her own," she wrote proudly. "She could be seen every day goose-stepping with her recruits over the cobbles of Belgrade."[30] The men of her *vod* also took great pride in their famous and unusual *vodnik*. Although they addressed her formally as "Mr Lieutenant", informally she became "*nasa Engleskinja*" ("our Englishwoman"), the fond nickname by which she was by then widely known throughout the army.

Flora had looked the men of her *vod* over worriedly the first time she met them, fearful that they would use every trick in the book to run rings around their new and inexperienced *vodnik*. Instead, to her relief, she found them a "loyal lot" who were willing to cover for her when, at first, she made the odd mistake.[31] The men were a mixed group. She had been put in charge of all the young recruits to her company, the veteran Macedonian-front men and the equally battle-weary Serbs who, by fate of living within Austria-Hungary in 1914, had had to fight for the enemy during the war. Some of the latter suffered language problems at first, she recalled. "They knew the Austrian drill, but not the Serbian, and at first some spoke more German and Hungarian than Serbian."

Loyal as they were, her men could be a handful, particularly her "old soldiers". After years of war, many were "utterly sick" of the army, resentful of army discipline and "incurably lazy". Still, Flora was far from without sympathy for them. "Small wonder," she remarked, "for some of these men, after fighting for four years, had not yet seen their homes."[32] Understanding though she was, they would occasionally tax her patience to the very limit. But soon, in her inimitable management style, she had brought even the most difficult men into line by sending them off with messages and assigning them odd jobs in an effort to keep them as busy as possible.

As the first icy breath of winter swept across the Danube, Flora was ordered to leave her makeshift encampment under the trees of the Gornji Grad. Initially she wondered where on earth she would go. Then, by fortuitous accident, she stumbled across the ruins of a whitewashed stone hut on the ramparts. It was doorless and roofless and not very large, but it had a spectacular view across the river to the flat, seemingly endless plains beyond. "It's a heap of rubble," sneered her colleagues. "Wait, you'll see," she haughtily told them as she staked a claim, cadged the materials she needed to fix it up and set half a dozen of the men of her *vod* to work. Within three days they had it windproof and watertight, and Flora proudly moved in. "See, I told you so," she crowed triumphantly when her fellow officers got their first look at her new winter quarters. "True... the approach was a bit chilly," she admitted, "but with the walls lined with [bast]-matting, a roaring stove going, and half a dozen of us sitting in there, one did not notice the outside cold."[33]

Every evening when she was not on patrol duty, they would drag her from her warm quarters into town. "Be a man," she would be told on the occasions she protested that she was too tired. "Oh, all right," Flora would invariably respond, powerless to resist such a loaded challenge. At the start of the month, after they had been paid, they frequented the restaurants, cinemas, the many cafés and the music hall. By the end of the month, with funds running low, they made do with sitting for hours listening to music in the smoky cafés, drinking local wine and sipping dark, sweet coffee. "Luckily for me I had always been pretty good at sitting up late," she commented later, "for we hardly ever got back before midnight, despite the fact that we had to be up again at 4 a.m." Tired as she often was, she loved the warm companionship of her fellow officers. "There was great camaraderie," she wrote later. "The barracks was our home, and all our interests were in common. It was that which always made the army so fascinating for me, and so different from any other kind of work... Our work and our play were all done together, and our whole life and interests revolved around the regiment."[34]

But for all the cosy camaraderie, Flora admitted to an acquaintance that she found life at the Gornji Grad in peacetime "dull and irksome" after the excitement of the war.[35] In March, in search of greater adventure, she applied to the army for a year's leave. She had thought her request through well. If they would grant it to her she offered to embark on a lecture tour of Australia to benefit Serbia's beleaguered agricultural industry. She would aim both to raise funds from her audiences and generate financial assistance from the Australian government. It would also give Flora, who spent money as fast as she earned it, the chance to travel to Australia for the first time to see her family.

On Thursday 3rd June she hopped off the ship in Adelaide, its first port of call, having assuaged the hardships of a long, tedious voyage by travelling first class. She then travelled by express train to Melbourne, en route to Sydney. Australian governmental, military and press circles were abuzz with the news of her arrival. "It is doubtful whether any woman in any sphere of life... is as wonderful as this soldier – a woman – a wonder – a woman who dared – and yet [is] so modest about her own achievements" trumpeted the *Daily Examiner* of Grafton, New South Wales.[36] She is the "Woman's champion", added the paper, while others feted the arrival of "a modern Amazon", "a real heroine" and the "new woman".[37]

Those unfamiliar with her exploits were instead able to recognize her as the sister of the renowned novelist, poet and journalist John Sandes, who had emigrated to Australia when Flora was just eleven years old. Watched by journalists and throngs of curious onlookers,

John proudly grasped her hands in welcome as she stepped down onto the station platform in Melbourne.[38] Her fifty-seven-year-old brother had returned to Australia only a few days previously, having been selected to accompany the Prince of Wales (the future King Edward VIII) on a seven-month-long colonial tour. He had been given this most prestigious, enviable and coveted post due to his unwavering support for the Empire and the King, and because he could therefore be trusted to send back suitably uncritical descriptions of the Prince's progress. By the time he met Flora he had already reported on the "tumultuous" welcomes and the "affectionate" farewells given to the Prince from Barbados, Hawaii, Fiji and New Zealand.

Flora stepped off the train in Sydney's busy Central Station two days later under chilly skies, as usual kitted out in full Serbian uniform, her medals pinned across her chest. On hand to extend an official welcome were the District Commandant of New South Wales and the Chief Staff Officer of the Australian Forces.[39] Pressing forward excitedly behind them were cheering crowds of Serbian-Australian well-wishers, who mobbed her from all sides in an attempt to shake the hand of the woman who embodied the pride they felt in the Serbian contribution to the Allied victory – "our brave warrior", they called her. A representative of the community stepped forward to present her with a large bouquet while another gave a brief speech in Serbian in her honour. "The name of Flora Sandes is engraved on every Serbian heart," he pronounced. She stumbled through a few impromptu words in gratitude to the shouts of *"Zivila!"* ("Long live [Flora]!") before she was whisked away to the Hotel Australia for a reception in her honour. There she posed for pictures draped in a Union Jack and a Serbian flag, signed autographs and graciously accepted an illustrated address that described her grandly as the "reincarnation of Joan of Arc".[40] Later that day, she had hardly caught her breath before she was introduced to the Prime Minister and was having tea with the Governor General and his wife.[41]

Over the days that followed Flora was flooded with invitations to various functions. Although all of New South Wales was then preoccupied with the royal visit, several members of parliament found time to welcome her and she was given the chance to explain the purpose of her visit to the Minister for Defence during an audience he granted her.[42] There were garden parties, dinners and formal receptions, along with an appearance at the horse races.[43] There was also an invitation to the most prestigious event of all, a ball attended by the Prince of Wales at Government House. While others looked on enviously, Flora's brother John introduced her to the Prince. "She... appeared in uniform, booted and spurred, her breast covered with decorations," recorded Louis Mountbatten, the Prince's nineteen-year-old cousin. "HRH chatted with her for some while, but couldn't bring himself to dance with her."[44]

"Perhaps you wonder why I have come all the way out here to Australia to tell you about Serbia which is so small and far away, and sometimes in danger of being forgotten," began Flora nervously from the stage of Sydney's King's Hall to her first audience on 3rd July. "Well it is just because Serbia is so far away that it is sometimes forgotten that the Serbian government asked me to come out and tell you something about the Serbian people, and the Serbian army to which I have the honour to belong, because I have lived with them for the last six years they think I know them better, and possibly understand them better than most people who have been over there."[45]

Her largely female audience looked up at her admiringly as she stood erectly before them dressed in khaki uniform, leggings and shiny, spurred top boots, an officer's swagger cane by her side, her short grey hair newly trimmed for the occasion. Her talk was a great success. It was colourful, unpretentious, self-effacing and full of humorous anecdotes. She started by outlining, briefly, the key points of Serbian history, before describing how she had nursed the grievously wounded in Kragujevac and survived the horrors of typhus in Valjevo. She explained how, during the retreat across Albania, she had joined the army and told them how she was rescued by her colleagues after she was wounded. She spoke about her recovery, of her time in the trenches, of the suffering, endurance and bravery of the ordinary Serbian soldiers and their great victory in 1918. After the interval she showed them lantern slides, some graphic, of photographs from the Serbian front. She ended her talk with an appeal for funds. "The men have lost their all in helping the Allies to win the war," she told them. "In peace they are a splendid, resourceful race, and with a little help they will soon be on their feet again."[46] As Flora thanked her listeners, she was given a standing ovation while the State Governor rose to his feet. "I have not heard of anything finer, or brighter, or more natural, or more modest, or more skilful than the work of Lieutenant Flora Sandes," he announced to the cheers of the audience, who pressed forward to shake her hand.[47]

The pending arrival of "Lt Flora Sandes" was advertised in newspapers all along the coast of New South Wales during the chilly month of July, as Flora slowly made her way north, on what was nothing short of a gruelling schedule. She gave both matinee and evening performances in larger towns, while virtually every hamlet en route, as long as it could provide a stage and a bed, also received a visit. Many of her appearances were accompanied by a flurry of activity. She was given civic receptions and tours of local hospitals and amenities. Red Cross ladies held afternoon teas and dinners in her honour, mayors welcomed her to the stage of their town halls and large audiences listened intently to her now-practised lectures.[48] But as her tour extended into the cold, wet month of August, the numbers at her lectures began, on occasion, to wane and the papers were sometimes only able to report "fair" or "moderate" attendances.[49]

Nevertheless, the press continued to comment widely on her visit. "She is a very manlike and martial lady, wearing military coat and cap over uniform top boots, and spurs, and carries a military cane," commented one paper. "The lieutenant is neither Amazonian nor petite," observed another. Still others speculated on what the ambiguous appearance of the chain-smoking, trousered second lieutenant meant for the future of womanhood. But most reports simply commented favourably on her lectures and her "amazing endurance and fortitude".[50]

She cared less about what the press said about her than her cause, in the knowledge that she needed to capitalize on her unusual appearance. But to her dismay, before she had stood behind her first lecture podium, she had received her first indication that she might struggle to attract much help for Serbia's agricultural industry. "We are not sure of Serbia," wrote one reporter from Sydney, "and our hands are very full of our own needs." The comment upset her deeply. "This hurts!" she scribbled miserably alongside it.[51]

Although Flora had isolated successes – she managed in one night alone to collect a staggering £300 (the equivalent today of over £9,350) from an audience in Sydney – by mid-August her hopes had been dashed that she would achieve her ambitions. Most of those who came to hear her speak paid a small admission fee, listened intently to her account of her adventures, clapped enthusiastically and left without making further significant donations. Flora was worried that her lectures might not even cover her costs. Forced to lower her aims, she told the press dejectedly that she was "not appealing for money but... to finance [the] tour from Belgrade and return, the Serbian government not being in the position to do so."[52] Nevertheless, she kept faith that her audiences with the Prime Minister, Governor General and Minister for Defence would result in offers to sell agricultural machinery and supplies to Serbia on beneficial terms. But these hopes too met with bitter disappointment when, as week followed week, she began to realize that their polite interest was unlikely to translate into practical help. Still, she continued her tour of the Australian coast into September and October, and was able to retreat into the warm embrace of her sister Meg's large family at their farm near the town of Inverell.

In late January an abrupt notice appeared in the papers. "Miss Sandes has been lecturing throughout New South Wales and Queensland, but her director [Rose Venn Brown] has found it necessary to cancel the lectures in this and the western States, as Miss Sandes is due back in Serbia."[53] However, Flora appears to have been in no rush whatsoever to rejoin her regiment. She applied to the army, who were expecting her back in March, for an additional six months' leave. With it duly granted – and declaring her occupation as "soldier" and her age as a relatively youthful thirty-eight (she was in reality forty-five) – she set sail on a round-the-world trip that encompassed Samoa, Honolulu, San Francisco, Los Angeles, Chicago and New York. Finally, in June, she arrived back in England en route for Belgrade, tired and penniless but happy.

All the while relief work had continued apace across Serbia. With the onset of warmer weather the previous spring, Emily had turned her attentions from the soldiers' canteen in the Gornji Grad to running the "Children's Fresh Air Camp" at Mount Avala, ten miles south of the capital, with the assistance of a Major Simpson of the Salvation Army.[54] Amelia was far from keen at the prospect of working alongside her. "I find that Miss Simmonds is to run a camp for three hundred poor children," she wrote gloomily to her mother. "Everyone is doing children's work, and I like soldiers much better."[55]

Still, at the beginning of August she joined Emily at the camp. With the help of Miss Tibbets, a "pleasant, middle-aged Englishwoman", and several German prisoners, they erected a dozen large tents, dining pavilions and a field kitchen on a hillside under some trees amid rolling, leafy countryside.[56] On 4th August the first three hundred children arrived from Belgrade. "Oh, but it's hot," Amelia scribbled in a letter to her sister later that month. "Our days are very full; they begin at half-past six and end at nine, or so. I go down and superintend the children's breakfast, nearly four hundred of them; then I dash up, and see that our breakfast is OK... Then I see who is sick, give out clothes, see about dinner and supper, and that the lanterns are lighted, and so forth." Any children identified by Amelia as sick were handed over to Emily, who was also in charge of its small dispensary. A multitude of children arrived for her to check over. She had cases of toothache, whooping cough, measles and malaria, along with the ubiquitous problem of head lice.[57] She sent the sickest down the slope to the nearby hospital camp run by the Girton and Newnham Unit of the Scottish Women's Hospitals.

The Unit had arrived in May from Salonika. They first established a small hospital in the centre of Belgrade while placing the bulk of their efforts and ambitions on their camp in Avala. With the help of the Serbian Relief Fund they planned to turn it into a flagship "rehabilitation colony" to provide orthopaedic treatment and occupational training for disabled soldiers. By June the women had erected a series of bell tents on a picturesque but muddy stretch of grassland and converted a number of wooden sheds into workshops. Once it was finished the camp could accommodate "half the disabled of Serbia", wrote Francesca Wilson, a veteran of relief work among the Serbs. But sadly, she added, "not many came".[58]

Francesca Wilson had travelled uncomfortably to Belgrade from central Serbia, where she had been working for the Serbian Relief Fund. Not only did her lorry keep breaking down on the rough, muddy roads, she had been travelling with Evelina Haverfield, and Evelina did not like her. "She was slender, dark and intense, and had a biting tongue," Francesca commented later as she recalled the awkward silences and haughty contempt that Evelina had subjected her to. "I admired her extremely – in any case there was a kind of loneliness and vulnerability about her that would have made it impossible for me to dislike her. But unfortunately she hated me. She had a fine scorn of people who, like me, had had soft jobs in soft places [Corsica and Bizerte] with Serbs in their exile."[59]

After her disagreement with Flora over the future focus of their relief efforts, Evelina had returned to Serbia in the spring of 1919 with money to open an orphanage. Francesca had met her as she was travelling, often with great hardship, through the country searching for a suitable site. In the autumn she finally decided to set up one in Bajina Bašta in mountainous, windswept western Serbia. The remote village appealed to her proclivity for discomfort. Not only was it over twenty miles from the nearest railway, it was also impossible to reach by car.[60] Its isolation virtually guaranteed from the outset that she would have to run herself ragged to ensure the delivery of sufficient supplies. Nevertheless, by the onset of winter, with the help of a handful of staff and her partner Vera Holme, she had managed to house sixty abandoned children in one of its few two-storey buildings.[61]

Autumn was in the air when Emily and Amelia packed up the Children's Fresh Air Camp on 6th October, in wooded countryside that was, by now, richly coloured with tints of red and orange. In the two months the camp had operated it had been a great success. Several hundred children had returned home with sun-browned faces, eager to tell their parents of their adventures and to show off the new clothes that Amelia had distributed to them. Although Amelia had continued to avow in her letters home that it was not work that she liked, she had thrown herself into it unreservedly, with relatively good grace. Her missives were soon littered with clumsy appeals, this time for children's clothing. As she neared the end of her stay, she worked proudly among her chattering, excitable young charges, and was pleased to see them all looking "much better for their stay here".[62]

The staff of the Girton and Newnham Unit remained behind in their adjacent camp, enjoying clear, brisk days outdoors. But within days, their rural idyll was shattered as the weather deteriorated. "It was foolish of the Serbs, who knew the climate, to have chosen this site," criticized Dr Isabel Emslie following a visit. Disaster struck in the middle of the month. The winds rose, thunder rumbled and heavy rain began to whip their tents. As the storm raged overhead, a nearby ravine filled with water before spilling tons of mud onto their camp below, sweeping away wooden walls and tents. Amid the chaos, lightning struck and killed one of their patients, "a poor fellow with trench feet who was just looking forward to going home".[63]

The storm was the final straw in what had been a slow process of disillusionment. The women had not been able to provide the orthopaedic treatment they had hoped to disabled soldiers and they had struggled with their Edinburgh-based organizing committee, which had steadfastly refused to sanction any of the alternative schemes they suggested.[64] Above all, they were utterly fed up with dealing with Serbian officialdom. "It gradually dawned on us that the Serbs didn't want us any more," commented one of their doctors bitterly.[65] With their camp in ruins, the women left Avala for good. They salvaged what they could of their equipment and joined the rest of their unit at their small hospital in the centre of Belgrade.

Theirs was now the sole unit of the Scottish Women's Hospitals in Serbia. In late September, Dr Emslie, the head of the Vranja Unit – who felt strongly that they *were* wanted by the Serbs – was left stunned when the "old committee ladies" ordered her to disband. After donating their equipment to a small civil hospital in the town, they closed their doors for the last time on 16th October.[66]

By the end of November Emily and Amelia were putting the finishing touches on their new project, the "American Free Canteen", in a large room on the ground floor of an ornate but dilapidated former hotel directly across from Belgrade's central station. The location, at least, was ideal for handing out tea and cigarettes to the shabby, tired soldiers, just discharged from the army, who were passing daily through Belgrade by train and boat. With the help of a number of POWs, Emily and Amelia had replaced the windows and doors, scrubbed and whitewashed it from top to bottom, and put in rough wooden benches and tables. By the time they had finished, the "very clean and cheerful" room was the only warm place where the near-penniless soldiers could sit without paying. Soon, the canteen was receiving between seven and eight hundred men per day.[67]

Within days of opening their doors, Emily and Amelia were scrambling to secure the permissions they needed to turn an adjacent room into a centre for soldiers who arrived in the dead of night with nowhere to go. "The [railway] station is unheated," explained Amelia in a letter to a donor. "And at four in the morning, the men are knocking at the door, begging to be let in out of the cold." Over the weeks that followed they begged and borrowed socks, gloves and shirts from other relief missions to hand out to the ill-dressed men and, when the city authorities began to use the rooms of the hotel to house destitute families and soldiers waiting to be fitted with artificial limbs, they helped care for those who fell ill.[68]

By December, with their POWs hard at work alongside them, they were able to steal a few moments to stand back and gaze over their warm, busy rooms with pride. Soon Emily felt able to leave Amelia to oversee the operations. "There was not enough work for both of us," she explained. "[The canteen] was entirely Amelia's. I only helped her get it started and in running order."[69] When she was approached by Helen Scott Hay, the European Director of Nursing Services for the American Red Cross, to take charge of the repatriation of POWs in Dubrovnik on the Adriatic coast, she accepted. Although she must have baulked initially at the thought of working for the organization that had treated her so harshly, she knew that the work would be challenging and interesting, and that it would allow her to make a difference to the lives of the ragged and ill men who were streaming home via the port town after years in captivity.[70] Recruiting Emily was nothing short of a coup for Miss Hay, who would have struggled to find anyone else with her combination of language and organizational skills. She had one further qualification that made her nearly unique – the Red Cross had decided to put her in charge of their efforts to combat typhus among the returning former prisoners, and Emily was immune.

On 26th January 1920 Emily caught the train to Dubrovnik. Although she knew that Amelia planned to keep the canteen open only until the onset of warmer weather at the end of March, she worried that she would push herself too hard. "Promise me you'll return home for a rest in April," Emily begged before leaving. "Don't worry. You know me. I'll be fine," Amelia responded reassuringly. But in a letter to one of her many beleaguered but generous donors, Amelia admitted for the first time that she was feeling tired. "I shall be awfully glad to go home," she wrote, "as I don't think my powers of working are inexhaustible."[71]

At quarter to four every morning Amelia dragged herself from her bed to the icy canteen kitchen downstairs. She lit the stove, made tea and, with the help of her soldiers, lugged the great can across the slippery, snow-covered road to the railway station. On the dim platform, she handed round steaming cups to the cold, exhausted soldiers who were waiting for the early-morning train. "I am very busy," she scribbled home to a friend.

> I also give cigarettes to the other soldiers on it, and, when I have them, socks, sweaters and shirts to the men who... are going home in old clothes, without coats or blankets... I also give cocoa or rice pudding to forty children in the house, look after the sick people, and am to run the kitchen for the invalided soldiers who spend a few days in Belgrade, seeing about artificial limbs... I have about seven hundred a day in the canteen, besides sleeping accommodations for about a hundred and fifty.[72]

Amelia had disregarded all of Emily's admonitions to rest. She struggled on through the bitterly cold, sunless winter seemingly unable to turn down any request made of her, despite her growing fatigue. On Wednesday 11th February she fell ill. Assuming that it was simply another attack of malaria that would soon pass, she retreated to her bed in her room above the canteen, shivering with cold and fever. Six days later, suffering from pneumonia, she was brought in critical condition to the nearby hospital run by the Scottish Women. There she was nursed night and day, but the attacks of malaria she had suffered since 1917 had weakened her heart. On 22nd February she died from heart failure brought on by pneumonia. She was one of their last patients. The following month, their Edinburgh-based organizing committee ordered them to disband. With that order, five years of remarkable work for the Serbs fizzled to a depressing and anticlimactic end.[73]

A wire reached Emily in Dubrovnik telling her of her friend's death. No doubt shocked to the very core at the news, she hurried back to spend early March packing away her possessions, closing the canteen and sorting out her financial affairs. She also spent long hours writing to Amelia's mother and sister, trying to comfort them as best she could. "You have cause to be proud of Amelia," she said. "Looking back, it seems to me that she somehow must have known, and was trying to get it all into the shortest space of time."[74] At her own request Amelia was buried in Belgrade.

A month later, on 21st March, Evelina Haverfield died following a battle with pneumonia in the village of Bajina Bašta. "My word did she love the Serbs and worked so hard for them to the very end," wrote Dr Isabel Emslie. "She would go through anything in the way of hardship and did till the time of her death."[75]

Few Allied women in Serbia had died so heroically. Although their irrational prejudices and, in some cases, unpleasant temperaments had sometimes made life a misery for those around them, their work had allowed them to transcend their own difficult and divisive characters while lending them a purpose that their leisured and privileged backgrounds had never hitherto been able to give them.

CHAPTER 17

FRONTIER TROOPS

1922

Throughout the war Flora's British nationality had never been a problem. She had been allowed to enlist and serve in the army for its duration, and had been promoted time and again. Even when she had been forced to fight to be commissioned as an officer her sex and not her nationality had been at issue. But on her return to Serbia in September 1921, after a summer spent vacationing with her family in England, she found that for the first time her foreign status put her at a disadvantage. Conflict with Italy was no longer likely, and all "reserve" officers – those who had joined the army for the duration of the war, like Flora – had been demobilized. Only "regular" officers – those for whom the army was a career – could serve as *vodniks*, and to be a regular officer it was necessary to be a Serbian citizen.

Still, she had a choice. Those who did not wish to leave the army could join the Granična Trupa – the Frontier Troops – instead. And Flora did not wish to be demobilized. "I never loved anything so much in my life," she said once of her time in the army.[1] She duly applied to join and, in February of the following year, was sent to the village of Cavtat on the Adriatic coast, near Dubrovnik, to become *vodnik* of the Second Vod, Thirteenth Company, of the Frontier Troops in Dalmatia. There she was charged primarily with helping to tackle the roaring trade in "excellent" tobacco that was smuggled over the mountains from nearby Herzegovina and across the water from Italy.

Flora had heard that her *vod* would be composed largely of White Russians, opponents of the Bolsheviks who had been forced to flee their homeland in 1920. She had also been told that high-ranking ex-officers of the defeated Imperial Russian army would be expected to serve under her as her sergeants. Flora's imagination ran wild as to what they would be like. "I had not previously met any Russians," she wrote, "so pictured to myself getting some fat, old colonel as sergeant; probably with a bushy beard… and was, if anything, rather pleased at the idea of getting some of my own back by making him take a bit of exercise."

Instead, when she stepped off the steamer that had carried her to the picturesque little bay at Cavtat, she was met by "a tall, clean-shaven young man, who stood at attention, and reported to me very correctly, but with a wicked and sarcastic twinkle in his eye." The thirty-three-year-old Russian artillery colonel introduced himself to Flora as Yurie Yudenitch. "Heaven help me if I am going to be held responsible for *that* sergeant's good behaviour for the next year or so," thought Flora to herself, all the while wondering "if there were many more like him".

And there were worse places that she could have been sent. As she was driven to her base of Mlin (now Mlini), to her left she looked out over the intense, azure blue of the Adriatic. To her right rose the rugged, scrub-covered peaks of the Dalmatian Alps, while fruit trees, palms and cypresses reached their branches upwards to the cloudless skies. Mlin too, she thought, with its rocky beaches and terracotta-roofed, tall stone houses, was "a lovely little village".[2]

Despite her intriguing reception and the beauty of her surroundings, she found the first weeks difficult. Not only had she been separated from her many friends in Belgrade, she had also been put in charge of men who, she strongly suspected, resented her presence. For once, she was intimidated. "Some of the men," she wrote, "were holding aloof and watching critically, or so it seemed to me." She was intimidated most by Yurie. "[He] had more at the end of his little finger concerning military matters than I could ever have learnt in a lifetime," commented Flora, who felt keenly that the former colonel must have found the obligation humiliating to have to "salute a lieutenant and take orders from him, or worst still, *her*."

Not only did she feel friendless and lonely at first, she soon realized that she had been given a near impossible task. From Mlin, where she was quartered with her batman Ivan, four or five men and a Russian sergeant, Flora was expected to patrol an irregular shoreline from Cavtat to Zaton, a headland beyond Dubrovnik. In all she had been given between thirty and forty men, distributed between five bases, to defeat an army of smugglers, many of whom were peasant women who simply tied sheaves of tobacco under their layered petticoats. "It was like a blind kitten being put into a haystack full of rats, and being expected to distinguish itself," explained Flora.[3]

The story behind the arrival of Flora's White Russians was one of almost unimaginable tragedy. By the autumn of 1920 the men of the anti-Bolshevik White Army had suffered defeat after defeat at the hands of the communist Red Army until they had been driven to the Crimean peninsula at the far reaches of Russian territory. With the Bolsheviks poised to hurl themselves on the cornered Whites, an assortment of Allied and Russian ships rushed to evacuate a mass of terrified refugees and bedraggled, defeated soldiers. Nearly one hundred and fifty thousand were taken first to Constantinople. The majority were then sent to camps in French-occupied Gallipoli, including twenty-five thousand White Russian officers and soldiers, among them Flora's sergeants.[4]

In 1921, after a winter of hunger and disease, the camps across Turkey began to empty as the refugees found homes in the capitals of Europe. Thirty thousand alone – many of them teachers, doctors, engineers and professional soldiers – were accepted by the Serbian government.[5] As they embarked on their new lives, they were haunted by the thoughts of what had become of the families they had been forced to leave behind. Those from aristocratic and privileged backgrounds suspected that, at best, they would face a life of penury and hardship and, at worst, they would be subjected to the same sort of savagery that had led to the brutal assassination of the Romanov royal family.

Flora had her hands full managing her Russians. Although they were a "rackety company", she also had great sympathy for them. "They were torn with anxiety about their families left behind in Russia, and were, besides, badly equipped and badly fed," she commented. She also implied they drank heavily. "Money was given in lieu of rations, so that it was no wonder that they sometimes tried to forget their troubles." Despite her difficult start, Flora was happy to report within weeks they had all become "good friends". "We all shook down," she explained.[6] And she returned their friendship and loyalty as only she could. Soon she had bales of clothes arriving not just for her *vod* but for her entire company.[7]

Of all of her men, she got on best with Yurie. By the early summer she was spending increasing amounts of time in the company of her polished, educated and handsome young sergeant. She was staggered by what she heard of his experiences. He was the son of a state advisor. His well-off family had sent him to a prestigious military college in St Petersburg where he had graduated with first-class honours. Athletic, hard-working and bright, he had risen rapidly through the ranks. In July 1914 the then twenty-six-year-old lieutenant had marched off to battle against the Austro-German army. The following month, in East Prussia, he was grievously wounded by a grenade in battle. He was later awarded the Order of St Vladimir for courage, which must have been scant recompense for the year he spent making a painfully slow recovery in hospital, so grave were his injuries. In 1916 he was finally able to return to the front as a commander of anti-air forces. Two years later, after the Revolution that swept the Bolsheviks into power, he was one of many ex-Imperial Russian army officers to join the White Army. Throughout 1919 and 1920, as part of the Artillery Division, he survived a continuous series of battles until he was evacuated from the Crimea. On 22nd November 1920 he arrived in Gallipoli, tired, exhausted and traumatized by his experiences. His aristocratic wife Elena and baby daughter Natalie had been unable to escape. He certainly knew that he would never see them again. It is also possible that he never knew what fate met them.[8]

Flora had at first, as the "new broom", thrown herself wholeheartedly into the task of catching a "real smuggler". She had spent every night for over a week perched halfway down a cliff overlooking a secluded bay with one of her Russians – almost certainly Yurie – who politely refrained from pointing out the utter futility of the exercise. "We… never got the sniff of a smuggler's lair or hide," she wrote dejectedly. From that point on she resigned herself to doing the only things that she could. She went through the motions of searching for ever-elusive smugglers, wrote a report to her captain every fortnight, and visited her men weekly at their posts, often rowing out to see them in her rowing boat, which she had promptly christened "Blighty".[9]

At weekends she would dash the seven miles north to the walled town of Dubrovnik in the company of Yurie and her Russians. As evening descended they walked through the maze of narrow streets, piled into restaurants and sat out in cafés in the soft heat, as swifts screamed and raced overhead. "I just slept at the hotel," she scribbled happily to her friend Vera Holme of her exploits one night, "and not very much of that as I make up there for lonely evenings in Mlin, I got carried off by force to the Ruski Dom [Russian Invalids "Club", for disabled war veterans] on Sunday evening about 11 p.m., drank until 3 a.m., then slipped away to leave them at it."[10]

It was, by and large, a happy summer, spent in the increasingly warm friendship of her new colleagues, along the rocky, sun-drenched shores of the clear, blue Adriatic. But content as she often was, she suffered severely with her men from poor provisioning. "The shortage of food here is growing worse, I only get a square feed when I go into Dubrovnik," she complained to Vera. And there were the flies to contend with in the sticky heat of summer. "What did you say kept [them] away?" she asked her. "They won't let me sleep now, please drop me a line."[11]

She also pined for British company. In Belgrade, the British "colony" had always been on hand. In Mlin, she had no one even to speak English with. When reports reached her in August that a ship had anchored off Dubrovnik carrying the First Lord of the Admiralty, Viscount Arthur Lee, Flora duly dashed over to introduce herself to him. "She came into his cabin; a most military figure with short grey hair, in Serbian uniform with sword, revolver, spurs and the smartest of salutes and clicking of heels," recorded his wife. "[Arthur] found her very interesting, and she seemed much gratified at being 'given an audience by a British cabinet minister'. She then saluted again and returned to her post on the mountain frontier."[12]

Flora's desire for British company would have been sharpened all the more by her knowledge that she had missed Emily by months and Katherine by weeks. By a strange turn of coincidence, both women had also worked in Dubrovnik in the early months following the war. At the end of January 1920 Emily had taken charge of American Red Cross efforts to combat typhus, particularly among former POWs. She organized hospitals and took charge of a disinfecting station where men were stripped, shaved and scrubbed before being handed clean, lice-free clothes from a warehouse she also ran. Over the course of the following months twenty-seven thousand men passed through her capable hands. When her efforts and the onset of warmer weather diminished the threat from the louse-borne disease, she took charge of the distribution of relief in the barren mountains of Dalmatia and Bosnia-Herzegovina. Finally, in October, when the American Red Cross withdrew from the region, she worked in conjunction with its non-Serbian speaking head, Major George Lyon, in ensuring the efficient transfer of their remaining supplies to hospitals and orphanages. He was full of praise for her. "Her duties frequently call[ed] her into conference with the highest officers of the Jugoslav government," he wrote, "when her tact, ingenuity and persistence enabled her to obtain excellent results."[13] It was her final remit of any note in the Balkans. In December 1920 the modest, unassuming nurse sailed for home.

In February 1920, just over a year after she had established Serbia's first children's hospital, Katherine opened a sanatorium in a borrowed villa in Lapad, a prosperous and leafy suburb of Dubrovnik. The convalescents were the dozens of children, many afflicted by tuberculosis, who crowded the wards of her "Anglo-Serbian Children's Hospital".[14] Although she had since transferred them from the bug-infested barracks to a large, grey-stone house in central Belgrade, she was all too aware that, light and airy as it was, it was inadequate to provide the only known treatment – rest, healthy food, fresh air and, above all, sun – for a disease that would otherwise progressively twist and contort their young limbs and bodies. For that, she needed an open-air facility that she could use all year round.

Her first patients were driven down a long avenue of tall cypresses, through a set of wrought-iron gates, into two acres of garden in which the limestone building lay among geranium-lined terraces. Within its spacious grounds roughly forty-five children were cared for by an assortment of British and Slav nurses and workers, including Katherine's sisters Annie and Isabel. "Every day a sister led a little band of children out through a postern door," wrote a visitor, "down cobbled paths and steps, among semi-tropical trees and flowers, to the little bay, and there they bathed and basked naked in the sun."[15]

Just as Flora prepared to travel to nearby Mlin to join the Frontier Troops, Katherine was informed that the villa had to be returned to its original owner. In February 1922, after she had helped hundreds of pale, sickly children return to health, she sadly closed the doors for the final time and handed over the keys.[16] Short-lived as the success was, it made her all the more determined to secure a permanent facility for such children.

Towards the end of the summer, Flora was deeply troubled by widespread rumours that the Frontier Troops were to be disbanded and its men demobilized. So too was Yurie, who must have been acutely aware that demobilization would leave him without a home or a job, let alone prospects of furthering the military career to which he had devoted much of his life. When word reached them that volunteers were being sought for companies to guard the Albanian and Bulgarian frontiers against irregular forces, they seized upon them. They spent long hours deeply engrossed in conversation about putting together a unit. Yurie eagerly sounded out the men. "Most of them will volunteer," he reported back to Flora, "but only on the condition that you'll agree to take charge, and that I'll be second-in-command." "I'll get some of the Salonika Front men together who were with me during the war," Flora replied enthusiastically.[17] But their fanciful musings of taking joint command of a "hand-picked company of devils, Russians and Serbs mixed" came crashing down about them with an order restricting Russians to the regular Frontier Troops.

During the final week of October, Flora received the news she had been dreading. "Collect your men at headquarters in Cavtat," she was ordered. Once there, she was told, they would all be handed their demobilization papers. So sudden was the news that, as she dashed along the coast that week to her outposts and hurriedly threw her belongings together, she had barely time to mull over the implications.

On 31st October 1922, after presenting herself at headquarters with her men, Flora became a civilian after almost seven years in the army. She hardly knew where to begin. The thought of building a new life for herself and becoming an "ordinary woman" again filled her with dismay. "It was like losing everything at one fell swoop," she wrote miserably, "and trying to find bearings again in another life and an entirely different world."[18] Demobilization must have turned Yurie cold with fear. Overnight he had become an unemployed refugee with few job prospects in a country with a war-ravaged economy. But by the time they were handed their papers – evidently unceremoniously – Flora and Yurie were inseparable friends, while their long hours of planning a jointly run unit had laid the groundwork for a decision they must have both taken at this time, to remain together after the war. When Flora made her way to Belgrade, it is almost certain that Yurie came with her.

Flora's first task in the capital was to buy herself some clothes. She peered dejectedly into windows and traipsed gloomily between shops, still dressed in Serbian uniform. As awkward as she felt, she retained enough of her sense of the absurd to be amused by the reactions that met her attempts. "I shall never forget one shop assistant's amazement when I went in uniform to try on a hat!" she exclaimed.[19] But when she returned home to put on her purchases, she felt almost ill as she looked in the mirror. "I felt neither fish nor flesh when I came out of the army," she said sorrowfully. "The first time I put on women's clothes I slunk through the streets."[20]

Just as difficult was remembering to behave as a woman. "For a long time, when walking down the street, I had to clench my hand to keep from saluting mechanically, and from taking off my cap when entering a house or restaurant," she wrote. "It was impossible, at first, to remember not to click the heels together when introduced to anyone... nor to wait until I was asked instead of saying, 'Come along, where shall we go tonight?'"[21] And, in December, when she arrived by taxi at the British legation for the annual Christmas party, Katherine MacPhail watched in dismay as Flora gingerly lifted the hem of her borrowed evening gown and thrust an army-booted foot out the door. The British minister looked at Katherine's horror-struck face and stepped in to the rescue. "Come on in, Sandes," he told her with a smile. "It really doesn't matter."[22]

Worse still, her discomfiture at her appearance was matched by that of her old comrades, who were shocked to see the former "Mr Lieutenant" in hats and dresses. "Run upstairs and find my old uniform," her former commander asked his wife when Flora visited him in the south of the country a few months later. "I can't stand seeing Sandes wearing women's clothes."[23] "I don't know where I am with you nor how to talk to you, dressed like that," he explained to Flora. "My metamorphosis... lost me all my old pals," she reflected sorrowfully. "Though still friendly they were now quite different. Never again could it be quite the same. As I had long ago had occasion to notice, men are never quite so naturally themselves where there are women present, as when among themselves. Formerly they had been so used to me that I did not count." She missed their company terribly. "It always seemed to me that men took life much more easily and straightforwardly than women," she commented.[24]

Peace came as little short of a calamity to many of the women who had worked in the Balkans. In war they had ably performed work that had until then been restricted to men. In so doing they had suffered – and enjoyed – hardship, danger and excitement. Difficult as their work had often been, it had given them a strong sense of purpose and had tasked their initiative to the limit of their abilities. It had also given them the sort of freedom that had been denied to them at home. Those who had wanted had cut their hair short, worn men's clothing, smoked endless cigarettes and raced about the countryside to the despair of the heads of their units who struggled to keep their exuberance in check. Just as the war had lent them these hitherto unheard-of opportunities, peace took them just as suddenly away, as much for them as it had for Flora.

They too found it difficult to adjust when they arrived home to find that their friends and families did not understand what they had experienced or accomplished in the Balkans. They had worked in spheres where their sex had been overlooked only to be forced on their return into traditional or domestic roles. Women doctors and surgeons who had proved themselves every bit as capable as their male counterparts found it near impossible to find work outside the fields of obstetrics and gynaecology, paediatrics or public health. One by one the London hospitals that had opened their doors to offer clinical training to women closed them again when they were no longer needed. And there were minor personal tragedies too, exemplified by that of Rose West from Scotland. The young, attractive head of Motor Transport for the American Unit, as able a mechanic as she was a driver, was forbidden by her family to own a car when she arrived home.[25]

"It's coming on me with a sort of cold horror," scribbled Australian Olive Kelso King in a letter to her father as she contemplated her return home. "What shall I do then? Live in London, with all one's interests in shops & theatres? Or in Sydney, going to teas & luncheons, playing tennis at the golf club, getting new dresses for the races, & always being gossiped about & disapproved of?"[26] For many, there was no real answer.

PART THREE

CHAPTER 18

INTERBELLUM

1922–1941

"I am not getting on at all happily in a perfectly respectable life and shall do something desperate soon," scribbled Flora miserably to Vera in August 1925 from Orford, Suffolk. She had submitted unwillingly to pleas by her family to stay put that summer, but life in the tranquil village did not suit her at all. "I am staying at present with a married sister here," she told her. "There's nothing in this world I should like better than to pay you a visit," she added gloomily, "but I have promised to stay here."[1]

Neither was life as a civilian suiting her. She had spent the first three years after demobilization drifting restlessly between England and the Kingdom of Serbs, Croats and Slovenes, often accompanied by Yurie. Her family at least uniformly approved of him, none more so than Betty, daughter of Flora's sister Fanny. When the self-described "fat, spotty, thirteen-year-old" first met him, he immediately came to attention, clicked his heels and bowed. For making her feel important, she loved him from that moment forth.[2]

Flora had enjoyed an idyllic few months with him in 1924 working at "Café Finish", a picturesque waterfront café in Lapad, Dubrovnik. There they had acquired a joint pet, "Ginger" the dog, and a joint motorboat for "motorboat picnics". But after they closed it that winter, she had returned to England with little idea what to do. She approached the Save the Children Fund for work as a lecturer and fund-raiser, apparently unsuccessfully, and began writing freelance articles but struggled to get them published.[3]

Restless and bored of village life in Orford and with Yurie evidently back in Belgrade, Flora was thumbing unenthusiastically through the daily papers when her eyes came to a sudden stop at headlines announcing "Sharp Fighting in Morocco". She avidly devoured reports of "Rifi Raids" – attacks by largely Berber tribespeople in a bid for self-determination against their Spanish and French colonial overlords – but kept her interest to herself.[4] In July, without telling anyone, she slipped from her sister's house across the Channel to Paris to ask the French military medical authorities to send her to the front as a nurse, confident that they could not refuse someone so uniquely qualified. To her dismay, they brushed her off. "We're only sending French nurses," they told her flatly.[5]

Flora returned dejectedly to Orford, all the while turning over thoughts in her mind about how she could join the fray. Pining for army life, she wrote to Vera with a proposal that was more wistful than practicable. "What about you, Curly [Margaret Ker, who had worked for the Scottish Women's Hospitals and Evelina Haverfield's orphanage] and I going there as a unit complete with Morris Oxford car? Doesn't that appeal to you? If we went on the side of the Riffs [the tribespeople] still better. I can add my motorboat which is still in Gruz [near Lapad] to the contingent, so we should be a mobile force by land or sea and could blow up a mole if we could find one (I don't mean to infer that anything faster than the quadruped could escape). You can take command at sea, Curly of the armoured car, and I will lead the storming parties. Must dry up now and leave you to digest this."[6]

By 1926 Flora had abandoned all hope of invading Morocco. The Rif rebellion had been crushed by a combined Franco-Spanish expedition and fighting was nearly at an end. Instead she decided to decamp to a "villa" that Katherine had purchased in the village of Sremska Kamenica, fifty miles north-west of Belgrade, to write her second autobiography. The villa had "highly original arrangements", wrote a later visitor, who found that she had to share it with numerous chickens, but its location in the rolling Fruška Gora hills more than compensated for any internal drawbacks.[7] Flora could step out of the back door onto its wide veranda and look for miles across orchard- and vineyard-clad slopes down to the winding Danube River in the distance, with forested mountains to the west. And if the Arcadian surroundings became too oppressive she could travel to the busy shops, restaurants and cinemas of nearby Novi Sad, a prosperous former Austro-Hungarian town. She also enjoyed the company of the villa's many guests and, at weekends, of Katherine.

Writing her autobiography had, if anything, sharpened her nostalgia for the war. "Sometimes now, when playing family bridge for threepence a hundred in an English drawing room, the memory of those wild jolly nights comes over me, and I am lost in another world," she wrote.

> So far away it all seems now that I wonder whether it was really myself, or only something I dreamt. Instead of the powdered nose of my partner I seem to be looking at the grizzled head and unshaven chin of the Commandant, and the scented drawing room suddenly fades away into the stone walls of a tiny hut lighted by a couple of candles stuck into bottles, and thick with tobacco smoke, where five or six officers and I sit crowded on bunks or camp stools. For evening dress, mud-stained, bloodstained khaki breeches and tunic, and for vanity bag a revolver. The camp table was covered by the thick brown folds of an army blanket, and before each was a pile of Serbian banknotes and gold, and a tumblerful of red wine. Then came a batman with another relay of little cups of the thick, sweet Turkish coffee, which he brought about every hour. But here comes a trim maid with tea, and I return to the prosaic drawing room with a start, and the realization that I am a "lady" now, not a "soldier and a man"; also that Serbian soil is resting lightly on the graves of many of those happy comrades I have been seeing in my dreams.[8]

In May 1927 *The Autobiography of a Woman Soldier* was published to positive if not particularly widespread or prominent reviews. "Miss Sandes writes easily and agreeably," commented the *Times Literary Supplement*. It was "quite good reading without the suggestion of offence", added the *Observer*, while the *Manchester Guardian* observed that it was "an unpretentious book of a brave and amusing woman which carries conviction with every page".[9] Despite her reviews, Flora was bitterly disappointed with her sales figures and wrote lengthy correspondence to her publisher in the suspicion that they could have done more to promote it. However, with a public increasingly tired of hearing about the war and her fame starting to wane, it remained only a moderate success.

Flora had written obliquely but affectionately about Yurie in the final pages of her autobiography, reticent about mixing a matter-of-fact account of life in the Serbian army with her growing fondness for her former sergeant. But he must have been at the forefront of her thoughts while she wrote her account, for a few months after she finished fifty-one-year-old Flora married Yurie, who was thirty-eight. This decision was not one that she would have taken lightly. She had not consciously chosen to stay single in her youth but the thought of a conventional English husband and conventional married life had held little appeal. Furthermore, her all-encompassing pursuit of adventure had long driven thoughts of settling down to the back of her mind. In her middle age she treasured her independence and her freedom to travel as much as she ever had, and she must have known that by entwining her life with Yurie's for the first time in her adult life she would have to take another person's wishes into account. But Yurie gave her the constant company she needed without ever suffocating her and, after five years together, the thought of life without him had become inconceivable. And for Yurie, who was just as adrift as Flora, marriage gave him a family again.

The civil ceremony was held on 14th May in Boulogne-Billancourt in the western suburbs of Paris. The wedding was small and quiet – their limited budget would have stretched no further – but they smiled happily for the camera in their finery, Flora in a smart, pale suit and Yurie in an elegant, dark one, a white corsage pinned to his lapel. They booked themselves into a local hotel, the Hôtel Billancourt, and travelled into central Paris to celebrate. The French capital, they had decided, was as good a place as any to begin their married life. Flora was fluent in the language, it was relatively inexpensive and it was also seen as the most glamorous capital city in the world. It was the home of Hemingway and F. Scott Fitzgerald, Picasso and Matisse, James Joyce and Gertrude Stein. It was where Josephine Baker electrified the audiences with her banana dance at the Folies-Bergère and where Coco Chanel revolutionized women's clothing with her "little black dress". It had a reputation for wild nightlife and wilder *"maisons de rendez-vous*" and was seen as modern, trendsetting and liberal. Above all it supported the largest White Russian community in the world – fifty thousand exiles in total – and it was therefore the closest thing that Yurie could get to home.[10]

Flora – now Sandes-Yudenitch – and Yurie moved to a street in the heart of the White Russian district in Boulogne-Billancourt. Although the industrial suburb was far removed from the glamour of the centre, it offered a tight-knit community that was full of restaurants and shops advertising their services in Cyrillic lettering. It was also close to the Citröen and Renault factories that hired White Russians in their thousands, for what were little more than ill-paid jobs without prospects.

Like most Russian exiles, Yurie was only able to find work as a "*manouvrier*" – unskilled labourer – most likely at one of the factories. Flora, who had declared herself "*sans profession*" at the time of their marriage, contributed her small army pension to their joint income while working at whatever jobs she could find. She returned to the secretarial work of her youth by spending hours "typing madly" and took on English pupils.[11] Somewhat incongruously, she also became temporary matron to a troupe of Tiller Girls, young precision dancers from northern-English working-class backgrounds who were performing at the Folies-Bergère. The girls, known as "the Eight Extraordinary Dancers", were housed at the "Reverend Cardew's Home for Theatrical Ladies" in the heart of seamy Place Pigalle. The ageing reverend had turned his hand to maintaining the purity of his charges, after an eccentric career that had included fighting the native Métis population in Canada in the 1880s.[12] He gave them a bed in a grey-painted dormitory, fed them bland, overcooked British food and placed middle-aged women like Flora in charge. She escorted them to and from the theatre and, under orders from Cardew to keep them on a tight leash, did her best to maintain discipline. While Flora's opinion of the reverend is unknown, she had a liking for her charges. "I think she had a certain sympathy with them," commented her grand-nephew Arthur Baker. "These were girls who were sticking their neck out and she kept them on the straight and narrow."[13]

After two years of scraping an unsatisfactory living in Paris, Flora and Yurie settled on a new plan. They invested their savings in a second-hand Panhard, a luxury French passenger car, which they hoped would be at the heart of a taxi business that they planned to set up in Belgrade. On a hot, July day they rose early, strapped their luggage on the car and placed a cage carrying Thompson, their canary, in the back. After a drive that took them through the vineyards of eastern France, the hills of Alsace-Lorraine, the forests of Bavaria and the mountains of Austria, they arrived in Belgrade in August 1929.

They had last left a parliamentary democracy; when they returned it was to a royal dictatorship. At the start of 1929, King Aleksandar, who had taken the throne upon his father's death in 1921, had abruptly suspended the constitution and dissolved the parliament. The "6th January Dictatorship", as it became known, had followed six months of political turmoil after the assassination, on 20th June 1928, of two Catholic Croatian parliamentary deputies by an Orthodox Montenegrin. Aleksandar had watched the Kingdom disintegrate around him in the fury that followed. Political, regional and religious hatreds, which were never far from the surface, began to escalate out of control. The Croats withdrew their deputies to Zagreb and, with parliament too splintered to run the country effectively, Aleksandar had stepped in forcefully.

The forty-year-old king was not a natural dictator, either in inclination or ability. Bookish in appearance, shy and somewhat gauche, he was first and foremost a believer in the Yugoslav ideal, that the ties of language and cultural tradition meant that the South Slavs formed a natural national unit. Although he was also a believer in Greater Serbia to the extent that he thought it self-evident that the Serbs should take the lead in the governance of the country, he was not as fanatical as many.[14] Still, to keep his country from disintegrating, he was willing to take whatever measures he deemed necessary.

He focused his efforts on attempting to impose a sense of national identity on his people as "Yugoslavs". One of his first decrees was to change the name of his divided and tumultuous country. The "Kingdom of Serbs, Croats and Slovenes" – which emphasized the separate national blocs – became the collective "Kingdom of Yugoslavia". Far less innocuous were his decrees banning political parties and giving the police new, draconian laws to use against political opponents.[15] Although he arguably had good intentions, the impact of his orders was to give virtual carte blanche to the secret and military police who arrested and imprisoned members of political parties and ruthlessly attempted to crush all dissent. "I found [Macedonia] being run as a police state from Belgrade, with the Serb army everywhere as though it were an occupied country," wrote Francesca Wilson in dismay when she revisited the country in 1929.[16] The situation, if anything, was worse in Croatia. State brutality in turn generated recruits for the Internal Macedonian Revolutionary Organization (IMRO) and prompted the formation of a sinister, ultra-nationalist Croatian organization with fascist undertones, the Ustaše ("Insurgents"), which began a campaign of violence and assassination directed against the Serbs.

"[I have] a permanent incapacity to settle down to anything," reflected Flora in frustration in 1926, as she placed the finishing touches on her autobiography.[17] Although she had found some contentment alongside Yurie, Paris had been unable to offer them a permanent home. They both now placed great hopes on their move to Belgrade.

In many respects, the Serbian capital fulfilled them. Flora was welcomed back by her many friends and began work as an English teacher at the "Anglo-Yugoslav Club". Known colloquially as the "English Club", it served as the busy social hub of the British colony. They also had many friends in common, including the President of the Club, Lilian Vidaković, and her daughter Mirjana (then known as "Cherry"), who recalls that Flora and Yurie spoke a "peculiar Serbian" to each other. Yurie too was ushered back into the fold of its large White Russian community. By 1931 they were well established in "our house", as Flora proudly labelled it – a large white, modern building with a spacious porch that they rented in the residential neighbourhood of Pašino Brdo. It also sported a garden big enough for their considerable menagerie – Thompson the canary, Vaška the rabbit, Kiko and Winkle the Pekinese puppies, Ginty, a dog of indeterminate breed, and Flora's pride and joy, a young Alsatian called Pat.

For reasons unknown their taxi business does not appear to have been a success. By the early 1930s Yurie was instead working at "Auto Commando", but Flora's diaries – and her often indifferent attention to spelling – leave it unclear whether he was working at

a taxi company of this name or in "Autokomanda", a district of
Belgrade. But what is clear is that, as the impact of the "Crash" of
October 1929 devastated the largely agricultural Yugoslav economy,
he worked long shifts for his employers, who made few allowances
for lateness or illness.[18] Still, with the added help of her small army
pension, they made a comfortable if not luxurious living that, at
the very least, allowed her to escape the domestic drudgery she so
hated by hiring a live-in maid, Marica.

Flora dutifully recorded the minutiae of their daily life in her
diary. They enjoyed warm summer days in their garden and cold
winter ones indoors in each other's company. On Yurie's free evenings they would travel into town to the cinema, or occasionally
splash out on dinner. Flora marked dates that were important
to her and Yurie in capitals – there was "RUSSIAN EASTER
SUNDAY" and "RUSSIAN XMAS", which they spent in the
company of their mutual friends, "YURIE'S BIRTHDAY" on
4th July and "OUR WEDDING DAY" on 14th May.

Although she had finally achieved a happy and relatively settled
existence, Flora remained nostalgic for the war. She was made a
reserve captain in September 1926, but her promotion only served
to remind her how much she missed the contentment that she had
found in the ranks of the army. She looked forward to the annual
regimental Slava which gave her the chance to squeeze into her old
uniform and she eagerly attended other veterans' events.[19] She was
there when King Aleksandar unveiled a statue to the war dead at
Šabac in northern Yugoslavia in 1934 and she held court at the
Russian Cabaret alongside Katherine the following year on the
occasion of the annual holiday to celebrate the "Reunion of the
Allies". A year later still, when six hundred British war veterans
arrived in Salonika to attend a commemoration ceremony at the old
British frontline, Flora travelled over three hundred miles south to
join them. "She was charmingly courteous and supremely happy at
meeting several old wartime friends," wrote one British observer.[20]

She also kept in touch with the many friends she had made among
the members of the units who had worked in Serbia during the war.
She sent them Christmas cards, postcards and the occasional letter,
and attended the annual dinner in London of the "British Serbian
Units" of the British Legion in 1925.[21] But by the 1930s she fretted
greatly at having lost contact with Emily. At the start of 1938, at

an utter loss of how to find her, she addressed and posted a letter to "Emily Simmonds, American Nurse, USA":

> Dear Simmonds: For the love of Mike if you ever get this letter write to me and say where and how you are. I once did get your address, in 1929, and then lost it again. I often think of you and how we'd never have survived the hospital at Kragujevatz and the gang there if we hadn't had each other, and ditto Valjevo. Good pals are scarce in this world so now what about it. When I hear from you will write again with all the news. I'm married (10 years) to a Russian colonel and we have settled here – for our sins, but are very happy in spite of it. You wouldn't know Belgrade or the Serbs now. Best luck for 1938 and all my love and when you get over the shock of hearing from me write pronto. Ever yours, Sandy.

The letter wound its way eventually to American Red Cross head-quarters, but the Red Cross too had lost touch with Emily by then.[22]

At least Flora had the company of other British women who had made Serbia their home. She travelled out on occasion to Lake Bohinj, Slovenia to visit her friend Constance Dušmanić who, as Constance Rowan, had met her Serbian husband while smoking an illicit cigarette in the laundry of the Salonika-based unit of the Scottish Women's Hospitals. She saw others at social events at the English Club. Above all, she spent time with Katherine, who by now was simply "Doc" to her.

"It is early yet, only eight a.m., but already work is in full swing in the outpatients department," wrote Flora in 1926, in an article published by the Save the Children Fund describing the work at Katherine's hospital. "The big waiting room is crowded to over-flowing, and still every minute brings some new arrival... Many have travelled all night by train from some distant part of the country; more have been, since dawn, jolting over the rough roads in a bullock wagon; more still have come on foot from some outly-ing villages; but, one and all, they await their turn, unhurried and uncomplaining, with that patience characteristic of the Serb."[23]

By the mid-1920s the hospital had treated nearly sixty thousand children, whose care Katherine had funded largely by voluntary contributions.[24] Those who visited it were impressed with what they saw. "Everything seemed to be running with extraordinary efficiency and yet with a kind of miraculous ease," praised Francesca Wilson. "Everyone obeyed Dr MacPhail but she was always quiet and relaxed and seemed to make no effort. It was natural that the nurses and the children and the anxious peasants who brought them should obey her but what was strange was that the Serb doctors and officials obeyed her too, they who had never before taken orders from a woman."[25] But by 1926, with ever-decreasing donations, she was barely keeping her hospital afloat. Flora, via her article, was one of many who stepped in to help. Others appealed for funds in the British press.[26] Their joint campaign raised enough to keep her hospital going until 1931, when her hospital finally received full official recognition and, with it, governmental funding.

With its future assured, Katherine made arrangements to sell her hospital to the government. She planned, with the proceeds, to build the convalescent facility for children with tuberculosis that she had dreamt of since 1922, when she had been forced to close her small home for them in Lapad. Eleven years later, the cornerstone of the building was laid in Kamenica on the crest of a hill overlooking the Danube. Overseeing the work was Vasa Srdić, a half-Serbian, half-Scottish agricultural engineer – known to everyone as "Mac" – whom, as a young army officer, Katherine had first met in Lapad. Although it remained unsaid, it was widely assumed by those who knew them that their relationship was like that of "husband and wife".[27]

By the summer of 1934, the hospital had been built according to her specifications. As the final preparations were made to admit her first patients, Katherine walked proudly through the double doors of the one-storey, cream-stucco building into the bright, spacious hall, past a centrepiece mosaic of a red "lion rampant" design, akin to the Royal Standard of Scotland, which had been worked into the shiny parquet floor. She gave the three wings of the hospital a final inspection and stepped out into the spacious terrace, which was large enough to allow the children to be wheeled outside in their beds to sit in the sun.

Katherine spent the summer months preparing for the official opening of the "Anglo-Yugoslav Children's Sanatorium for Tubercular Disease of the Bones and Joints", set for 23rd September, all the while caring for her first thirty patients, who had been admitted on 1st August. She secured the patronage of Queen Marie, the wife of King Aleksandar, issued invitations, oversaw the planting of flower beds and, as the date neared, decorated the wards.[28] In the days before the opening her guests descended upon Belgrade, including Vera Holme and several other veterans of relief work who had sailed from Britain to attend. On Saturday 22nd September Flora and Katherine travelled into town to meet fifteen of them at Belgrade's Park Hotel for an emotional and joyous reunion. Many had not seen each other for years. It was a "jolly party" enthused Vera in her diary. "[We had] a smoke and a grand crack."[29]

At ten o'clock the following morning, the first of the cars and horse-drawn cabs carrying Katherine's guests parked outside her hospital, which had been decorated with greenery and the entwined flags of Yugoslavia and the United Kingdom. They were ushered up the pathway through the entrance into the central hall. Over the course of the morning, Flora – dressed in the crisp white tunic and cap of a Serbian captain – joined the other British guests alongside the British minister, representatives of the Orthodox Church, the royal family, the medical profession and local authorities. After a formal ceremony, the guests were taken on a tour of the facilities and to meet the excited young patients who were lying in their beds in the warm sun on the terrace.[30] The opening was a triumph, the importance of which was considerably understated by Flora in her diary. "Big crowd," she commented simply.[31] But absent among them was Queen Marie, who was on her way to Marseilles to join her husband for a state visit. Also en route to Marseilles was Vlado Chernozemski, a Bulgarian assassin who was travelling there at the joint behest of IMRO and the Ustaše.

Content as she was with her life with Yurie in Belgrade, Flora's urge to travel remained as strong as ever. In the 1930s, she returned frequently to both the Dalmatian coast and England, sometimes sharing her adventures with a friend but rarely, according to her patchy diaries, with Yurie. Perhaps he had to work, perhaps he did not trust his increasingly indifferent health or perhaps he simply had no such peripatetic inclinations. Whatever the reason, Flora missed him terribly on such trips. "Felt horrible leaving him standing lonely on the quay," she wrote as she set out in July 1936 for

London. "Wish he was here," she scribbled plaintively on another occasion when she found herself away on his birthday.[32]

If no friend was available she would set out on her own. "When one travels alone one gets more of the 'human interest'," she concluded during one such journey from Belgrade to the Dalmatian coast in August 1931. There was plenty such interest on this particular trip, all jotted carefully and in unusual detail in her diary. "One passenger was in a high fever and was flopping about with chattering teeth," recorded Flora of a bus trip between Dubrovnik and Cavtat, where she had travelled to revisit the place she had first met Yurie. "I diagnosed it as either very bad malaria or else smallpox, and was relieved when he got out before he was sick over me." The following day, she caught a steamer to Prčanj, Montenegro where she visited the Ruski Dom, a home for war-disabled Russians. "Was ushered into a room where two men were having lunch," she wrote. "One a good looking man about 38 simply clad in a pair of scanty bathing shorts, and the other an old fellow in his shirt and panties, much to their embarrassment poor things, in fact they couldn't have looked more alarmed if I'd been a man-eating tiger." She felt keenly at their discomfiture. "I don't know which are the more pathetic, the young ones whose lives are done for, or the old chaps ending their days in a home, they must get so bored with each other always, and they are all incurable either from wounds or old age." There were lighter moments too, which gave free rein to her finely tuned sense of the ridiculous. "The waiter asked if I preferred [a] cheese or sausage sandwich," wrote Flora of an encounter that had amused her greatly in Budva, "and when I said cheese, replied pleasantly that there was no cheese."[33]

The cameras of Fox Movietone News were fixed on King Aleksandar as he arrived at the Old Port of Marseilles just before four in the afternoon on 9th October 1934. He had arrived alone on the light cruiser *Dubrovnik*, Queen Marie having decided to travel instead by train to the southern French city to meet him. They filmed his open-topped car as it drove him, at walking pace, behind a mounted guard of honour over the cobbled streets and into one of the main thoroughfares. One of the cameramen recorded him waving to the massed crowds. He then jogged ahead to film the visit from a different angle. His camera was rolling as Vlado

Chernozemski broke through the crowds and a cordon of French troops, leapt on the running board of the car and fired shots from a Mauser pistol into the King's heart and liver.[34]

The news of Aleksandar's murder stunned the whole of Yugoslavia. For a brief moment, in the outpouring of grief that swept the country, he achieved in death what he had failed to in life, the unification of his people as "Yugoslavs".[35] Equally shaken by the news were the many British women and men who had developed genuine affection for him during the war for the great courtesy he had unfailingly showed them. Many, in the days before television, would have watched in silent horror at the cinema as the newsreel footage of the assassination flickered across the screen before them.

Flora's diary entry on the day – "King Alexander assassinated at Marseilles" – was typically factual and unembellished, but she was shocked and saddened enough at the news to insist on paying her respects by seeing him lying in state in Belgrade's National Cathedral on 17th October.[36] His funeral cortège was watched the following morning by "immense and utterly silent crowds". Following a service at the Cathedral, the cadets of the military academy led the procession. Behind them marched soldiers of every regiment of the Yugoslav army, followed by detachments of the French, British, Greek, Turkish, Romanian and Czech armies. Then the elite holders of the Karadorđe Star for Bravery under Fire marched past. In their ranks was Flora in her captain's uniform. "I walked in the procession with the other Kara George Stars," she scribbled later. "Had to leave home very early. We met near Kalemegdan, stood for hours, then processed. Very fine procession."

The gun carriage carrying Aleksandar's coffin, covered by the Royal Standard of Yugoslavia, followed near the end of the long cortège. Behind it walked Queen Marie draped in mourning black alongside her eleven-year-old son Petar, who had become king upon the death of his father. Paying their respects a few steps back were the official representatives of foreign governments. Among them, in the grey-green and crimson uniform of the Reichswehr, walked a symbol of the growing fascist menace to Europe – General Hermann Göring.[37]

The death of King Aleksandar marked the beginning of the end of the attempt to turn his heterogeneous subjects into "Yugoslavs".

With the appointment of Prince Pavle (Paul), a cousin of Aleksandar's, as chief regent until the young king came of age, it also marked a shift away from the worst abuses of naked dictatorship. Under the more liberal hand of Pavle's rule, the press was allowed to report more freely and political parties permitted to resume their activities.[38] But the peace and prosperity that might have otherwise followed in the wake of this liberalization were threatened by the sinister motives of the fascist regimes in Germany and Italy, both of which had a view to exploiting Yugoslavia's weaknesses.

Hitler's ambitions were fundamentally economic. He hoped to bind the Yugoslav economy closely to Germany's, thereby guaranteeing him access to the country's rich agricultural and mineral resources. By the late 1930s he had largely succeeded, having offered agreements to supply the industrial goods that Yugoslavia could ill afford in exchange for the raw materials he needed for Germany's armaments industry.[39] The aim of Mussolini's Italy was instead political, to gain influence over the Adriatic coast by exploiting ethnic tension between Serbs and Croats. It duly nurtured, financed, armed and trained Croatian separatist extremists, among them the murderous Ustaše.

"The governments of Japan, Germany and Italy consider it a prerequisite of a lasting peace that every nation of the world shall receive the space to which it is entitled," stated the disingenuous preamble to the Tripartite Pact. "It is furthermore the desire of the three governments to extend cooperation to nations… for the purpose of realizing their ultimate object, world peace…" In reality, the Pact, which was presented by the Nazis to the governments of central Europe and the Balkans for signature in the autumn of 1940, was designed to prostrate them into the political, economic and military submission that Hitler required before he could mass his troops for an invasion of the Soviet Union. Behind its rhetorical flourishes lay the threat that, should they refuse to sign, they would instead be overrun by the mechanized forces of the German army.

The first to acquiesce to the Pact was Germany's neighbour Hungary, on 20th November, followed that week by Romania and Slovakia. Hitler then turned his attention to the governments of Yugoslavia and Bulgaria, who had looked on grimly as he had "protected" the new signatories by pouring German troops into their territory. On 27th November he invited the Yugoslav foreign minister to Germany. There he used a mixture of threats and inducements to encourage him to sign. He reminded him that most of his country's trade was with Germany, all the while offering the kind of terms that none of the earlier signatories had been presented with. He would guarantee the sanctity of Yugoslavia's frontiers, and would present the country with the port of Salonika. He would neither ask for military assistance nor allow the passage of German troops through Yugoslav territory. The foreign minister would need solely to agree to suppress any anti-Axis activity and permit his territory to be used for the passage of German war material. Although the Yugoslavs saw these amendments to the terms as a "diplomatic triumph", they looked in profound distaste at the Nazi regime and stalled for time in the forlorn hope that the changing fortunes of war would somehow turn in their favour.[40]

The echoes of the opening shots of the Second World War carried a profound sense of unease throughout Europe, even in countries distant from the approach of German jackboots. As the first months of the war had unfolded, the Serbs had watched with growing alarm as Poland, Denmark, Luxembourg, Holland, Belgium and Norway had fallen to the might of the German army. Then, in June 1940, they had heard in disbelief the news that France, their "heroic Ally of the last war", had surrendered.[41] That autumn Greece, their closest ally in the region, was invaded by Italy.

Life on the surface remained normal. The restaurants and cafés of Belgrade were crowded, there was plenty of food in the shops, the trams, buses and trains ran as usual and people went about their business as they had always done. But all that they could talk about was what would happen to their homeland. "We'll be left alone like Switzerland and Sweden," some stated optimistically. "Or invaded like Poland," others responded grimly.[42]

By mid-February 1941, Hitler had had enough of Bulgarian and Yugoslav equivocations. He summoned the recalcitrant Yugoslav foreign minister and prime minister to Salzburg on 14th February and, in a four-hour conversation, urged them to sign the Pact. Yet again, they shuffled their feet evasively and stalled for time. At the same time, Hitler's foreign minister, Ribbentrop, peremptorily informed King Boris of Bulgaria that if he refused to sign Germany would simply invade. On 1st March 1941, after Hitler had backed up the threat by massing thirteen German divisions on Bulgaria's northern frontier, the King capitulated. On the same day Hitler poured his army into Bulgaria to take up positions along the frontier with Yugoslavia. Next, on 19th March, he gave Prince Pavle five days to sign or face invasion.[43]

The situation facing the Prince and his government was impossible. Yugoslavia now stood alone in south-eastern Europe and the Balkans. Its thousand mile frontier was bordered by seven countries, all of which, with the exception of beleaguered Greece, were Axis signatories. The country was economically dependent upon Germany. It was also split, with the Croats strongly in favour of signing the Pact and the Serbs just as intransigently opposed. The army was equipped with obsolete weaponry, most of its ageing tanks were "quite useless" and it was led by brave but out-of-touch veterans of the First World War who trusted ox wagons more than motorized vehicles.[44]

As Hitler stepped up the pressure on Yugoslavia to sign the Pact, the Serbs' desperate hopes of staying neutral gave way to a realization that he would force on them an unpalatable choice – sign the Pact and be forced into a shameful compromise with their hated enemy or refuse and face invasion. Neither were they under any illusion that their antiquated and ill-prepared armed forces stood any chance against columns of German panzers. They joked blackly about an imagined telephone call between Hitler and Prince Pavle. "Pavle, I need some more tanks," Hitler said. "Can you let me have some of yours?" "Yes, of course," replied Pavle. "At once, Adolf. How many do you want? One, two or three?"[45]

From the terrace of her hilltop hospital Katherine looked with a worried eye across the Danube to the flat Bačka plain that stretched seemingly endlessly northwards towards German-occupied Hungary. She had watched anxiously through the autumn and winter of 1940 as the Yugoslav army dug trenches and built gun emplacements in the surrounding countryside, twenty of which were in the immediate vicinity. "If we're attacked, the children won't stand a chance," she thought to herself. In vain she had visited the Ministry of Health to ask that they make plans for their evacuation. By

February 1941 she was fraught with worry. At the end of the month, sensing that every passing day was bringing the country closer to war, she knew she would have to take the matter into her own hands. With a heavy heart she put her approximately one hundred and fifteen young patients in plaster and sent them home. "Take them to villages in the mountains," she told their parents. "They should be safe there." Next she sent her staff home on indefinite leave. She remained behind with Alice Murphy, her half-Russian, half-English hospital secretary, confident that the two of them could make their escape in time.[46]

By March the ranks of the English Club had noticeably thinned. For weeks Flora had listened as others at the Club deliberated endlessly about what they should do. Many in the end had obeyed the Minister, Ronald Campbell, when he quietly requested their evacuation.[47] A number, among them several women who had met their Serbian husbands whilst working for British units in the First World War, decided to remain.[48] For Flora, there was no debate. "I'm staying too," she avowed to anyone who asked, her spirit of defiance undiminished. But as much as anything, the thought of what the upheaval would do to Yurie's health made a move back to England inconceivable. Throughout the 1930s he had suffered from attacks of malaria that left him bedridden, sometimes for days on end. By 1940, aged only fifty-two, he was also suffering from blood pressure so high that, at times, he struggled for breath at the least exertion.

The precarious state of his health had been brought home to Flora during a disastrous holiday. In August 1940 they had set aside all thoughts of war to travel back together to their beloved Dalmatian coast. First they spent a few happy days in and around Dubrovnik. They visited Cavtat, where they had first met eighteen years before and sat reminiscing in Lapad, where they overlooked the former site of Café Finish. Then, after they had travelled up the coast by steamer to Makarska to take a room in a quiet pension, he became ill. "Yurie got a chill late in afternoon, and was bad in the night, couldn't breathe, or sleep," scribbled Flora in her diary a week into their trip. Three days later she called a doctor. His breath must have caught in his throat when he took the reading from his arm. "Yurie's B.P. 280, and he must not be in the sun or drink anything alcoholic. Seaside not good place for him," she commented anxiously after the consultation. Two days later she cut their holiday short. "We think Yurie had better come home," she wrote sadly, as she vowed to herself to live quietly with him in the hope that his health would stabilize.[49]

The tension in the air was almost palpable by the middle of March 1941. Although the government had publicly divulged not a word of Hitler's ultimatum, the Serbs sensed the growing crisis. In Kamenica, Katherine and Alice were joined nightly by the officers of the nearby batteries who came to listen in with them to the news from London.[50] In Belgrade, more grey-green uniforms of the Yugoslav army appeared in the streets following a slow call-up of reserves while the authorities began to take half-hearted measures to prepare the capital for the eventuality of a German bombing raid. A few public shelters were hastily dug in parks and squares while householders were ordered to clear their attics of lumber and keep quantities of sand and water at hand. "What's the point of all this? There are no military targets here," they grumbled to each other but, under threat of fines, they complied with the edict.[51]

On the morning of 25th March news broke that Yugoslavia had capitulated. In an atmosphere of "funereal gloom", the Prime Minister and foreign minister had signed the Pact in front of Ribbentrop in Vienna. Across Belgrade grizzled, scarred veterans of the First World War sat silently in *kafanas*, heads bowed, weeping silently in shame and disbelief, while "passers-by slunk along with their eyes on the ground".[52] "We were... humiliated before the world," wrote Lena Yovitchitch, a half-Serbian, half-English acquaintance of Flora's.[53] That evening, Katherine reported, not a single officer came to listen to the radio. "They were ashamed," she wrote.[54]

Across Serbia, there were signs of growing fury. Children smashed the windows of their schools, cabinet ministers stepped down, civil servants resigned and Orthodox priests preached to their congregations that they must not allow their government to consign them to foreign domination. Peasants flooded towns and villages to protest the signing of the Pact while university students took to the streets with a refrain of "Down with the traitors!"[55] "Everyone was simply sick," wrote Flora in a letter to her sister Fanny. "The people said they would never be slaves, better death. When a special edition came out at two o'clock with the news of the definite signing everyone was in the streets simply snatching the papers from the boys and poring over them with curses… The kids in the schools all demonstrated and refused to learn their German lesson. One small boy pupil of mine told me all about it with great glee – that they hadn't done any work at all… He said they'd sung patriotic songs all morning."[56]

"Something seemed to be in the air," commented Katherine. With a sense of unease, she had returned that day from Kamenica to the small flat she owned in Belgrade. The flat, down the hill from the busy intersection known as "London Crossing", overlooked the Ministries of War and Internal Affairs. That night, Wednesday 26th March, she went to sleep as normal, but was suddenly wakened by noises from the street below. "In the stillness of the night I heard the tramp of soldiers and beneath my window I saw a small gathering of officers and men," she wrote breathlessly.

> At first I did not realize what was afoot until I heard the salute and the signal for action, "Long live King Peter" and the answer, "Long live the King". The sentries guarding the ministries were then disarmed and a cordon of soldiers were placed across the street thus barring all ways to the ministries. Quietly and with the swiftness of lightning, heavy field guns, machine guns and small armed tanks were brought out from the courtyard behind the Ministry of War and mounted in the streets facing in all directions… As the officers and men who were taking part in this passed beneath my window they seized each other with wild enthusiasm, kissing each other as free men and beside themselves with joy. Quickly I realized that this was an overthrow of the government and that a handful of officers and a few picked troops had taken power into their own hands.[57]

The events that Katherine had seen and heard from her window were later described as "one of the most magnificent gestures of this age".[58] In a bloodless military *coup d'état*, the blue-uniformed officers of the Yugoslav Air Force had overthrown the government that had bound them into Nazi vassalage. They had done so in full knowledge that their actions made a German invasion – and their defeat – imminent and inevitable. What mattered to them was that they had redeemed the honour of the nation.

The news that a small power had defied the armed might of Germany was met in the capitals of the world first with incredulity, then with "emotional exhilaration". It was "a lightning flash illuminating a dark landscape", declared the *New York Times*. "Yugoslavia has found its soul," rejoiced Winston Churchill. It was met in Berlin with disbelief. "I thought it was a joke," Hitler is reported to have said.[59]

Flora's maid Marica woke her at seven thirty that morning with a rush of words. "No one's allowed into the town," she told her anxiously. "Everyone's being turned back. It's full of machine guns and tanks." "Are they German?" asked Flora with excitement as she sat bolt upright in bed. "I don't know what they are," responded Marica apprehensively.[60]

Flora threw on her clothes, drew the curtain, gulped the last of her tea and told Yurie that she was going to explore. "Don't get into a row with anyone," he told her worriedly. "I won't; I'll be fine," she reassured him breezily as she sailed out the door. "Never shall I forget the scenes of enthusiasm in the town that morning," she recalled later. "It was a fine sunny day. Everybody in Belgrade was in the streets; men, women and children marching in processions waving flags, singing patriotic songs, laughing and cheering. Shouts of the old Serbian slogan, '*Bolje grob nego rob*' ('Better the grave than slavery') were caught up by the crowd and became a roar of defiance."[61]

Flora rushed home to tell Yurie that young King Petar had been brought to the throne, the government arrested and Prince Pavle sent into exile. "[He] is just as delighted as I am," she wrote to her sister Fanny that day. "He says this is the fourth revolution he has seen." That afternoon she walked through the dust and heat of the tumultuous streets to visit Katherine at her flat in the town. As she neared, she was stopped. "Do you have a permit?" demanded an officer as Flora peered past the barricades into the street beyond. "No, but I have the Kara George," she replied hopefully, as she showed him the medal in her buttonhole. "Are you Flora Sandes?" he replied in "excellent" English. When she nodded, he shook her warmly by the hand. "Go wherever you like," he smiled as he waved her past.

That evening, after listening intently to Katherine's account of the coup, she returned to celebrate the news with Yurie. "Although [he's] not supposed to drink," she told Fanny, "he is so much better now and we have drunk the health of King Peter several times." She finished her letter with an attempt to forestall the anxious thoughts she knew would have entered her sister's head as the clouds of war gathered on the horizon. "Don't worry about me anyhow," she told her. "I'm too old to fight now with a game leg, and, as Yurie politely remarks, what would the Germans want to bother with an old woman like me for even if they did succeed in taking the country."[62]

That week, in the knowledge that she was too old and "war disabled" to be conscripted, she presented herself at the War Office in Belgrade to volunteer "in case of war". "They were rather amused," she later commented drily. "They asked whether the last war had not been enough for me, and then they formally accepted me."[63]

Throughout Serbia and Montenegro crowds flocked to the towns and streets waving improvised Union Jacks and the Stars and Stripes, carrying the Yugoslav flag and banners aloft, holding up photographs of King Petar and singing and chanting at the top of their lungs. Better the grave than slavery! Better war than the Pact! Long live King Petar! Long live England! In Belgrade, they smashed the windows of the German "Travel Bureau" – in reality a hotbed of German intelligence – threw the contents in the streets, tore the picture of Hitler from the wall, dumped it on top of the heap and burned the lot. In the window frame they hung instead a huge picture of the seventeen-year-old King. On the Terazije, Belgrade's central boulevard, crowds looked up at the towering Albanija Building – then the tallest building in the Balkans – as an old Montenegrin appeared on the balcony between a British and American flag and spread out his arms in joy, in unconscious imitation of the crucifixion.[64]

"Reports from the country revealed the same enthusiasm everywhere," recorded Flora. "Peasants had not forgotten how they fought shoulder to shoulder with the English and French in the war of 1914–18, how they were cared for by British nurses, how they fraternized with British Tommies in Salonika… A young officer said to me, half in joke but half in earnest, 'If the English and French together can't beat the Germans, why we must.'"[65]

In the streets of Zagreb, the Croatian capital, the news of the coup was met with silence.[66]

After a few days of elation the mood in Belgrade changed. People hurried through the streets looking worried, while others flocked to the railway station with their children and piles of baggage in the hope of returning to their villages. The German minister left abruptly for Berlin, followed two days later by the remaining staff of his legation. The new government back-pedalled furiously. To consolidate control over the whole of Yugoslavia, they realized, they needed the support of the Croats, and that could only be won if they agreed to abide by the terms of the Pact.[67]

It was already too late. Hitler had ordered "the destruction of Yugoslavia militarily and as a national unit" on hearing the news of the coup. He had thrust aside the Pact in fury, declaring that "politically it is especially important that the blow against Yugoslavia is carried out with pitiless harshness and that the military destruction is done with lightning rapidity".[68]

On 5th April, as Hitler readied his forces to attack, an interview with Flora reached the English papers, to what must have been the horror of her family. "I am ready and willing to fight again for the people with whom I have lived for half a century," she declared.[69]

CHAPTER 19

OCCUPATION

1941–1946

For ten days the citizens of Belgrade had waited, sick with anxiety, for Hitler to make his next move. "He'll at least issue an ultimatum first," they reassured each other.[1] Instead, there had been silence from Berlin. It was broken over the skies of Belgrade just after seven a.m. on Sunday 6th April.[2] On that clear, spring morning a faint vibration of engines roused the sleepy inhabitants from their beds. They peered out of their windows and stepped out of their front doors to squint east into the rising sun. By the time they spotted a perfect formation of bombers, flanked on either side by fighters, the uneven drone had grown into a deafening roar. All at once the boom and ack-ack-ack of anti-aircraft guns thundered across the city while the sky filled with little black-and-white puffs. Suddenly, while the inhabitants watched motionless, around half of the bombers wheeled sharply towards Zemun aerodrome, while the other aircraft held their course. A few seconds later the earth shook with the thudding concussion of the first explosions to hit the city. As a further formation appeared on the horizon, they turned and ran for cover.[3]

"Waked at 7 a.m. by bombs and firing. Went in to Yurie who is still sleeping in the sitting room on the couch," wrote Flora in her diary. "We both got up and went into the little room for breakfast which we ate to the accompaniment of bombs which sounded very close... All the windows in the attic-studio broken and glass showering down, and the whole house shook. Pat [the Alsatian] very scared." During a pause in the attack their terrified landlady and her two children appeared at their gate in their nightclothes. Flora and Yurie ushered them in. For the rest of the day they sat huddled together in the sitting room while explosions shook the district.[4]

Fifty miles north-west, in Kamenica, Katherine too had been jolted awake that morning. "We were awakened by planes flying over the hospital," she wrote. "We thought they were Yugoslav planes exercising. But as we watched them we saw bombs being dropped on the local aerodrome across the Danube and fires started in Novi Sad, our nearest town. Then we realized that war had begun."[5]

Wave after wave of dive-bombers screamed over Belgrade, targeting royal and government buildings and destroying the railway station and university. In the city centre they targeted in particular the Terazije, the main boulevard where jubilant crowds had flocked following the coup. They roared and shrieked over the residential districts, dropping bombs, many of them incendiary, on the terrified residents.[6] With no mains water, the fire brigade could only watch helplessly while fire raged furiously, burning sections of the city to the ground. "There was no pretence of bombing 'military objects'," wrote Flora angrily. "It was a punitive expedition." During a lull in the attack many survivors prepared to flee the city. "I went to the end of our lane and watched the crowds of refugees tearing along the main road leading up from the town," she recorded. "They were carrying children or pushing perambulators. They had handcarts piled with such goods as they had been able to seize. All were making for the open country in flight from a holocaust."[7]

The survivors had emerged blinking from their cellars into virtually unrecognizable streets. The sun was shining but a strong wind whipped clouds of plaster dust around their faces as they crunched across broken glass, stepped past burning debris, stumbled over rubble and inched their way around craters. Strange smells filled the air, first from an acrid yellow-white smoke redolent of sulphur from the incendiary bombs and then from the fires that were sweeping through parts of the town. There were sounds too: the sporadic wail of sirens, the smash of tiles falling off roofs, the moans of the dying and the screams of those trapped in the debris.[8]

The Luftwaffe bombed Belgrade for four days in what Hitler termed "Operation Punishment". By the time the last bomber turned for home, the capital had no phones, no water and no electricity. Seventeen thousand civilians lay dead in the ruined, burning city.[9] Katherine's flat, adjacent to the War Office, was completely destroyed.[10] Flora and Yurie, in their suburban house, had been lucky. "Even there bombs fell close," she wrote. "Nearly all the windows were shattered, and three incendiaries fell in the garden."[11]

The savagery and suddenness of the attack threw the government and army into disarray. They provided no effective leadership and they organized no systematic mobilization of troops. Even if they had, it would have made little difference to the outcome of the attack.

In the deceptive calm following the coup, Katherine had returned to her hospital at Kamenica. The children had long since been sent home, and she had spent the days in the quiet wards with her hospital secretary Alice Murphy slowly packing up the supplies and equipment while they decided what they were going to do. The first roar of bombers overhead sent them into a desperate flurry of activity. They immediately sent some of their equipment to the village to use as a first-aid station and packed the rest hurriedly in the cellar. That afternoon they threw a few things into the back of Katherine's car and left the village for Dubrovnik, hoping that the rumours were true that the Yugoslav army was planning to defend the Dalmatian coast.[12]

The first columns of German panzers rumbled across the Bulgarian border towards Niš on the day that Luftwaffe began raining destruction on Belgrade. They made no attempt to disguise their objective of paralysing communications by cutting Serbia in two.[13] "[We passed] an interminable column of ox-drawn wagons," wrote an American journalist. "This miserable, crawling thing bore supplies and munitions for the defense of Nish – that vital road and railhead of eastern Serbia on which so much depended – at approximately half a mile an hour."[14] By the evening of 8th April the Germans had captured the town and turned towards Belgrade. Across Serbia and Montenegro reservists struggled desperately to find their units. In Croatia many local soldiers in the ranks of the Yugoslav army refused to fight while, in Slovenia, the "Volksdeutsche" – Yugoslavs of German extraction – flocked treacherously to the aid of the Germans.[15]

"The Germans will arrest you for a spy once they discover you're British and a captain in the army. If they find you in civilian clothes, you'll be the first to be hanged. They'll probably string you up in your own front garden in front of your husband," speculated Nikola, Flora's former captain from the Frontier Troops. She received his opinion cheerfully enough. There was after all a solution – to put her uniform back on and join the army. Perhaps because he knew how badly Flora wanted to be off, his words were echoed by Yurie. She needed little urging. Not only was there the possibility of adventure, her pride was also at stake. "You can't stay out of the fighting – can't let other people do it for you – not if you hold the Kara George Star," she explained later.[16]

At six o'clock on the morning of 10th April, four days after the start of the attack, Flora – then aged sixty-five – rose and pulled on her uniform. This time though her feelings were mixed. "I cannot say that I felt as enthusiastic as I did on joining up in the war of 1914–18, when I was considerably younger [and] not married," she said later. "My husband was ill, and though as a 'White' Russian he would be safe, Germany not then having declared war on Russia, it was a wrench saying 'goodbye to all that'." She picked up a blanket, raincoat and her kitbag (into which she had stuffed five hundred cigarettes), said goodbye to Yurie and set off in a blizzard to report to the nearest headquarters. With Marica by her side to help her carry her things, she walked for six miles through the snow and bitter cold, before she stepped wearily into a chaotic scene at headquarters. "I've already got three hundred officers here all clamouring for orders," the beleaguered adjutant told her. Still, he wrote her out an order to present herself to army headquarters in Užice in western Serbia, gave her a pass for the train and a driver to take her to the station. "Maritza, in floods of tears, was convinced that she would never see me again," said Flora. "I embraced her, and assured her that of course I should come back. Then I set out into the blue."[17]

* * *

At dawn on 10th April, just as Flora was preparing to march off with the army, the Germans began their final advance on Belgrade. The following day, the Italians began to drive down the Dalmatian coast and the Hungarians marched south towards Novi Sad. In Zagreb, Croats wearing homemade swastika armbands welcomed the Germans enthusiastically as liberators.[18] With German support they declared the establishment of the "Independent State of Croatia" across both Croatia and much of Bosnia-Herzegovina, under the leadership of the head of the Ustaše, the fanatically anti-Serbian and anti-Semitic Ante Pavelić.

Two mornings later the inhabitants of Belgrade were wakened by the sound of explosions as the Serbs blew up the bridges over the Sava and Danube in an attempt to slow the German advance.[19] Their efforts were futile. That afternoon, the first German motor-cycle patrols appeared in the streets. "There was no spectacular entrance into the city," wrote Lena Yovitchitch. "The primary detachments of the Wehrmacht seemed as bewildered as we were."[20] That evening, the mayor surrendered his capital to a captain of the SS.[21]

"There are no trains from here to Užice," the transport officer told Flora after she had been dropped off on the platform at Topčider. He paused, then added, "Perhaps, if you're willing to wait, there might be one to Palanka. You can change there." In the middle of the afternoon, he finally found her a seat in the mail van of a train carrying families of refugees from Belgrade. The train steamed out of the station and began to crawl south. At three thirty p.m. it stopped in the middle of snow-covered fields. There it remained stationary. "At first we thought the engine had run out of water, but presently we learnt that German tanks were ahead of us," recalled Flora. "[We feared they were] preparing to make matchwood of our train, to say nothing of the aeroplanes which we could hear in the distance."

Around midnight the train began to inch back along the route they had already travelled. It halted finally in a siding near the small town of Mladenovac. "Back to the army at last," Flora thought happily to herself when she spotted the captain of a labour battalion, Major Stefan Buković, authoritatively issuing orders. When she introduced herself and suggested she join them as their *vodnik*, he nodded his assent and gestured her into a horse car with the men of her new *vod*. "He showed no surprise," she commented flatly, "nor would if the devil himself had dropped from the skies into their midst, provided he wasn't German."

At daybreak, the train came to a stop. Under the charge of Buković, Flora and the eighty men of his heterogeneous unit piled out and began to march. All day long they walked across hills and through mud under the burning sun. "The going was hard," commented Flora tersely. By the end of the first day she wrote in her diary that she was "lame". As darkness fell she gratefully accepted a bed at a house in the village of Rogača, in which the major was also quartered. That night she watched as he wordlessly changed his epaulettes to hide his rank from the Germans.[22]

The next morning she rose again at dawn, rubbed her aching feet and put on her boots for another day's march. "We wandered along all day through roads like a morass, knee deep in mud," wrote Flora. Several times they were forced to dive suddenly under hedgerows when German aeroplanes appeared overhead, scouring the lanes and roads for targets. The sound of heavy firing echoed round them from the right and they looked to the horizons expecting any moment to be chased down by columns of panzers. By the time they reached the mineral spa town of Aranđelovac after nightfall, forty miles south of the capital, Flora was dropping with exhaustion. There they were met by the news that the Germans were entering the town at the same moment. "We numbered only 80, of whom only 40 had rifles," explained Flora. "So our major led his force back to a wood, dispersed them, and told them to make their way to their homes by devious routes."[23] She was too fatigued to go on. Instead, in the company of two others, a man she called either "the old gasbag" or the "Sudija" – Judge – and her sole fellow officer, Lieutenant Dušan Miloradović, "a sick man with an awful cough", she limped slowly through the dark streets to the hospital, a former hotel, knowing full well that they would shortly be taken prisoner.

Across Yugoslavia one defeat had followed another. By the middle of the month the royal authorities and government realized that the battle was all but over. They fled the country on 14th and 15th April respectively. On the 17th, after the fall of both Sarajevo and

Dubrovnik, the army surrendered. It had taken the Germans only eleven days to crush and humiliate the Yugoslav army.

The capitulation of the army marked the end of Yugoslavia as a political unit for the duration of the war. The brown-uniformed fascist Ustaše took charge in Croatia, while Italy, Bulgaria, Albania and Hungary seized territory adjacent to their borders.[24] The Germans annexed part of Slovenia, occupied Serbia in force and set up a puppet government. Next, they moved to consolidate their authority over the defeated Serbs.

The news of the surrender reached Katherine and Alice in the small coastal town of Herceg Novi. "You must leave at once," they were told by a harried messenger from the British legation. "There's no time. You need to get to Perast where you'll find the minister [Ronald Campbell]. There's a chance of getting you all off from there in a British destroyer." Twelve hours later they reached the ancient grey-stone village, where they joined a "strange collection of British people who had come from every direction".[25]

Only eight days earlier Katherine and Alice had reached Dubrovnik hoping to set up a hospital unit, unaware that enemy pincers were beginning to close around them. Other British nationals from across Yugoslavia had also begun to converge on the coast. Many had travelled there in the false hope that the British and Americans were advancing north from Greece to come to the assistance of the Yugoslavs.[26] When it became clear that no help would be forthcoming they turned their hopes instead to rumours that the British would be able to evacuate them in time to allow them to escape capture.

The British Defence Attaché had done his very best to arrange just that. He had spent the last few days scrambling in an attempt to buy vessels to take them all to safety in Corfu but had been rebuffed at every turn by the Croat element of the population who had become noticeably more hostile to the British with the announcement of every German victory. All the while the Germans were reported to be less than twenty miles away.[27]

None of them were overly worried. News had reached them that a British destroyer was on the way to pick them up that evening. "At 11 o'clock at night we heard voices calling us to collect at once at the village inn," reported Katherine. "We gathered together by light of candles and then began our exit into the pitch-dark night." They emerged at the quay four miles away into a scene of chaos. Among the British were nearly two hundred Yugoslav officers and men, all hoping to be evacuated.[28] At four thirty a.m. those holding British passports were ordered to embark on a wine boat to carry them to the entrance of the Bay of Kotor to meet the destroyer.[29] It was barely large enough to hold the British, let alone the panicked Yugoslavs. "Just before we pushed off," recalled Flavia Kingscote, one of the nine women in the British party, "one of these desperate men on shore pulled a hand grenade out of his pocket and said if we refused to let him and his friends on board he would blow the whole boat sky high. We called his bluff, as there was no alternative, and pushed off, whereupon he took a running jump across the intervening space and clung despairingly to the side of the ship. I am glad I was below in the hold then and never saw the horrible scene that followed." The boat eased out into the dark waters and made its way cautiously through the winding bay. "Everything looked grey and unearthly," wrote Flavia. "A fine rain was falling. The drowned body of a soldier floated very slowly past the side of the boat. It was to us a presage of defeat."[30]

The rays of the sun were framing the mountains in warm silhouette by the time the ship rounded the last headland. Katherine and Alice scanned the horizon expectantly with the other passengers hoping to catch the first sight of the destroyer. Instead the expanse was empty. For several hours the boat cruised up and down the entrance to the bay while, in the direction of the shore, they could hear distant firing. The British Defence Attaché sent out repeated SOS messages searching for news of their rescue. Other than the crackle of the wireless, he was met with silence. Finally, at eleven a.m., the Minister huddled together his legation staff, then announced grimly that they were returning to shore. They stepped onto land near the village of Herceg Novi to await their fate at the hands of the enemy.[31]

The doctors and nurses ushered Flora, the lieutenant and judge into the hospital, a former hotel. Then they led them into the soldiers' ward, gave them coffee and cognac and tucked them up side by side.[32] The next morning Flora sat up brightly in her hospital bed to keep watch for Germans. "We haven't seen any yet, though always expecting to," she recorded, with a twinge of disappointment at the anticlimax. Instead, she spent the week resting quietly in bed and sitting in the sun on the terrace in the company of the lieutenant, until the doctors isolated him in a room for officers with tuberculosis. "He has it," they told her.[33]

All the while, Flora fretted terribly about the worry she knew she was putting Yurie through. When a young sergeant she had befriended offered conspiratorially to secrete her on board a lorry evacuating the wounded to the military hospital in Belgrade, she leapt at the chance. At least if she was in Belgrade she would have a chance of getting word to Yurie that she was safe. "We'll have to smuggle you in," he told her. "The Germans are disarming the soldiers and letting them go home, but they're taking the officers prisoner. If there's trouble en route just stick by me."

On a grey and bitterly cold morning Flora crowded into the open lorry with around seventeen others, wrapped a blanket around her and lay down shivering on a mattress. As the lorry neared the town of Mladenovac, Flora was gestured urgently to hide when a German sentry post was spotted ahead. She lay still and covered herself from head to toe with the blanket. The truck slowed and came to a stop while the Germans peered into the back. Then they waved them impatiently on. "I got through safely," Flora wrote triumphantly, "feeling very much as if I were being rescued by the Scarlet Pimpernel."[34]

By dusk Flora was wrapped up in bed in the military hospital in Belgrade, which was packed to capacity with victims of the bombing and the fighting. The staff had gone to great lengths to find her a room. Many knew her already – she had spent weeks in their wards the previous December and January after her old injuries had played up again. The next day she sent a note to Yurie to tell him that she was alive. Sick with worry about him in turn, she waited anxiously overnight for a response. It came in the form of Marica. Flora hurried down to meet her at the gate of the German-controlled hospital. The maid passed her a note and packet from Yurie through the bars. "He's been very ill while you've been away but he's a bit better now," she told her. "He would have come himself but he's not strong enough." Relief and emotion flooded over her at the news. "He knows now thank goodness that I am alive," she wrote in a rush. "I was determined he should know by [Russian] Easter."[35]

Flora was desperate to find a way to return home to him. "I thought it might be fun to stay and puzzle the Germans," she commented, "but I decided I must get out." But how to get past the armed sentries at the gate, she wondered. There was no way that they would permit a captain in the Yugoslav army to sally forth past them. Then she struck on a simple plan. She knew that she was on the hospital register as Captain Sandes. The answer was obvious; she would leave instead as "Mrs X". Flora sent another message to Marica to bring her women's clothes. The next morning, her maid bribed her way through the gates to hand her the package. Flora thanked her, said goodbye to a junior doctor and a few officers in whom she had gleefully confided her plans and hurried into a lavatory to change. Then she walked through the gate past the sentries without a second glance. "I arrived home very fit, very sunburnt and looking – so my husband and friends declared – 10 years younger, and as if I had been away for a holiday."[36]

Sinister rumours had gathered pace in Belgrade that the Germans would finish with the gallows what they had started with the bombing. Instead, to the great surprise of everyone including Flora, the behaviour of the first detachments of the Wehrmacht to enter the capital was "exemplary". The Germans put an end to widespread looting, calmed the first fears of starvation by forcing shop owners to open their doors, ordered everyone to be inoculated against typhoid and drew up plans to restore electricity, running water and the tram service. The behaviour, too, of German officers billeted on resentful families was "very correct".[37]

Within days, as one edict followed another in rapid succession, the Germans began to tighten their grip on the capital. Loudspeakers were set up across town to bellow orders to the population, who were expected to stand still and listen obediently, while notices were posted in public spaces across the city.[38] "They ruled with an iron fist; but if you strictly obeyed orders you were safe," commented Flora. "If you did not you were shot out of hand. There were no two ways about it."

One of their first measures was to impose a six-p.m. curfew. They sent out armed patrols to every part of town to ensure it was obeyed. "At first the Serbs, who do not take kindly to discipline, could not grasp the seriousness of curfew," Flora observed. "All night one heard shooting, and in the morning there were bodies lying in the streets with a paper pinned to the chest, 'found out in the street after 6 p.m.' One woman living near us went a few steps outside to call in her cat, and she was shot."[39] On 16th April, three days after the occupation of Belgrade, a new series of diktats were posted. "All Jews must report to Tašmajdan Square at 8 a.m. on 19th April. Those who do not report will be shot," they read. Those who obeyed were handed yellow armbands and were later set to work sweeping streets, tearing down ruined buildings and digging out corpses from fire- and bomb-damaged buildings.[40] Another set of orders were designed to shut down all but German-controlled press and media. First they announced that anyone caught listening to a foreign radio station would face the death penalty. Later they insisted that anyone with a wireless radio needed to register it. Finally they simply outlawed their possession. With no independent radio, no post and only a single permitted newspaper, the *Novo Vreme* (*New Times*), which published a continuous stream of fascist propaganda, the population were shut off from the outside world.[41]

Flora had returned home after twelve days away to a jubilant reunion with Yurie. "Great rejoicings," she wrote that evening in her diary. But during the days that followed she had to face the harsh reality of life in the occupied capital, made harder still by her knowledge that she was liable to be arrested at any time. For the first week after her escape from hospital she stayed at home with her husband. "Didn't like to go into the town," she commented miserably. But soon the edicts forced her out. Initially she only dared go in company, in fear that she would be simply lifted from the streets with no one to tell Yurie what had happened. First she walked into town with him to get their typhoid inoculations, one of a requisite two to protect them from the water-borne illness. ("Yurie got out of his second one on account of his heart," she noted.[42]) Then they queued repeatedly over subsequent days to register for their papers, as required by their new overlords. Finally, "expecting to be arrested every step", Flora furtively ventured out alone for the first time, certain that her British nationality, her

Yugoslav military rank and her recent escape from the clutches of the Germans were evident from her bearing. She returned home safely, having received hardly a second glance. From that moment on, she walked to and from town as she pleased.

Although life was increasingly difficult and she could never escape the fear of arrest, Flora returned to the same sort of mundane tasks that had occupied her before the war. She mended jumpers and darned socks, shopped at the grocer's, fought to keep moths under control, visited friends during the day and spent evenings playing cards with Yurie, the details of which she dutifully jotted in her diary along, regularly, with comments on the state of the weather, Yurie's health and what she had eaten for lunch.

In many respects, Flora and Yurie were better off than most. Their house was situated well away from the worst of the destruction, unlike many others who were forced to live in proximity to the stench of bodies, buried under collapsed houses, which grew worse following rain or on torrid spring days.[43] They had a nearby well from which they could obtain clean water and friends who checked in on them frequently. They also had the "invaluable" Marica (along with her "worthless" husband Sava) as live-in help. Although they were by no means wealthy – particularly as Yurie's health no longer allowed him to work – they had enough to get by.

For others in the capital life was a daily struggle to survive. Those who had lost their homes and possessions were forced to rely on the charity of others. Men and women, their faces drawn with hunger, spent their days in search of the little food remaining that had neither been commandeered by the Wehrmacht nor purchased by its soldiers with the Reichsmark at rates of exchange that made them feel wealthy. All municipal services had ceased to operate, leaving stinking heaps of rubbish to pile in the already rubble-clogged and cratered streets. There was no running water or operational toilets – hence the edict about typhoid inoculation. Instead the citizens were forced to use makeshift and foul "conveniences" in courtyards and cellars.[44]

Certain services were re-established with remarkable efficiency, given the extent of the damage, as gangs of Jews and starving, ragged Yugoslav POWs appeared in the streets to mend roads, lay tramlines, rebuild sewers and fix electric wires.[45] "The electricity came on," wrote Flora on 7th May, only a month after the bombing.

But against the backdrop of some seeming improvements in conditions, she was unsettled. A friend had related a conversation to her he had had with a German sergeant on the subject of German discipline. "'Yes,' said the sergeant, 'it is all right now we are the army, and are here only to do our own job. Our discipline is very severe. It is the death penalty for molesting a woman. But you just wait till the Gestapo comes along. It has been the same in every country. When we have done our own bit, the Gestapo follows on our heels.'"[46]

Katherine and Alice dejectedly traipsed up the steep main street of Herceg Novi in the company of the other British refugees to await capture by enemy troops. They dragged their few possessions into the abandoned Hotel Boka and laid claim to a corner. Late that afternoon, as they all sat wearily on the wisteria-covered terrace, the drivers of four motorcycles equipped with machine guns raced through the main street, looked up at the British party in amazement and drove on. They were wearing the green uniforms and plumed helmets of the Italian army.[47] "[We were] only thankful it was not the Germans," said Katherine in relief. The next morning, 18th April, a motorized unit arrived at the hotel to take them prisoner.[48]

For days the Italians imprisoned them within the confines of the hotel. Although they became increasingly "emboldened and arrogant" as their numbers in the town rose, by and large they did not mistreat their prisoners, thanks partly to the efforts of David Edge, an opera singer among the British. His Italian arias delighted their captors. "Edge will always sing us out of trouble," commented the Minister.[49] But suddenly, in the middle of their tenth night in captivity, they were wakened abruptly. "Pack your things," the Italians ordered impatiently. "We're taking you to Durazzo." At noon thirteen buses pulled up outside the hotel to take them to the Albanian port where, a quarter of a century before, the starving remnants of the Serbian army had gathered.[50]

On the evening of 25th April the bus carrying Katherine and Alice finally pulled up outside the Albergo dei Dogi, the swankiest hotel in Durazzo. The semicircular building was relatively new. It had real beds. It also had running water and baths – at least for two days, until the water supply gave out. From one side of its flat roof the British prisoners could look over the town, whose Ottoman-style architecture was swathed with Italian slogans and posters depicting the slightly comical features of Mussolini. From the other, they could look across to the Adriatic where, only fifty yards away, the town's main drain pumped effluent into the sea. "Added to this horror," shuddered Flavia, "the inhabitants of the place, through force of suggestion... used that spot quite openly as a public convenience." As the wind blew the contaminated air back at them, they would dash downstairs to the lounge with handkerchiefs across their mouths, only for "clouds" of flies to descend upon them. When, after a week, news arrived that they were to be taken to Italy, it came as a relief to all. Katherine was only too pleased to escape the town of "little water, hot weather, flies, mud flats and smells", for whatever awaited her there.[51]

With unambiguous menace, the green-grey uniformed Gestapo reached the capital shortly after the Wehrmacht. "The first thing [they] did was to hang three men from lamp posts on the Terrazia, the main street, one Sunday morning," said Flora. "They advertised their intention [to terrorize the Serbs], so that all could see." They set up their headquarters on the Terazije and a prison just off it, and began rounding up those they designated as enemies, including communists, intellectuals, Jews, Gypsies, Serbian politicians, criminals and those with links to the Allies. "The Gestapo by now were arresting people right and left; even taking them from their beds at night," she added. "These people simply disappeared, and one heard no more of them."[52]

On 24th June Flora went about her business as usual, still reeling from the news that Germany had declared war on the Soviet Union two days earlier, an event she considered important enough to record in capital letters in her diary. She had much weighing heavily on her mind. They were nearly out of wood for the fire, the price of food was soaring and she had had to visit Karl Rankin – the American legation's commercial attaché – for what she called the "dole". More worrying still, Yurie's health had taken a turn for the worse. That morning she sat to write a long letter to her sister Fanny in England, which she then had smuggled out of the country. "I am very well," she told her, and I wish I could say the same of Yurie, but he is really very ill, very high blood pressure, which affects his heart and lungs, and doesn't sleep well, at least not consecutively, though a good deal off and on and in the daytime… He has his bed in the sitting room, which is lighter and more cheery, and he can get up and sit on the porch and wander about a bit, but is too weak to walk far. He has been like this before and got quite well apparently last month, and used to go down town and all, and then it all came back again, but I hope and trust it will pass off again soon. He won't hear of going into a clinic, and really they did him more harm than good last time as he was starved. He is quite cheerful, and lies and reads most of the day.[53]

That evening, Flora had tucked him up in bed, as usual, in the sitting room. The streets had emptied when dusk fell, as the inhabitants rushed indoors to comply with the curfew. Only the occasional barking of dogs or the crack of a rifle could be heard to break the silence.[54] The day had been hot and humid and it promised to be an equally warm night, so she prepared to sleep on the porch where, at least, a breeze would reach her. Around ten o'clock, just as she was climbing into bed, the doorbell rang. Startled, she leapt up and ran to answer it. "Who's there?" she demanded. "Never mind who's here, open the gate," barked the reply. "I certainly won't, unless you tell me who you are. Besides, my dog will fly at you," exclaimed Flora as she struggled to hold on to Pat, who was growling ferociously. "Gestapo," answered the abrupt voice.

She pulled open the gate to two officers. "We're going to search the house," they informed her. "What's going on?" asked Yurie when he saw them. "Gestapo," she said simply. They walked from room to room, turned out her desk and confiscated a suitcase full of old letters and papers. Then they waited patiently while Flora dressed in the bathroom. "Come with us," they ordered them both. "They had been so correct and polite that it never dawned on me that they were taking my husband and myself to prison," recalled Flora. "So we took nothing with us, not even a blanket. I protested that my husband was very ill, but I suppose they didn't believe it. They would not hear of taking me only. We certainly must have been the most naive pair they had ever arrested. When we were in their car I said I hoped we would not have to walk back as my husband had a very bad heart and could not walk far. The officer looked at me queerly and said no, we would not have to walk back."[55]

Flora and Yurie were driven to the centre of town, past the shadowy ruins of numerous buildings. At the Terazije the car turned off onto Bulevar Kralja Aleksandra and through a dark archway. It came to a stop in a small courtyard. In the dim light Flora and Yurie were escorted to a thick iron door, set in a featureless wall. They waited momentarily while, on the other side, they could hear the rattle of keys and the sudden heavy shot of a bolt. Fully expecting to be beaten mercilessly as soon as the door clanged shut behind them, Flora was momentarily relieved when they were instead led across an enclosed, cobbled yard, through another door, into a stone passage, past a cell, and up a short flight of steps. There they were directed into an office that contained two beds pushed up against a wall, some filing cabinets, a washbasin and a central desk.[56] They sat while officials checked their details before ordering them to empty their pockets and Flora her handbag. Their money was counted out before them and placed with the rest of their possessions in two large envelopes, which were then sealed. Then two "grinning" guards stepped forward and gestured Flora and Yurie to stand. They patted down Yurie half-heartedly before leading them out. One took Yurie up another flight of stairs to a cell, while the other took Flora back to the cell that they had passed on the way to the office, unlocked it and shoved her in.

Even before the first incarnation of the Yugoslav experiment had emerged from the wreckage of post-1918 Europe, the signs had been there that all would not end well. "The Serbs are denying flatly the Croatian right to a name, a history and even a language," declared a Croatian spokesman before the international press in 1916. "[They] expect and are working through the diplomatic channels of the Entente powers to create a Greater Serbia. If they succeed, peace in that section of Europe will never be permanent; for the Serbs are not likely to diminish or quench the flames of their religious or national fanaticism."[57] Twenty-five years later, Serbian heavy-handedness and fanatical Croat nationalism had converted such brooding resentment into unbridled fury. The German invasion allowed them to unleash it on the two million Serbs living within the borders of the fascist "Independent State of Croatia".[58]

Two days after the State had been declared under the leadership of Ante Pavelić, the Ustaše began putting their plans into action to end Serb hegemony once and for all. In a campaign that combined genocide, forced conversions to Catholicism and ethnic cleansing, the Ustaše, with the assistance of units of equally merciless Bosnian Muslims, threw Serbs into concentration camps, burned their villages, massacred the inhabitants, destroyed churches and executed the Orthodox clergy. In an orgy of violence they conducted a campaign so savage that even the Germans stepped in to try to restrain them, in the knowledge that they were driving recruits into the resistance movements that were forming as a result of the German invasion.[59] According to the Simon Wiesenthal Center half a million Serbs were killed during this period. History would repeat itself half a century later. The names of the towns and villages where the Ustaše round-ups and atrocities occurred — such as Sarajevo, Vukovar, Banja Luka and Mostar — would appear in the press once again, but in the context of the Serbs acting as equally savage perpetrators. The victims had again become the aggressors.

There were two routes of escape for the Serbs. They could "go to the hills" to join the resistance movements or find sanctuary in the Italian-occupied zones. The Italians who twenty-five years previously had allowed them to die of neglect on the Albanian coast, now tried to come to their rescue. "The Italians again and again tried to intervene to save the defenceless Serbs and often succeeded," commented an American observer.[60] They also allowed them to travel north towards Split, a port that was solely under Italian control. Other targets of fascist hatred, including Jews, also found refuge in the Italian zones. The Jewish population of Split, three hundred before the war, expanded almost overnight to three thousand. Almost all survived the war. In another region, where the Italians shared authority with the Ustaše, the Italian commander refused them permission to round up the Jews. To do so would have been "incompatible with the honour of the Italian Army", he is reputed to have said.[61]

The Jews of Serbia had no such route of escape. In "the most comprehensive campaign of annihilation throughout Axis-occupied Europe", the Germans were assisted by the Volksdeutsche and the supporters of the Zbor, the Serbian fascist party, although their anti-Semitism reflected no widespread local prejudice.[62] The men were rounded up in the summer of 1941. Most were shot by soldiers of the Wehrmacht, the German regular army. In December six thousand women and children were interned in the Exhibition Grounds in Zemun, along the Sava River. They were housed in buildings of glass and concrete, where they died of starvation and exposure. One of the victims was Ruža Vinaver, who had befriended Flora and Emily in Valjevo in early 1915.[63] Those who survived such imprisonment were murdered in the early incarnations of gas chambers. In late 1942, having completed their genocidal mission in Serbia, the Germans closed their "Jewish Section" office in Belgrade.[64]

War crimes of staggering enormity were also carried out by the Germans against the Serbs in reaction to their insurrection. Fuelled by a tradition of armed uprising and the fierce, proud nationalism of the heroic sort that led to their victory in the First World War, only the Serbs – of all the peoples in Europe to suffer German occupation – rose up against their oppressors from the very beginning.[65] They flocked to two organizations – the royalist Četniks, who were led by a former Serbian Colonel, Draža Mihailović, and the communist Partisans, headed by Josip Broz, known as "Tito". In a remarkable campaign in August and September 1941 they liberated large areas of Serbian territory from German occupation.

The armed opposition took the Germans by surprise. In the belief that his motorized forces had cowed the recalcitrant Serbs, Hitler had quickly redeployed the forces that he had used to defeat their army for the invasion of Russia. To compensate for his deficiency of manpower he issued the infamous edict that for the death of every German one hundred Serbs would be killed, and for each German wounded fifty would die. The full horror of this decree was put into play in October when, in retaliation for an attack in a nearby village that left ten dead and a number wounded, the Germans marched into Kragujevac, the town where Flora and Emily had worked in the autumn of 1914. By the end of the day they had executed 2,324 men, among them boys from the upper year of the high school.[66] To underline their intention to pursue this policy to its full extent, the Germans took prominent men from towns and villages across Serbia hostage, including Vasa "Mac" Srdić,

Katherine's half-Serbian, half-Scottish partner. They announced that, if they were attacked, the men would be killed.

At first the Četniks and Partisans had collaborated uneasily in their pitched battles against the Germans. However, their long-term goal, to take over the reins of government at the end of the war, put them on a collision course with each other. The impact of Hitler's edict – one that even he had not foreseen – was to turn growing tensions between them into outright civil war. The Partisans held that individual lives were of little account against their goal of replacing the old system with one based on the Soviet model. The more savage the Germans, they reasoned, the more recruits they could win, and they were accordingly willing to provoke attacks against civilians. In stark contrast, Hitler's order had paralysed the Četniks' operations. Those of Mihailović's generation remembered all too vividly the horrific losses that the Serbians had suffered during the First World War. In the belief that the cost in lives of attacking the Germans was too high to justify any short-term advantages, they planned instead to build up their power to fight them when they could be assured of long-term success and Allied help. Not only did they see the behaviour of the Partisans as a threat to innocent civilians, the Četniks also believed that they posed their greatest challenge to re-establishing the old royalist order. In some instances these beliefs drove them into the murky waters of appeasement and collaboration with Germans with whom they now shared a joint enemy.[67]

Mac Srdić did not survive. He was executed as a hostage by the Germans in 1942.[68]

Reeling from the shock of her arrest, Flora paused for a moment just beyond the wide, low door to the cell as it slammed shut behind her. In front of her, on two long rows of mouldy straw mattresses, lay thirteen women under ragged blankets who stirred and looked over curiously at the new arrival. With the exception of two narrow cots, the room was otherwise empty of all furniture.[69] Although it was relatively large, at fifteen by twenty feet, it felt claustrophobic. Its two small, glassless windows, above head height, were heavily barred and covered with wooden screens. In one corner was an odorous "night bucket", while the stagnant, foul air buzzed with flies. The bottom half of the walls was painted dark brown, above which they were white. They were otherwise undecorated, the drab expanse broken only by clothes hanging from a handful of crooked nails and the smudged remains of flies. Strung from one wall to another was a washing line on which grey towels were hung. As Flora stood taking stock, several of the women stood up to greet her warmly. They handed her a spare blanket and squeezed up further on the straw mattresses to make room for her.[70]

The women were mixed in terms of both nationality and class.[71] "There were also streetwalkers," Flora commented, "but we were bound together by our common misfortunes and became astonishingly good comrades." Among them, fifty-three-year-old Ruth Mitchell from Milwaukee cut an incongruous figure. She had joined the Četniks the month before the German invasion. A journalist for the Associated Press had encountered her before she had been arrested. "It seemed to me that Miss Mitchell was just looking for some à la Hollywood adventure," he wrote. "Well, I thought, she'll probably get all she wants and more before long."[72] The American woman Četnik was awed by the veteran Englishwoman soldier. She was a "really magnificent old lady of sixty-seven, stocky, weather-beaten, with short-cropped white hair," Mitchell wrote admiringly.[73]

Each morning, after an armed guard threw open the door at seven o'clock and bellowed the order "*Aufstehen!*" ("Get up!"), the women would jump up and queue at the door. In pairs they were led down to the "ladies' room" at the end of the stone passage. When Flora's turn came she splashed across the wet floor to wash at one of the two taps, both cold. There was one toilet in the passage, the sole facility to serve between thirty and forty women, while the contents of the night bucket were poured down the urinal in the cobbled yard.

The women spent the mornings doing the "housework". They swept and scrubbed the floor of their room, the passage, the office and guardroom. They shook their blankets to rid them of dust and the latest generation of bedbugs, aired their straw mattresses and polished the boots of the prison warders. And once a week they were assigned the laundry for the prison. "The clothes were sometimes exceedingly dirty and often – how often! covered with blood," wrote Ruth.[74] But the work at least broke the monotony of the day, gave them some exercise and allowed them out of the confines of the cell into the yard. "This yard was a hot, cobble-stoned place enclosed by a high wall, but it might have been the Garden of Eden, we were so keen to get into it," recalled Flora.[75] At twelve thirty they were handed their only food of the day, a plate of beans and a slice of maize bread. The women's relatives were allowed to drop off food for them at the gates, but much was stolen by the guards.[76]

"The days were very long," wrote Flora. "We had no books or pencils. I used to gaze up at the narrow strip of blue sky and think that I would never keep an animal in a cage."[77] It was also apparent to the other women how wracked with worry she was about Yurie. "Her anxiety about him, her efforts to catch the smallest glimpse of him were agonizing," remembered Ruth.[78]

By the end of the first week of May, Katherine and Alice had left the stinking Albanian town of Durazzo behind. With the other British prisoners, they had been flown in groups to the east coast of Italy. German officers were everywhere, lending their Axis ally the appearance of being yet another country that they had conquered. The arrival of the British allowed the Italians to show their contempt for the Germans. "There we were treated like princes," commented Patrick Maitland of the *Times*, one of the interned journalists. "Under the noses of German officers we were stood drinks and all payment was refused."[79] The prisoners were taken by train and bus through Italy. "At each stage we found our transport ready and waiting, and we were treated with consideration and good humour throughout," reported Flavia. The last leg of their long journey took them through countryside of olive groves, vineyards and picturesque villages to the hilltop walled town of Chianciano, in the province of Siena.[80] They stepped out in disbelief into a spa resort that had been built around famed mineral springs.

The prisoners were taken to three adjacent hotels and given unlimited food and drink, access to the gardens, which were thick with lilacs and irises, along with the use of a former horse-show ground as an exercise field. "It was impossible to believe that we were in an enemy country," wrote David Walker, another journalist. "Not one of us had been interrogated, not one of us had received anything but kindness at the hands of the Italian Foreign Office and the Italian people."[81] Within days they had their own newspaper, cricket, baseball and football teams and, for the less athletically inclined, bridge, chess and draughts. Every afternoon they were allowed out on walks in the company of detectives, while in the evenings they could go shopping for half an hour. "The Italians gave us a very generous rate of exchange for our now practically worthless Yugoslav money," praised Flavia.[82]

All the while, as the chilly month of May gave way to the hot, long days of early June, the American embassy in Rome worked hard on securing their release. Finally, on 10th June, they received the news that they could leave the next day. The prisoners packed their bags, drank the rest of their wine and prepared to leave. "Our departure from Chianciano was marked by friendly gestures from the inhabitants," wrote Patrick Maitland. "They hoped to see us again in better times and were certainly going to miss our trade. Within five weeks, they admitted, the British prisoners had drunk more beer than the whole village normally consumed in two whole years."[83]

"The prison was exceptional, perhaps unique, in that it was an amateur affair hastily organized," wrote Flora's cellmate Ruth, who spent two months languishing in its confines before she was sent into internment in Germany. "It was staffed by half-witted local scum, who were ludicrously unsure of themselves and who therefore vacillated between needless ferocity and lazy apathy." The guards had been selected from the Volksdeutsche for their ability to speak both Serbian and German. The most senior staff in the prison were also Volksdeutsche. Most day-to-day authority was invested in Richter, the chief warder, and Hahn, the second warder. Richter, in peacetime, had been a carpenter and a good one at that, by reputation. He was also a sadist. "He was constantly telling women that their husbands or sons were going to be shot that night and then eagerly watching for a twitch of agony," wrote Ruth. "He seemed to be always a member of the firing squads." Cruelty came less easily to blond, blue-eyed Hahn. "He had obviously been born with decent instincts, and it was strange to watch him slowly deteriorate," she commented. "Several times he did small kindnesses to the women but was furious if thanked." Like Richter, he also joined the firing squads but struggled to cope.

"For four days Hahn drank steadily and could not eat a mouthful," recalled Ruth after one hundred and twenty-eight Serbs were executed, not all from that prison. "I knew, because I had to place and remove his meals. As conditions in the prison became steadily more frightful, Hahn drank more and more."

The "frequent" executions took place at two a.m., although it is unclear whether any occurred while Flora was there. At first the men and women selected for death were dragged out of the prison to a nearby park, almost certainly Kalemegdan. Then, one day, Hahn announced to one of the women that as such detours were "a waste of time" they would henceforth take place in the cellar. The steps to it lay off the same passage as the women's cell. Although the guards first slammed and bolted the door and turned up the radio in the office to drown out the sound, they could still hear the muffled bursts of firing above the dance music.[84]

The women lived day by day with the threat that they might be shot. Flora refused to be intimidated. "Had a row with Hahn because he shouted at me and was threatened with the cellar," she scribbled.[85] The other women looked on with a mixture of alarm and admiration. "Flora Sandes knew how to handle [the guards]," commented Ruth. "She possessed a wonderful fund of Serbian swear words which she launched at [them] with such devastating effect that while she was there they behaved almost respectfully."[86]

4th July 1941 was Yurie's fifty-third birthday. That day Flora heard that he had become so ill that even the prison doctor – a man of brutal instincts named Jung – had agreed that he needed to be taken to hospital. The women in the cell could see the almost physical impact the news had on her. They spoke to her quietly in sympathy while Ruth, as "head woman", approached Hahn to ask that she be allowed to say goodbye to him first. Brusquely, he agreed. That afternoon she accompanied Flora into the cobbled yard. "Out stumbled her thin, dying husband, supported by a stick," she wrote. "He fell on the bench; his head bowed as he coughed." Without words, Flora sat down next to him and put her hand on his arm. Shortly after he was "roughly" removed and taken through the prison doors on his way to hospital. "He looks terribly ill, shall I see him again?" Flora wrote in despair after seeing him.[87]

The next morning, Hahn threw open the door to their cell. "*Achtung*," he shouted. "Flora Sandes. Take your things and come." He paused for effect while the other women stood still with horror. Then he broke the tension with a single word. "Home," he said. The women burst into applause, crowded round her and enthusiastically wished her luck. "I could hardly believe it," wrote Flora, "and I felt, in an odd way, rather mean at leaving those women there."[88]

She was taken to the office, handed her possessions and money and told that she first needed to visit Gestapo headquarters on the Terazije to complete some paperwork. "I said goodbye quite friendlily with Hahn and Richter," she scribbled, "and we shook hands and I showed R[ichter] my Kara-G[eorge] legitimation with my photo as an officer, which seemed to tickle him very much, and when we got to the Gestapo the young man who escorted me there asked for it too, and showed it to the others." There, she was introduced to "Mr Huber" who became, in effect, her Gestapo parole officer. In his presence she signed some paperwork in promise of good behaviour, agreeing to speak only to Serbs, to show any letters she received to him first and to say or do nothing that might "offend Germany". She also had to agree to report to him weekly.

In disbelief that she was free, she was escorted to the door and told to return home. She hurried through the streets feeling "dazed" and "very dirty", all the while expecting to be rearrested at any moment. She was nearly at her door when someone called out to her. She turned to see Yurie waving at her from a carriage. He had been released from hospital at the same time that she had been sent home. "Richter had fetched him himself, and got him a carriage and even carried his bag, as Yurie was so ill and weak," she wrote.[89] They stepped through their front door together after eleven days in prison.

"We sat on the porch and had breakfast and talked," recorded Flora on the day of her release. "M[arica] and the dogs overjoyed to see us... Yurie went to bed very soon. He had a very bad night, and called me (I was sleeping in the other room then) about 11.30, and I sat up with him all night, in the armchair. His heart [is] very bad." The next morning, a Sunday, he was so ill that in desperation

Flora raced through the streets trying to find a doctor from a local practice. None were open. On her return, she sent Marica out with instructions to fetch Dr Svetislav Stojanović, Katherine's former chief surgeon. He came at once to give him an injection. That night Flora stayed with Yurie on a campbed. "He had a bad night," she wrote simply.[90]

The next morning he was no better. In despair about what best to do, she ordered a taxi to take him back to the clinic that had "starved" him when he had stayed there last, comforting herself with the knowledge that at least he would have medical care on hand. "He was put into a nice little room by himself," she wrote that evening. "I am only allowed to stay from 12 to 1 with him. I came home feeling very sad." Every day for the rest of July Flora walked to the clinic to see him for the solitary hour she was permitted. She brought him his lunch, kept him company and noted the state of his health each day in her diary. His arms and hands swelled and he had had to have fluid removed from his lung – "one litre (4th time)", she noted flatly.[91]

Meanwhile she kept as busy as she could. When she was not with Yurie she passed her time searching the shops in the sticky July heat for food she thought he might like. She also gave English lessons, something that the Gestapo had forbidden her to do, but she felt she had no choice. With prices in Belgrade soaring, her invalids' pension bought her almost nothing, and she needed money to care for Yurie. She had a steady if not abundant succession of students – most people in Belgrade believed that the Allies would win the war and enough were willing to take the risk of running foul of the Germans by taking lessons.[92]

She also had Mr Huber to visit weekly. She would dress in full Serbian uniform, recalls Mirjana Harding (née Vidaković), to stand up to him. "Paid my visit to Gestapo as ordered, at 11, all most pleasant," she wrote in her diary after her first interview with him on 12th July. Soon she felt confident enough to make queries and requests of her own. In late July she marched into his office to ask him about a man who had questioned her. "If anyone comes to see you again they must show you their badge, unless they're in Gestapo uniform," he told her. Feeling emboldened at his response, next she asked him if she could visit Miss Jane Allison, a "stern old Scottish spinster" whom the Gestapo had thrown into prison. Her request was too much for Huber. "He most indignantly refused," she reported.[93]

Flora's request was symptomatic of her attitude towards abiding by the Gestapo's rules. If she thought she might get away with it, she did as she pleased. Not only did she continue to teach English "under the noses of the Germans", she had no intention of obeying the order that she speak only to Serbs.[94] But as the weeks passed, she had fewer opportunities to savour each small victory. The small colony of British women dwindled rapidly, as one arrest followed another. Most, after a stay in the same prison as Flora, were interned in Liebenau, a civilian internment camp in southern Germany. And of those who remained free, many were too fearful to be seen with her. "I abruptly realized the folly of being seen speaking to an Englishwoman... especially one who had lately been to prison," wrote Lena Yovitchitch of a chance encounter with her.[95] It meant, for Flora, an increasingly isolated and lonely existence.

By the third week of July, Yurie's health had seemingly begun to stabilize. On 2nd August, after nearly a month at the clinic and a final check by the doctor, he was released. Flora was overjoyed. So too was Yurie. "Yurie came home," wrote Flora happily, another event she considered important enough to merit capital letters in her diary.[96] For the first couple of days, all went well. He rested in the shade on the porch, slept in the afternoons and sat with Flora sipping the "real tea" that she had saved for special occasions. But on 4th August his health took a turn for the worse. His feet and legs swelled, his thin frame was wracked by coughing fits and he barely slept. Flora now began to voice a fear in her diary that had lingered unwritten for months. "Yurie about the same," she noted six days later. "I made cakes for tea and we had tea together by his couch – perhaps for the last time?"[97]

The following morning she brought him back to the clinic. For the first few days he was so ill that the doctors, contrary to regulations, allowed her to sleep there. She spent every possible moment with him, sometimes hiding from them after they began reinforcing their strict visiting rules. Yurie too began to face the fact that he was dying. "Yurie seemed awfully bad," wrote Flora on 29th August after a visit that left her deeply shaken, "and for the first time said to me he thought he was going to die, and would like to die at home but 'it would be more trouble for me!'... I went home feeling very miserable and wondering if Yurie would be alive tomorrow."[98]

Two days later he was carried home by ambulance for what his doctors almost certainly assumed would be his final days, although Flora may have held lingering hopes that he would stage a temporary recovery of the sort he had enjoyed time and again. "Great rejoicings," she scribbled that day. "I can hardly believe my eyes that he is home again, and he is so delighted himself." But the strain must have been almost unbearable for her over the days that followed. With the help of Marica she looked after him, sitting with him during the day and often for much of the night. She got little sleep and called the doctor frequently. One told her quietly, after giving Yurie a morphia injection, that the "end was very near".[99] Flora already knew as much.

"I went to find Milenka after tea and get his wife to come and help, long walk and couldn't find the place and was away for two hours, and Yurie was worried about me," wrote Flora with remarkable presence of mind on 11th September.

> He only had milk for supper and coughed a lot. I went to bed and slept from 9 till 12 and Yurie didn't wake me though he had been coughing, he says softly so as not to wake me. But at 12 he asked for tea, and we had it together and we sat and talked and smoked and he seemed all right. Then he said he wanted to sleep so I tucked him up and heard no more coughing and thought he was asleep. At 1.30 heard a little gasp and then a sound – the death rattle, rushed to Yurie but it was all over. Yurie had died in his sleep. Could not believe it and spoke to him frantically, but no heartbeat and no pulse. His eyes were closed as if asleep.[100]

It was pouring with rain and very cold when, two days later, Flora and Marica shivered through the grey, wet streets on their long walk to Belgrade's New Cemetery. They walked through the elaborate stone and wrought-iron gates, past the ornate sepulchres to the small Russian chapel. Crowded inside were several of Yurie's Russian friends. So too was Lilian Vidaković (née Allen), the former president of the English Club who, along with her twelve-year-old daughter Cherry, was one of the few Englishwomen who had so far escaped arrest.[101] She was putting herself at risk by being seen with Flora, as Flora realized. "A great help she was to me," she commented appreciatively. The solemn group attended the long, Orthodox service, then trailed behind the hearse in the mud and rain to the grave. "Flowers on coffin. Cherry fainted from the incense but recovered afterwards," noted Flora simply. Then the sad group turned away, walked out through the great gates to a café across the road. "Then walked to Alex. St [Bulevar Kralja Aleksandra] and all went our ways, Maritza and I walked home. Terrible day," concluded Flora. "I slept for an hour after lunch on the sofa. M[arica] lit the fire as it was so cold. Wrote up diary." It was the last time she did so for the duration of the war.[102]

For three and a half long years Flora remained in German-occupied Belgrade. Her life in recent months had revolved almost entirely around her beloved Yurie and, alone with her thoughts, she suffered his loss both constantly and keenly during what must have seemed like an interminable and often forlorn wait for Allied victory. Not only was she largely cut off from the few British women who had avoided arrest and internment, with nothing but propaganda in the newspapers and over the airwaves, she was also cut off from her family and the rest of the world.

The feeling of loneliness must have been particularly acute during the long, cold winter evenings after the six o'clock curfew when she sat indoors alone, listening to the sound of gunfire as it broke the eerie silence. "I cannot remember a night when there was no shooting; but later, when the people had learnt their bitter lesson, I think it was only the patrols keeping in touch to encourage themselves," she commented. She also lived with a constant weight of worry. "I never went to bed without placing a dressing gown handy in which to receive the police; and a pair of slacks, warm jumper and thick shoes in case of acute emergency."[103]

She also suffered grinding poverty. Many of the wealthier inhabitants of the capital had been able to move to the outlying villages where they swapped comfort for relative freedom and more plentiful food, but Flora could not have afforded the luxury even had she wanted. She was reliant for income on teaching English and her students were in the capital. "As everyone in Belgrade seemed to be learning English I was kept busy teaching it," she wrote. Busy as she remained, her work earned her barely enough to make ends meet. No longer able to afford the services of Marica and Sava, she moved from her large house to a smaller one in the same district, with only Pat for company. And difficult as it had been for her to buy food and fuel during her first summer under occupation, by winter it had become far worse. The cold had swept in on the back of a howling Arctic wind at the end of November, driving flurries of thick snow before it and coating the streets thickly with ice. "Neither firewood nor coal was obtainable, and winter fell exceptionally hard, even for the Balkans," recalled Flora. "So I had to break up tables and chairs to make fires… Had it not been for the black market, which flourished openly, we would have starved."[104]

Throughout the war she continued her weekly trips into town to see Huber. As the weeks passed, something that might have passed for friendship if circumstances had been different arose between them. "H[uber] very amiable and looks much better after his holiday," she reported brightly after one early meeting.[105] He treated her very well, Flora later reported, and would reputedly pour her a glass of schnapps before sitting chatting to her.[106] It is also far from inconceivable, in light of the fact she was virtually the only woman of British nationality to retain her freedom in Belgrade during the occupation, that he helped to protect her from rearrest and internment.

News of German victories followed one after another that first year, settling like a blanket of depression on Flora and the other inhabitants of Belgrade. German media barked the news to them of each Russian city that fell to their armies until, by the end of November, they crowed that they were at the gates of Moscow. A few days later, they were told of the devastating Japanese surprise attack on the US Pacific Fleet at Pearl Harbour and, in the New Year, of Rommel's march towards the Suez Canal. Every report of a German victory served to make their belief in their ultimate liberation feel ever more remote.

But by late 1942, although the stream of German propaganda continued unabated, whispers of an Allied victory against Rommel reached the ears of the Serbs, lending credence to their belief that the Allies would, in the end, be victorious. Then, in 1943, they heard rumours of German defeats in Russia and North Africa, the Allied invasion of Sicily, the surrender of Italy and the gathering pace of British and American air raids on Germany.

Although each new rumour of victory led to "secret rejoicings", the morale of the Serbs was tempered by increasing hardship.[107] Inflation was raging out of control. The shelves and counters of shops were bare, people were ill fed and disease, particularly tuberculosis, began to take hold as it had done during the previous global conflict. By the middle of the war, Flora too was tired, ill nourished and utterly fed up with the daily struggle to make ends meet. Following one particularly trying week, she sat herself down in front of Huber and glowered at him. "I've had enough," she told him. "Things have got to be better in one of your camps. I want you to send me to one." Huber roared with laughter. "Put your request in writing," he replied.[108] If she did, he almost certainly ensured that it went no further than his desk.

Cordial as her relations were with Huber, she took great pleasure in the news of the Allied victories. She took particular delight in a story that spread like wildfire through the capital. "One day the Germans paraded some British prisoners of war through the streets of Belgrade, with the idea of impressing the Serbs," Flora relayed with mischievous pleasure. "It proved a terrible flop, for the prisoners marched whistling, their guards could not prevent the crowds from cheering and pressing cigarettes on them. One prisoner, on passing a donkey, shot out his arm in the Nazi salute and shouted 'Heil Hitler', whereupon the rest of the column followed suit."[109]

Easter Sunday 1944 dawned cloudy but dry over Belgrade. All across the city, as church bells tolled, families rose and greeted each other with the traditional greeting "*Hristos voskrese*" ("Christ is risen"), to which they replied "*Vaistinu voskrese*" ("Truly He is risen"). This spring, the fragrant April winds had carried particular promise with them. Shrubs and fruit trees were in full bloom and flowers were in profusion everywhere. Equally ubiquitous were tales of recent Allied victories and German defeats, lending people confidence for the first time that this would be their final Easter under occupation.

As the citizens of the capital sat down at their breakfast tables, their conversations were interrupted by the sudden drone of engines overhead. The hum, this time, was unfamiliar. As they peered upwards into the sky, wave upon wave of American Flying Fortresses and Liberators appeared overhead in breaks in the cloud, almost three years to the day since German bombers began the attack that left seventeen thousand dead. It was all the proof they needed that the Allies were on the verge of winning the war.[110]

The first explosion in the centre of the capital turned their joy instantly to disbelief. One bomb after another whistled down onto the residential districts in a series of earth-shaking concussions, driving dense pillars of smoke high above the rooftops. For Flora, it was the most terrifying experience of the war. There were no air-raid shelters for her to run to, since there were no military targets for miles around. Instead, she dashed for the only cover she could find. "I sheltered in a tiny shack and held the head of an old woman on my lap," she recalled later, "telling her not to be frightened, while the ceiling crashed down on my head."[111]

When the skies finally cleared of American aircraft, Flora – then sixty-eight years old – and the "old woman" were shaken but unhurt. She returned home to find that her windows had been broken, but that otherwise her house was intact. Those on either side of her had been hit.[112] "It is bad to be bombed by the enemy, but doubly so to be attacked by one's friends," she later wrote angrily. "The casualties numbered 2,000 in a radius of half a mile round my house. Not a single German suffered, for they were safely ensconced in deep dugouts in the town."[113] No adequate explanation was ever given of how the Americans had managed to rain over one hundred bombs on the centre of Belgrade while targeting a German aircraft-component factory over three miles outside of the city. "It was an accident," they simply shrugged.[114]

The bombers continued their sorties time and again over Belgrade that summer and autumn, terrifying the inhabitants, who feared a repetition of the mistake. They left their capital in droves to seek shelter in the villages, as they had done in 1941.[115] Others, too poor, tired or ill to flee, stayed in their homes but fled to the outskirts at the first warning of attack. Flora stayed put. "Almost every morning the air-raid siren sounded," she said later. "I sat on my balcony drinking tea made of lime-tree flowers or – a rare luxury – tea made of the stalks of morello cherries. I watched endless streams of men, women and children passing my gate on their way to the open fields. At sundown they came back weary, footsore and sun-scorched, or wet through in one of those frequent thunderstorms."[116]

"I've come to say goodbye," Flora said to Huber during a visit to his office. He looked up with a start. "And where do you think you're going?" he demanded, spluttering with indignation. "You're not going anywhere." "No," she smiled, "but you are."[117]

By the end of the summer Flora knew the Germans had lost the war. So too did the rest of the country. When word of the Normandy landings reached the ears of the Serbs after 6th June they were filled with renewed hope that their liberation from the enemy would be soon at hand. Their hope turned to certainty that summer as they watched columns of Wehrmacht retreat north, after Hitler began to withdraw his forces from Serbia in a desperate attempt to shore up his other fronts.

Events now moved rapidly. Across Yugoslavia, the Partisans inflicted a series of crushing defeats on the Četniks, leaving them the only serious contender to take over post-war authority. Romania declared war on Germany in August while in September Bulgaria followed suit. In France the Allies drove the Germans back towards their borders while the Soviet Red Army won victory after victory against them in the east. The vanguard of a massive Soviet invasion force crossed the Serbian frontier on 22nd September.[118] In loose collaboration with the Partisans they battled their way towards Belgrade. The fighting was savage and merciless. "Corpses littered the sides of the road, piled one on another, some in the field-grey of the Wehrmacht, others stripped of their boots and uniforms and left lying half-naked; hundreds and hundreds of them," wrote Fitzroy MacLean, the head of a British liaison mission to the Partisans, who had travelled with them on their approach to the capital. Some, he noted, bore the signs of execution.[119]

"Early one morning in October 1944, we heard that the Russians were coming," wrote Flora. "At first we did not believe it. Yet actually they were there; with tanks 'Katushkas' [rocket launchers], armoured cars and all." She rushed out of her house to cheer them as they passed. "We gave them a terrific reception," she said later. "All young, tough looking fellows, dusty and dirty after marching and fighting for days, but full of high spirits and splendid soldiers."[120] For ten days street fighting raged across the capital, as the Russians and Partisans fought to clear the city of the last pockets of resistance. "Bullets whiz[zed] along every street as the Russians hunted out isolated groups who were in hiding," Flora recalled. By 20th October, after three and a half years of brutal occupation, the capital had been cleared of Germans.

The population of Belgrade gave the Partisans as euphoric a welcome as they had given the Russians. They flew red flags from their windows and flocked to the streets to cheer a parade marking Tito's triumphant entry into the capital. "It was impossible not to be moved by the sight of the ragged, battle-stained throng of Partisans of all sizes and ages who marched past us," wrote MacLean. "Veterans of Salonika and the Balkan Wars marched next to boys of sixteen and seventeen; here and there a girl strode along with rifle and pack beside the men."[121]

With the support of much of the public the Partisans under Tito moved rapidly to establish their authority across the length and breadth of Yugoslavia. Their political, military and administrative structures became the new government, they took control over the written press and radio and instituted conscription to give their authority the backing of their armed forces. They also established a court for "trying crimes against the national honour" and set their secret police – the "OZNA" – to root out those they viewed as counter-revolutionaries, collaborators and traitors.[122]

Even before the last of the Germans had been driven from the city agents of the OZNA were rounding up their opponents, in the first ominous sign that liberation from the Germans would not be all that many Serbs had hoped for. Soon it became clear that the same ruthlessness that had allowed the Partisans to continue their attacks after the 1941 massacres was being applied to the persecution of their opponents. Just as the Germans had done, they imposed a curfew from six p.m. until daylight while, during the day, the streets rang with the shouts of "Death to the traitors!" and "Long live the Soviet Union!" as parades of Communist supporters marched through the streets carrying framed portraits of Stalin.[123] They requisitioned homes, appropriated their contents and took what food and fuel they wanted, leaving little for anyone else. "Most people considered themselves lucky if they secured potatoes and other vegetables," recalled Lena Yovitchitch.[124] Then, on 27th

November, the papers announced the execution of over a hundred people accused of being war criminals. "There was little in common among them, except perhaps that none was a war criminal," wrote one dismayed onlooker.[125] It was rapidly becoming clear to all but the most ardent Communists that they had exchanged one set of oppressors for another.

While the Partisans were manoeuvring to establish their unequivocal control over the machinery of state, Flora was interviewed by Reuters. Her words, less than a month after they had marched into Belgrade, were already subject to censorship. "I must express my admiration for the Russians who took Belgrade without using artillery on the town, and without wrecking a single house," she was quoted as saying.[126] Although there is no evidence that the Russians actually targeted civilians, this statement was blatantly untrue.[127] She was also visited on occasion by the Partisans, who would have viewed her with suspicion from the start, both as an English national and a "bourgeois". But now she had no one like Huber to look out for her or to whom she could air her grievances.[128]

Life over the following months became increasingly difficult for Flora and the remaining British nationals, as the suspicion of the new Communist authorities hardened towards their country of birth. Not only were they hostile on ideological grounds, in the post-war scramble to claim territory and define borders, the British had sided with the Italians in their claim over the largely Italian-populated city of Trieste that lay near the old border between the two countries. The airwaves rang with verbal attacks against Britain while the newspapers were peppered with equally antagonistic commentary. The hostility not only left the British vulnerable to maltreatment at the hands of the authorities but also put at risk those who were friendly towards them. "Denunciation was to be a great factor in the lives of all of us for a long time," commented Isabel Božić, an Englishwoman married to a Serb. "It followed that a newly converted Partisan might be able to win the confidence of Russian and other communists by denouncing someone who had spoken in favour of the British."[129] With great sadness Flora began to turn over the hitherto unimaginable thought that she would have to leave the country that had been her home for much of the last thirty years and for which she had served in two world wars.

* * *

At a time when most British nationals were struggling to come to terms with the fact that they were no longer welcome in their adopted country, Katherine began to make plans to return to Yugoslavia. She had spent the remainder of the war, after being released by her benevolent Italian captors, in Lanarkshire, Scotland, where she had run baby clinics while serving as chairman of the West of Scotland Committee of the Yugoslav Relief Society, an organization that included many other "old campaigners", including Vera Holme.[130]

In the spring of 1944 the Save the Children Fund had approached her to ask if she would head a relief unit that they were putting together to work in Yugoslavia. Under the auspices of the United Nations Relief and Rehabilitation Administration (UNRRA), an organization whose remit was to provide immediate aid and assistance to all such liberated countries, Katherine set out with her unit in early June to await transportation first to Italy and then to Yugoslavia. With her travelled Alice Murphy, her old hospital secretary.

The need for emergency relief was enormous. Three and a half years of war, occupation and civil strife had ravaged the country from end to end. Transportation links had been destroyed, agriculture and industry lay in ruins and the population was threatened by both starvation and disease, particularly tuberculosis, in conditions virtually identical to those that had beset the nascent kingdom at the end of the First World War.[131] All the while the negotiations for the unit's entry to Yugoslavia went on and on and on. "The talks... were... unforgivably slow," commented a contemporary Serbian observer. "Foreigners from Western countries were unwelcome, and, contrary to the situation after the First World War, the attitude towards them was one of considerable hostility and fear... However, in the end Yugoslavia had to accept help from UNRRA... the simple reason was that the country was devastated and the people hungry."[132]

In March 1945, after a nine-month wait, Tito grudgingly gave his consent for the first representatives of UNRRA to leave for Yugoslavia from Italy.[133] Soon after arrival Katherine and Alice received permission from the Ministry of Health to travel from their base in Budva, Montenegro, to Belgrade to discuss the future of the Anglo-Yugoslav Children's Sanatorium. It was a "harrowing and distressing" trip, reported Katherine. The streets were thick with snow and slush and every café and public building was overflowing with the wounded, in a scene that reminded her of "Kragujevatz in 1915". Before she visited the site of her hospital in Kamenica, she went to visit Flora and her former chief surgeon, Dr Svetislav Stojanović. "They looked older and worn out," she recalled.[134]

The hospital that Katherine had had built largely at her own expense in 1934 was now "an empty shell". It had been used, then abandoned, by the Partisans during the war. In disbelief she walked grimly from room to room. "We found the hospital standing but entirely bare, the windows broken and the doors off," wrote Katherine.[135] But the sight of her mosaic of the red lion rampant lying intact in the central hall gave her a small but significant glimmer of hope.[136] When she returned to Montenegro with Alice, she was all the more determined to see her hospital restored to its former glory.

CHAPTER 20

"FOLLY'S END"

1945–1956

Near the end of February 1945, Flora turned the key in her lock one last time, picked up her bags and left for the airport to catch a British military flight to Bari. As she looked out over the familiar streets, she must have wondered if she would ever pass through them again. She carried with her the precious exit visa that granted her the right to leave, and which were granted so rarely. "I regretted having to leave behind so many good friends among the Serbs, who would have got out too, had it been possible," she wrote mournfully.[1]

Aged sixty-nine, Flora had lost none of her wanderlust. Although she had not been home to England for years, she chose instead to catch a ship from Naples to Jerusalem to visit her nephew Gerrard Baker, a police forensic scientist. In June, she sailed again, this time for Africa, to stay with Dick Sandes and his wife Joan at their home in Bulawayo, Rhodesia. Flora had last seen her nephew in London in early 1920, just before he had left to join the British South Africa Police, Rhodesia's police force. The boy whom, aged five, she had taken on a road trip across America in 1905 after his mother had died was now a detective inspector. His nine-year-old daughter Allison and her younger brother Richard bubbled with excitement at the news that their father's "favourite aunt and hero" was coming to stay, while their maternal grandmother, who lived with them, was sent to live with her son to make room for their esteemed guest.

On Saturday 21st July, Dick, Joan, Richard and Allison drove to the railway station to meet Flora, who had travelled the long distance to Bulawayo across grasslands and bushveld from the port of Durban. Their car had not been driven for years as petrol was so scarce, but in honour of her arrival it had been taken off its bricks so that she could be collected in style. Flora arrived in the leafy town during its cool, dry winter to a flurry of press interest. "Seven-Medalled Irishwoman Comes to Bulawayo", trumpeted the local paper.[2] There were parties and dinners, interviews and public appearances. "For the first time two 'colonial' children were exposed to the press and dignitaries who were clambering to meet this famous woman," remembered Allison.

She soon made herself at home. "Flora was not an early riser and would appear in a sort of sleeveless 'apron' which wrapped around her body and tied with strings at the back," recalled Allison. In the evenings, she would reappear in a "very smart skirt and blouse", although her mannerisms often failed to match her otherwise respectable appearance. "Flora was a heavy smoker and... took the stance of a man while smoking her cigarette or small cheroot. Her legs and feet would be apart with her elbow balanced on one knee, the cigarette held between thumb and first finger," described Allison.

Her forceful and – with age – somewhat truculent character made her an overbearing house guest but such was her esteem in Dick's eyes that she was given almost carte blanche to behave as she wished. "I personally owe most of the moral standards I have, and still try to keep, entirely to her," he wrote years later.[3] His wife Joan behaved with remarkable forbearance, but Flora's presence must have been hardest of all on her. "She was not long in our home before she took over the running of the household and needless to say, my father," Allison wrote. "There being no place for two women in the home my mother took an unpaid job with Sanders, an upmarket store in Bulawayo, as an alteration hand. Work even unpaid was not readily available and my mother was only too pleased to get it."[4]

But although she was near penniless – and thus reliant on the goodwill of Dick and his family to put a roof over her head – she was either unaware of how domineering she could be or simply too set in her ways to behave any differently. Worse still for Dick, she transferred her familiarity with dealing on the black market in occupied Belgrade to Bulawayo. "Butter was one of the commodities that was strictly rationed," wrote Allison. "It was not long before Flora made friends with Mr Kay the local dairy farmer who supplied us with milk and soon Flora was getting more than an adequate supply of butter. Can you imagine the horror of my father, a detective inspector in the CID [Criminal Investigation Department], when he found out that Auntie was buying butter on the black market! The butter was quickly returned to its origin; but as Auntie had to have her butter the family rations were given to her and we had to make do with beef dripping."[5]

Full of hope that she would finally be granted the necessary permission from the Ministry of Health to renovate and reopen her Anglo-Yugoslav Children's Sanatorium, in July, Katherine left Budva for Belgrade with Alice and her small team. She was thrilled on arrival to be informed that the ministry had agreed provisionally to repair the hospital building, and that it would also lend much needed financial support to help meet its running costs.[6] But soon disturbing reports reached her that her unit instead would almost certainly be forced to leave Yugoslavia, in a renewed push by Tito and his Partisan authorities to rid their country of foreigners.

Angered by the abrupt volte-face of the authorities, she booked an appointment to see the Minister of Health. To her surprise, when she was ushered into his office, the slight but feisty fifty-seven-year-old doctor recognized him. As a young medic he had been a frequent visitor to her wards. "Is it true we might have to leave?" she asked him directly. In response, he shamefacedly stuttered the official line that his government was trying to take charge of its own people. "Do you know doctor," Katherine replied determinedly, as she pulled herself up to her full height in front of him, "I was looking after your Yugoslav children before you were born, or when you were a very small boy, so you can't really look on me as an outsider in your country." He laughed, then considered his response. "All right," he replied. "I'll make an exception for you and your team. You'll be allowed to resume work at Kamenica."[7]

At first Flora had found plenty of distractions in Bulawayo. She had the town to explore, the well-stocked local library to visit, local "leading lights" to meet and black-marketeering to keep her busy. But as the weeks passed in the provincial Rhodesian town, she grew increasingly restless. She began to slip from the house after dinner without a word to anyone about where she was going. When she returned in the early hours of the morning, she was invariably worse the wear for alcohol. "No one seemed to know where she went," recalled Allison. Then, one day, Dick was hauled in before his superiors at the BSAP only to be informed that they had received a series of complaints about her behaviour. "It turned out that… she had been fraternizing with the local African peasant population, sitting around an open fire and drinking beer made from sorgum," wrote Allison. "This beer was brewed in a barrel which had originally contained oil or petrol. In those days this was called kaffir beer." When he returned home, Dick confronted her. She was "extremely difficult", he recorded. "When I spoke to her about it all she would say was 'I have done what I like all my life and will continue to do so, and will not stay here if I can't.'"[8]

Dick's superiors had already told him she had to go. "We said goodbye to Auntie at the railway station," recalled Allison. "The car had again been taken out of mothballs for the occasion."[9]

Katherine raced back to Kamenica, bursting with enthusiasm at the prospect of finally beginning the work for which she had left Scotland thirteen months previously. With her came Alice, her secretary, Marion Tew, her matron, and Alwyn Griffiths, a teacher of handicrafts. Under the orders of the Minister of Health the local authorities began work repairing the building and re-establishing the water and electricity supplies, while Katherine took charge of re-equipping it. Alongside her driver Vasilj, a White Russian refugee who had worked for her before the war, she passed through the village knocking on doors to reclaim her furniture, much of which had been secreted away, while the equipment for her operating theatre was returned to her from a nearby military hospital. Much of what she lacked was given to her. UNRRA supplied the beds and bedding while, as word spread among her many overseas contacts that Katherine was yet again accomplishing the near-impossible, gifts and supplies began to arrive in volume including linen, blankets and boxes of children's clothes from Canada and Britain. On 19th December, when she admitted her first five young tubercular patients, she also opened the country's only joint post-Communist Anglo-Yugoslav enterprise.[10] Not only had Katherine triumphed in her battle with the Partisan authorities, she had managed to reopen her hospital despite her increasing deafness, a legacy of the damage to her hearing that she had suffered while lying gravely ill with typhus in 1915.

Desperate parents travelled to Kamenica from across Yugoslavia, all hoping for a bed for their child – often their only chance of survival. By the autumn of 1946, sixty-six children were being cared for in the wards by Katherine, her staff and Dr Stojanović, her former chief surgeon who had returned to work alongside her. "When I planned to spend a week in it, I thought the experience would be rather sad," wrote Francesca Wilson, who was also now working for UNRRA. "I was quite unprepared for its gaiety. The… children at Kamenitza were as gay as a covey of birds, chattering, singing and laughing most of the day."[11]

But there was a darker side that Francesca – an admirer of the Partisans – did not report upon. As the months had passed the authorities had put the hospital under increasingly oppressive surveillance. The first step was innocuous enough. Katherine was informed that it would need a Yugoslav "administrative director", but that she could choose who she wanted.[12] Other measures soon followed. She was ordered to place a large photograph of Tito shaking hands with Stalin in the main hall. The telephone line between her villa in the village and the hospital was cut and a nurse was sent to her from Belgrade, whose furtive behaviour gave her away as a police informer. There was little Katherine could do about the telephone and the nurse, but she made short work of the photograph by mounting it alongside one of Tito shaking hands with Churchill. Both were removed shortly thereafter "by mutual agreement".[13]

Worse still, the Communist propaganda began to affect the children. The older ones refused to say their evening prayers while on Christmas Eve 1946 they sang Partisan songs instead of carols. "We're celebrating the birthday of Jesus Christ," Katherine remonstrated to the eldest girl. "I don't believe in that," she shrugged in response. Katherine at least had the protection of UNRRA, under whose auspices the hospital was being run. But that autumn she was notified that their reconstructive work in Yugoslavia was coming to an end. When she wrote to the Ministry of Health about the future of her hospital, this time she received no response.[14]

* * *

Flora arrived in Muizenberg, a seaside resort near Cape Town, in late October, after spending three months with Dick and his family. There she booked into the local YWCA hostel, dusted herself down and presented herself at Thomas Cook's to arrange a passage to England, certain that she would be able to jump aboard the next transport home. "We've got nothing at all," she was told instead by the manager. "We've already got hundreds waiting and there's no boat at all next month. It will be months before we can find you a place." "So what happens to people like me who can't get away and have no money to stay long?" she asked dejectedly. "I'm sorry, there's just nothing available. We'd help if we could," he replied.

The news threw Flora into a panic. "My dear Dick," she wrote from her room that night. "Saw a nice young man who could do nothing... However dear Dick don't worry about me something will turn up," she continued as bravely as possible, "at present I have a roof over my head if they don't turn me out for smoking in my bedroom, the only place I can, as it's forbidden elsewhere, also card playing, and prayers every morning to which you are invited, but not compelled. Did you ever hear of such old fossils, 100 years behind the times. They want to uplift the younger generation, the only result is that no people will come here, most of them look as though they have been buried and dug up again." Not only did she miss him terribly, she felt both vulnerable and alone. "I felt very lonely and unhappy last night but feel better now, it hardly seemed worth while getting through the war alive to land up in a YWCA hole. I could hardly bear saying goodbye to you at the station, but we will meet again in Jersey or somewhere please God."[15]

The day after arrival she began to trudge the streets in a frantic search for work, all the while recording her efforts in her diary. She approached a Jewish-owned wholesale dress shop ("we agreed not the job for me"), an insurance office ("Mr Arnold. Tested me with forms and I told him it would drive me mad"), a lawyer ("too late"), and a broker ("took someone else"). She also put an ad in the local paper. "No answers," she wrote miserably a week after arrival. But the next day she scribbled that she had received "one answer to ad", from Barnacks, a small typewriting company in Cape Town's central Longmarket Street. Five days later she began work for them. The work – typing and copying letters – was monotonous, but the manager and his wife were friendly and kind, as were their handful of staff.

Flora made the best of things. She moved from the "YWCA hole" to a room in central Cape Town. During her spare time she travelled by bus and train around the city and its environs, to walk along the beaches at Sea Point, Camps Bay and Fish Hoek. And she had people to look after her. She had a cousin, surgeon Dr Thomas Lindsay Sandes, in nearby Claremont, while a couple, the Sitters, took it upon themselves to invite her frequently to lunch, tea and social events. She wrote regular letters to her family and friends, and she recorded sending letters and parcels to "Simmonds" – Emily – to which she received regular replies.

Still, it was a hand-to-mouth existence. She was paid enough to allow her the occasional beer, ice cream or inexpensive lunch or dinner out, but little more. To keep her expenses to a minimum she bought herself an "electric pot" so she could cook in her room and carefully recorded all her expenditures in her diary, from how much she paid for Marmite to how much she had left as a tip.

Hard as she found things financially, she was relatively content. She passed the weekdays – and sometimes even her free Saturdays – typing happily in Mr Barnack's small office. She spent her weekends tidying her room, doing chores, going into town or in walks along the coast, all the while filling her diary daily with the comfortable minutiae of her existence. "My free Saturday," she jotted on 24th November in a typical entry. "Went to Barclays Bank. Sent parcel to Simmonds from Stuttefords. Had hair permed, 2 hours, awful ordeal. Mr & Mrs Sitters took me to Henry V at 5.20. Awfully good. I had supper at Greek Café." Finally, around the start of April 1946, Flora received news from Thomas Cook's that a place had been secured for her on a ship. Well aware that her stay in South Africa had been little more than a working holiday, she handed in her notice, said her many farewells, paid her bills and set sail.

"They want the place but not us," commented Katherine bitterly at the news that her Anglo-Yugoslav Children's Sanatorium was being nationalized by the Partisan authorities.[16] The Minister of Health had finally delivered the news to her in person that the hospital could remain open but the British staff would have to leave. It was with a feeling of utter wretchedness that Katherine walked around the wards of the hospital that had become the culmination of her life's work, knowing that it was nearing an end. "It was with a heavy heart that I left the work which I had begun, then carried on for so many years," she wrote later. In June 1947, over thirty-two years after she had first stepped onto Serbian soil as a young junior doctor, she packed what little she could and left for Scotland.[17]

Katherine retired to windswept St Andrews, to a two-storey, terraced stone house that she shared with her sister Annie. She missed her work dreadfully, and kept in close touch with her former members of staff and with other veterans of work in Serbia, travelling often to London to see them. In 1949, following Tito's ideological break with Stalin and a corresponding warming of Anglo-Yugoslav relations, Katherine was invited back to Kamenica to complete the final formalities of handing her hospital over to government ownership. In the company of her former matron, Alice Murphy, she returned in October. The hospital, from the outside, appeared just as it always had but, inside, it was overcrowded, there were shortages of material, no toys and few staff with adequate training. "Instead of lying immobilized, fixed to the bed in good comfortable positions, the children sat or lay without much attempt to straighten their deformities," wrote Katherine. She was deeply upset when she returned home to St Andrews. "[The visit] really broke her heart," recollected her niece. "I've never seen her in tears, but my sister Ann told me… that… she found Aunt Kathie, sitting on the floor, arranging her books in a bookcase, and crying bitterly. She was never really happy again."[18]

"To think after all I've done and the places I've been to that I should have to settle down in Wickham Market!" commented Flora wryly to one of her neighbours.[19] Her family had set her up in "Folly's End", an ancient brick two-storey cottage on the main street of the Suffolk village after she had returned to English shores, near penniless, in August 1946. The irony of the name would not have been lost on her, nor the fact that she had come full circle. It was only one mile south-west of Marlesford, where she had spent much of her childhood.

Her family welcomed her back with open arms. Several of her relatives lived nearby, including her sister Fanny. From the moment of her arrival she was invited along to their many family outings, including bathing picnics to Orford Ness, which gave her young relations the chance to glance surreptitiously at her when the famous, battle-scarred aunt donned a bathing costume. "When I saw her... I noticed there was rather a lot missing," remembered her grand-nephew Arthur Baker. "She lost a lot of muscle in the small of her back and walked very stiffly."[20]

The villagers too had welcomed the return of the old soldier whose reputation had long preceded her arrival, and Flora also received a steady stream of visitors, including many Serbians.[21] She repaid such visits, often turning up unannounced with the full expectation that she would be fed and watered. She had a "talent for imposing on others", Arthur recalled, but she was also good company. "She did what she wanted to do," he said. "She smoked, she drank fairly heavily – things that ladies didn't do you know – and she was very funny. She had an interesting sense of humour – not something you'd expect in an old lady."[22] She would also travel regularly to London to visit friends, on one occasion taking her young grand-nephew Ben Johnston and his sister with her. "It was very exciting," remembered Ben. "She took us to the railway carriage and ordered a coffee for herself and drinks for us. Later a conductor came round and told her that we would have to go to our seats as they were about to start the meal service, but she refused to move. 'We don't have seats,' she told him. She simply ordered another coffee. We were in awe of her audacity."

As her old wounds caught up with her and she became less mobile, she took to using a battery-powered electric chair given to her by her sister to travel between the local villages and would set off, white hair streaming behind her in the wind, as she pushed it to its full speed. "Quite often she couldn't get back because the batteries had run flat and my father would have to bring her back," recalled Arthur. "She would sometimes also have to be rescued between the villages when it ran out of juice."[23] Yet despite the best efforts of her family and friends they were unable to give her the sort of constant companionship that she had so thrived upon in the army and she reported feeling lonesome in the pages of the diary that she continued to keep. She also missed Yurie terribly, recalled one of the villagers.[24]

* * *

"But I must say, it gets a little dull at times," Flora sighed to a journalist who asked her about her life in 1954. She had ushered him through her low front door, which was framed by a fragrant tangle of honeysuckle and roses. Limping ahead of him with her walking stick in hand, she had led him to her tiny but tidy parlour for the interview and poured him tea. Duly, a few days later, his story appeared within the pages of the *Weekend Reveille*. "Kind Old Lady Led Me into Battle", read the sensational headline, alongside a martial-looking photograph of Flora from the First World War.[25]

His was one of several newspaper interviews to appear in the popular press in Flora's later years. She was even more forthright in others. "Give me a cigarette first – never could talk without a smoke," she demanded of another reporter who had come to interview her on behalf of the *Woman's Sunday Mirror*. "BORED" declared one of the paragraph headings when the article was published. "I hate old age and retirement," she bemoaned forcefully. "I'm bored to tears. I miss soldiering. I loved it." She looks straight at the camera in the accompanying photograph, with only the smallest hint of a smile to soften her challenging stare, her revolver firmly clenched in her hand. "The police allow me to keep it as a souvenir, but they won't let me have any ammunition," she added miserably. Later that week an enormous bouquet arrived for her, which allowed the paper to end the article on a particularly patronizing note. "To a gallant old soldier, who remains charming and feminine even with the light of battle still burning in her eye, *Woman's Sunday Mirror* presents this week's bouquet of two dozen red roses."[26]

As the years passed she became increasingly nostalgic for army life and sought out, in particular, the company of her wartime friends. In late 1949 she received a Christmas card out of the blue from Colonel Lloyd Smellie, whom she had known briefly in 1918 when, as a young officer of a British Motor Transport company, he had been stationed in Macedonia. He was now living with his wife in the Lake District. "I was indeed astonished and very pleased to receive the Christmas card from you and your wife, it was a breath of the past from the old days of war which I still think of so often," she wrote back enthusiastically. "I am now living alone in the country near nephews and nieces," she told him. "Very safe but not very exciting!"[27] In the brisk correspondence between them that month, he mentioned his membership of the Salonika Reunion Association and the *Mosquito*, their journal. Flora's eyes lit on the references and she took out a year's subscription to the latter forthwith. "I did not even know there was a Salonika Reunion Association, and should so much like to become a member but I suppose I should not be eligible as I was not serving in HM Forces," she replied sadly to one of his letters. "If you think I could join the Association I would be very grateful if you would tell me how to do it."[28]

Smellie set to work convincing the Association to accept Flora into their ranks. By September, with their annual "muster" only a month away, they had passed a resolution making her an honorary member.[29] For thirty-one years its members had gathered at Horse Guards Parade for a service of remembrance, before parading the short distance to the Cenotaph to lay wreaths. Such was the importance to her of attending the thirty-second ceremony on Sunday 1st October that she became increasingly nervous as the date neared. "Also I'm wondering where I'll stand, as I can't of course go with the men, and don't belong to the nursing sisters, and don't know anybody, but I suppose someone will tell me there," she wrote worriedly to Smellie. "Hoping we shall meet somehow, don't forget that I am now a very old lady, not a bit like the sergeant you know."[30] As soon as she joined the ranks of the twelve hundred other veterans, all her concerns fell away as she stood proudly behind the President and Honorary Secretary of the Association, dressed in a smart dark suit, a dark hat with a pale feather, her long row of medals pinned across her chest.[31] At the luncheon that followed she was "besieged" by autograph hunters and veteran nursing sisters who pressed forward to shake her hand. She was the "the Joan of Arc of our campaign and one of the finest women that ever lived", declared the Honorary Secretary grandiosely as he led a toast in her honour. "Thank you very much, indeed, all my friends here," replied Flora shyly.[32]

The Association opened up a new world for her. She began attending the meetings of her local Suffolk branch and she met old friends at the summer reunion held at the start of July by the veterans of the Serbian units.[33] The annual parade, she once said, was "the one bright spot" in her life and she avidly read every word of the *Mosquito*.[34] In turn, the Association took great pride in her public appearances alongside them, and littered its pages with references to her. In the following years, when she joined them again at their autumn muster, her presence among them was reported in the press and journalists would muscle in to try to meet her.[35] "Miss Sandes has a simple technique that I like [to get rid of them]," commented one of her friends. "She tells all inquisitive papers that she is ninety, and they doubtfully report her words."[36] Duly, seventy-six-year-old Flora's words reached the pages of the *Daily Mirror* and the *Daily Express* in 1952. "I'm aged round about ninety," they recorded her saying, no doubt to her considerable amusement.[37]

Not only did Flora keep in touch with British veterans via the Salonika Reunion Association, she also maintained links with its Serbian equivalent. In 1954 she received and accepted an invitation to join them as their guest at a reunion in Belgrade. On arrival she was fêted as their guest of honour. "The Savez Boraca (Soldiers' Association) took me round by car to the Tomb of the Unknown Soldier which is an enormous monument by Mestrovic [Ivan Meštrović, sculptor], and to many other places, and welcomed me most warmly... I think any small thing one can do to help good relations is all for the good, and we never mentioned politics," she wrote on her return, sensitive to the still-delicate political situation.[38]

By a remarkable coincidence Katherine was in Yugoslavia at the same time. In a rush to make amends to those whom they had treated badly, the Yugoslav medical authorities had invited her to celebrate the twentieth anniversary of the opening of her Anglo-Yugoslav Hospital in Kamenica. In the company once again of Alice Murphy, on 22nd September Katherine was ushered through the hospital – noticing with amusement that her photograph was sandwiched between ones of Lenin and Tito in the office – out into the sunny courtyard, where she was welcomed by more than one hundred guests. Among them was Flora.[39] Katherine took great pride not only in the reception she received, but also in that extended to her old friend. "People from far and near came to see her," she recalled later. "Her name was known and honoured all over Serbia."[40] On 2nd October, regretful only that she had had to miss the muster that had taken place the day before, Flora arrived back at Wickham Market brimming with enthusiasm about her visit. "I had a wonderful month's holiday and met more friends than I could have thought possible," she wrote to the Association on her return.[41]

Two years later, on 30th September 1956, walking stick in hand, she paraded proudly once again within the Association's ranks on their march to the Cenotaph and joined them afterwards for their luncheon, apparently as hale and hearty as ever. It was Flora's last muster. "'If I be spared', as the village people here say," she commented once, as she promised to attend in future years.[42] 1956 did not spare her. After a brief and sudden illness, she died at Ipswich and East Suffolk Hospital on 24th November of "obstructive jaundice".[43] She was cremated at Ipswich Crematorium three days later and her ashes buried in the Garden of Remembrance. She had renewed her passport shortly before she died, still dreaming of places to see and trips to take.

AFTERWORD

Nearly one hundred years since the start of the First World War, interest remains centred on the fighting along the Western Front, from which women were barred. Thus the prevailing view of the contribution of women to the war effort is that they dutifully "kept the home fires burning" while waiting for their men to return home, cheerfully stuffed shells full of explosives at munitions factories and worked devotedly as "ministering angels" in hospitals safely behind the frontlines. This view, however, overlooks the fact that when women were able to seize the freedom to work as they wished their contribution to the war effort was as important and competent as that of their male equivalents. They ran hospitals, worked as army and ambulance drivers, survived untold hardship and carried out acts of staggering courage – and, of course, in one exceptional case, fought bravely throughout the duration of the war.

Flora did not view her actions as political. It was the "love of adventure" instead that motivated her, she once stated.[1] But her actions had political consequences. In an age when women were denied the right to vote, she pushed the boundaries of what was considered acceptable behaviour – and work – for women. In so doing she became symbol of what could be achieved and an inspiration to many. Hundreds of women eagerly bought her books and stuck newspaper clippings about her in between the well-thumbed pages. Others collected the postcard issued by Raphael Tuck showing her in full military regalia. Even more listened eagerly to her speak about her adventures among the Serbs when she took the stage.

On a personal level, she met with remarkably little prejudice. There were of course people who disapproved of her pursuit of what was seen as an exclusively male profession, but by and large she was widely admired. "I am convinced that she earned promotion not because she happened to be a woman but because she displayed qualities which would have deserved recognition in a man," commented a reviewer from *Punch* on reading her 1916

book, *An English Woman Sergeant in the Serbian Army*.[2] "She has
solved the riddle often put, 'Should women be soldiers?' and has
answered it so far as she is personally concerned," wrote another in
the pages of the *Liverpool Weekly Post*.[3] Not only was she widely
celebrated in the British press, she was accepted as a comrade by
British officers and ordinary soldiers. Even the crusty old officials
of the British War Office gave her the permits she needed to lecture
to their men at camps across northern France.

Nonetheless the widespread acceptance that Flora received was to
a great extent the exception that proved the rule. Only in April 1915
was the War Office forced by a shortage of male doctors to recruit
women, but they refused to allow them to work near the front and,
by denying them officer status, they were also able to withhold
the privileges of rank that were given to their male counterparts.[4]
One of the most disgraceful forms the discrimination took was in
the government's refusal to recognize the foreign awards bestowed
on British women by publishing them in the *Gazette*, a journal
which publishes official British Government information. Only
those granted to men were "gazetted". Even Flora's receipt of
the Karađorđe Star with Swords – the highest award in Serbia for
bravery under fire – received the same official slight.

Snubbed at home, the British women who worked in Serbia during
the First World War were treated there as equals. Although few in
Britain today have heard of their achievements, they are still remembered widely in the country they came to love. The fervent nationalism of the Serbs, which lay at the heart of the appalling atrocities
committed in their name in recent years, has also had a remarkable
and honourable counterpart. Not only did it permit them to win
some of the most extraordinary victories of the First World War, it
drove them to oppose the Nazis in the Second. Today it helps keep
alive the memory of the British women who worked and so often
died in their service. There are streets and buildings named after
Katherine MacPhail, Elsie Inglis, Lady Leila Paget and Elizabeth
Ross. Towns abound with plaques and memorials, while heavily
attended commemorations are held annually in Kragujevac and
Mladenovac. In 2006 a Serbian film was released about the retreat,
Where the Lemon Blossoms Bloom, that featured Flora Sandes. Every
schoolchild was sent to see it. Three years later, in 2009, a street in
Belgrade's affluent Dedinje district was named after her.

EPILOGUE

ADA BARLOW

Hardly had the "fat and plain, elderly and rather pasty" nurse returned to England with the Paget Unit following their release from captivity in the spring of 1916 before she left again to work for the Serbs. She demonstrated the same extraordinary dedication to her patients in her work with Serbian refugees in Corsica for the Serbian Relief Fund.[1] By the end of the war she was living in Manchester, where she played a leading role in the committee that ran the Lord Mayor of Manchester Fund, which aimed to raise money for her beloved Serbs.[2] In 1937, she is identifiable one final time in the newspaper archives that are currently accessible online. In March of that year, sixty-six-year-old Slavko Grouitch, the then Yugoslav Ambassador, died in London of heart failure. The funeral brought together many of the men and women who had worked devotedly for Serbia in one of the largest gatherings of its kind. Mrs Barlow was listed as being among them.[3]

BARTON COOKINGHAM

The young doctor discovered by Flora and Emily lying next to a coffin gravely ill with typhus in Valjevo arrived home to Red Hook, New York, in June 1915.[4] He returned to his pre-war work as a physician and surgeon in Poughkeepsie, New York, and, in April 1919 married Edna.[5] Two years later they had a son, Harris.

Shortly thereafter, pursued by personal demons, his life slowly began to unravel. In 1926 the courts awarded a divorce to his wife on the grounds that he had been "intimate with women in cities near his home". In 1930, aged forty-one, he married a teacher seventeen years his junior. They divorced in 1933. In February 1934, a month before he married for the third time, he spent five days in the county jail for contempt of court over his failure to pay alimony. In 1938 he testified for the defence in the case of a woman who was found guilty of killing a twenty-four-year-old man while drink-driving. When asked how long he had been drinking in the same bar as her on the day in question, he was evasive. "You do drink rather extensively, don't you doctor?" the prosecution alleged, while observing that he had been suspended that summer from the staff of the Northern Dutchess Health Service centre in Rhinebeck, New York.[6]

In 1944 he stood trial for carrying out an elective abortion, a criminal offence. In 1946 he was arrested by agents of the US Narcotics Division, accused of issuing prescriptions to drug addicts without the necessary licence.[7] Four years later his medical licence was revoked after he was charged with carrying out another termination. He turned his hand instead to real estate, all the while continuing to run a sideline in abortions. In 1955 he divorced for the third time.[8] In 1962, following a tip-off, he was arrested and found guilty of carrying out an abortion on a twenty-six-year-old unmarried woman. Only his counsel's argument that prison would almost certainly mean death at his "advanced age" of seventy-three saved him from a custodial term.[9] This brave man, fallen from grace, died on 8th February 1968.

MABEL GROUITCH

The American woman who led the first volunteer medical unit from British shores during the First World War worked tirelessly for the rest of her life on behalf of Serbia. After seeing the Anglo-American Unit to Kragujevac she returned to New York in early 1915 to raise funds. That summer she sent a second unit to Serbia, to open the "Grouitch Baby Hospital" in Niš.[10] When Serbia was invaded by Germany, Austria-Hungary and Bulgaria that autumn, she turned her hospital into a frontline field ambulance – the First American Field Hospital in Serbia. Once it became clear that Serbia was on the verge of defeat, she was forced to leave her staff in Niš by virtue of the fact that she could not, as the wife of a Serbian government official, afford to be taken prisoner. She survived a punishing twenty-day trek south to Monastir.[11]

After the war Mabel opened an orphanage, the American Home for Yugoslav Children, in Selce on the Dalmatian coast. In 1937, following the death of her husband, she returned to the Home. As the threat of war loomed in 1941 she hurried to Belgrade to seek advice, where she was caught up in the bombing by the Nazis.[12] She survived but was forced to retreat once again before the Germans. To escape capture, she fled through Croatia towards the Adriatic coast, at times disguising herself as a Hungarian peasant. She later credited her survival to the Croatian people who fed and hid her.[13] At the end of June, she finally reached New York, where she spent her retirement. In August 1956, aged eighty-four, she died of leukaemia.[14]

KATHERINE MACPHAIL

Katherine's visit to Serbia in 1954 was her last. She greatly missed her "second homeland" and listened to Belgrade on the radio until her loss of hearing made it impossible. Her deafness also made it increasingly difficult for her to make new friendships and she "lived for" meetings with her old friends. "When one of them died she was deeply sad and dejected for several days," remembered her niece. She suffered keenly when her sister Isabel – who had worked alongside her in Macedonia in the First World War and who had introduced her to Flora – died in 1955, and she became increasingly lonely when Annie, the sister with whom she shared her house in St Andrews, died in 1966.[15]

But there were also happy moments. In 1969 she was delighted to be reunited with Anna Christitch, Dorothy Newhall and Francesca Wilson, all veterans of work in Serbia, for a BBC documentary, *Yesterday's Witness*.[16] The researcher for the programme, Jean Bray, spent time with her over the next couple of years recording her memories. Her deafness had come to isolate her to such an extent that she revealed that she had grown to regret that her work had come before marriage and children.[17] In 1973, the now eighty-six-year-old Katherine received the news that she had been elected an honorary member of the Serbian Medical Association. "You have given me the greatest possible pleasure," she wrote back in a strong hand. "I am glad my work among your people is still remembered and that friends and colleagues in Belgrade still remember me… This gesture on your part has given me great happiness especially after so many years." By then her health was beginning to fail. She had chronic bronchitis and, in the summer of 1974, suffered two disabling strokes. She died on 21st September, missing by a few hours a letter from the Yugoslav ambassador in London letting her know that her name had been put forward to receive the Order of the Yugoslav Flag with Gold Star in honour of her work.[18]

Her hospital remained open as an orthopaedic ward of the Novi Sad School of Medicine until 1992, when the building was used to house destitute Serbian refugees from the former territories of Yugoslavia. Katherine's building – the greatest memorial to the work of the British women in Serbia during the First World War – is now sadly abandoned and a plaque in her honour stolen, but her red-lion-rampant design is perfectly preserved. A retired Serbian orthopaedic surgeon, Dr Želimir Mikić, is spearheading an attempt to raise sufficient funds for the "English Hospital" to be renovated and returned to its medical purpose, as a memorial to her work.

DR EDWARD RYAN

Dr Ryan left Macedonia at the end of the war for Berlin to become second-in-command of a Red Cross unit tasked with overseeing the return of Russian prisoners. In the summer of 1919, after he took charge of Red Cross activities in northern Russia and the Baltic states, he imposed draconian but almost certainly essential travel restrictions across Estonia in an effort to combat a typhus epidemic.[19] No stranger to controversy, he reported back to the US State Department that the Bolshevik government was a "social adventure become a ghastly failure", invoking the full fury of the Russians.[20] In August 1921 he was accused by both the Russians and a Bolshevik-sympathizing US senator of helping to foment the Kronstadt rebellion – a short-lived and brutally suppressed uprising against the Bolsheviks led by the sailors of the Baltic Fleet – an accusation of which he was later exonerated by another Red Cross Commission.[21] In early 1923, as a sanitary advisor with the rank of lieutenant colonel in the US Army Medical Corps, he left for Tehran, Persia (now Iran), to design water and sewage plants. Aged only thirty-nine, he died in September of the same combination of overwork and heart failure brought on by malaria that had killed his chief detractor in Macedonia, Amelia Tileston.

In February 1924 his body was repatriated to his home town of Scranton, Pennsylvania.[22]

DICK SANDES

In 1948 Flora's nephew became the warden of two national parks and the curator of the Great Zimbabwe Ruins, now a UNESCO World Heritage Site, near the town of Fort Victoria (now Masvingo), southern Rhodesia, which enabled him to pursue his "hobby" of archaeology. It was a "peaceful life out in the bush looking after my farm – the Ruins – and National Parks," he wrote. But the savage guerrilla fighting that eventually put an end to oppressive British white minority rule in 1980 also rent the new country of Zimbabwe in an orgy of violence. At the age of eighty-two Dick became a refugee from the country that had been his home for sixty-two years. "My neighbours were murdered – my wife had died," he wrote, "so I had to set about trying to dispose of my assets and get over the border." He packed a suitcase and fled to stay with his daughter in South Africa but missed his old life. "I hate concrete jungles, and miss my boat, sailing and fishing," he wrote. Three years later, in 1984, he died in exile.[23]

MILUNKA SAVIĆ

The twenty-eight-year-old woman soldier with whom Flora shared a tent at the 41st General Hospital was later sent to Bizerte and then France, where she was fêted and awarded the Legion d'Honneur and Croix de Guerre, which she added to her string of Serbian and Allied medals.[24] She remains the most decorated woman in history. She left the Army in 1919, married and moved to Belgrade, had a daughter, divorced and remarried. She worked first as a seamstress in a factory producing military uniforms, then as a cleaning lady at a bank, then as a manager of its cleaning staff, making what must have been an adequate if not luxurious living.[25] During the course of her working life, she adopted three homeless girls and fostered many more children. By the 1950s her husband had died and her exploits were largely forgotten, although she kept in close touch with her fellow soldiers during veterans' events.[26] In 1972, a newspaper article recalling her remarkable war service and highlighting her predicament as an elderly, impoverished widow prompted the city authorities to give her a tiny one-storey house in a village outside of Belgrade, amid rolling cornfields, which is now marked with a plaque in her honour. She is remembered to this day by the inhabitants of what is now "Milunka Savić Street", which has long since been subsumed in the conurbation of Belgrade. "She used to go out for hours whatever the weather," one recalled. "She was tough and energetic and used to be collected to go to ceremonies."[27] She died on 5th October 1973.

EMILY SIMMONDS

After seven years of work in the Balkans, Emily returned to New York in March 1921.[28] Afflicted by the same failure to settle back into normal existence that had blighted the lives of so many women who had seen war service, six weeks later she applied to the Quakers for relief work under their auspices.[29] Over the next year she bided her time working as a private-duty nurse. In September 1922 she finally received the summons she had been hoping for.[30] Her referees, knowing how desperate she was to return to the work she loved, had already written her glowing references. "She is almost over-conscientious, intensely loyal, clear-headed, quick witted, scrupulously honest, cheerful, a hard worker, understands and gets on with all sorts and conditions of people," wrote her friend Marjorie Daw Johnson, who had worked alongside Emily during her brief posting in Italy during the war.[31] "She would I think have to have an allowance beside her full expenses as she has no money at all and no one to turn to, but she is so indifferent on that subject she would demand little and possibly not mention it at all, but knowing her circumstances do not feel she might be asked to go for only her expenses... She is the personification of self-sacrificing devotion."[32]

At the end of September, presumably having agreed to pay her a small salary, the Quakers sent Emily with a small team to the "worst place in the world" – the Volga famine district in Bolshevik Russia.[33] There she put on the grey Quaker uniform with its distinctive red-and-black star and set to work inspecting hospitals, orphanages and warehouses to help determine how their limited resources could be best used to keep the population alive.[34] After

Emily had completed her year's contract she left for war-devastated
Berlin, where passport and passenger records indicate she may have
remained for five months. She travelled back to New York in March
1924, where she again returned to the private-duty nursing of her
pre-war years.[35] In 1926 she applied for the position of superin-
tendent of a nursing school in the Caucasus with the Near East
Relief, a charitable organization founded in response to the Turkish
campaign of genocide against the Armenians, but the American
Red Cross dashed the hopes of the nurse who had served them so
loyally by sending her prospective employers such a scathing reference as to make it impossible for them to hire her. "[She is] not of
such a character as would make it possible for me to recommend
her for service with your organization," wrote Clara Noyes, the
National Director of the Nursing Service. "While she is capable
and resourceful she is very individualistic, likes to go her own way,
and would not I believe be a particularly good teamworker... Our
records would not indicate that she was the type that would serve
best as a leader for young people."[36] Denied a posting that she
longed for, Emily instead had to scrape an impoverished living
from private-duty nursing into the early 1930s, in a succession of
what must have been dreary and spirit-sapping postings.

From the early 1930s the outlines of her life become sketchy. By
1934 she had moved to Hollywood, California, although the reason
for this is unknown. In 1940, in her mid-fifties, she crossed the
Atlantic, giving her destination as Ramsgate, where it is likely she
found work in a war hospital.[37] She moved permanently to California in 1950, where she shared a house in Pasadena with nurse Jean
MacKay, a friend since their days together at the Roosevelt Hospital
Training School in New York, until the latter's death in 1958.[38]
In 1962, Emily moved to Chino, California. On New Year's Eve,
1965, she fractured her hip during a fall. According to her death
certificate, after six weeks in hospital in Los Angeles she succumbed
to pneumonia on 18th February 1966. Her brief and shamefully
inadequate obituary mentioned only that the woman who had done
so much – nursed the wounded in Kragujevac, survived typhus in
Valjevo, rescued refugees in Albania and Serbian boys in Corfu,
fought cholera on refugee ships, cared for children in Brod and
refugees in Vodena, set up soldiers' canteens in Macedonia and
Belgrade, helped defeat typhus in Dubrovnik and fed the starving

in Russia – had been a Red Cross nurse.[39] After she was cremated at Pomona Cemetery, no one claimed her ashes, which were buried in one of two sites used for unclaimed remains. In 2006, with the help of the American Red Cross and the cemetery authorities, a small stone memorial was erected in her memory, and a Serbian Orthodox ceremony was held in her honour.

ACKNOWLEDGEMENTS

I am indebted to many for helping to make this book possible, none more so than Arthur and Nan Baker, who shared their recollections of Flora and allowed me access to her diaries, papers and photographs. I am also obliged to the late Allison Blackmore for sending me her father's vivid accounts of Flora and for taking the time to send me her own. I also appreciate the generous help given to me by Ben and Sue Johnston and am grateful to other members of Flora's extended family, including Brian Evans for his assistance over many years. I am thankful too to Mike Sandes, Frank Sandes, Steve Sandes and Isabelle Abu-Hejleh.

I feel humbled by the hospitality I have received during several visits to Serbia, which could not have been dissimilar to that extended to the British women who worked there during the war. I would like to thank, in particular, my "Serbian family" – Žarko, Vera, Nenad, Ana Vuković and Iva Brajović – for making their country feel like my second home. I am deeply grateful to the late Žarko who, by force of character and determination, helped to keep alive the memory of women, like Dr Elsie Inglis, who risked their lives in their work for the Serbs. So too would I like to thank my friends Bojan Dragićević, Daniel Sunter and Igor Sunter of the Euro-Atlantic Initiative for their valuable research, friendship and support. Acknowledgements are also due to Nataša Djulić of RTS, Goran Vuković, Professor Želimir and Marija Mikić, Dr Sladjana Filipović, Elena Vidić, Slobodan Kovačević, John White and Slavko Jugović. I would also like to thank Miloje Pantović, Liljana Naumova and Trajche Slaklevski for their memorable tours of Serbia and Macedonia, the staff of the Serbian Red Cross and, in particular, Nevenka Bogdanović for allowing me to participate in the ceremony held annually in Kragujevac in honour of Dr Elizabeth Ross.

I should also mention my obligation to my great friends Dr Jonathan Standley and Elizabeth Greene of Kingston, Ontario,

354 A FINE BROTHER

for their support and assistance. I also appreciate the help of Mrs Edith Ross, Mrs Mirjana Harding, Colonel Simon Vandeleur, Dr Vivien Newman, Lynette Beardwood, Jean Waldman, Sarah Frankenburg and Gethyn Rees. I am indebted to Ella Skrigitil for her painstaking work translating Yurie's service document. I would also like to thank Charles R. Furlong for giving me permission to use a photograph taken by his great-grandfather for the front cover. Thanks are further due to Marijana Matić and Ann Trevor.

Many others, from the following archives and libraries, have been of great assistance: Donald Davis of the American Friends Service Committee; Christina V. Jones, Archivist, the National Archives at College Park, Maryland; Jennie Levine Knies and Elizabeth A. Novara of the University of Maryland Libraries; Paul Barth of the St Luke's Roosevelt Hospital Center Medical Library; Pamela Bonham of the University of Kansas Libraries; Jocelyn K. Wilk of Columbia University Archives; Clare Ellis of the East Anglian Film Archive; Robin Bray of News Anglia; Frances E. O'Donnell of the Andover-Harvard Theological Library; Stephen E. Novak and Henry Blanco of the Augustus C. Long Health Sciences Library; Stephen Greenberg of the National Library of Medicine; John Tarring of Brooklands Museum; Janel Quirante of the Hoover Institution Archives; Trish McCormack of Archives New Zealand; Steven Kerr and Marianne Smith of the Royal College of Surgeons of Edinburgh; Bill Cronauer of the Albright Memorial Library, Scranton, and the Lackawanna Historical Society. I would also like to thank the staff of the Croydon Council Local Studies Library, Leeds and Edinburgh University Libraries, the Countway Library of Medicine, the Seeley G. Mudd Manuscript Library, British Colombia Archives, the Imperial War Museum, the Women's Library, the Wellcome Library, the Mitchell Library, the National Library of Scotland, the British Newspaper Library and the British Library.

My research into the life of the extraordinary Emily Simmonds brought me to Pomona, California in September 2006. I am deeply grateful to the following for their assistance and for helping me to erect a small memorial in her honour: Patti and Jack French, Joe Blackstock of the *Inland Valley Daily Bulletin*, Dan McLaughlin of Pasadena Public Library, Alan Beadle of the American Red Cross,

Melody Baxter of the Pomona Cemetery Association, Permeco (Monument Company), Don Ebbeler, and Father Petar and Mrs Ljiljana Jovanović and the congregation of the St Sava Serbian Orthodox Church, San Gabriel.

I am also obliged to Alexander Middleton, Caroline Miller, Peter Martin, Ajda Vučićević and David Smith for their considerable editorial assistance.

Finally, I would like to thank my family for their considerable forbearance during the research and writing of this book. I am grateful above all to Caroline, Claire and Laura Miller, Jennie and Peter Newton and, above all, Paul and Tom Newton.

NOTES AND REFERENCES

CUE TITLES

I. BOOKS

AFT	Wilson, Francesca M., *Aftermath* (West Drayton, Middlesex: Penguin, 1947)
AMM	Wheelwright, Julie, *Amazons and Military Maids* (London: Pandora, 1989)
APT	Tileston, Amelia Peabody, *Amelia Peabody Tileston and her Canteens for the Serbs* (Boston, MA: Atlantic Monthly Press, 1920)
ASF	Stebbing, E.P., *At the Serbian Front in Macedonia* (London: John Lane, the Bodley Head, 1917)
ASSA	van Tienhoven, A., *Avec les Serbs en Serbie et en Albanie* (Paris: Imprimerie Typographique H. Richard, 1918)
AWS	Sandes, Flora, *The Autobiography of a Woman Soldier* (New York, NY: Frederick A. Stokes Co., 1927)
BAL	Glenny, Misha, *The Balkans* (London: Granta Books, 1999)
BBF	Komski, Victor, *Blackbirds' Field* (New York, NY: Rae D. Henkle, 1934)
BE	Kingscote, Flavia, *Balkan Exit* (London: Geoffrey Bles, 1942)
BLGF	West, Rebecca, *Black Lamb and Grey Falcon* (Edinburgh: Canongate Press, 1993)
BSL	Hilton-Young, E., *By Sea and Land*, 2nd edn. (London: Methuen & Co., 1924)
BTR	Allsebrook, Mary, *Born to Rebel: The Life of Harriet Boyd Hawes* (Oxford: Oxbow Books, 1992)
CCD	Whitsed, Juliet de Key, *Come to the Cookhouse Door!* (London: Herbert Joseph, 1932)

CE   Wratislaw, A.C., *A Consul in the East* (Edinburgh and London: William Blackwood & Sons, 1924)

CTC   Adie, Kate, *Corsets to Camouflage* (London: Hodder & Stoughton, 2003)

DAB   Manson, Cecil and Celia, *Doctor Agnes Bennett* (London: Michael Joseph, 1960)

DH   de Ripert d'Alauzier, Lieutenant Colonel, *Un Drame historique: Résurrection de l'armée serbe Albanie-Corfou 1915–1916* (Paris: Payot, 1923)

DMH   Walker, David, *Death at My Heels* (London: Chapman & Hall Ltd, 1942)

DOS   Fryer, Charles E.J., *The Destruction of Serbia in 1915* (New York, NY: Eastern European Monographs, 1997)

EA   MacLean, Fitzroy, *Eastern Approaches* (London: Reprint Society, 1951)

EWB   Graham, Stephen, *Europe – Whither Bound?* (London: Thornton Butterworth, 1921)

EWD   Matthews, Caroline, *Experiences of a Woman Doctor in Serbia* (London: Mills & Boon, 1916)

EWS   Sandes, Flora, *An English Woman Sergeant in the Serbian Army* (London: Hodder & Stoughton, 1916)

EYS   Mikić, Želimir, *Ever Yours Sincerely: The Life and Work of Dr Katherine S. MacPhail* (Cambridge: Perfect Publishers, 2007)

FBF   Evans, Martin Marix, *Forgotten Battlefronts of the First World War* (Stroud, Gloucestershire: Sutton Publishing, 2003)

FHFC   Thurstan, Violetta, *Field Hospital and Flying Column* (London: G.P. Putnam's Sons, 1915)

FIS   Chivers Davies, Ellen, *A Farmer in Serbia* (London: Methuen & Co., 1916)

FLSP   St John, Robert, *From the Land of Silent People* (London: George G. Harrap & Co., 1942)

FMC   Moffet, Una P., and Yovitchitch, Lena A., *Florence Maw: The Chronicle of Her Lifework in Serbia* (London: privately printed for Nellie Hooker, 1957)

FNS   Allan, Sheila, *Fear Not to Sow: A Life of Elsie Stephenson* (Penzance: Jamieson Library, 1990)

FPW   Popham, Hugh, *The FANY in Peace and War*, revised edn. (Barnsley: Leo Cooper, 2003)

FSJ	Gordon-Smith, Gordon, *From Serbia to Jugoslavia* (New York, NY, and London: G.P. Putnam's Sons, 1920)
FSS	Stobart, M.A. St Clair, *The Flaming Sword in Serbia and Elsewhere*, 2nd edn. (London: Hodder & Stoughton, 1917)
FW	Adams, John Clinton, *Flight in Winter* (Princeton, NJ: Princeton University Press, 1942)
FY	Dragnich, Alex N., *The First Yugoslavia. Search for a Viable Political System* (Stanford, CA: Hoover Institution Press, 1983)
GS	Palmer, Alan, *The Gardeners of Salonika* (London: Andre Deutsch, 1965)
HARCN	Dock, Lavinia L., et al., *History of American Red Cross Nursing* (New York, NY: Macmillan, 1922)
HD	Downer, Earl Bishop, *The Highway of Death* (Philadelphia, PA: F.A. Davis Co., 1916)
HSWH	McLaren, Eva Shaw, ed., *A History of the Scottish Women's Hospitals* (London: Hodder & Stoughton, 1919)
IMC	Wilson, Francesca M., *In the Margins of Chaos* (London: John Murray, 1944)
ISL	Leneman, Leah, *In the Service of Life* (Edinburgh: Mercat Press, 1994)
JBM	Bruce, James, *Memoirs* (Baltimore, MD: Gateway Press Inc., 1997)
JEB	Bellows, John Earnshaw, *Miscellaneous Writings* (Gloucester: John Bellows, 1958)
LBN	White, Leigh, *The Long Balkan Night* (New York, NY: Charles Scribner's Sons, 1944)
LFH	Dearmer, Mabel, *Letters from a Field Hospital* (London: Macmillan, 1916)
LGP	Dixon, Jess, ed., *Little Grey Partridge* (Aberdeen: Aberdeen University Press, 1988)
LLV	Bosanquet, Robert Carr, *Letters and Light Verse* (Gloucester: John Bellows, 1938)
LOS	Holland, D., Serbia: *The Land of 'Sutra'* (London: Harrods Ltd., [*c.* 1917])
LS	Burgess, Alan, *The Lovely Sergeant* (London: Heinemann, 1963)
LSW	Alport, Major A. Cecil, *The Lighter Side of the War* (London: Hutchinson & Co., 1934)

MAS	Rutherford, Colonel N.J.C., *Memories of an Army Surgeon* (London: Stanley Paul & Co., 1939)
MBL	Abraham, J. Johnson, *My Balkan Log* (New York, NY: E.P. Dutton & Co., 1922)
MC	Villari, Luigi, *The Macedonian Campaign* (London: T. Fisher Unwin, 1922)
MFS	Frothingham, Helen Losanitch, *Mission for Serbia* (New York, NY: Walker & Co., 1970)
MMH	Morrison, Kenneth, *Montenegro: A Modern History* (London: I.B. Tauris, 2009)
MOMI	Falls, Cyril, *Military Operations Macedonia*, Vol. I (London: Imperial War Museum, 1996)
MOMII	Falls, Cyril, *Military Operations Macedonia*, Vol. II (London: Imperial War Museum, 1996)
MP	Dodds, E.R., *Missing Persons* (Oxford: Clarendon Press, 1977)
MSY	Fitch, Henry, *My Mis-Spent Youth* (London: Macmillan, 1937)
NAB	Farnam, Ruth S., *A Nation at Bay* (Indianapolis, IN: Bobbs-Merrill Co., 1918)
NAV	Brock, Ray, *Nor Any Victory* (New York, NY: Raynal & Hitchcock, 1942)
NQY	Banac, Ivo, *The National Question in Yugoslavia* (Ithaca, NY: Cornell University Press, 1984)
OWW	King, Hazel, ed., *One Woman at War: The Letters of Olive King, 1915–1920* (Victoria: Melbourne University Press, 1986)
PAR	Macmillan, Margaret, *Paris 1919* (New York, NY: Random House, 2003)
PSS	Wilson, Francesca M., *Portraits and Sketches of Serbia* (London: Swarthmore Press, 1920)
PTC	Saramandic, Ljubomir, *Pilgrimage to Corfu*, 3rd ed. (Belgrade: Tetraton, 2004)
QA	Fry, A. Ruth, *A Quaker Adventure* (London: Nisbet & Co. 1926)
QM	Krippner, Monica, *The Quality of Mercy* (London: David & Charles, 1980)
RCS	Corbett, Elsie, *Red Cross in Serbia 1915–1919* (Banbury, Oxon: Cheney & Sons Ltd, 1964)

RD	Wilson, Francesca M., *Rebel Daughter of a Country House: The Life of Eglantyne Jebb* (London: George Allen & Unwin, 1967)
RND	Fryer, Charles E.J., *The Royal Navy on the Danube* (Boulder, CO: East European Monographs, 1988)
SCW	Mitchell, Ruth, *The Serbs Choose War* (New York, NY: Doubleday, Doran & Co., Inc., 1943)
SEG	Sturzenegger, C., *La Serbie en guerre 1914–1916* (Paris: Neuchâtel, Delachaux & Niestlé s.a., 1916)
SF	Wood, William T., and Mann, A.J., *The Salonika Front* (London: A&C Black, 1920)
SH	Burr, Malcolm, *Slouch Hat* (London: George Allen & Unwin, 1935)
SJ	Abraham, J. Johnston, *Surgeon's Journey* (London: Heinemann, 1957)
SMFL	Djordjevic, Dimitrije, *Scars and Memory: Four Lives in One Lifetime* (Boulder, CO: East European Monographs, 1997)
SRCU	Berry, James, et al., *The Story of a Red Cross Unit in Serbia* (London: J.&A. Churchill, 1916)
TF	Strong, Richard P., *Typhus Fever with Particular Reference to the Serbian Epidemic* (Cambridge, MA: Harvard University Press, 1920)
TM	Staley, Mildred E., *A Tapestry of Memories* (Honolulu, HI: Hilo Tribune Herald, 1944)
TSC	Gordon-Smith, Gordon, *Through the Serbian Campaign* (London: Hutchinson & Co., 1916)
UDE	Wakefield, Alan, and Moody, Simon, *Under the Devil's Eye* (Stroud, Gloucestershire: Sutton Publishing, 2004)
UTF	Livingston, St Clair, and Steen-Hansen, Ingeborg, *Under Three Flags* (London: Macmillan, 1916)
WBH	Fairclough, Henry Rushton, *Warming Both Hands* (Stanford, CA: Stanford University Press, 1941)
WCF	Yovitchitch, Lena A., *Within Closed Frontiers*, 2nd edn. (London: W.&R. Chambers, 1956)
WEE	Reed, John, *The War in Eastern Europe* (New York, NY: Charles Scribner's Sons, 1916)
WIY	Alexander, Nora, *Wanderings in Yugoslavia* (London: Skeffington & Son, 1936)

WRY   Tomasevich, Jozo, *War and Revolution in Yugoslavia: 1941–1945* (Stanford, CA: Stanford University Press, 1975)

WSA   Paget, Lady, *With Our Serbian Allies, Second Report* (Woking and London: Gresham Press, 1916)

WSB   Walshe, Douglas, *With the Serbs in Macedonia* (London: John Lane, The Bodley Head, 1920)

WSE   Jones, Fortier, *With Serbia into Exile* (New York, NY: Grosset & Dunlap, 1916)

WV   Rayner, Louisa, *Women in a Village* (London: William Heinemann, 1957)

WWU   Hutton, I. Emslie, *With a Women's Unit in Serbia, Salonika and Sebastopol* (London: Williams & Norgate, 1928)

2. NEWSPAPERS, MAGAZINES AND JOURNALS

A/ITB   'In the Balkans', *Argus* [Melbourne], 1st January 1916

A/MA   'A Modern Amazon', *Argus* [Melbourne], 7th June 1920

AG/RD   'Rothbury: Death of Dr W.R. Ridley', *Alnwick & County Gazette*, 14th November 1914

BC/SMI   'Seven-Medalled Irishwoman Comes to Bulawayo: Soldier in Two Wars', *Bulawayo Chronicle*, 27th July 1945

BJN/BN   'British Nurses in Serbia', *British Journal of Nursing*, 9th January 1915

BJN/NW   'Nursing and the War', *British Journal of Nursing*, 8th April 1916

BM/DD   Fraser, L.E., 'Diary of a Dresser in the Serbian Unit of the Scottish Women's Hospitals', *Blackwood's Magazine*, June 1915

BM/MAW   de Liaison, Officer, 'My Albanian Winter', *Blackwood's Magazine*, January 1917

BMS/TG   MacGlade, A., 'Two Girls and a Car in France', *Badminton Magazine of Sport and Pastimes*, November 1911

CA/ASW   Baker, Sophia, 'Among the Servian Wounded' [letter to the editor dated 6th April 1915], *Croydon Advertiser* [date unknown]

CT/SS   'Serbia's Sacrifice', *Croydon Times*, 16th March 1918, in the Flora Sandes Collection

DC/DL   'Dartford Lady's Experiences in Serbia', *Dartford Chronicle and District Times*, 9th July 1915

DE/FSI   'Lieut. Flora Sandes', *Daily Examiner* [Grafton, Australia],
              19th August 1920

DE/FSII   'Lieut. Flora Sandes', *Daily Examiner* [Grafton, Australia],
              24th August 1920

DE/FSIII   'Lieut. Flora Sandes', *Daily Examiner* [Grafton, Australia],
              26th August 1920

DE/LS   'Lieut. Sandes', *Daily Examiner* [Grafton, Australia], 21st
              August 1920

DM/HF   'Heard First War News', *Daily Mirror*, 24th March
              1937

DM/HGS   'Heroic Girl Soldier', *Daily Mirror*, 11th May 1916

DX/WSM   'Woman Sergeant Major Appeal for Comforts for the
              Serbian Army', *Daily Express*, 21st December 1917

EAT/FH   'Flora, Heroine of the Trenches', *East Anglian Times*, 15th
              March 1988

FWDN/ND   'Nurse Decorated by Serbian Royalty', *Fort Wayne Daily
              News*, 7th July 1916

HFWW/DB   Palmer, Alan, 'Defeat of Bulgaria', *History of the First
              World War: Collapse of Bulgaria*, Vol. VII, No. 11 (London:
              BPC Publishing, 1971)

HM/WBF   Folks, Homer, 'War, Best Friend of Disease', *Harper's
              Monthly Magazine*, March 1920

HOM/WP   Fedunkiw, Marianne P., 'Women Physicians Serving in
              Serbia, 1915–1917: The Story of Dorothea Maude', *History
              of Medicine*, Vol. IV, No. 1, 2007

HT/RB   Palmer, Alan, 'Revolt in Belgrade', *History Today*, Vol. X,
              No. 3, March 1960

HT/SOS   Palmer, Alan, 'Shadow over Serbia: The Black Hand',
              History Today, Vol. VIII, No. 12, December 1958

II/KSS   'Kerrywoman Soldier in Serbia', *Irish Independent*, 2nd
              January 1917

IS/OMS   Corey, Herbert, '"Our Miss Simmonds" of America Is
              Heroine of the Stricken Serbs', *Idaho Statesman*, 11th
              February 1917

JMH/AHC   Rothenberg, Gunther E., 'The Austro-Hungarian Campaign
              Against Serbia in 1914', *Journal of Military History*,
              April 1989

JS/WE   'War Experiences of a Woman Soldier in Yugoslavia', *Star*
              [Johannesburg], 2nd October 1945

L/NWB   Phillips, I.E., 'The Nurse Who Became a Soldier', *Legionary*, Vol. XXX, No. 2, July 1955

LDN/VD   'Victims Dying like Flies', *Lincoln Daily News*, 21st May 1915

LI/HM   Simmonds, Emily, 'With the Hungry in Macedonia', *Leslie's Illustrated Weekly Newspaper*, 15th December 1917

LI/WW   Estep, Edwin Ralph, 'Women's Work on the Serbian Front', *Leslie's Illustrated Weekly Newspaper*, 7th June 1917

LM/CY   Lane, Arthur Bliss, 'Conquest in Yugoslavia', *Life Magazine*, 15th September 1941

LP/HW   'Hospital Work in Servia', *Lady's Pictorial*, 30th January 1915

MO/ED   'The Editor's "Dump"', *Mosquito*, No. 108, December 1954

MO/WPI   'Women's Pages', *Mosquito*, No. 91, September 1950

MO/WPII   'Women's Pages', *Mosquito*, No. 97, March 1952

NG/OMR   Corey, Herbert, 'On the Monastir Road', *National Geographic*, Vol. XXXI, May 1917

NR/WFS   Sandes, Flora, 'A Word for Serbia', *National Review*, No. 75, March–August 1920

NT/IWM   [Unnamed article], *Nursing Times*, 19th September 1915, Private Papers of Flora Sandes, Imperial War Museum [67/332/1]

NT/NS   'Nursing in Serbia', *Nursing Times*, 14th November 1914

NYT/HSD   'Hero Surgeon's Diary of Devotion', *New York Times*, 10th May 1915

NYT/NB   'Nurse in Belgrade When Shells Fell', *New York Times*, 15th January 1915

NYT/RC   'Red Cross at Work in Many Fields', *New York Times*, 18th April 1915

NYT/SCH   Capser, L.W., 'Serbian Children's Hospital', *New York Times*, 23rd October 1921

NYT/SF   'Senator France Assails Col. Ryan', *New York Times*, 3rd August 1921

NYT/WEG   'Wounded English Girl Wins Serbian Cross', *New York Times*, 31st December 1916

NYTR/AN   'American Nurse Tells How She Plies Knife to Ease Wounded in Serbian Field Hospital', *New York Tribune*, 20th June 1915

OWH/WF   Corey, Herbert, 'Woman Fights in Ranks with Serbian Soldiers', *Omaha World Herald*, 6th April 1917

PH/OP	Palmer, Alan, 'Operation Punishment', *Purnell's History of the Second World War: Hitler's Revenge on Yugoslavia*, No. 14, 1972
RCM/S	Hendrick, Ellwood, 'The Serbians', *Red Cross Magazine*, December 1916
RCM/WSR	Simmonds, Emily, 'With the Serbian Refugees', *Red Cross Magazine*, April 1916
S/FS	'Miss Flora Sandes Fought with Servia: Interview with Her Sister-in-Law', *Sun* [Sydney, undated], Private Papers of Flora Sandes, Imperial War Museum [67/332/1]
SC/LIB	'Captain Flora Sandes: Lived in Belgrade During German Occupation', *Scotsman*, 17th November 1944
SC/TOS	'The Tragedy of Serbia: Madame Grouitch's Story', *Scotsman*, 1st February 1916
SMH/FSI	'Lieut. Flora Sandes', *Sydney Morning Herald*, 7th June 1920
SMH/FSII	'Lieut. Flora Sandes', *Sydney Morning Herald*, 9th June 1920
T/ABL	'Adventures of a British Legation', *Times*, 20th June 1941
UHD/SIN	'Servia Is Now a Vast Pest House: Typhus Spreading', *Utica Herald-Dispatch*, 2nd June 1915
WMJ/ES	Simmonds, Emily, letter dated 14th July 1917, *Woman's Medical Journal*, Vol. XXVII, No. 10
WSM/IF	'Is Flora the Bravest Woman Alive?', *Woman's Sunday Mirror*, 24th June 1956

3. LETTERS, DIARIES AND OTHER DOCUMENTS

THE FLORA SANDES COLLECTION, IN THE POSSESSION OF ARTHUR AND NAN BAKER [FSC]

FSC/ALN	'Australian Lecture Notes'
FSC/BB	'A Brief Biography of S.D.S. Wanderings in the Wilderness from Nov. 4th 1856 till July 16th 1894'
FSC/D	Flora Sandes's diaries
FSC/HWL	'How We Lived under the Nazis' [original draft for JS/WE]
FSC/LET	Flora Sandes's letters

IMPERIAL WAR MUSEUM, LONDON [IWM]

IWM/BOS Memo from Professor Bosanquet to the Secretary, 27th January 1917, Women at Work Collection [Serbia 7.1/34]

IWM/EA Bray, Jean, The Extraordinary Ambassador: An Unpublished Biography of Dr K.S. MacPhail [78/17/1]

IWM/FS Private Papers of Flora Sandes [67/332/1]

IWM/IFS Interview with Sergeant Major Flora Sandes, 29th January 1918, Women at Work Collection [Serbia 11/10]

IWM/KM Private Papers of Dr K S MacPhail [Documents.6767]

IWM/LC Private Papers of Miss L. Creighton [Documents.1898]

IWM/LPS Private Papers of Lieutenant Colonel L.P. Smellie [Documents.11391]

IWM/MM Private Papers of Dr M.L. McNeill [Documents.12043]

IWM/RCW Report on Civilian Work in Corfu, Women at Work Collection [Serbia 5/11]

IWM/SS Pamphlet: The Serbian Soldier. Victorious–, Suffering, Women at Work Collection [Serbia 11/4]

IWM/WS Private Papers of Miss W. Seymour [Documents.7165]

IWM/WW Women at Work Collection

MISCELLANEOUS

AHL/HF Papers of Professor Henry Wilder Foote and His Family, Andover-Harvard Theological Library, Harvard University [bMS 00575]

ANZ/MMA Rigg, Theodore, Mission to Montenegro and Albania: Experiences of a Relief Worker on the Adriatic Coast at the Time of the Retreat of the Serbian Army 1915/16 [unpublished manuscript], Archives New Zealand [AALT W3082/126]

CLM/FTL Papers of Frederick Taylor Lord, Countway Library of Medicine, Harvard University [Rare Books GA50.5]

ESF Emily Simmonds's file, American Friends Service Committee Archives, Philadelphia

ESRC Emily Simmonds's American Red Cross file, National Archives and Records Administration, College Park, Maryland

ESRC/HA Emily Simmonds's handwritten account of her work dated January 1919, Emily Simmonds's American Red Cross file,

National Archives and Records Administration, College Park, Maryland

ESRC/LET   Emily Simmonds's letters, Emily Simmonds's American Red Cross file, National Archives and Records Administration, College Park, Maryland

INT/AB   Arthur Baker in discussion with the author, 2005

LET/AB   Letter from Allison Blackmore to the author, 28th December 2007

LET/BCWW   Letter from Barton Cookingham to Whitney Warren, 6th February 1915, the Whitney Warren Collection, Houghton Library, Harvard University

LET/DSAB   Letter from Dick Sandes to Alan Burgess, 19th February 1962, in private hands

LET/DSJS   Letter from Dick Sandes to James Sandes, undated [1981/2], in private hands

LET/ES   Letter from Emily Simmonds, quoted in: Jane A. Delano, 'The Red Cross', *American Journal of Nursing*, April 1915, pp. 580–82; Mabel T. Boardman, *Under the Red Cross Flag at Home and Abroad* (Philadelphia: J.B. Lippincott, 1915), pp. 298–99

LET/FSDS   Letter from Flora Sandes to Dick Sandes, 1945, in private hands

LU/LPS   Colonel Lloyd Piercy Smellie Papers, Special Collections Department, Leeds University Library [SAL 060]

LU/RV   Ruth E. Verney (née Conway) Papers, Special Collections Department, Leeds University Library [WO 127]

NAK   National Archives, Kew

PCL/NY   Passenger and Crew Lists of Vessels Arriving at New York, New York, 1897–1957, Records of the Immigration and Naturalization Service, National Archives, Washington DC [Microfilm Publication T715]

SNW/APT   The Testimony of a Nurse (Amelia Peabody Tileston), Samuel Newell Watson Papers, Hoover Institution Archives, Stanford University [XX033]

SNW/TYE   Three Years' Experiences in Serbia as Related by Miss Simmonds, Samuel Newell Watson Papers, Hoover Institution Archives, Stanford University [XX033]

SWH   Scottish Women's Hospitals Collection, Mitchell Library, Glasgow

SWH/LET   Letter from Dr Bennett, 16th November 1916, Scottish Women's Hospitals Collection, Mitchell Library, Glasgow [Circulated Letters, Tin 42, November–December 1916]

WL/ML   Miscellaneous Letters, Scottish Women's Hospitals, Women's Library, London [GB/106/2/C]

WL/VH   Papers of Vera Holme, Special Collections, Women's Library, London [7VJH]

WL/VHI   Letter from Flora Sandes, 17th August 1925, Papers of Vera Holme, Special Collections, Women's Library, London [7VJH]

WL/VHII   Letter from Flora Sandes, 13th June 1922, Papers of Vera Holme, Special Collections, Women's Library, London [7VJH]

4. OTHER MEDIA

BBC/OH   'Our Heritage: Flora Sandes', BBC, broadcast 5th August 1965, in the archives of East Anglian Television

BBC/YW   'Yesterday's Witness: Mission to Serbia', BBC2, broadcast 22nd February 1970

MWWI   Šrámek, Josef, 'Memoirs of the World War I', www.svobodat. com/sramek/sramek02_eng.html

CHAPTER 1

1   FHFC, p. 3.

2   BBC/OH.

3   FHFC, p. 3.

4   I have attempted to ensure that both place and surnames reflect
     their Serbian spelling. However, where people habitually Anglicized
     their surnames, I have retained their preferred spelling. Thus, for
     example, Mabel Grouitch remains "Grouitch" instead of the Serbian
     "Grujić".

5   IWM/IFS; 'Lieut. Flora Sandes', *Australian Bystander*, 8th July 1920;
     'The Woman Soldier', *Glen Innes Guardian* [Australia], 18th October
     1920.

6   DM/HF.

7   LS, p. 13.

8   'Credentials from Training School', ESRC.

9   NYT/NB.

10   FSC/ALN. They were not quite the first to leave British shores to
     nurse near the front. The first group of women left on 9th August for
     Belgium. See 'Active Service', *British Journal of Nursing*, 15th August
     1914.

11   FSC/ALN; FSC/D, 13th August 1914.

12   The stated number of nurses in the Unit varies according to source. Flora
     mentions seven in total, Emily eight and Mabel nine. FSC/ALN states
     that the eighth left to work elsewhere and FSC/D, 7th September 1914,
     states "Mrs Hartley and Miss Mann went to Hospital XIX", which
     almost certainly accounts for the inconsistency.

13   FSC/ALN.

14   FSC/D, 14th, 17th August 1914.

15   SNW/TYE; FSC/D, 17th August 1914.

16   FSC/ALN.

17   The identity of Emily's father is unknown, although she stated that he
     was from Aberdeen.

18   Inez Haynes Gillmore Papers 1872–1945, Schlesinger Library, Radcliffe
     Institute, Harvard University [A25].

19   NYT/NB.

20   FSC/D, 17th August 1914.

21   FSC/D, 17th–25th August 1914.

22   DC/DL.

23   FSC/ALN.

24   Mary H. Frances Ivens, 'The Part Played by British Medical Women in the War', *British Medical Journal*, 18th August 1917, p. 205.

25   FSC/ALN; IWM/IFS.

CHAPTER 2

1   L/NWB.

2   INT/AB; Brian Thompson, *Imperial Vanities* (London: HarperCollins, 2002), pp. 160–66.

3   FSC/BB.

4   FSC/BB.

5   *John Bull*, 13th April 1878, p. 230.

6   See: 'Bazaar and Fête at Monewden', *Ipswich Journal*, 12th July 1884; 'Marlesford', *Ipswich Journal*, 8th July 1887; 'Marlesford', *Ipswich Journal*, 5th January 1888.

7   'Monewden: Concert', *Ipswich Journal*, 10th January 1882.

8   'Monewden', *Ipswich Journal*, 27th January 1883.

9   *History, Gazetteer and Directory of Suffolk* (Sheffield: William White Ltd, 1891–92), pp. 547–48.

10   1891 and 1901 census information.

11   Diaries of Mary Baker (née Sandes), FSC.

12   FSC.

13   AWS, p. 9.

14   INT/AB.

15   'Letter to the Editor', *Times*, 29th August, 22nd September 1891.

16   See William Besnard Sandes's Discharge Document, War Office: Soldiers' Documents from Pension Claims, First World War, NAK [Microfilm Publication WO364].

17   Geoffrey Serle et al., eds., *Australian Dictionary of Biography* (Melbourne: Melbourne University Press, 1988), p. 518; Richard Evans, 'Reporting "a Mercenary and Inglorious War": The Argus, the Boer War and Breaker Morant', in Muriel Porter, ed., *The Argus: The Life and Death of a Great Melbourne Newspaper, 1846–1957* (Melbourne: RMIT Publishing, 2003), pp. 139–57.

18   FSC/BB.

19   The 1901 Census lists them both as "correspondents".

20   *Local Studies Pack: Thornton Heath*, 2nd edn. (Croydon: Croydon Libraries, 1993).

21 Little is known of Flora's work in London, but in January 1900 she appears to have been employed by the "Colonial Trading Co." at 130 London Wall. See India Office Records, British Library, London [IOR/L/PJ/6].

22 LET/DSAB.

23 PCL/NY.

24 'Typing Round the World', *Pitman's Phonetic Journal*, 19th November 1904.

25 'Girl Starts Journey on Foot to San Francisco', *St Louis Republic*, 9th August 1904.

26 S/FS.

27 'Deaths on Cassiar – Two Occurred While Steamer Was Southbound', *Nanaimo Free Press*, 7th December 1904. See also: Margaret A. Ormsby, ed., *A Pioneer Gentlewoman in British Columbia: The Recollections of Susan Allison* (Vancouver, BC: University of British Columbia Press, 1991).

28 LET/DSAB.

29 'A First Impression of Van Anda', *Coast Miner* [Van Anda, British Columbia], 15th January 1900.

30 'Texada Island, the Gem of the Gulf', *Coast Miner* [Van Anda, British Columbia], 15th January 1900.

31 LET/DSAB.

32 Flora, by one likely exaggerated account, took "a trip – by bicycle – through Central America [to Panama]… young Dick spending the first part of the journey through the jungle in her bicycle basket." See CTC, p. 55.

33 LET/DSAB.

34 INT/AB.

35 LET/DSJS.

36 LET/DSAB.

37 S/FS.

38 LET/DSAB. Flora's name does not appear in Brooklands' archives. She most likely drove her car around the track when it was open to the public, on non-race days.

39 Letter from Dick Sandes, FSC.

40 S/FS.

41 'Correspondence', *Autocar*, 9th May 1914.

42 See 1911 Census. At the time it was taken, Nan was staying with Flora and her family in Thornton Heath. See also BBC/OH.

43 BMS/TG, pp. 539, 540; FSC.

44   BMS/TG, p. 541.

45   S/FS.

46   LET/DSAB. See also S/FS.

47   LET/DSAB.

48   S/FS.

49   FSC/LET to unnamed friend, 14th October 1916.

50   CTC, p. 20; FPW, p. 1. Baker was not a relation.

51   Information provided by Lynette Beardwood, FANY archivist.

52   M.A. St Clair Stobart, *War and Women* (London: G. Bell & Sons, 1913), p. 5.

53   Lyn MacDonald, *The Roses of No Man's Land* (London: Penguin, 1993), p. 16; Yvonne McEwen, *It's a Long Way to Tipperary* (Dunfermline: Cualann Press, 2006), pp. 39, 45.

54   Irene Ward, *FANY Invicta* (London: Hutchinson, 1955), p. 27. Ward was quoting an early member of the FANY.

55   'England's New Woman – A Woman of War', *San Antonio Light and Gazette*, 8th July 1909. Although this article is from an American publication, its original source would have been one of the British papers.

56   LS, pp. 10–11.

57   FPW, p. 6. See also M.A. St Clair Stobart, *Miracles and Adventures: An Autobiography*, 2nd edn. (London: Rider & Co., 1936), p. 83.

58   'Nursing Echoes', *British Journal of Nursing*, 3rd July 1909, p. 13.

59   FPW, pp. 6–7.

60   Information provided by Lynette Beardwood, FANY archivist.

61   LET/DSAB.

62   An exception was made for Mairi Chisholm and Elsie Knocker, two women who worked at a frontline first-aid post in Pervyse, Belgium.

63   Nineteen died in Serbia itself. Two died of disease shortly after arriving back in England.

64   IWM/EA.

65   EYS, pp. 16–17.

66   The Scottish Women's Hospitals were not used for suffrage propaganda for fear that it would backfire. See ISL, p. 110.

67   ISL, p. 70.

68   WWU, p. 139.

69   Nurses, some of whom were paid, came from more diverse backgrounds. See ISL, p. x.

70   LET/DSAB.

71   Jan and Cora Gordon, *Two Vagabonds in Serbia and Montenegro* (Harmondsworth, Middlesex: Penguin, 1939), p. 152. The 1916 edition of this book, published under the title *The Luck of Thirteen* (London: John Murray, 1916), omits this information.

CHAPTER 3

1   Vučetić is the most likely original spelling of the Anglicized "Woutch-etitch". See SEG, p. 48.

2   BM/DD, p. 782.

3   LET/ES.

4   FSC/ALN.

5   See SEG, p. 56 [illustration].

6   LET/ES. See also SEG, p. 48.

7   See: LP/HW [right-hand illustration]; SEG, p. 56 [illustration].

8   FSC/D, 30th August 1914.

9   FSC/D, 7th September 1914.

10   FSC/ALN.

11   NT/NS.

12   NT/NS. See also: FSC/ALN; DC/DL.

13   FSC/ALN.

14   See: SEG, p. 107, 'Typhus Takes Toll', *Stillwater County Democrat*, 29th May 1915.

15   LET/ES.

16   LET/ES.

17   FSC/ALN.

18   LP/HW. The source of this anecdote was almost certainly Flora.

19   BJN/BN.

20   BBF, p. 108.

21   Josephine, Newcombe, 'Serbia: The Second Onslaught', *History of the First World War: Serbia: Defeat into Victory*, Vol. II, No. 2 (London: BPC Publishing, 1970), p. 484.

22   BAL, p. 314. See also: Stanley Naylor, 'The Serbian People in War Time', *Scribner's Magazine*, March 1916, p. 375; JMH/AHC, p. 134.

23   FW, p. 19.

24   BAL, pp. 314–15.

25   Quoted in BAL, p. 315.

26   BAL, p. 316; WSB, p. 272. See also TF, p. 18.

27   R.A. Reiss, *How Austria-Hungary Waged War in Serbia* (Paris: Librairie Armand Colin, 1916), p. 37. Reiss's investigation was far from impartial, as his investigation was sponsored by the Serbian government. However, other eyewitnesses corroborated his reports of atrocities. See ASSA, p. 16.

28   JMH/AHC, p. 138.

29   FSC/ALN.

30   LET/ES.

31   SEG, p. 51.

32   FSC/D, 15th February 1915.

33   HARCN, pp. 187–88.

34   See John E. Mackenzie, ed., *University of Edinburgh Roll of Honour 1914–1919* (London: Oliver & Boyd, 1921), p. 85.

35   Edinburgh University Special Collections, records of the School of Medicine.

36   FSC/D, 12th October 1914.

37   FSC/D, 13th, 17th October 1914.

38   AG/RD.

39   FSC/D, 1st, 3rd November 1914.

40   AG/RD.

41   FSC/D, 5th November 1914; LP/HW.

42   See SEG, pp. 108–109.

43   NYT/NB. See also FSC/ALN.

44   'The Care of the Wounded', *British Journal of Nursing*, 24th October 1914.

45   'Mme Grouitch Begs Aid', *Oakland Tribune*, 20th May 1915. Violet O'Brien had trained in Cork and worked in Calcutta. See 'Appointments', *British Journal of Nursing*, 29th May 1915.

46   NYT/NB.

47   'Lauds US Red Cross', *Washington Post*, 17th January 1915.

48   NYT/NB. Nonetheless, they managed to save most of their patients. Of the two thousand that passed through the hospital during their time there, only fifty died. See BJN/BN.

49   Lady Paget, *With Our Serbian Allies* (London: Serbian Relief Fund, 1915), p. 3. See also EWD.

50   DC/DL.

51   'The Needs of Our Serbian Ally', *Daily Mail*, 10th December 1914.

52   FSC/D, 13th November 1914.

53   FSC/D, 14th November 1914.

54   NYT/NB.

55   JMH/AHC, p. 143.

56   MOMI, p. 144.

57   SJ, p. 145.

58   Claire Hirshfield, 'In Search of Mrs Ryder: British Women in Serbia Dur-
      ing the Great War', *East European Quarterly*, Vol. XX, No. 4, January
      1987, p. 389.

59   See 'Alarming State of Disease in Servia', *Brooklyn Daily Eagle*, 4th
      April 1915.

60   'Nursing Typhus in Serbia', *British Journal of Nursing*, 22nd May 1915;
      SJ, p. 60; MBL, p. 103.

61   'The Passing Bell', *British Journal of Nursing*, 9th January 1915.

62   WEE, p. 42.

63   MBL, p. 118. See also MWWI.

64   MBL, p. 54.

65   HARCN, p. 188.

CHAPTER 4

1   AWS, p. 10. Today's equivalent is roughly £124,000.

2   NYT/NB. See also: ESRC/LET, from Helen Fidelia Draper to Miss Jane
      A. Delano, 18th November 1915; ESRC/LET, from "Chairman, National
      Committee, Red Cross Nursing Service" [Jane Delano] to Mrs Wm K.
      Draper, 20th November 1915.

3   AWS, p. 10; letter on British Red Cross paper, 16th January 1915, IWM/
      FS.

4   NT/IWM.

5   FSC/D, 14th February 1915.

6   UTF, p. 114; HD, p. 19; Monica M. Stanley, *My Diary in Serbia* (London:
      Simpkin, Marshall, Hamilton, Kent & Co., 1916), p. 25.

7   UTF, p. 115.

8   See: HD, p. 30; HARCN, p. 180; NYT/HSD.

9   'Making a War', *Lima Daily News*, 8th July 1915.

10   NYT/HSD.

11   NYT/RC.

12   Today, with proper treatment, the mortality from typhus fever is around
      one per cent.

13   See 'Report of the Death of an American Citizen' [3rd March 1915],
      Reports of the Deaths of American Citizens, General Records of the
      Department of State, National Archives, Washington DC [Record Group

59]. See also: 'American Doctor Suicides in Serbia', *Coshocton Morning Tribune*, 28th April 1915; 'Talks to Medical Society', *Orange County Times*, 7th December 1917; 'Serbian Nurses Come Home', *Emporia Gazette*, 16th July 1916.

14   NYT/RC.

15   WSE, p. 72. See also TSC, p. 248.

16   ASSA, p. 11.

17   Pamela Bright, 'A British Nurse in Serbia', *History of the First World War: Mackensen's Balkan Victory*, Vol. III, No. 8 (London: BPC Publishing, 1970), p. 1120, EWD, pp. 36–37; ASSA, pp. 84–86.

18   ASSA, p. 109.

19   The Anglo-American Unit were the first "mission" per se to start work in Serbia during the war, although the first foreign medical workers were in fact Dr van Tienhoven and his head nurse, Miss de Groote. They had been travelling in Eastern Europe when war was declared. They began work in the provincial hospital in Valjevo on 7th August 1914. See ASSA.

20   ASSA, p. 88.

21   ASSA, p. 113. See also 'Dr Cookingham, 79, Dies; Was Surgeon in Rhinebeck', *Poughkeepsie Journal*, 9th February 1968.

22   UHD/SIN.

23   LET/BCWW.

24   ASSA, p. 114.

25   LDN/VD.

26   MBL, p. 203.

27   LET/BCWW.

28   NT/IWM.

29   MBL, p. 238. See also: EWD, pp. 30–31.

30   DC/DL. At least two Greek doctors were also at work there, as were about twenty members of the Russian Red Cross.

31   FSC/D, 16th February 1915.

32   MBL, p. 239.

33   See 'The Cry of Serbia', *Nursing Times*, 19th December 1914.

34   MBL, pp. 239–40.

35   MBL, p. 240; FSC/D, 17th February 1915.

36   FWDN/ND.

37   FSC/D, 18th February 1915.

38   NYT/RC.

39   FSC/D, 21st February 1915.

40   FSC/ALN.

41   See 'Hannah Jessie Hankin-Hardy', Raunds War Memorials Research Project, www.raundswarmemorials.org/2918/18738.html.

42   See letter dated 21st February 1916, 'Prisoners: Balkan Files 1915', NAK [FO 383/131].

43   BM/DD, pp. 793–94.

44   FSC/D, 20th February 1915.

45   FSC/ALN. Flora's notes state that Cooke had died the "day before", i.e. 19th February, but Cooke in fact died on 10th February 1915. See: 'From a Surgeon's Notebook', *Graduate Magazine of the University of Kansas*, Vol. XVI, No. 8, May 1916, p. 255; LET/BCWW.

46   APT. See also UHD/SIN.

47   FSC/D, 22nd February 1915.

48   See ASSA.

49   IS/OMS.

50   FSC/D, 3rd March 1915.

51   SNW/TYE. See also: WEE, pp. 48, 90–91; CA/ASW; 'Typhus Epidemic in Serbia, Where Washington Doctor Gave His Life, Kills 30% of Population', *Washington Post*, 21st June 1915.

52   CA/ASW.

53   SNW/TYE.

54   IS/OMS.

55   FSC/D, 3rd March 1915.

56   See: LFH, p. 144; EWD, p. 38.

57   MP, p. 47.

58   'Mrs Farwell Describes Her War Experiences', *Chicago Daily Tribune*, 3rd May 1916.

59   See: SEG, pp. 108, 109 [illustration captions]; HARCN, p. 191; 'The Passing Bell', *British Journal of Nursing*, 20th March 1915; UTF, pp. 127–28; WWU, p. 115.

60   Nan had been a member of another all-women unit that Mabel had taken to Antwerp the previous year, which had been forced to retreat ahead of the German capture of the Belgian city.

61   FSC/D, 22nd February 1915.

62   SNW/TYE.

63   NYTR/AN, 20th June 1915.

64   FSC/D, 3rd March 1915.

65   Herbert Corey, *The Army Means Business* (Indianapolis, IN: Bobbs-Merrill Co., 1942), pp. 190–91.

66   CA/ASW.

67   FSC/ALN.

68   FSC/ALN. She did not name the explorer.

69   CA/ASW; A/ITB.

70   FSC/D, 25th February 1915.

71   FSC/ALN.

72   NYTR/AN.

73   LI/WW.

74   FSC/D, 1st March 1915.

75   FSC/ALN.

76   FSC/D, 22nd February 1915. According to Dr Jeanneret Minkine, a
     remarkably similar mindset existed at the French Mission in Pirot.
     "It is a curious psychological phenomenon that the fact of seeing
     so many people die, causes one to regard death as a very common
     event, even when it is a question of one's own death." See TF,
     p. 16.

77   Dr Josif and Mrs Ruža Vinaver's son, Stanislav, whom Flora would later
     meet, is believed to be "Constantine the Poet" of BLGF.

78   His name does not appear within Irish or British medical registers.
     Therefore he was unlikely to have been a doctor, but it is possible he
     was some sort of engineer.

79   MAS, p. 190.

80   FSC/D, 8th March 1915.

81   See: 'The War: Serbia', British Medical Journal, 28th August 1915; 'Fever
     Takes More Victims than War', Lincoln Daily News, 11th May 1915;
     TF, p. 22.

82   TF, pp. 23, 33. See also MBL, p. 307.

83   WEE, p. 31.

84   IWM/IFS; FSC/ALN.

85   LDN/VD; IWM/IFS.

86   FSC/ALN.

87   FSC/D, 14th March 1915.

88   UTF, p. 195.

89   FSC/D, 14th–21st March 1915, written on 22nd March when she had
     sufficiently recovered.

90   UTF, p. 195.

91   SNW/TYE.

92   FSC/D, 2nd, 6th April 1915.

93   FSC/D, 7th–15th April 1915.

94   FSC/D, 20th February 1915. Within one three-week period in Valjevo
      alone, twenty-one doctors died.

95   FSC/D, 18th–27th June 1915. See also: ISL, p. 25; 'Nursing and the War',
      British Journal of Nursing, 1st May 1915, p. 363.

96   IWM/EA.

97   IWM/EA. See also EYS, p. 30. Coincidentally, Katherine's father, who
      was also a doctor, was an expert on typhus fever. See Donald MacPhail,
      'Statistical Comparison of Typhus and Enteric Fevers', *Glasgow Medical
      Journal*, No. 10, October 1879.

98   See CLM/FTL.

99   TF, p. 20.

100   TF, p. 3. See also: WSB, p. 273; HM/WBF, p. 456.

101   TF, p. 6; LDN/VD. See also: 'Magazines', *Scotsman*, 2nd September
      1915; 'Dr Cookingham Receives Award', *Poughkeepsie Eagle-News*,
      22nd May 1915.

102   SRCU, p. 42.

103   TF, p. 5. See also: Michael D. Nicklanovich, 'Rebecca West's "Constan-
      tine the Poet"', *Serb World*, Vol. XV, No. 4, March–April 1999; Papers
      of Richard Pearson Strong, Countway Library of Medicine, Harvard
      University [Rare Books GA82].

104   FSS, p. 26.

105   LFH, pp. 156–57.

106   Letter from Dr Elsie Inglis, 22nd June 1915, quoted in Anne Powell,
      Women in the War Zone (Stroud: History Press, 2009), p. 172.

107   SNW/TYE.

108   FSC/D, 9th July 1915.

109   SNW/TYE.

110   FSC/D, 29th July 1915.

111   FSC/D, 3rd, 4th August 1915.

112   With thanks to Dr Jonathan Standley for providing the modern-day
      diagnosis for what Flora described as "infective jaundice".

113   See 'Austro-German Menace to Serbia', *Times*, 5th October 1915.

114   Peter Kemp, 'Gunboats on the Danube', *History of the First World War:
      Bulgaria: Germany's New Recruit*, Vol. III, No. 7 (London: BPC Publish-
      ing, 1970), p. 1086. Troubridge and the other members keenly felt that they
      had been sent as punishment to what the British Admiralty considered an
      operational backwater. See WSE, p. 105. Troubridge, for example, had
      had a long and distinguished naval career until he was subjected to a court
      martial, accused of letting two German cruisers escape from the Adriatic

in August 1914 without engaging them in battle. He was later "fully and honourably acquitted". See: RND, pp. 44, 45, 53, 187; DOS, p. 136.

115 See: SC/TOS; MP, p. 51; TSC, p. 285.

116 EWS, p. 183. Emily left Liverpool for New York on 22nd September 1915.

117 See: IWM/WS; WWU, p. 36.

118 ISL, p. 236.

119 WWU, p. 37.

120 FSC/D, 23rd October 1915.

121 See 'Ships Torpedoed Without Warning', *Nevada State Journal*, 15th October 1915.

122 IWM/WS.

123 FSC/D, 23rd October 1915.

124 FSC/D, 3rd November 1915.

125 During 1917, the dangerous voyage between Marseilles and Salonika was practically abandoned, in preference to a route through Italy and mainland Greece that minimized sea travel. That year, on 21st November, south-west of Sicily, the *Mossoul* was sunk by a torpedo.

126 EWS, p. 55.

127 WWU, p. 67.

CHAPTER 5

1   EWS, pp. 9–10.

2   EWS, p. 4.

3   FSC/D, 3rd November 1915.

4   OWW, p. 12.

5   A/ITB.

6   EWS, pp. 5–6; FSC/D, 6th, 8th November 1915.

7   FSC/D, 8th, 9th November 1915.

8   EWS, p. 6.

9   FSC/D, 8th November 1915.

10   WWU, pp. 48–49.

11   EWS, p. 13; FSC/D, 9th November 1915.

12   EWS, pp. 15–16.

13   FW, p. 90.

14   See: FW, p. 96; TSC, p. 67.

15   FSS, p. 20.

16   FSJ, p. 131.

17 EWS, pp. 22–23.

18 EWS, p. 21.

19 FSC/LET to Sophia, 21st November 1915.

20 FSC/D, 14th November 1915.

21 EWS, p. 23.

22 IMC, p. 21.

23 EWS, pp. 27–28.

24 FSC/D, 14th November 1915.

25 EWS, p. 29.

26 FSC/LET to Sophia, 21st November 1915.

27 EWS, p. 33.

28 FSC/D, 15th November 1915.

29 FSC/LET to Sophia, 21st November 1915.

30 FSC/LET to Sophia, 21st November 1915.

31 EWS, p. 38.

32 EWS, pp. 63, 89.

33 FSC/LET to Sophia, 21st November 1915.

34 EWS, p. 30.

35 FSC/D, 19th November 1915.

36 EWS, p. 51.

37 FSC/D, 20th November 1915.

38 EWS, p. 64.

39 FSC/D, 24th November 1915; EWS, pp. 68–70.

40 FSC/D, 24th November 1915.

41 EWS, p. 72.

42 EWS, pp. 74–75.

43 EWS, p. 47.

44 FSC/D, 20th November 1915.

45 FSC/LET to Sophia, 21st November 1915.

46 EWS, p. 80.

47 FSC/D, 26th November 1915; EWS, p. 81.

48 EWS, p. 81.

49 Diary entry, 28th June 1917, IWM/MM. They had two children. Greig
    died in 1958.

50 FSC/LET to Sophia, 21st November 1915.

51 EWS, p. 85.

52 AWS, p. 13.

53 AWS, pp. 13–14.

54 EWS, p. 91. See also FSC/ALN.

CHAPTER 6

1   EWS, p. 94.

2   FSC/D, 29th November 1915. In fact, the flesh had been stripped by POWs and refugees, who sometimes ate it raw. See: MSY, p. 209; FSJ, p. 150; ANZ/MMA. The women of the Stobart Unit were also forced to eat the fallen animals. See IMC, p. 65.

3   EWS, p. 101.

4   MFS, p. 318.

5   FW, pp. 150, 158.

6   See TSC, p. 150.

7   See: FW, p. 168; K. Peball, 'Serbia – The Long Retreat', *History of the First World War: Mackensen's Balkan Victory*, Vol. III, No. 8 (London: BPC Publishing, 1970), p. 1,119.

8   EWS, pp. 104–106.

9   EWS, pp. 113, 120.

10   EWS, pp. 109–10.

11   See for example SRCU, pp. 201, 203.

12   Fortier Jones, 'Glimpses of Serbia in Retreat', *Century*, August 1916, p. 513.

13   FSC/D, 11th December 1915.

14   FIS, p. 191. See also: SRCU, p. 228; TSC, p. 291.

15   WSA, pp. 72, 74.

16   'Germans Showed No Mercy to Her Patients in World War I', *Kansas City Star*, 5th July 1942.

17   HSWH, p. 165. See also: EWD, pp. 180, 204; 'In Man's Attire', *Irish Times*, 13th February 1916.

18   HARCN, p. 215. See also: FIS, p. 130; RND, p. 66.

19   WSA, p. 20.

20   EWS, pp. 125, 135.

21   EWS, p. 140.

22   EWS, p. 141.

23   AWS, p. 40.

24   EWS, pp. 142–43.

25   See: 'Saving Serbia', *Western Morning News* [Plymouth, MA], 24th April 1920; Jan and Cora Gordon, *The Luck of Thirteen* (London: John Murray, 1916), p. 236; SMH/FSII; RCS, p. 39; EWD, p. 59; LGP, p. 23; BBF, pp. 107–108; SH, p. 153; LLV, p. 203.

26   AWS, p. 17. See AMM for a feminist interpretation of the phenomenon of women soldiers, including Flora. Serbian women did not always achieve

instant acceptance among their male colleagues. See for example BBF, pp. 108–109. Women combatants were not unusual elsewhere in the east, particularly along the Russian front. The Russian "Women's Death Battalion" achieved widespread publicity during the war although its actual performance under fire was questionable. See Florence Farmborough, *Nurse at the Russian Front* (London: Constable, 1974), p. 305. Flora too had heard of it. "I'd very much like to see it but I don't think I'd like to be in it," she scribbled in a telling letter to her sister. See AMM, p. 129.

27   EWS, pp. 144–50.

28   EWS, p. 159; FSC/ALN.

29   EWS, p. 158.

30   See: HSWH, p. 155; Olive M. Aldridge, *The Retreat from Serbia* (London: Minerva Publishing Co., 1916), p. 70; LOS, pp. 69–70.

31   TSC, pp. 267–68.

32   ISL, p. 41.

33   FSS, p. 245.

34   TSC, p. 275.

35   LOS, p. 67.

36   Two were lucky to survive. The cook, Selina "Tubby" Tubbs, caught paratyphoid and had to be held on horseback across the mountains to Scutari, and nurse Florence Clifton was shot through both lungs during an affray. See 'A Unique Experience', *British Journal of Nursing*, 11th January 1919.

37   EWS, p. 160.

38   EWS, pp. 161–62.

39   EWS, pp. 166–67.

40   EWS, pp. 167, 169.

CHAPTER 7

1   EYS, p. 240.

2   See: IMC, p. 15; BLGF, p. 586; MFS, p. 318; ISL, p. 42. Estimates of civilian dead varied wildly from 50,000 to 200,000 depending on whether deaths during the retreat but prior to the mountain crossing were taken into account. The lower of the two figures is almost certainly the more accurate.

3   BSL, p. 102.

4   See DH.

5   MOMI, p. 36.

6   FW, pp. 204–205.

7   FW, p. 242.

8   EWS, pp. 170, 172, 180.

9   EWS, p. 172.

10   ASSA, p. 123.

11   EWS, pp. 172–73.

12   FSC/LET to unnamed friend, 14th October 1916.

13   EWS, pp. 173–74.

14   'Nurse Goes Back to Serbia', New York Times, 3rd December 1915.

15   Roughly ten thousand refugees reached Salonika. See: SNW/TYE; Private
     Papers of Miss K.E. Royds, IWM [Documents.12811].

16   SNW/TYE. They likely told her disingenuously, as they had other relief
     workers, that there were "no Serbs in Durazzo". See also: ESRC/HA;
     ASSA, p. 121.

17   See: BTR, p. 143; SNW/TYE.

18   EWS, p. 184.

19   See: Dorothy and Carl J. Schneider, Into the Breach: American Women
     Overseas in World War I (New York, NY: Viking, 1991), p. 84; SNW/TYE.

20   LLV, p. 195; EWS, p. 184.

21   SNW/TYE.

22   See: MSY, p. 287; ASSA, p. 48; Jeannette Grace Watson, Our Sentry Go
     (Chicago, IL: Ralph Fletcher Seymour, 1924), p. 158.

23   RCM/WSR, p. 119.

24   FWDN/ND; IWM/IFS.

25   RCM/WSR, p. 119.

26   See: LLV, p. 187; ESRC/HA.

27   See: RND, pp. 180–81; MSY, pp. 225–27; 'American Red Cross Nurse
     Tells of Terrible Experiences in Albania', Augusta Chronicle, 5th Febru-
     ary 1916.

28   RCM/S, p. 415.

29   RCM/WSR, p. 120.

30   EWS, p. 185; QA, p. 126; LLV, p. 187.

31   FSC/ALN; ASSA, p. 138; FW, pp. 247–48.

32   EWS, pp. 187–91.

33   FSJ, p. 169.

34   Report of Miss M. Barclay, IWM [Documents.4320]. See also: FSJ, p. 240;
     IMC, p. 15.

35   FSJ, p. 198.

36   FW, p. 218.

37 BSL, pp. 107–11.

38 LOS, p. 93; BM/MAW, p. 112; ANZ/MMA; Alice and Claude Askew, 'The Great Serbian Retreat: A Personal Narrative', *The Great War*, No. 85, 1st April 1916.

39 FW, pp. 250–51, 260.

40 FW, p. 215.

41 ASSA, p. 126; RCM/WSR, p. 117.

42 RCM/WSR, p. 119.

43 FW, p. 215. While they waited on the coast, there were rumours that some of the men resorted to cannibalism. See MWWI.

44 See: JEB, pp. 74, 81; MC, p. 87.

45 Figures are commonly cited to the effect that twenty of a total of thirty thousand schoolboys died in the mountains. See: WSB, p. 101; MFS, p. 318; NAB, p. 59; HSWH, p. 238. However, according to Corbett, who had the Yugoslav embassy in London as a source, roughly twelve thousand did not attempt the mountain crossing and turned back. See RCS, p. 45.

46 'How 30,000 Serbian Boys Perished', *Weekly Dispatch*, 28th January 1917.

47 See: FW, p. 244; MWWI, diary entry 20th December 1915.

48 See QA, p. 37.

49 See: Helen R. Hughes, *A Quaker Scientist: The Life of Theodore Rigg KBE* (Rotorua, New Zealand: Beechtree Press, 2005); ANZ/MMA.

50 See: JEB, pp. 73, 74, 82; QA, p. 126; RCM/WSR, p. 119; LLV, pp. 189–90.

51 RCM/WSR, p. 120.

52 JEB, pp. 74–75.

53 'American Woman Saw Serbs Fight', *New York Times*, 24th November 1916.

54 JEB, p. 75.

55 EWS, pp. 195–96. See also FW, p. 251.

56 BM/MAW, p. 115.

57 FW, p. 260.

58 Dr Alice Hutchison, 'In the Hands of the Austrians', *Blackwood's Magazine*, April 1916, pp. 457–60.

59 FIS, pp. 227, 235; 'Nursing and the War', *British Journal of Nursing*, 26th February 1916, p. 181.

60 SRCU, pp. 274–81.

61 WSA, pp. 93–94; BJN/NW, p. 314; 'Nursing and the War', *British Journal of Nursing*, 15th April 1916, p. 337. See also: 'Austrian Government

Pays Tribute to Former American Girl', *Fort Wayne Daily News*, 20th
January 1917; 'Hungarian Tribute to Lady Paget', *Scotsman*, 13th
March 1916.

62   JEB, p. 82.

63   RCM/WSR, p. 122.

64   JEB, p. 76.

65   IS/OMS.

66   EWS, pp. 198–200. Two days later, with the Austrians pressing from the
     north, the last of the Serbs were evacuated from Durazzo. FW, p. 257.

CHAPTER 8

1   EWS, pp. 204–205.

2   FSC/ALN.

3   EWS, pp. 208–11; FSC/ALN.

4   FSJ, pp. 203–204.

5   RCM/S, p. 416.

6   EWS, p. 206. See also BTR, p. 145.

7   It was also used to rid healthy soldiers of lice before reclothing them.
     See LLV, p. 190.

8   BTR, p. 147.

9   FW, pp. 264–65; ASSA, p. 158; PTC, p. 24; BTR, p. 145.

10   MOMI, p. 119. In total, around ten thousand Serbian soldiers died
     on both Corfu and Vido. See FW, p. 265. Flora visited Vido in the
     company of Robert Carr Bosanquet on 15th February 1916. However,
     her visit coincided with that of the Crown Prince and the island had
     been "swept and disinfected" and all bodies removed. See LLV, p. 190.

11   FSC/D, 25th November 1915.

12   EWS, p. 212.

13   In fact, Flora had met Bosanquet previously, as he had sailed on the
     Arménie from Durazzo as far as Gallipoli.

14   EWS, pp. 215–16.

15   EWS, pp. 231–32.

16   EWS, p. 216.

17   FSC/LET to an unnamed friend, 14th October 1916.

18   EWS, p. 217.

19   See HOM/WP, p. 55.

20   See: Alice and Claude Askew, 'With the Serbian Army in Corfu', *Windsor
     Magazine*, Vol. XLIV, June–November 1916; BJN/NW, p. 313.

21 Private Papers of Miss F.E. Latham, IWM [Documents.5592].

22 HOM/WP, p. 55; 'Care of the Wounded', *British Journal of Nursing*, 22nd July 1916.

23 TM, p. 169; 'Care of the Wounded', *British Journal of Nursing*, 29th July 1916.

24 Report No. 3 on Corfu Hospital, IWM/WW [Serbia 6.2/11].

25 RCM/S, p. 416, See also: FSRC/HA; IWM/RCW.

26 See: LLV, p. 193; ESRC/HA.

27 IWM/RCW.

28 LLV, p. 194.

29 TM, p. 172.

30 EWS, pp. 220–23.

31 EWS, pp. 225–29.

32 Anthony Dell, Report for Week Ending, 10th June 1916, IWM/WW [Serbia 5/19]. See also Society of Friends, War Victims' Relief Committee, IWM/WW [Relief 4.1/46].

33 SNW/TYE.

34 RCM/S, p. 416.

35 PTC, pp. 51–55, 67.

36 See: BTR, p. 150; WWU, p. 77; HFWW/DB, p. 2986.

37 During this reorganization, Flora's Morava Division became part of the First Army. Previously, it had been part of the Army of the New Territories. See DH, p. 56; MOMI, p. 120.

38 GS, p. 60. See also FSJ, p. 244.

39 EWS, pp. 235–41.

40 See: NG/OMR, pp. 385–87; GS, p. 61.

41 EWS, p. 241.

42 IWM/FS.

CHAPTER 9

1 FSC/D, 12th September 1916.

2 FSC/D, 16th August–11th September 1916.

3 See ASF, pp. 99–103.

4 See RCS, p. 69.

5 See: Lesley M. Williams, *No Easy Path: The Life and Times of Lilian Violet Cooper* (Brisbane, Queensland: Amphion Press, 1991), p. 59; ASF, p. 157; NAB, p. 168; SWH/LET.

6 FSC/D, 11th, 13th September 1916; AWS, p. 26.

7   From a photograph of Major Pešić, FSC.

8   AWS, p. 44.

9   AWS, p. 39.

10   See: LS, pp. 112–14, 121, 129–30; AMM, pp. 53, 60, 147.

11   FSC/D, 21st September 1916.

12   AWS, p. 30.

13   AWS, p. 22.

14   DAB, p. 87.

15   FSC/D, 30th September 1916.

16   DAB, pp. 85–86.

17   'Miss Beauchamp's Report', SWH [Circulated Letters, Tin 42, November–December 1916].

18   LGP, p. 37.

19   SWH/LET. See also OWW, p. 35.

20   See: Letter from Miss Agneta F. Beauchamp, 27th December 1916, SWH [Circulated Letters, Tin 42, November–December 1916].

21   FSC/D, 9th October 1916.

22   AWS, pp. 27–28. See also FSC/D, 9th October 1916.

23   AWS, p. 27.

24   FSC/D, 14th October 1916.

25   AWS, p. 30.

26   AWS, pp. 16, 24.

27   AWS, pp. 30, 17, 19, 26.

28   FSC/D, 11th September 1916.

29   AWS, pp. 42–43.

30   AWS, p. 32.

31   FSC/D, 19th October 1916.

32   AWS, p. 64; FSC/D, 20th October 1916.

33   AWS, pp. 46–47; FSC/D, 20th October 1916.

34   AWS, pp. 34–35.

35   FSC/D, 20th October 1916.

36   AWS, p. 29.

37   FSC/D, 22nd October 1916.

38   FSC/D, 3rd November 1916.

39   AWS, p. 40.

40   FSJ, pp. 318, 320–21. See also: NG/OMR, pp. 391–92; MOMI, p. 236.

41   AWS, p. 58.

42   AWS, p. 59.

43   CT/SS. See also L/NWB.

44   'Flora Sand's [sic] Own Story', *Kansas City Star*, 2nd June 1917. See also:
     NYT/WEG; II/KSS; 'Women in the War', *Indiana Evening Gazette*, 10th
     October 1917; 'A Woman in the Serbian Army – Sergeant Flora Sandes',
     Morning Post, 14th December 1916.

45   AWS, pp. 63–66.

CHAPTER 10

1   AWS, p. 67.

2   See OWH/WF.

3   AWS, pp. 67–68.

4   AWS, p. 60.

5   AWS, p. 68.

6   OWH/WF.

7   AWS, p. 69; FSC/ALN; DAB, p. 100.

8   RCS, pp. 86–87.

9   WSB, p. 68.

10   LSW, p. 139.

11   LSW, pp. 145–46.

12   AWS, p. 72.

13   See: F.G. Hemenway, 'Letter to the Editor', *Mosquito*, No. 101, March
     1953; LGP, p. 16; SF, p. 160.

14   See UDE, p. 168.

15   See Marguerite Fedden, *Sisters' Quarters: Salonika* (London: Grant
     Richards, 1921), p. 75.

16   MAS, pp. 122–26.

17   AWS, p. 72.

18   AWS, pp. 76–77; PTC, p. 90. See also DM/HGS.

19   AWS, p. 77.

20   AWS, p. 73.

21   FBF, p. 216.

22   See: MOMI, p. 240; FBF, p. 216; WSB, p. 143.

23   See for example WL/ML.

24   LI/HM, p. 824.

25   See: ESRC/HA; NAB, p. 151; LLV, p. 196.

26   ISL, p. 111.

27   NAB, pp. 184, 194.

28   APT, p. 58.

29   Corey, Herbert, 'Davison Is Man with Punch for Red Cross Work', *Idaho Statesman*, 4th June 1917. See also SNW/APT.

30   AWS, p. 74.

31   AWS, p. 75.

32   AWS, p. 80.

33   See MO/WPI, p. 81 [illustration].

34   AWS, p. 78.

35   Order AD N. 83064, FSC.

36   F.J. Calvert, 'Woman Sergeant Wounded', *Daily Express*, 30th December 1916; 'British Nurse "Who Was Always First over the Top" Decorated with the Serbian VC', *Daily Mirror*, 9th February 1917; 'Brave Irishwoman Who Fought in the Trenches with the Serbians', *Daily Mirror*, 15th February 1917; 'Sergeant Flora Sandes', *Argus* [Melbourne, Australia], 1st January 1917; 'Salonika Front', *Mercury*, [Hobart, Tasmania], 1st January 1917; NYT/WEG; II/KSS. See also 'A Woman in the Serbian Army', *Times*, 30th December 1916.

37   MSY, p. 258.

38   AWS, pp. 77–78.

39   AWS, pp. 80–81.

40   IMC, p. 26.

41   AWS, p. 81.

42   PTC, p. 21.

43   IMC, p. 28.

44   See HT/SOS, p. 840.

45   DAB, p. 105.

46   See: HT/SOS, p. 845; GS, pp. 134–35; FBF, p. 221.

47   IMC, pp. 28–29.

48   PSS, pp. 20–21.

49   IMC, pp. 41–42; PSS, pp. 33–34.

50   IMC, p. 26.

51   IMC, p. 38.

52   AWS, p. 84.

53   FSC/LET to Sophia, 2nd May 1917.

54   AWS, pp. 85–86.

55   MC, p. 53.

56   FSC/LET to Sophia, 2nd May 1917.

57   AWS, pp. 87–88.

CHAPTER 11

1   AWS, p. 89.
2   AWS, p. 91.
3   See: Letter from Amelia Peabody Tileston to Mary W. Tileston, 2nd January 1917, AHL/HF; LLV, p. 202.
4   See APT, p. 35.
5   LI/HM, p. 824.
6   LI/HM, p. 824. See also: NG/OMR, p. 398; EYS, p. 57.
7   See: IWM/EA; IWM/BOS.
8   LI/HM, p. 840. See also ESRC/HA.
9   LI/WW.
10 LI/HM, p. 840.
11 See: APT, p. 74; NG/OMR, p. 398.
12 LI/HM, p. 840.
13 LI/WW.
14 AWS, pp. 108–109. Flora later changed her mind, particularly following a visit after the war. See AWS, p. 106.
15 FSC/D, 31st May 1917; AWS, p. 92.
16 See: AWS, p. 91; MC, pp. 185–87; MOMI, p. 343.
17 FSC/LET to Bessie Stear, 6th June 1917.
18 TSC, p. 326; AWS, p. 92.
19 AWS, pp. 93–99.
20 AWS, p. 94.
21 AWS, pp. 93, 134.
22 AWS, p. 93,
23 AWS, p. 95.
24 FSC/LET to Bessie Stear, 6th June 1917.
25 AWS, p. 98.
26 See IWM/MM.
27 AWS, p. 100.
28 AWS, p. 23.
29 See: ESRC/HA; WL/ML; IWM/LC, 17th March 1917.
30 LI/HM, p. 824.
31 See SNW/APT.
32 APT, pp. 76–77.
33 Letter from Amelia Peabody Tileston to Mary W. Tileston, 8th April 1917, AHL/HF.
34 WMJ/ES.

35   The doctor was almost certainly Dr Fred Burnham, from Winnipeg. WMJ/ES; SNW/APT.

36   Letter from Amelia Peabody Tileston to Mary W. Tileston, 28th April 1917, AHL/HF.

37   APT, p. 34.

38   George Horton, *Recollections Grave and Gay* (Indianapolis, IN: The Bobbs-Merrill Company, 1927), p. 280.

39   See OWW, pp. 134–35.

40   See CLM/FTL.

41   CLM/FTL, Notebook IV.

42   Letter dated 24th June 1917, AHL/HF.

43   LI/HM, p. 824.

44   See LSW, p. 139.

45   G. Ward Price, *The Story of the Salonika Army* (London: Hodder & Stoughton, 1918), p. 177.

46   FSC/D, 26th February 1917; IWM/LC; R.A. Reiss, *Lettres du front macédono-serbe* (Geneva: Éditions d'Art Boissonnas, 1921), p. 71.

47   DAB, p. 96.

48   IWM/LC, 24th February 1917.

49   FSC/D, 26th February, 7th March 1917; IWM/LC; WWU, p. 104; DAB, p. 108; ISL, p. 105; Ethel Daniels Hubbard, *Lone Sentinels in the Near East* (Boston, MA: Woman's Board of Missions, 1920), pp. 30–31.

50   ISL, p. 105.

51   FSC/D, 27th July 1917.

52   FSC/D, 4th August 1917.

53   IMC, p. 10.

54   Handwritten account for a speech, IWM/KM.

55   See IWM/KM, 8th May, 1st June 1916.

56   Diary of Miss C.U. Barnett, IWM [Documents.10778].

57   See EYS, pp. 51–52.

58   See: 'Serbia's Suffering', *British Journal of Nursing*, 19th July 1919, p. 48; EYS, p. 57.

59   IWM/EA.

60   Letter from Amelia Peabody Tileston to Mary W. Tileston, 14th August 1917, AHL/HF.

61   FSC/LET to Bessie Stear, 6th June 1917.

62   AWS, p. 106.

63   H. Collinson Owen, 'I saw Salonika Burn', Hammerton, Sir John,

ed., *The Great War... I Was There!*, No. 29, 18th April 1939 (London: Amalgamated Press, 1938–39), p. 1147. See also: SF, p. 16; MOMII, p. 22; UDE, p. 162; WSB, p. 35.

64   WWU, p. 121; HSWH, p. 343.

65   FSC/D, 20th–23rd August 1917.

66   FSC/D, 3rd September 1917.

67   AWS, pp. 114–15.

CHAPTER 12

1   AWS, p. 116.

2   'Sergeant Major Sandes in London', *Daily Mirror*, 19th December 1917; 'Woman Sergeant Major in the Trenches', *Daily Mail*, December 1917; DX/WSM.

3   AWS, p. 120.

4   See: 'Explanatory Notes', WL/VH; WL/VHI.

5   Flora Sandes, 'Serbia's Skeleton Army', *Weekly Dispatch*, 23rd December 1917. See also DX/WSM.

6   See: HSWH, pp. 244, 257; APT, p. 74.

7   Its full name was "The Hon. Evelina Haverfield's and Sergt. Major Flora Sandes's Comforts Fund for Serbian Soldiers and Prisoners".

8   AWS, p. 117.

9   [Article], *Sunday Times*, 20th January 1918, IWM/FS.

10   Untitled, undated article, IWM/FS.

11   AWS, pp. 118–19.

12   See: 'A York Heroine', *Yorkshire Herald*, 21st March 1918, IWM/FS; 'An Appeal for the Serbians', *Belfast News-Letter*, 16th February 1918, IWM/FS; 'Serbia Heroine Visits Brixton', *South London Press*, 8th March 1918, IWM/FS; 'Serbia's Joan of Arc', *Daily Mirror*, 23rd February 1918; 'Sergeant Flora Sandes on Vacation from Trenches', *Brooklyn Daily Eagle*, 27th February 1918.

13   CT/SS.

14   AWS, pp. 119–20.

15   LET/DSAB.

16   AWS, pp. 116–18.

17   AWS, pp. 121–22.

18   Letter dated 15th February 1918, AHL/HF.

19   APT, p. 89.

20   See AHL/HF.

21   APT, pp. 99–100.

22   See CLM/FTL, Notebooks III, IV, VI.

23   See CLM/FTL, Notebooks III, IV.

24   See: 'Red Cross Nurse Makes Appeal for Serbia', *New York Times*, 15th July 1917; 'Red Cross Will Aid Serbia Victims', *Trenton Evening Times* [Trenton, NJ], 28th August 1917; 'Red Cross Sends Commission to Serbia', *Wichita Daily Times*, 30th August 1917.

25   See CLM/FTL, Notebook IV.

26   See CLM/FTL, Notebook III.

27   See CLM/FTL, Notebook IV.

28   Elizabeth H. Ashe, *Intimate Letters from France* (San Francisco, CA: Philopolis Press, 1918), p. 41.

29   See: ESRC/LET from Clara D. Noyes, 16th July 1934; ESRC/LET, 22nd July 1934.

30   SNW/TYE; Charles M. Bakewell, *The Story of the American Red Cross in Italy* (New York, NY: Macmillan, 1920), p. 243.

31   Letters dated 21st January, 15th February 1918, AHL/HF.

32   See ESRC/HA.

33   AWS, p. 122.

34   See IWM/FS.

35   AWS, p. 124.

36   AWS, p. 125.

37   'A Serbian Infantrywoman', *Times*, 7th May 1918.

38   See: APT, pp. 34–36, 114; letter dated 15th February 1918, AHL/HF.

39   FSC/LET to the Hon. Evelina Haverfield, 15th June 1918.

40   APT, p. 122.

41   See: MC, pp. 207, 224; UDE, pp. 200, 224; BAL, p. 335; CE, p. 355.

42   See: SF, pp. 133–34; FBF, p. 235; MC, pp. 192–94; MOMII, p. 68.

43   See: GS, p. 192; MC, p. 216; TSC, p. 332.

44   AWS, pp. 135–36.

45   LU/LPS.

46   Letter of Thanks from General Boiovitch, commanding First Serbian Army, in *The Hon. Evelina Haverfield & Sergeant Major Flora Sandes: Comfort Fund for Serbian Soldiers and Prisoners, Annual Report*, IWM [Serbia 11/18]. See also AWS, p. 120.

CHAPTER 13

1   See: GS, pp. 185–86; HFWW/DB, p. 2981; CF, p. 355.

2   See MOMII, pp. 113, 329.

3   AWS, p. 136.

4   TSC, p. 335; HFWW/DB, p. 2983.

5   HFWW/DB, p. 2981.

6   TSC, p. 342.

7   AWS, p. 138.

8   See: HFWW/DB, p. 2983; MOMII, pp. 124–25; UDE, p. 198; TSC, p. 330;
    MC, p. 214.

9   FSC/D, 5th September 1918. Between 31st August [13th Septem-
    ber] and 14th [27th] October 1918 Flora followed the Julian
    calendar used by the Serbs at the time. The Western date is 18th
    September.

10 FSC/D, 6th [19th] September 1918.

11 ISL, p. 27.

12 AWS, p. 139.

13 AWS, p. 139.

14 AWS, p. 152; FSC/D, 10th [23rd] September 1918.

15 FSC/D, 10th [23rd] September 1918.

16 AWS, pp. 150–53; FSC/D, 15th [28th] September 1918.

17 FSC/D, 7th [20th] September 1918.

18 AWS, p. 140.

19 FSC/D, 9th [22nd] September 1918.

20 MOMII, p. 199.

21 MC, pp. 244–46. See also: H. Collinson Owen, *Salonika and After*
    (London: Hodder & Stoughton, 1919), p. 287; FBF, p. 249; MOMII,
    pp. 202, 206; UDE, pp. 220–21; BAL, p. 354; GS, pp. 213–14; HFWW/
    DB, p. 2985; MC, p. 233.

22 HFWW/DB, p. 2,987.

23 Mention in dispatches, 8th December 1918, FSC.

24 AWS, p. 155.

25 See: 'Fiendish Massacres', *Weekly Dispatch*, 3rd June 1917; MOMI,
    p. 300.

26 AWS, p. 156.

27 See: J. Purves-Stewart, *Sands of Time* (London: Hutchinson & Co.,
    1939), p. 158; WWU, p. 97; ASF, pp. 117–18; FSC/D, 17th [30th] Sep-
    tember 1918.

28   Aubrey Herbert, *Ben Kendim: A Record of Eastern Travel* (London: Hutchinson & Co., 1924), p. 26.

29   AWS, pp. 158–59; FSC/D, 26th September [9th October] 1918. See also RCS, p. 160.

30   FSC/D, 29th September [12th October] 1918.

31   AWS, pp. 158–59.

32   FSC/D, 26th September [9th October] 1918.

33   AWS, p. 158.

34   AWS, pp. 159–60.

35   FSC/D, 29th September [12th October] 1918.

36   AWS, p. 164; FSC/D, 2nd [15th] October 1918.

37   MOMII, p. 274; TSC, p. 359; APT, p. 11.

38   MC, p. 250.

CHAPTER 14

1   AWS, pp. 165–66; FSC/D, 7th–11th [20th–24th] October 1918.

2   FSC/D, 7th–11th [20th–24th] October 1918.

3   AWS, p. 172.

4   MOMII, p. 276.

5   AWS, p. 173.

6   FSC/D, 12th [25th] October 1918.

7   AWS, pp. 173–74.

8   AWS, p. 175.

9   AWS, pp. 175–77; FSC/D, undated final entry for 1918.

10   MOMII, p. 276; GS, p. 233.

11   AWS, pp. 179–80; FSC/D, undated final entry for 1918.

12   AWS, p. 171; FSC/D, undated final entry for 1918.

13   MAS, pp. 138–39.

14   APT, pp. 37, 130.

15   See: ISL, p. 177; HSWH, p. 225. In relation to Spanish influenza, see: CCD, p. 135; MSY, p. 293; HSWH, p. 304.

16   WWU, p. 149.

17   Isabel Hutton, *Memories of a Doctor in War and Peace* (London: Heinemann, 1960), p. 171.

18   IWM/SS. See also Extracts from Miss MacGlade's Letters, IWM/WW [Serbia 11/1].

19   IMC, p. 66. See also BBC/YW.

20   AWS, p. 182.

21 'Serbia's 322,000 Dead', *Daily News*, 13th November 1918. See also John Keegan, *The First World War* (London: Hutchinson, 1999), p. 7.

22 CCD, p. 149. See also WWU, p. 164.

CHAPTER 15

1 AWS, pp. 182, 184–85.

2 Andrej Mitrović, *Serbia's Great War, 1914–1918* (London: Hurst & Co., 2007), p. 320; PAR, pp. 120–21.

3 Bogdan Krizman, 'The Belgrade Armistice of 13th November 1918', *Slavonic and East European Review*, Vol. XLVIII, No. 110, January 1970, pp. 72, 83.

4 IWM/SS; AWS, pp. 185–86.

5 AWS, pp. 188–89.

6 PAR, p. 116.

7 EWB, p. 73.

8 See: WWU, p. 167; TF, p. 5.

9 See: IWM/EA; HM/WBF; Edward Stuart, 'Sanitation in Serbia', *American Journal of Public Health*, Vol. X, No. 2, February 1920, p. 130.

10 See ESRC/HA.

11 See: ESRC/HA; AWS, pp. 192–93.

12 WWU, p. 185. See also QA, p. 129.

13 WSB, p. 237.

14 See: IMC, p. 63; JEB, pp. 109–19; 'The Serbian Relief Fund', *British Journal of Nursing*, 22nd February 1919.

15 See Esther Pohl Lovejoy, *Certain Samaritans* (New York, NY: Macmillan, 1933), chapters 4–8.

16 'The American Red Cross in Serbia', *Red Cross Bulletin*, Vol. III, No. 37, 8th September 1919; HARCN, pp. 1,117–25.

17 QA, p. 132. See also John Forbes, *The Quaker Star under Seven Flags* (Philadelphia, PA: University of Pennsylvania Press, 1962), pp. 73–74.

18 See: FMC; IMC, pp. 102, 104; EYS, pp. 85, 244.

19 NYT/SCH.

20 Troubridge's diary, 29th October 1915, quoted in DOS, p. 148.

21 IWM/EA.

22 NYT/SCH.

23 See: NYT/SCH; IWM/EA; EYS, pp. 74–77.

24 IWM/SS.

25   'Entertainments', *Times*, 20th February 1919; 'Misery in Serbia', *Times*,
     1st April 1919; 'Serbian Destitution', *Times*, 13th May 1919; 'The Slavo
     Dance', *Daily Express*, 24th February 1919.

26   [Untitled], *Times*, 17th May 1919.

CHAPTER 16

1   AWS, p. 193.

2   See: PAR, p. 116; OWW, p. 206; MC, p. 91; EWB, p. 75; BLGF, pp. 85–86,
     583.

3   BAL, p. 372; PAR, p. 291.

4   NR/WFS, p. 412.

5   PAR, pp. 299–301.

6   AWS, p. 194.

7   See BAL, p. 374.

8   See: MMH, pp. 36–40; NQY, p. 285.

9   BLGF, p. 492.

10   JBM, p. 108. See also: NQY, p. 285; MMH, pp. 41–43; Merton Emerson,
     'Serbian Victories of Peace', *New York Times Magazine*, 15th June 1919;
     Ronald Tree, 'Montenegrin Situation' [letter to the editor], *New York
     Times*, 7th May 1922.

11   See: MMH, p. 35; NQY, p. 288.

12   JBM, p. 109.

13   NQY, p. 286. See also Brigadier General F.E. Burnham, 'The Betrayal of
     the Helpless', *Foreign Affairs: A Journal of International Understanding*,
     Vol. V, No. 11, May 1924.

14   Alice and Claude Askew, *The Stricken Land: Serbia as We Saw It* (Lon-
     don: Eveleigh Nash Co., 1916), p. 276.

15   JBM, pp. 106–107, 120–21.

16   See: JBM, pp. 120, 128–29, 140–42; WBH, pp. 330, 336; 'Serbs Arrest
     de Salis', *New York Times*, 4th April 1920; Henry Baerlein, *The Birth
     of Yugoslavia*, Vol. II (London: Leonard Parsons, 1922), p. 309.

17   See: 'The Annihilation of a Nation', *New York Times*, 16th April 1922;
     Ronald McNeill, 'Martyrdom of Montenegro', *The Nineteenth Century
     and After*, Vol. LXXXIX, January 1921.

18   NR/WFS, p. 414.

19   Inside leaf of flyer publicizing Flora's Australian tour. In author's per-
     sonal collection.

20   NR/WFS, pp. 414–15.

21   See: AWS, p. 194; NR/WFS, p. 415.

22   See: FSC/D, 9th May 1919; diary entry, 9th May 1919, LU/RV; 'Red
     Cross Cleans Up Turkish Capital', *Iowa City Citizen*, 9th July 1919;
     JEB, pp. 110, 112–13; OWW, p. 113; WWU, pp. 198, 214–15.

23   See: MOMII, p. 251; WWU, pp. 173–78; HSWH, pp. 319–20; CCD,
     p. 163; MC, p. 267; PSS, p. 77; IMC, p. 72.

24   WWU, pp. 174, 177–78.

25   See: IMC, p. 68; PSS, pp. 77–81.

26   See: JEB, p. 110; WWU, p. 198; LU/LPS; diary entry, 30th June 1919,
     LU/RV.

27   AWS, pp. 194–96.

28   CCD, p. 179.

29   AWS, p. 202.

30   WWU, p. 220.

31   AWS, p. 204.

32   AWS, p. 205.

33   AWS, p. 211.

34   AWS, pp. 208–10.

35   SH, p. 158.

36   DE/LS.

37   AMM, p. 105.

38   'With the Serbians' [unnamed and undated Melbourne paper],
     IWM/FS.

39   SMH/FSII.

40   See: 'Serbia's Heroine' [unnamed and undated Sydney paper], IWM/FS;
     Card: Serbian Citizens of Sydney: Dinner to Lt (Miss) Flora Sandes,
     IWM/FS; 'The Sydney Address' [unnamed paper], 6th June 1920,
     IWM/FS; SMH/FSII; DE/LS.

41   'A Woman's Adventures', *West Australian*, 7th June 1920; 'Vice-Regal',
     Argus [Melbourne], 8th June 1920; SMH/FSI; A/MA.

42   SMH/FSI.

43   'Near and Far', *Sydney Morning Herald*, 10th June 1920; 'Ross Smith
     Flight', *Sydney Morning Herald*, 12th June 1920; 'Near and Far', *Syd-
     ney Morning Herald*, 16th June 1920; 'Near and Far', *Sydney Morning
     Herald*, 28th June 1920.

44   Philip Ziegler, ed., *The Diaries of Lord Louis Mountbatten, 1920–1922*
     (London: Collins, 1987), p. 82.

45   FSC/ALN; 'Carnival Nights', *Sun* [Sydney], 18th June 1920.

46   See: A/MA; DE/FSII; DE/FSIII.

47 DE/FSI. See also 'Lieut. Sandes', *Sydney Morning Herald*, 5th July 1920.

48 See: DE/LS; DE/FSI; DE/FSII; DE/FSIII; 'Lieut. Flora Sandes', *Brisbane Courier*, 16th September 1920.

49 See: 'Lieutenant Flora Sandes', *Wingham Chronicle*, 6th August 1920; 'Lieut. Flora Sandes', *Eastern Telegraph*, 6th August 1920.

50 DE/FSI. See also AMM, p. 105.

51 'Sydney Day by Day', *Argus* [Melbourne], 12th June 1920. The annotated article is in IWM/FS.

52 DE/FSI. See also: 'For Serbia's Sake', *Herald* [Melbourne], 7th June 1920; SMH/FSII.

53 'Personal', *Argus* [Melbourne], 22nd January 1921.

54 She was then at work for the Ministry of Child Welfare. See: ESRC/HA; diary entry, 3rd September 1919, IWM/MM.

55 APT, p. 142.

56 Diary entry, 3rd June 1919, LU/RV; APT, pp. 142–43.

57 APT, pp. 146–48.

58 IMC, pp. 77–78. See also: diary entry, 3rd June 1919, LU/RV; ISL, p. 196.

59 IMC, p. 74.

60 WWU, pp. 224–25.

61 Boyce Gaddes, *Evelina: Outward Bound from Inverlochy* (Gloucester: Merlin Books, 1995), p. 118. See also 'Account of the Work of Evelina Haverfield in Serbia', WL/VH.

62 APT, p. 149.

63 See: WWU, p. 216; diary entry, 22nd October 1919, IWM/MM; IMC, p. 84; ISL, p. 198.

64 See ISL, p. 197.

65 Transcript of Tape 480, LU/RV.

66 ISL, pp. 197–98; WWU, p. 212.

67 APT, p. 152.

68 See: APT, p. 155; ESRC/HA.

69 APT, p. 153.

70 See 'Nursing Service, American Red Cross, Commission to Europe', ESRC.

71 APT, p. 162.

72 APT, pp. 28, 31–32, 167.

73 See ISL, pp. 200–201.

74 APT, p. 191.

75 ISL, p. 203.

CHAPTER 17

1   AWS, p. 195.
2   AWS, pp. 214–17.
3   AWS, pp. 216–17.
4   MAS, p. 186. See also HARCN, p. 1180.
5   See: FWB, p. 79; WWU, pp. 223, 285–86.
6   AWS, pp. 217–18.
7   WL/VHII.
8   Yurie's service document, FSC.
9   AWS, pp. 215–17; WL/VHII.
10 WL/VHII.
11 WL/VHII.
12 Alan Clark, ed., *A Good Innings: The Private Papers of Viscount Lee of Fareham* (London: John Murray, 1974), p. 228.
13 ESF.
14 See: NYT/SCH; EYS, p. 78; IWM/EA.
15 See: EYS, p. 81; OWW, pp. 192, 194.
16 EYS, p. 81.
17 AWS, p. 218.
18 AWS, p. 220.
19 AWS, p. 220.
20 BC/SMI.
21 AWS, p. 220.
22 IWM/EA.
23 IWM/EA.
24 AWS, pp. 210, 221.
25 ISL, pp. 208, 213, 218.
26 OWW, p. 169.

CHAPTER 18

1   WL/VHI. Flora did not specify which sister she was staying with, but it would have either been Fanny or Sophia, both of whom lived there.
2   With many thanks to Ben Johnston for passing on his aunt's recollection.
3   WL/VHI.
4   See *Times*, 30th April, 6th May, 16th May, 22nd May, 4th June 1925.
5   WL/VHI.
6   WL/VHI.

7   WIY, pp. 201–202.

8   AWS, p. 38.

9   *Times Literary Supplement*, 26th May 1927, p. 378; George Sampson, 'Seven Stories and a Dream', *Observer*, 10th April 1927; 'New Books', *Manchester Guardian*, 4th April 1927. See also: 'Woman Soldier', *Daily Mirror*, 1st April 1927; 'A Woman Soldier', *Scotsman*, 11th July 1927.

10 See James E. Hassell, *Russian Refugees in France and the United States Between the World Wars* (Darby, PA: Diane Publishing, 1991), p. 58.

11 Flora's notes on what she was doing on 1st January 1928 and 1929, FSC.

12 See 'Milestones', *Time Magazine*, 27th July 1942.

13 EAT/FH. See also: 'Lowdown on High Kicks', *Daily Mirror*, 22nd August 1979; Doremy Vernon, *Tiller's Girls* (London: Robson Books, 1988), pp. 74–76.

14 See: BLGF, p. 601; WBH, p. 392; BAL, p. 430.

15 See: BAL, p. 428; MMH, p. 48.

16 RD, p. 222.

17 AWS, p. 221.

18 FSC/D, 15th May 1932, 29th September 1934.

19 FSC/D, 19th April 1932.

20 See: 'English Woman Honoured', *Observer*, 10th June 1934; 'The Gallipoli Pilgrimage', *Manchester Guardian*, 5th June 1936; 'Editor's Dump', *Mosquito*, No. 117, March 1957; WIY, p. 189.

21 See 'Medical News', *British Medical Journal*, 19th December 1925.

22 ESRC/LET.

23 Flora Sandes, 'British Magic, A Glimpse of the Anglo-Serbian Children's Hospital', *The World's Children* [the magazine of the Save the Children Fund], January 1927.

24 See 'Belgrade Hospital' [letter to the editor], *Times*, 28th December 1927.

25 RD, p. 188.

26 See: 'Scottish Enterprise', *Scotsman*, 27th October 1927; 'Children's Hospital, Belgrade', *Times*, 1st October 1929; 'Scottish Serbian Hospital', *British Medical Journal*, 12th November 1927.

27 See EYS, p. 110.

28 See EYS, pp. 127, 143.

29 Diary entry, 22nd September 1934, WL/VH.

30 See EYS, p. 128.

31 FSC/D, 23rd September 1934.

32 FSC/D, 4th, 13th July 1936.

33 FSC/D, 13th–17th August 1931.

34 See 'King of Yugoslavia Murdered', *Times*, 10th October 1934.

35 See BLGF, p. 615.

36 FSC/D, 18th October 1934.

37 See: 'Funeral of King Alexander', *Scotsman*, 19th October 1934; 'Last Rites in Belgrade', *Times*, 19th October 1934.

38 See FY, p. 104.

39 BAL, p. 436.

40 See: BAL, p. 473; BLGF, p. 1135; HT/RB, p. 193; PH/OP, p. 376.

41 BE, p. 29.

42 BE, p. 42.

43 See: PH/OP, p. 376; BAL, p. 472; HT/RB, p. 194.

44 See: HT/RB, p. 192; FY, p. 131; WCF, p. 22; PH/OP, p. 376.

45 BE, p. 72.

46 EYS, pp. 143–44.

47 DMH, p. 186.

48 See: ISL, p. 212; WCF, p. 21; QM, p. 210.

49 FSC/D, 16th, 20th, 22nd August 1940.

50 EYS, p. 146.

51 WCF, p. 24.

52 SCW, p. 70; HT/RB, p. 195; NAV, pp. 131, 137, 143.

53 WCF, p. 26. She Anglicized her surname from Jovičić.

54 FYS, p. 146.

55 See: BLGF, p. 1136; SCW, p. 71; HT/RB, p. 195; NAV, pp. 137, 147, 149.

56 LS, pp. 178–79.

57 EYS, p. 147.

58 BAL, p. 475.

59 HT/RB, p. 192; PH/OP, p. 378.

60 LS, pp. 179.

61 JS/WE.

62 LS, pp. 179–80.

63 JS/WE.

64 SCW, p. 74. See also: NAV, pp. 165–69; LBN, pp. 206–207.

65 JS/WE.

66 WCF, p. 23; BE, p. 49.

67 FLSP, pp. 26–28; WV, p. 10; NAV, pp. 179–81; BAL, p. 476; LM/CY, p. 105.

68 PH/OP, p. 378.

69 'Sergeant Flora', *Daily Herald*, 5th April 1941.

CHAPTER 19

1   PH/OP, p. 379.
2   See: LM/CY, p. 108; SCW, p. 86; JS/WE; Boris Todorovich, *Last Words: A Memoir of World War II and the Yugoslav Tragedy* (New York, NY: Walker & Co., 1989), p. 4.
3   NAV, p. 193; FLSP, pp. 38–39.
4   FSC/D, 6th April 1941; FSC/HWL.
5   EYS, p. 149.
6   See: PH/OP, p. 379; NAV, pp. 190–204; LBN, p. 225.
7   JS/WE. See also NAV, p. 203.
8   See: FLSP, p. 41; WCF, pp. 39–40; LBN, p. 233.
9   PH/OP, p. 379; DMH, p. 198.
10 EYS, p. 147.
11 JS/WE.
12 EYS, p. 167.
13 See NAV, pp. 177–78.
14 NAV, p. 220.
15 See: HT/RB, p. 193; PH/OP, p. 391; James L. Collins, Jr, ed., *The Marshall Cavendish Illustrated Encyclopedia of World War II*, Vol. IV (New York, NY: Marshall Cavendish Corporation, 1972), p. 466.
16 BC/SMI.
17 JS/WE.
18 Cecil Brown, *Suez to Singapore* (Garden City, NY: Halcyon House, 1943), p. 6.
19 NAV, p. 279; LM/CY, p. 111.
20 WCF, pp. 68–69.
21 See: PH/OP, p. 391; LM/CY, p. 111.
22 JS/WE; FSC/D, 13th April 1941.
23 JS/WE.
24 See: PH/OP, p. 391; AFT, pp. 154–56.
25 EYS, p. 168; IWM/EA. See also BE, pp. 101, 156.
26 See: SCW, p. 105; BE, p. 64.
27 BE, p. 132. See also NAV, p. 264.
28 T/ABL.
29 See: BE, p. 133; NAV, pp. 266–67.
30 BE, p. 134.
31 EYS, p. 169; NAV, p. 267; BE, pp. 135–36.
32 FSC/D, 13th April 1941; JS/WE.

33 FSC/D, 14th, 16th April 1941.

34 JS/WE.

35 FSC/D, 20th April 1941.

36 See: SCW, p. 192; JS/WE.

37 JS/WE.

38 WCF, p. 89.

39 JS/WE.

40 LM/CY, p. 111; NAV, p. 281.

41 WCF, p. 198.

42 FSC/D, 8th May 1941.

43 See: SCW, p. 166; NAV, pp. 280, 283.

44 WCF, pp. 77–78, 80.

45 WCF, pp. 78–79.

46 JS/WE.

47 NAV, p. 268.

48 IWM/EA; BE, pp. 136–37, 139; DMH, p. 224.

49 EYS, p. 170. See also NAV, p. 269.

50 See NAV, p. 270.

51 BE, p. 155; EYS, p. 171.

52 JS/WE.

53 FSC/LET to Fanny, 24th June 1941.

54 See WCF, p. 77.

55 JS/WE.

56 See SCW, p. 174.

57 Revd M.D. Krmpotić, 'Serb and Croat Rivalry for Bosnia', Current History, September 1916, pp. 1080, 1082. See also 'Jugo Slavs Quit Serbian Corps in Defense of Autonomy', Washington Post, 7th August 1917.

58 BAL, p. 498.

59 See: EA, p. 265; BAL, pp. 486–87.

60 SCW, p. 253.

61 See: BAL, pp. 497–98; Edward Alexander, The Holocaust and the War of Ideas (New Brunswick, NJ: Transaction Publishers, 1994), p. 116.

62 See: WCF, pp. 94–95; WV, p. 76.

63 Jovo Anđić, 'On a Quest for the Essence of Things: Stanislav Vinaver', Belguest, Vol. IX, Spring 2009, p. 24.

64 See: WCF, p. 95; BAL, pp. 504–506; WV, p. 77; SCW, p. 262.

65 See BAL, p. 486.

66 One of the boys was the brother of my friend, the late Dr Žarko Vuković,

who did more than anyone to keep the memory alive of the work of British women in Serbia in the First World War. That same month, over seventeen hundred men and a handful of women were also massacred in the town of Kraljevo. See BAL, pp. 490–91.

67 WRY, pp. 146, 166; EA, p. 243; BAL, p. 489; WV, pp. 101–103.

68 EYS, p. 244.

69 Flora was given one of these when one of the women was transferred out. See FSC/D, 25th June 1941. Her diary entries for 24th June to 5th July 1941 must have been written after her release from prison. See also SCW, p. 174.

70 SCW, p. 175; JS/WE; FSC/D, 24th June 1941.

71 FSC/HWL; JS/WE.

72 FLSP, p. 55.

73 SCW, p. 192.

74 SCW, pp. 177–79.

75 JS/WE; SCW, pp. 178–79.

76 SCW, p. 181; FSC/HWL.

77 FSC/HWL.

78 SCW, p. 192.

79 T/ABL. See also BE, p. 162.

80 See BE, pp. 163–65.

81 See EYS, p. 172.

82 BE, p. 169.

83 T/ABL.

84 SCW, pp. 183–91.

85 FSC/D, 25th June 1941.

86 SCW, p. 192.

87 SCW, p. 193; FSC/D, 24th June–5th July 1941.

88 JS/WE.

89 FSC/D, 5th July 1941; JS/WE.

90 FSC/D, 5th, 6th July 1941.

91 FSC/D, 7th, 19th July 1941.

92 See: WV, pp. 10–11; BC/SMI.

93 FSC/D, 25th July 1941; SCW, p. 197.

94 IWM/EA; BC/SMI.

95 WCF, pp. 117–18.

96 FSC/D, 2nd August 1941.

97 FSC/D, 10th August 1941.

98 FSC/D, 29th August 1941.

99   FSC/D, 9th September 1941.

100 FSC/D, 11th–12th September 1941.

101 She was arrested soon after. See WCF, pp. 133–34.

102 FSC/D, 13th September 1941.

103 JS/WE.

104 JS/WE. See also WCF, p. 151.

105 FSC/D, 24th July 1941.

106 See: IWM/EA; CTC, p. 57.

107 WCF, p. 199.

108 BC/SMI.

109 JS/WE.

110 See WCF, p. 204.

111 SC/LIB; JS/WE.

112 BC/SMI.

113 JS/WE. Contrary to what Flora said, a handful of German soldiers were killed.

114 See: WCF, pp. 218–19; 'Belgrade Bombed by Accident Last April Is Report', *Vidette Messenger* [Valparaiso, IN], 5th December 1944; 'Flying Fortresses Bomb Belgrade by Mischance', *Monessen Daily Independent*, 4th December 1944.

115 See WCF, p. 219.

116 JS/WE.

117 QM, p. 210.

118 WRY, p. 417.

119 EA, pp. 389–90.

120 JS/WE.

121 EA, p. 397.

122 SMFL, p. 223.

123 SMFL, p. 223.

124 See WCF, p. 245.

125 SMFL, p. 223.

126 SC/LIB.

127 See: WV, p. 221; WCF, p. 241; EA, p. 394.

128 JS/WE.

129 WV, p. 184. See also FMC, pp. 47–48.

130 EYS, p. 173; 'King Peter of Yugoslavia – Visit to the West of Scotland', *Scotsman*, 25th January 1943; WL/VH.

131 See: IWM/EA; AFT, pp. 163–64.

132 EYS, pp. 178–79.

133 AFT, p. 212; EYS, p. 183; FNS, p. 40.
134 IWM/EA.
135 EYS, p. 184.
136 'Yugoslav Surgeons Handicapped by Germans' Destruction', *Scotsman*, 24th September 1946.

CHAPTER 20

1   JS/WE.
2   BC/SMI.
3   LET/DSAB.
4   LET/AB.
5   LET/AB.
6   IWM/EA.
7   IWM/EA.
8   LET/DSAB.
9   LET/AB.
10 AFT, p. 234; EYS, p. 190.
11 RD, p. 194.
12 EYS, p. 195; AFT, p. 234.
13 IWM/EA; EYS, p. 195.
14 EYS, pp. 197–96.
15 Letter from Flora Sandes to Dick Sandes, 1945, in private hands.
16 IWM/EA.
17 EYS, pp. 198–99.
18 EYS, pp. 202–204. See also 'The London Letter', *Scotsman*, 14th January 1950.
19 BBC/OH.
20 EAT/FH.
21 See FNS, p. 94.
22 EAT/FH.
23 INT/AB. See also EAT/FH.
24 BBC/OH.
25 'Kind Old Lady Led Me into Battle', *Weekend Reveille*, 23rd July 1954.
26 WSM/IF.
27 Letter from Flora, 4th January 1950, IWM/LPS.
28 Letter from Flora, 18th January 1950, IWM/LPS.
29 LU/LPS.
30 Letter from Flora, 10th September, IWM/LPS.

31   See *Mosquito*, No. 92, December 1950, p. 103 [illustration].
32   'The Tie that Binds', *Mosquito*, No. 92, December 1950, p. 112; 'Joan of Arc', *Mosquito*, No. 92, December 1950.
33   Flora attended reunions of the "British Serbian Units Branch" of the British Legion on 1st July 1950 and 7th July 1951, according to a book of attendance in the author's personal collection. See also MO/WPI, pp. 80, 82.
34   WSM/IF.
35   She was unable to attend the Parade in 1951 due to a family tragedy. Her nephew, Stephen Johnston, was murdered by communist guerrillas in Malaya and his wife and children were flown back to Britain almost immediately. See MO/WPII.
36   'Women's Pages', *Mosquito*, No. 104, December 1953.
37   'Captain Flora Hides Her "VC"', *Daily Express*, 6th October 1952; 'Captain Flora "V.C." Parades with the Men', *Daily Mirror*, 6th October 1952.
38   MO/ED, p. 121.
39   EYS, p. 215.
40   IWM/EA.
41   MO/ED, p. 121.
42   MO/WPII.
43   This is medical shorthand for a blockage of the bile duct. The blockage was, at her age, likely caused either by cancer of the pancreas or a stuck gallstone. Many thanks to Dr Jonathan Standley.

AFTERWORD

1   RD, p. 193.
2   'Our Booking-Office', *Punch*, 1st November 1916, p. 324.
3   'An English Woman Sergeant', *Liverpool Weekly Post*, 7th October 1916.
4   See: Leah Leneman, 'Medical Women in the First World War – Ranking Nowhere', *British Medical Journal*, 18th–25th December 1993, p. 1592; Leah Leneman, 'Medical Women at War, 1914–1918', *Medical History*, No. 38, 1994, pp. 171–72; HSWH, p. 373.

EPILOGUE

1   Reports of Work in Corsica Nos. 75, 76, 77, IWM/WW [Serbia 6.2/24]; Report of Work in Corsica No. 186, IWM/WW [Serbia 6/4].
2   'The Plight of Serbia', *Manchester Guardian*, 5th November 1918; 'The

Needs of Serbia', *Manchester Guardian*, 23rd December 1918. See also 'The Serbian Relief Fund' [advertisement], *Manchester Guardian*, 20th November 1918.

3   'Funeral Services: Yugoslav Minister', *Times*, 27th March 1937; DM/HF.

4   'Gave Reception for Dr Barton Cookingham', *Poughkeepsie Eagle-News*, 28th June 1915.

5   'Dr Cookingham Appointed', *Poughkeepsie Eagle-News*, 3rd March 1919.

6   'Doctor's Wife Wins Divorce', *Poughkeepsie Eagle-News*, 12th July 1926; 'Dr Cookingham Wed to Miss Janet Kehm', *Register and Herald* [Pine Plains, NY], 24th April 1930; 'Other Weddings', *New York Times*, 25th March 1934; 'Mack Moves for Mistrial in Stormy Cleveland Session', *Poughkeepsie Star-Enterprise*, 15th December 1938.

7   'Dr Cookingham Freed in Bail', *Poughkeepsie Journal*, 14th January 1944; 'Cookingham Saved a Life, Dow Says Defense Will Prove', *Poughkeepsie Journal*, 30th March 1944; 'Son Testifies for Cookingham', *Poughkeepsie Journal*, 31st March 1944; 'Dr Cookingham Acquitted by Jury', *Poughkeepsie Journal*, 1st April 1944; 'Dr Cookingham Provides Bail', *Poughkeepsie Journal*, 7th June 1946; 'Physician Arrested', *Greene County Examiner-Recorder* [Catskill, NY], 27th June 1946.

8   Florida Divorce Index, 1927–2001, Florida Department of Health, Jacksonville, Florida.

9   'Ex-Doctor Being Held in Operation', *Troy Record*, 4th August 1962; 'Advanced Age Saves Physician from Jail Term', *Times Record* [Troy, NY], 24th October 1962.

10   See HARCN, p. 216.

11   SC/TOS; 'All Serbia Starving', *Washington Post*, 27th November 1915.

12   See LM/CY, p. 108.

13   'American Wife of Slav Envoy flees Europe', *Mansfield News-Journal*, 11th February 1943; Mme Slavko Grouitch, 'Now Back in America, Has Seen Both World Wars Break on the Balkans', *Christian Science Monitor*, 30th October 1942, p. 15.

14   'Mme Grouitch Aided Refugees', *New York Times*, 14th August 1956.

15   EYS, pp. 202, 206, 209.

16   BBC/YW.

17   IWM/EA.

18   EYS, pp. 212–14.

19   NYT/SF.

20   'American Found Soviet Crumbling', *New York Times*, 14th May 1920.

21 NYT/SF.

22 'Denies Knee Dress Is Back in France', *New York Times*, 4th February 1924.

23 LET/DSJS.

24 See DM/HGS.

25 'Milunka Savić: Heroina, pa čistačica', *Novosti*, 12th March, 2011.

26 PTC, p. 90, AWS, p. 79; 'Two Fine Fighters', *Mosquito*, No. 155, September 1966.

27 With many thanks to Nenad and Goran Vuković for spending a cold February evening in 2007 helping to find her house.

28 PCL/NY.

29 Letter from Emily to Miss Rhoades, 2nd May 1921, ESF.

30 Telegram from the American Friends Service Committee to Emily, 13th September 1922, ESF.

31 Reference dated 9th January [1922], ESF.

32 Letter from Marjorie Daw Johnson to the American Friends Service Committee, 12th January 1922, ESF.

33 See Dorothy Detzer, *Appointment on the Hill* (New York, NY: Henry Holt & Co., 1948), p. 10.

34 Letter from Emily to Miss Longshore, 2nd December 1922, ESF.

35 Letter from the American Friends Service Committee to Marjorie Daw Johnson, 28th October 1923, ESF.

36 ESRC/LET, from "National Director, Nursing Service" [Clara D. Noyes] to "Dr William S. Dodd, Medical Secretary, Foreign Department, Near East Relief", 13th May 1926.

37 Inwards Passenger Lists, Board of Trade: Commercial and Statistical Department and Successors, NAK [Series BT26].

38 With thanks to Dan McLaughlin, Librarian, Reference Services, Pasadena Public Library. See also 1910 US Census for Emily Simmonds and Jean MacKay.

39 'Obituary', *Ontario Daily Report*, 21st February 1966; 'Obituary Notices', *Independent* [Pasadena, CA], 22nd February 1966.

INDEX

ILLUSTRATIONS

1, 2, 3, 4, 6, 7, 8, 11, 14, 16, 17 and 20 are reproduced courtesy of the Flora Sandes Collection.

5 is reproduced courtesy of Royal BC Museum, BC Archives (Image G-08303).

13 and 15 are reproduced courtesy of Allison Blackmore.

18 is reproduced courtesy of Stephen Sandes.

19 is reproduced courtesy of Elena Vidić and Slobodan Kovačević of Fotodokumentacija Borba, Belgrade.